Rabbi Jack H Bloom, PhD
Editor

Jewish Relational Care A-Z
We Are Our Other's Keeper

Pre-publication
REVIEWS,
COMMENTARIES,
EVALUATIONS . . .

"**T**his is an exceptional book on a relational approach to professional caring relationships. Jack Bloom has assembled an extraordinary community of writers who talk as much about how to give care to others as how to care for one's self. This makes the book a remarkably practical and healing gift to its readers. I highly recommend it."

Stephen Gilligan, PhD
Psychologist; Author,
The Courage to Love:
Principles of Self-Relations
and *Walking in Two Worlds*

"**J**ack Bloom's life and career have been devoted to demonstrating that the Jewish tradition and the discipline of psychotherapy can only enrich each other. This thesis was at the heart of his previous book, *The Rabbi As Symbolic Exemplar.* It is now illustrated in each of the articles that make up this treasure house of papers by authorities in one or the other of these disciplines (and frequently both). This book is directed not only to rabbis and therapists, but to all of us who are inevitably engaged in caring for the significant others in our lives. The list of these 'others' addressed here is exhaustive. If the book has one central message, it is that before we care for all of these others, we must learn to care for the 'others' within ourselves. For that piece of cautionary advice alone, we must be particularly grateful to Dr. Bloom and his associates."

Rabbi Neil Gillman, PhD
Chairman and Professor
of Jewish Philosophy,
Jewish Theological Seminary
of America

More pre-publication
REVIEWS, COMMENTARIES, EVALUATIONS . . .

"*Jewish Relational Care A-Z* is a treasure house of wisdom possessing both religious and intellectual depth about care and caregiving, grounded in the insights of contemporary psychotherapy and a traditional yet present-day reading of the world of Judaism. The editor, rabbi and psychotherapist Jack H Bloom, has assembled as contributors a group of seasoned, knowledgeable, compassionate caregivers, primarily rabbis. It is truly a book from A to Z. The contributors share with their readers many lifetimes of religious and practical experience, as well as intellectual and spiritual development, concerning almost every conceivable situation rabbis are likely to encounter in their caregiving role. These include their own inner struggles, their own and others' life cycle crises, sexuality in all of its manifestations, marriage and intermarriage, and the divine-human encounter.

Jewish Relational Care A-Z is fundamentally a book about relationships, to self, family, friends, lovers, community, tradition, and God. It is an extremely helpful book of exemplary honesty and depth about men and women in the real world. Unlike some books of this genre, there isn't a false emotional or spiritual note within it. As with Bloom's *The Rabbi As Symbolic Exemplar,* this book can be read with very great profit by congregants as well as rabbis, by churchgoers as well as clergy."

Richard L. Rubenstein, PhD
President Emeritus,
and Distinguished Professor
of Religion,
University of Bridgeport;
Lawton Distinguished Professor
of Religion Emeritus,
Florida State University

The Haworth Press
New York • London • Oxford

Jewish Relational Care A-Z
We Are Our Other's Keeper

THE HAWORTH PRESS
New, Recent, and Forthcoming
Titles of Related Interest

Shared Grace: Therapists and Clergy Working Together by Marion A. Bilich, Susan T. Bonfiglio, and Steven D. Carlson

A Memoir of a Pastoral Counseling Practice by Robert L. Menz

The Pastor's Family: The Challenges of Family Life and Pastoral Responsibilities by Daniel L. Langford

A Theology for Pastoral Psychotherapy: God's Play in Sacred Spaces by Brian W. Grant

Pastoral Counseling: A Gestalt Approach by Ward A. Knights Jr.

The Rabbi As Symbolic Exemplar: By the Power Vested in Me by Rabbi Jack H Bloom

Jewish Relational Care A-Z
We Are Our Other's Keeper

Rabbi Jack H Bloom, PhD
Editor

The Haworth Press
New York • London • Oxford

For more information on this book or to order, visit
http://www.haworthpress.com/store/product.asp?sku=5440

or call 1-800-HAWORTH (800-429-6784) in the United States and Canada
or (607) 722-5857 outside the United States and Canada

or contact orders@HaworthPress.com

The Haworth Press, Inc., 10 Alice Street, Binghamton, NY 13904-1580.

PUBLISHER'S NOTE
The development, preparation, and publication of this work has been undertaken with great care. However, the Publisher, employees, editors, and agents of The Haworth Press are not responsible for any errors contained herein or for consequences that may ensue from use of materials or information contained in this work. The Haworth Press is committed to the dissemination of ideas and information according to the highest standards of intellectual freedom and the free exchange of ideas. Statements made and opinions expressed in this publication do not necessarily reflect the views of the Publisher, Directors, management, or staff of The Haworth Press, Inc., or an endorsement by them.

Some names have been changed to protect the privacy of individuals; some individuals are composite characters created from the authors' experience.

Cover painting, "On the Journey," by Ingrid Bloom.
Cover design by Jennifer M. Gaska.

Library of Congress Cataloging-in-Publication Data

Jewish relational care A-Z : we are our other's keeper / [compiled and edited by] Jack H Bloom.
     p. cm.
     Includes bibliographical references and index.
     ISBN-13: 978-0-7890-2705-4 (hard : alk. paper)
     ISBN-10: 0-7890-2705-4 (hard : alk. paper)
     ISBN-13: 978-0-7890-2706-1 (soft : alk. paper)
     ISBN-10: 0-7890-2706-2 (soft : alk. paper)
     1. Social service—Religious aspects—Judaism. 2. Caring—Religious aspects—Judaism. 3. Helping behavior—Religious aspects—Judaism. 4. Spiritual life—Judaism. 5. Caregivers—Religious life. I. Bloom, Jack H, 1932-   .

BM729.S7J49 2006
296.6'1—dc22

2005013143

To my colleagues whom I love and the tradition to which we are heir

To Steve Gilligan whom I love and the traditions to which he is heir

To the covenant I love and struggle with, to which I am heir

To God, matchmaker extraordinaire, who one beautiful autumn evening took Ingrid, my beloved *Schatz,* by the hand and had her take the seat on my right

And to our heirs whom we love

May they, standing on our shoulders, lovingly treasure what we have done, enhance it a thousand times over, and pass it on to their heirs

CONTENTS

About the Editor   xv

Contributors   xvii

Acknowledgments   xxiii

A Guide for the Reader   1
Jack H Bloom

THE ABC'S OF JEWISH RELATIONAL CARE

1. Premises of Jewish Relational Care   7
Jack H Bloom

Presents the underlying model and presuppositions of this
book

**2. Language As a Relational Tool:
Using Your Mouth with Your Head?**   17
Jack H Bloom

Discusses language, its relation to reality, and how to use it
wisely to achieve rapport as well as to frame and reframe
one's own and others' experiences

CARING FOR THE CAREGIVER'S RELATIONAL "SELF"

3. Taking Care of Ourselves: It's About Time!   51
David J. Zucker

Describes how to use time more effectively and create
healthy boundaries by being fully at work, taking time off,
using technology wisely, and employing methods of self-
care

4. Managing Compassion Fatigue   67
David J. Stern

Defines compassion and compassion fatigue; informs and
advises on how to deal with compassion fatigue, acknowledging that life, though wonderful, sometimes hurts like hell

5. Maintaining Balance: The Kabbalah As a Resource   81
Susan Gulack

Makes use of the Kabbalah's understanding of the physical, emotional, mental, and spiritual world in which we live as a resource for maintaining balance in our lives

HEALING MUSES FOR JEWISH RELATIONAL CARE

6. The Muse of Visiting   87
David J. Zucker
Bonita E Taylor

Talks about the use of visiting, in and of itself, in the healing armamentarium; covers how to plan a purposeful visit and the blessings that ensue from such visitation

7. The Muse of Silence   97
Jeffery M. Silberman

Recommends the benefits and sacredness of silence as a tool in caregiving work

8. The Muse of Relational Listening   101
Samuel Chiel

Considers what it means to truly listen and hear what the other has to say; highlights the importance of this practice for those in caregiving roles

9. The Muse of Music and Song   105
Shira Stern

Discusses music, a traditional Jewish response, as universal, as a link to places we thought our minds had long forgotten, and as a resource that can assist the release of endorphins and help healing take place

10. The Muse of Chanting   111
Bonita E Taylor

Offers a biblically grounded chant for use as a tool in healing work

11. The Muse of Creative Ritual for Relational Healing   **117**
     Marcia Cohn Spiegel

Presents examples of new healing rituals, such as a ritual of purification, a celebration of wisdom, and a ritual for rage; discusses how to create group prayers and caveats in the creation of new rituals

**12. The Muse of Spontaneous Prayer for All
the [*Tzelem* ⇔ *N'shamah*] Relationships**   **127**
     Charles P. Rabinowitz

Offers thoughts about spontaneous prayer: what it is and how we use it in our healing work; suggests a variety of ways to create one's own spontaneous prayers

HOW SPACIOUS IS OUR TENT?

13. Caring for the Non-Jews Within Our Community   **139**
     Gordon M. Freeman
     Stuart Kelman

Teaches how our community is defined by our foundation myth and the various layers of the myth from early times to today; proposes that we need to relate to, and make room for, the new reality and widen our circle to include the non-Jews in our community; presents a new category, *Karov Yisrael,* a relationship that delineates issues of obligation and community

14. Caring for Non-Jews Outside Our Community   **153**
     Judith B. Edelstein

Shares the vast experience gained by one caregiver working with the non-Jewish community in a hospital setting

**15. What We Gentiles Need in Jewish Relational Care:
A Minister's Perspective**   **159**
     Richard L. Rush

Tells us what Christian clergy and congregations need from the rabbi and Jewish community; offers ways for the two communities to strengthen their connection and understanding of each other

WHEN LIFE CHALLENGES
OUR HUMAN "BEING"

16. Caring for and Supporting Those Going Through Divorce
Judith Levitan

165

Discusses how divorce is a stressful, often crazy time when life's anchors, or "containers," disintegrate and one's own sense of self as well as the nuclear and extended family are severely threatened; describes how clergy can help and support through the most difficult times, as the healing begins; discusses the *get,* the Jewish bill of divorce

17. When a Pregnancy Is Unwelcome
Bonnie Margulis
Douglas Maben

175

Covers the issues women with unwelcome pregnancies face and the three options available; presents a model counseling session as well as rituals for pregnancy loss and for healing after abortion

18. Caring for Those Whose Sexual Orientation and Gender Identity Vary
Nancy H. Wiener

191

Deals with the coming-out process for individuals within the Jewish community and what the community needs to do to respond openly and lovingly, such as same-sex ceremonies

JEWISH RELATIONAL CARE WHEN
THE RELATIONSHIP IS FRAGILE

19. Relating to and Caring for Those Who Don't Care About You
Steven Bayar

205

Uses our understanding of the rabbi as symbolic exemplar as a means for dealing with and loving those who don't care; discusses minimizing and dealing with destructive dynamics

20. Blessing Those We Have Trouble Blessing
Jack H Bloom

209

Presents thoughts on how we bless those we have trouble blessing using the "blessings" of Yaaqov at the end of the book of Genesis as a teaching paradigm

21. A Story of Brokenness and Healing:
   The Relationship of Rabbi and Congregant   221
         Rena Halpern Kieval
         Dan Ornstein

   Shares a poignant story of tragedy, loss, and disconnection
   between a rabbi and a committed congregant; discusses how
   the break in the relationship happened, how they healed the
   break and re-created their relationship, and what they have
   learned in the process

22. *T'shuvah* in Sexual Violations with Direct Implications
   for Other Situations: Relational Care for Those
   Who Have Sinned and Wish to "Return"   241
         Jack H Bloom

   Critiques the traditional model of *t'shuvah,* commonly mistranslated as repentance; presents a new model based on Jewish relational care; discusses its application to those who
   have violated sexual boundaries as well as the Jewish clergy's
   special role in re-creating a new relationship to self and community

23. Jewish Relational Thinking and a Difficult Text:
   Amalek and Us   269
         Jack H Bloom

   Analyzes, in a Jewish relational manner, a classic biblical
   text demanding unremitting revenge

JEWISH RELATIONAL CARE IN THE "GOLDEN" YEARS

24. Jewish Relational Care with the Healthy Aging   277
         Richard F. Address

   Addresses the new challenges and opportunities presented to
   the Jewish community and clergy by the "longevity revolution"; discusses the need to broaden our thinking about care
   of the aging from simply end-of-life care to reflect the large,
   growing population of healthy, active, older community
   members

25. Jewish Relational Care and Retired Clergy   289
Jack H Bloom

Considers the crucial question of whether one is retiring "from" or retiring "to"; discusses resources that can help and the usefulness of new tasks that absorb one's whole being

JEWISH RELATIONAL CARE
WITH THE TRAUMATIZED

26. There and Back Again—
Journey into the "Death Zone":
Jewish Relational Care and Disabilities   307
Judith Z. Abrams

Presents a personal memoir of the author's traumatic experience with chronic pain and illness; discusses managing the practical issues of navigating the medical maze as well as the blessings and the tragedies that come with this painful journey

27. When the Rabbi Needs Care   315
Andrew R. Sklarz

Offers a personal memoir of a rabbi facing a life-threatening illness; explains what he needed during this time from those near to him and from his congregation

28. Caring for Those Violated by Child Sexual Abuse and Incest   329
Rachel Lev

Examines t'shuvah in the context of child sexual abuse as well as the impact on the victim and the community; asks the question of when and if t'shuvah can ever be done; looks at how our communities can help to heighten awareness and promote healing

JEWISH RELATIONAL CARE
WITH THE IMPAIRED

29. Relating Gently and Wisely with the Cognitively Impaired   339
Cary Kozberg

Offers touching wisdom about dealing with those who suffer from Alzheimer's disease and other cognitively degenerative conditions

30. Caring for the Mentally Ill   **357**
Judith Brazen

Discusses how clergy caregivers must be open to alternative, often idiosyncratic, relationships with God and alternative relationships with the community; offers specific guidelines for working with, and caring for, the mentally ill

31. Caring for the Institutionalized Developmentally Disabled   **365**
Bernie Robinson

Describes how participation in communal worship is often the only avenue for the institutionalized person with developmental disabilities to actively identify with the Jewish People and tradition; suggests ways of achieving this goal

JEWISH RELATIONAL CARE AT LIFE'S END

32. Relating to the Sick and Dying   **369**
Steven Moss

Examines ways, based on personal experience, in which the [*Tzelem*⇔*N'shamah*] relationship is crucial to the care of the sick and dying

33. The *Vidui:* Jewish Relational Care for the Final Moments of Life   **375**
Alison Jordan
Stuart Kelman

Emphasizes the importance of liturgy and ritual in the final moments of life; offers some truly beautiful versions of the *Vidui,* a prayer for the final moments of life

34. Jewish Relational Care with the Grieving   **389**
Mel Glazer

Gives caregivers ways to help those experiencing a loss deal with their pain; also provides many "dos and don'ts" for caregivers to observe when dealing with the grieving; stresses the importance of the use of "positive grief language" for anyone interacting with the grieving; touches on working with children after they've experienced a loss

Healing Notes. Frames for Blessing All *"Selves"*
As [Breath-Taking⇔Models of Divinity] **401**
Jack H Bloom

Index **435**

ABOUT THE EDITOR

Jack H Bloom, PhD, Rabbi and Clinical Psychologist, is one of a handful of rabbis who is a full member of both the Central Conference of American Rabbis (Reform) and the Rabbinical Assembly (Conservative). In addition to his private practice at the Psychotherapy Center in Fairfield, Connecticut, Dr. Bloom serves as Director of Professional Career Review for his Reform colleagues, for whom he created a program to assist rabbis seeking to shape their futures. Working closely with Conservative rabbis, Dr. Bloom mentors and has taught regularly at the Rabbinic Training Institutes sponsored by his alma mater, the Jewish Theological Seminary of America.

Dr. Bloom earned a bachelor's degree at Columbia College and a BHL (Bachelor's of Hebrew Literature), an MHL (Master's of Hebrew Literature), and rabbinical ordination at the Jewish Theological Seminary of America. He served as rabbi of Congregation Beth El, Fairfield, Connecticut, for ten years, during which time he completed an STM (Master's of Sacred Theology) in Pastoral Counseling at New York Theological Seminary. Dr. Bloom earned a PhD in Clinical Psychology at Columbia. Dr. Bloom's book *The Rabbi As Symbolic Exemplar: By the Power Vested in Me* (Haworth, 2002) is now in use in rabbinic training throughout the country and is used by non-Jewish clergy and laity to understand what it is like to be clergy.

Dr. Bloom has become known as a rabbi's rabbi. In 2001, Dr. Bloom was awarded an honorary doctorate "in recognition of the enormous contribution [he has] made to improving the personal and professional lives of Conservative and Reform rabbis." Dr. Bloom's "concern for colleagues at the center of [his] professional life" as well as his "love and respect for the work of [his] colleagues" makes him "the quintessential rabbi for rabbis."

Dr. Bloom and his beloved wife, Ingrid, a German teacher, reside in Fairfield, Connecticut. They are the parents of four children and the grandparents of seven.

CONTRIBUTORS

Rabbi Judith Z. Abrams, PhD, is Founder and Director of Maqom: A School for Adult Talmud Study (www.maqom.com) and the author of many books. Her book *Judaism and Disabilities* (Gallaudet University Press, 1998) won the Koret Jewish Studies Publications Program Publication Subsidy in 1998.

Rabbi Richard F. Address, DMin, directs the Department of Jewish Family Concerns for the Union for Reform Judaism. Caregiving issues are an integral part of the department's movement-wide program on sacred aging.

Steven Bayar, BA, MA, is Rabbi of Bnai Israel Congregation in Millburn, New Jersey, since 1989; co-founder of Ikkar Publishing; author of Ziv/Tzedakah curricula; and co-author of *Teens & Trust: Building Bridges in Jewish Education* (Torah Aura, 1992).

Judith Brazen was ordained from Hebrew Union College—Jewish Institute of Religion (HUC-JIR), New York City, in 1990. She serves as Rabbi and Pastoral Counselor with Jewish Chaplaincy Services of the Jewish Social Service Agency and Hospice of Metropolitan Washington. She has recently trained and worked in behavioral health at the National Institutes of Health.

Rabbi Samuel Chiel, BSS, MHL, received his bachelor's degree in social science from the City College of New York and was ordained as a rabbi at the Jewish Theological Seminary of America, both in New York City. He is Rabbi Emeritus of Temple Emanuel, Newton, Massachusetts, where he served as Senior Rabbi for twenty-seven years. In retirement, he has become Scholar in Residence at the Combined Jewish Philanthropies of Greater Boston and Director of the Rabbinic Institute and special advisor to Dr. David Gordis, President of Boston Hebrew College.

Rabbi Judith B. Edelstein, BA, MA, DMin, works at the Jewish Home & Hospital Lifecare System in New York City as the Director of Religious Life. She is also Chair of the Board of the Academy for Jewish Religion, Riverdale, New York, from which she was ordained.

Rabbi Gordon M. Freeman, PhD, was ordained by the Jewish Theological Seminary, New York City, and received his PhD in political science from the University of California, Berkeley. After a tour of duty as a U.S. Air Force Chaplain, he has served as Rabbi of Congregation B'nai Shalom in Walnut Creek, California, since 1968. He has published extensively on the Jewish political tradition and is a Hebrew calligrapher.

Mel Glazer, BA, BHL, MA, DMin, a pulpit Rabbi and Grief Specialist for over thirty years, believes that we learn the emotional truth about ourselves only when we grieve our losses and move forward. He received his BA from Columbia University; his BHL and MA from the Jewish Theological Seminary, where he was ordained in 1974; and his DMin from Princeton Theological Seminary. He is Rabbi of Temple Israel of the Poconos in Stroudsburg, Pennsylvania.

Rabbi Susan Gulack, BA, received her bachelor's degree in Hebraic Studies, Elementary and Special Education, from Rutgers University in 1980 and was ordained at the Academy for Jewish Religion in 1986. A member of the Rabbinical Assembly and the National Association of Jewish Chaplains, she serves as a chaplain in three prisons, a psychiatric hospital, and a VA hospital, as well as being the mother of two special-needs children. Climbing the Tree is one of the ways she maintains her balance.

Alison Jordan, RN, MS, MFT, is a psychotherapist and member of Congregation Netivot Shalom in Berkeley, California. She has particular interest in Jewish responses to illness, death, and bereavement and has been developing relevant new liturgy as well as a handbook on the deathbed confession.

Stuart Kelman, PhD, is Rabbi at Congregation Netivot Shalom in Berkeley, California. A graduate of the Jewish Theological Seminary, New York City, he holds a PhD in education from the University of Southern California, Los Angeles; has created a Chevra Kadisha at the congregation; and has written books about death and dying and Tahara. He is on the Board of Directors of Kavod v'Nichum, a national organization of Chevra Kadishas.

Rena Halpern Kieval, BA, MSW, was ordained as a rabbi at the Academy for Jewish Religion, Riverdale, New York, in May 2006. She serves as Rabbinic Associate at Congregation Ohav Shalom and as Jewish Chaplain at Albany Medical Center, in Albany, New York, where she lives with her husband and two sons.

Rabbi Cary Kozberg is Director of Religious Life at the Council for Jewish Elderly in Chicago. He has been working with older Jewish and non-Jewish adults for over sixteen years. Through his work and writings, he hopes to promote more sanctity in contemporary culture. He believes that Jews and all people of faith are God's "walking commercials."

Rachel Lev, MSW, is the author of *Shine the Light—Sexual Abuse and Healing in the Jewish Community.* A psychotherapist for over twenty-five years, she has engaged in clinical work primarily with adult survivors of childhood loss or trauma.

Judith Levitan, CSW, is Director of Clinical and Community Support Services for the Jewish Connections Division of the Jewish Board of Family and Children's Services, which developed and runs the Divorce Support and Single Parent Family Projects in partnership with the Jewish Community Center (JCC) in Manhattan. She is also in private practice in Manhattan.

Douglas Maben is a theologically trained carpenter and practicing psychotherapist. He serves the Religious Coalition for Reproductive Choice, Washington, DC, as an All Options Clergy Counselor and Trainer.

Rabbi Bonnie Margulis is Director of Clergy Programming and Associate Director of Field Services for the Religious Coalition for Reproductive Choice (www.rcrc.org), Washington, DC.

Rabbi Steven Moss, DMin, has served B'nai Israel, Oakdale, New York, for over thirty years as its spiritual leader. He also has served as a chaplain in many hospitals in New York City and the surrounding metropolitan area, including Memorial Sloan-Kettering Cancer Center, and with various local police departments.

Dan Ornstein, BA, MA, is Rabbi of Congregation Ohav Shalom and a writer living in Albany, New York. He received a BA in sociology and history from Columbia University and a BA in Talmud from the Jewish Theological Seminary of America, where he also earned an MA in Jewish education and his rabbinical ordination.

Rabbi (Dayan) Charles P. Rabinowitz, AB, MA, is a bereavement counselor, a Reform Jewish educator (RJE), and a board-certified chaplain. After being a visiting rabbinical student at Leo Baeck College in London, England, he was ordained by Tifereth Israel Rabbinical Seminary as a Rabbi and Dayan.

Rabbi Bernie Robinson, BA, MAHL, JD, served full-time as California State Chaplain at Napa State Hospital (a psychiatric facility) and at Sonoma and Agnews Developmental Centers for twelve years (1987-1999). He resides in San Rafael, California, with his wife, Yetta.

Reverend Richard L. ("Dick") Rush, BA, MDiv, served as Pastor of First Church Congregational of Fairfield, Connecticut, for thirty-three years and as Adjunct Assistant Professor in Communication Studies at the University of Bridgeport, Connecticut, for more than twenty-five years concurrently. He was deeply involved in community Jewish-Christian issues during that same period. Now retired, he lives in Concord, New Hampshire.

Rabbi Jeffery M. Silberman, DMin, DD (hc), has been a hospital chaplain for more than twenty years and has directed Clinical Pastoral Education programs at Lenox Hill Hospital in Manhattan, New York; UCSF Medical Center at Mount Zion, San Francisco, California; Albert Einstein Medical Center, Philadelphia, Pennsylvania; Beth Israel Medical Center, New York City; and, currently, Norwalk Hospital, Norwalk, Connecticut.

Rabbi Andrew R. Sklarz, MA, MSW, serves as spiritual leader of Old York Road Temple—Beth Am in Abington, Pennsylvania. In addition to his rabbinical training and ordination at Hebrew Union College—Jewish Institute of Religion (HUC-JIR), Rabbi Sklarz holds master's degrees in school psychology and social work. Passionately devoted to the concept of spiritual healing, Rabbi Sklarz has served in a variety of congregations and hospital settings, including Memorial Sloan-Kettering Cancer Center. Rabbi Sklarz celebrates his many blessings in life, most of all his wife, Susan, and their two children, Daniella and Alexander.

Marcia Cohn Spiegel, Doctor of Jewish Communal Service, Hebrew Union College—Jewish Institute of Religion (HUC-JIR), Los Angeles, California, is working to create change in the attitudes of the Jewish community toward addiction, violence, and sexual abuse. She works with both women and men to create rituals of healing and celebration.

David J. Stern, PsyD, is a licensed psychologist, healer, teacher/trainer living and working in Providence, Rhode Island. In addition to individual counseling, he consults with organizations and helps them to explore and develop relevant spiritual practices within the workplace. He is currently developing a spiritual mentoring program to help clergy develop peer support and growth groups and transform the spiritual life of their congregations.

Rabbi Shira Stern, DMin, BCC, is Director of the Center for Studies in Jewish Pastoral Care, part of the HealthCare Chaplaincy in Manhattan. She has been a pulpit rabbi, a full-time community chaplain, the East Coast Director for MAZON: A Jewish Reponse to Hunger, and a community activist.

Rabbi Bonita E Taylor, MA, BCC, is Associate Director of Clinical Pastoral Education (CPE) for the HealthCare Chaplaincy in Manhattan. She is Pastoral Care Educator at the Jewish Institute for Pastoral Care, New York

City; the Academy for Jewish Religion, Riverdale, New York; Yeshivat Chovevei Torah, New York City; and Spiritual Leader for Congregation Gan Eden in Maui, Hawaii. She serves on the National Association of Jewish Chaplains (NAJC) Board of Directors and has been published in several Jewish and secular journals.

Rabbi Nancy H. Wiener, DMin, is Clinical Director of the Jacob and Hilda Blaustein Center for Pastoral Counseling and Adjunct Associate Professor of Pastoral Care and Counseling, Hebrew Union College—Jewish Institute of Relgion (HUC-JIR), New York City. She is Rabbi of a Reform Chavurah in Pound Ridge, New York.

Rabbi David J. Zucker, PhD, BCC, is full-time Chaplain/Rabbi at Shalom Park, a senior continuum-of-care center, in Aurora, Colorado. Author of three books, *Israel's Prophets: An Introduction for Christians and Jews* (Paulist, 1994); *American Rabbis: Facts and Fiction* (Jason Aronson, 1998), and *The Torah: An Introduction for Christians and Jews* (Paulist, 2005), he has contributed chapters to several books, and he publishes regularly in both Jewish and secular journals and magazines.

Acknowledgments

With gratitude to Tara Maquire Knopick, an exemplar that humankind is modeled after and molded by Divinity, whose unstinting loyalty and talent helped make this book possible.

With appreciation to Arnie Sher, longtime beloved friend who, though he didn't finish the chapter he was supposed to, nonetheless, with his unswerving support, helped birth this book.

And respect and thanks to Amy Rentner, superb editor and human being, whose commitment, talent, and caring have made this a better book.

And admiration for Bill Palmer, who suggested this enterprise, and for all the folks at Haworth whose consistent decency and good grace have helped bring it to fruition.

A Guide for the Reader

Jack H Bloom

A thing and its opposite
stood at the door,
and came in.
Someone invited them.[1]

I was a rabbi who had fled congregational life, returned to Columbia to get a PhD, and was working full-time as a clinical psychologist when I met Stephen Gilligan. The location near the Continental Divide, high in the Colorado Rockies, might well have been a metaphor for the divisions within me. Stephen, then twenty-eight, was coleading a hypnosis workshop. I needed all the trance I could get to navigate the rapids of an exquisitely painful divorce. That we would become beloved friends was unimaginable to me. An even greater bonus was Steve's developing Self-Relations, a model of human "being" that by inviting "them" in enabled me to reclaim fully the estranged religious half of my identity and then to fashion a [Both/And] relationship so that I am now at one and the same time [rabbi⇔psychologist], with both parts interacting with each other in a respectful, loving, sometimes tumultuous relationship. Affirming both, at the same time, I realized how the Self-Relations concept of the relational self is not only rooted in our Jewish foundational myth but also ever present in the centuries of biblical and postbiblical insights and learning that comprise our Jewish inheritance. The playing out of a covenantal sacred relational dynamic involving human beings, their nature, and the Divine is at the core of what Jewish tradition is about. In recent years a major focus of my work has been being a "sponsor," witnessing in Jewish tradition the presence of relational thinking, naming it where it appears, and blessing it.[2] Self-Relations concepts provide a framework, rationale, and methodology for inviting in the multiple *"selves"* of each of us, as well as our relations to all others of our

---

1. Yehuda Amichai, *Posthumous Fragments,* trans. Leon Wieseltier, excerpted in *The New York Times Book Review,* November 21, 2004.
2. See Jack H Bloom, *The Rabbi As Symbolic Exemplar: By the Power Vested in Me* (Binghamton, NY: The Haworth Press, 2002), Chapter 10, "Witnessing, Naming, and Blessing."

species and to the Holy and Bountiful One. This book is heir to a long history of our tradition's witnessing, naming, and blessing the very best aspects of the environment in which we live, bringing them into relationship within Jewish life and thought, into a loving, respectful [I–You] relationship.[3]

According to Gilligan,

> a sponsor does not operate in a vacuum . . . [sponsorship] requires that the sponsor surrender to a larger field than him or her *Self*. [The sponsor] is a part of a beautiful tradition of awakening the human spirit. . . . [The tradition—JHB] is the real "sponsor." There are many streams in this river of consciousness. . . . [The sponsor] must walk and swim in at least one to be a good sponsor. Thus, being a good sponsor requires that [the sponsor] connect with those that have gone before . . . and those who have started a little bit after . . . [on that particular path].[4]

I walk in the footsteps of my Jewish antecedents. Being God's recalcitrant servant, I wrestle with the very tradition of which I am a product. I, following in the footsteps of my biblical namesake, am blessed by that struggle. Jewish tradition influences and sometimes determines both the ground and boundaries of the struggle. Jewish experience is the particular stream of human experience into which I was born and educated, and in which I live and breathe. That is not all of me. I also swim in the stream of Self-Relations. The two are I hope in a loving relationship. These are not the only paths. Others may choose to walk on paths that differ. They are no less holy, for either all of us are modeled after and molded by Divinity, or each of us is in deep trouble.

Following the wide and positive reception of *The Rabbi As Symbolic Exemplar*, The Haworth Press enouraged me to undertake a book on Jewish caregiving. I decided early on that the book you hold in your hands, to which so many have made vital contributions, would be coherent rather than scattershot in approach. Each contribution would need to fit within a [Self-Relations⇔Jewish Tradition] model. All of the authors, given their

---

3. After Walter Kaufmann, who, in "I and You: A Prologue," in Martin Buber's *I and Thou: A New Translation* (New York: Simon and Schuster, 1970), spends sixty pages demonstrating conclusively that I–You is better English usage than I–Thou, and in consultation with my wife, Ingrid, a native German speaker and teacher of German, who affirms that "you" is a better expression of what Buber meant by the German intimate "Du." The publisher, concerned about market share, no doubt retained the more familiar *I and Thou* title as better for sales.

4. Stephen Gilligan, in private correspondence with the author, February 1998, as quoted in Bloom, *The Rabbi As Symbolic Exemplar*, p. 165.

own widely different styles, were asked to follow some of this editor's guidelines, which adhered to certain given premises of Self-Relations.

An example of one such premise and the changes it made: The use of *Tzelem Elohim* in glorious isolation, rather than in relationship, and its six-teenth-century translation as "image"[5] as a mantra is an inadequate half-truth.

If we accept Maimonides' understanding of *Tzelem* as being our cogni-tive being, the isolated use of *Tzelem Elohim* is a well-intentioned distortion of our biblical underpinnings. It, first and foremost, deals only with Genesis 1:25-27 and totally disregards the second creation myth of Genesis 2:5-7, which the biblical author clearly felt needed to be added. It is simplistic and does not deal with the reality of how we are as human beings, how we are with those "independently" existing parts of us that are clearly not "in the image." It has become a truism, widely accepted, tripping too easily off the tongue, a truism that, though having served us well, is now less than ade-quate and has seen its day. Whenever a contributor used the phrase, it was edited out and changed to the affirmation that humankind *is modeled after and molded by Divinity.*

Though the reader will no doubt read different chapters at different times, I strongly recommend beginning with the first section, *The ABC's of Jewish Relational Care,* particularly Chapter 1, "Premises of Jewish Rela-tional Care." The concepts presented in this section are the foundation on which the entire book is built.

To further achieve some sense of unity, virtually all translations of the Torah text used by the editor in his chapters are from the magnificent trans-lation by Everett Fox in *The Five Books of Moses.*[6] Given my stance on the use of "image," I have taken the liberty of slightly altering the Fox transla-tion in one vital place, the story of creation. Fox's translation of Genesis 1:26-27 reads:

> God said: "Let us make humankind, in our image, according to our likeness." . . . God created humankind in his image, in the image of God did he create it, male and female did he create them.

---

5. Used in the King James Bible of 1611. "Image" according to *Merriam-Webster's Collegiate Dictionary* (Eleventh Edition, 2003), is a Middle English word that means "a reproduction or imitation of the form of a person or thing; *esp.:* an imitation in solid form," or, alternatively, "exact likeness: SEMBLANCE," as in God created man in His im-age. Certainly in modern usage "image" has much more of a visual sense to it. It does not mean what *Tzelem* meant, then or now. An Italian saying puts it best: *Traduttore traditore*—"The translator is a traitor." The only question is degree.

6. Everett Fox, *The Five Books of Moses: A New Translation with Introductions, Commentary, and Notes* (New York: Schocken Books, 1995).

The emended translation in this book reads:

> God said: "Let us **model** humankind after us, according to our like-
> ness." . . . God created humankind **modeled** after Himself, in the
> **model** of God He created it, male and female He created them.

Fox's translation in Genesis 5:1-2 is:

> This is the record of the begettings of Adam/Humankind! At the time
> of God's creating humankind, in the likeness of God did He then make
> it, male and female He created them, and gave blessing to them and
> named them "Humankind" on the day of their being created.

The emended translation reads:

> This is the record of the begettings of Adam/Humankind! At the time
> of God's creating humankind, **modeled after God** did He then make it,
> male and female He created them, and gave blessing to them and
> named them "Humankind" on the day of their being created.

Where the translation is neither that of Everett Fox nor mine, it is noted as
being by the author of the piece.

Transliterations were a problem. The transliteration system used here
follows the Union of American Hebrew Congregations (now the Union for
Reform Judaism) Transliteration Guidelines and Master Word List prepared by Debra Hirsch Corman and Rabbi Hara Person, February 1, 2001.
Translations and the meaning of Hebrew transliterated terms are virtually
identical throughout the book and appear as footnotes within the chapters.
This is done for the convenience of both those who know Hebrew and can
move on effortlessly and those others who do not know Hebrew and would
want ready access to the English explanation.

The authors whose work makes up *Jewish Relational Care A-Z: We Are
Our Other's Keeper* responded magnificently to my call for contributions
and graciously to my suggested changes. Representative of the best around,
they have covered a wide range of topics, though not all. Some await a second edition.

Conceiving, partially authoring, and learning what it means to edit a
book of this magnitude has turned out to be a most exciting project. I am
profoundly grateful to all contributors, and to the God with whom I have
wrestled for sparing me to reach this day.

THE ABC'S OF JEWISH RELATIONAL CARE

The כשמה *(N'shamah)* is always present
at the core and essence of each person
The כשמה *(N'shamah)* is the Breath-Taking Somatic self
Life moves through you, except when it doesn't
Life is great, but sometimes it hurts like hell
There is a second you, always present the צלם *(Tzelem)*
The צלם *(Tzelem)* is the Cognitive self-mindfulness
whose task is to witness sponsor, name and bless
whatever comes through
the Breath-Taking Somatic self כשמה *(N'shamah)*
The [כשמה⇔צלם] *[Tzelem⇔N'shamah]*
[Breath-Taking⇔Model of Divinity]
is in balance and life works,
when both are in an [I–You] reciprocal relationship.
Relationship is the basic religious and psychological unit.
There is an intelligence greater than you present in the world.

דע לפני מי אתה עומד

Know in Whose Presence you exist.

B'rachot 28b

You are an incurable deviant.

Mishnah Sanhedrin 4:5

5

1

Premises of Jewish Relational Care

Jack H Bloom

It is told that Mendel of Kotzk (1787-1859) would shock a disciple by asking: ***"Where does God live?"***

Certain of his learning, the disciple responded: "The whole world is filled with God's glory." The "Kotzker" answered his own question—perhaps with an edge in his voice: ***"God lives wherever one lets God in."***

Or, we might say, daring to update the Kotzker: ***"God lives in relationship."***

Let God in?! Be in relationship with God?! It's an untidy mess inside, all those unspoken thoughts, unworthy aims, hidden acts, splits between what we let the world see and who we think we really are. Besides, there are all those "negative *selves*" living in our attic/basement, closeted away from others' view, and most often our own. We barely keep them at bay! They shouldn't be with us at all! If we open the doors just a crack they'll overwhelm us and trash the place! Let God in? When our inner life is not a fit place to bring anyone home to, and we can barely care for ourselves? Let God in?! Who are you kidding? And we're expected to do caregiving for others?! No way! Get someone else!

We are the inheritors of an incredibly rich 5,000-year-old tradition dealing with what it is, and means, to be human. We are charged both to remain loyal to that tradition and to explore what modern models can teach us. This is an audacious challenge. What can we moderns bring to a tradition that has spent thousands of years dealing with the human condition? What new understandings will make a difference, and what new means are usable beyond the well-worn, still indispensable tools of the past. As Jewish relational caregivers linked to the ongoing search represented in the creation of our tradition, how do we use our best understanding today to assert what *"they"* would have interpreted had *"they"* known? Exhorted to "Reinvent Yourself—Find Your Real Self,"[1] we live in an era where, despite all evi-

---

1. "Reinvent Yourself—A Chat with Judith Sills," appearing in *Psychology Today*, June 2004, pp. 38-40.

dence to the contrary, the Self is still envisioned as a unit. We talk endlessly of the sovereign self and personal autonomy. The right, even more than the ability, to make choices seems not only a given but also a self-evident truth, a desideratum to be pursued with vigor. How can we who live in this time understand being in relationship and caregiving for our *"selves"* and for others? How can we respond to those in our ranks, and to those others for whom we care, to promote well-being and healing? To have a shot at being competent caregivers, we need a grounding that is both authentically Jewish and currently meaningful, and that has a chance of working.

This book presumes a specific and eminently practical model of relationship, useful in Jewish relational caregiving. The model flows from biblical underpinnings and is consonant with current psychological understandings. It is a model of individual, Jewish, and human "beingness."

The model proposes that, first and foremost, we are not unitary selves. The *"self"* we present to the outside world is not all of us. From a very young age we are taught to think of our "being" as a singular Self. This singular Self is to be shaped and molded into a Self that family, society, and religious community consider to be socially appropriate and desirable, whether that be living by the Boy Scout Oath or the Commandments of the Living God. We are taught that things, ideas, emotions, and *"selves"* are either good or bad, either one way or the other. The *"self"* of "To thine own *'self'* be true"[2] refers to one's good, worthwhile, acceptable *"self"* with the other *"selves"* having been educated out or in hiding. When, inevitably, unacceptable *"selves"* show up and take over center stage, despite our best efforts to quash them, we describe ourselves and others in me or not me terms:

> "It wasn't like **ME** to do that."
> "That's just not **HER**."
> "If only you knew the **TRUE ME**."
> "What I did is just **NOT ME**."
> "The **REAL HIM** is always cheating."
> "I just wasn't **MYSELF** when I hit her."
> "**I** didn't know what **I** was doing."

A *New York Times* sports page report about an altercation their star pitcher David Wells was engaged in says it as well as anything: **Yank's Wells Testifies That He Was Attacked.** In court he recounted what he said to 911: "I said a lot of things I probably shouldn't have said on the tape," he told the jurors. **"I wasn't myself at the time."** Furthermore, he told the jury

---

2. William Shakespeare, *Hamlet,* Act 1, Scene 3.

that *part of him would have really liked to go back into the diner and settle things himself.*[3]

Such phrasing is not just a manner of speaking. These words are a description of our "reality." Language is an attempt, sometimes superb and sometimes totally inadequate, to capture and communicate our experience. The "reality" is that each of us is not a Self, and the people we have undertaken to care for, each of them is not a Self. To think of each of us as a Self is to misconstrue how we are, and what our experience is. The human being we are dealing with is also not a Self, as we have hitherto understood that concept, but a relationship. Each person is a relationship between *"selves,"* rather than the position of any given *"self."* The relational self at its best is the experience of both selves simultaneously. Each is the field that holds, and the spirit that connects, the differences. Self is a pattern of me/not me connections experienced in a relational field. Self is the experience of a dynamic relatedness between differences: Self is neither here nor there, me nor you; it is the conversation that bridges, the spirit that unites, the pattern that connects the differences.[4] It is difficult for any caregiver to hold on to that. When dealing with people in who are in pain, hurting, confused, angry, or going through difficult times, the *[Tzelem⇔N'shamah]* seems absent, missing in action. Our task as caregivers is to look for who else is in the room, for evidence of the *[Tzelem⇔N'shamah]*, while not losing contact with our own. Only when that is witnessed, brought forth, loved, appreciated, and blessed can healing begin. SELF comes to be when all those wounded "negative others," both/all *"selves,"* are simultaneously blessed and valued, acknowledged and appreciated, and in loving, respectful contact. SELF occurs in the relationship between our various *"selves."* When we are at our best that relationship can be loving and respectful. When that relationship is wounded and breaks down, we get into trouble and our experience is marked by self-hatred and anger toward others.

Relationship is the basic psychological and religious unit.[5] As Gilligan points out, "nothing exists on its own; something [someone] is known only in relationship to something [someone] 'other' than itself. The simplest relationship is complementary."[6] Perhaps that is why Eve was created: "Now

---

3. See *The New York Times,* Sports, Wednesday, November 20, 2002.

4. Stephen Gilligan, *The Courage to Love* (New York: W.W. Norton and Company, 1997).

5. Ibid.; see "Presuppositions of Self-Relations," to which I have added *"and religious."*

6. Stephen Gilligan, in Stephen Gilligan and Dvorah Simon, eds., *Walking in Two Worlds: The Relational Self in Theory, Practice, and Community* (Phoenix, AZ: Zeig, Tucker, and Theisen, Inc., 2004), p. xxvi. The "[someone]" is my addition.

YHWH," God said, "it is not good for the human to be alone; I will make him a helper corresponding to him."[7] Without relationship we are impaired, and, indeed, only in relationship can life be sustained, creation happen, and life go on.

These are the core foundational religious facts:

ויאמר אלהים נעשה אדם בצלמנו כדמותנו
ויברא אלהים את האדם בצלמו בצלם אלהים
ברא אתו זכר ונקבה ברא אתם

God said: "Let us model humankind after us, according to our like-ness." . . . *God created humankind modeled after Himself, in the model of God* **He created it, male and female** **He created them.**[8]

The biblical author, recognizing the manifold and plural nature of the Creator, perceived that the Divine *Tzelem* was not an adequate description of the human condition. He no doubt noticed that people did unspeakable things, without a shred of good judgment, which they "knew" were not in keeping with the *Tzelem*. She no doubt had heard tales told around the well of Cain and Abel, by thirsty caravan travelers of Sodom and Gomorrah, and countless other stories never recorded. Humans just got carried away and did all kinds of things. That this happened in all arenas of human behavior was evident to any and all who dealt with their own *"selves"* and with other humans. Despite being created *Tzelem*, modeled after Divinity, humanity seemed dragged around by that which was not *Tzelem*. The *Tzelem* could go along on "trips" it knew made no sense. The *Tzelem* all too often seemed just to disappear, abandoning the field. *"You want to do THAT! You know it's wrong! You know you shouldn't! How many times have I told you? Go ahead if you must, but I'm out of here."*

The author, evidently unsatisfied with the partial truth of chapter one, hastens to add the complementary truth of chapter two: that each of us is a *living* being because the Divine breath, the *N'shamah,*[9] was breathed into us by the living God.

---

7. Genesis 2:18. Translation of Torah text by Everett Fox, *The Five Books of Moses: A New Translation with Introductions, Commentary, and Notes* (New York: Schocken Books, 1995), p. 20.

8. Genesis 1:26-27. Author's change from Fox, *The Five Books of Moses,* p. 15. This translation deals with the difficulties that the King James translator created for us by using the word *image* for the Hebrew *Tzelem.* See note 15 for further elucidation.

9. Genesis 2:7, from the Hebrew root, *N-Sh-M*—to breathe.

ויּיצֶר יהוה אלהים את האדם עפר מן האדמה ויפח באפּיו
נשמת חיים ויהי האדם לנפש חיה

YHWH, God, molded the human of dust from the soil, He blew into his nostrils the breath of life; and the human became a living being. [10]

The *N'shamah* can best be understood as our somatic being, marked by pulsation and throbbing, feelings of all sorts, pleasant and painful, and a sense of corporeal aliveness. Beyond being a model of the Divine, we are blessed by the Living God [YHWH][11] who has infused in us the breath of life, saturating each with the precious gift of *N'shamah* [נשמה].

The two are inextricably linked in relationship, forming the [*Tzelem* ⇔*N'shamah*] [Breath-Taking⇔Model of Divinity].[12] The *Tzelem* provides thought, form, and direction. The *N'shamah* gives life, energy, and vitality. The [*Tzelem*⇔*N'shamah*] is at one and the same time both indivisible and yet with each vulnerable part having a life of its own. Thought, form, and direction alone would lead to a useless spinning of the wheels. Life, energy, and vitality alone would be directionless, and we would be dragged around aimlessly by our feelings. We are thus not either *Tzelem* or *N'shamah,* but both simultaneously, interacting reciprocally. When "things" are going well, each part is in living interaction and respectful relationship with the other, and life goes on easily. When one is ignored, incapacitated, or traumatized, the other is grievously wounded. We are truly blessed when the *N'shamah* sustains the *Tzelem* and the *Tzelem* shapes the *N'shamah.*

The [*Tzelem*⇔*N'shamah*] is the basic interacting relationship—in me, in you, and in all others. This is a new and different way of using these terms and will no doubt take some getting used to. *N'shamah* here is not meant as "soul," nor as in the Yiddish description of a kindly person, *"guteh n'shamah."*[13] That has a completely different overtone. In this meaning, the

---

10. Genesis 2:7. Fox, *The Five Books of Moses*, p. 19.

11. This name of God derives from the Hebrew root meaning "to be." Its best meaning is: **[Was! Is! Will be!]**, thus The Eternal. Sarna points out that YHWH "is the . . . immanent, personal God . . . who shows concern for the needs of human beings." Nahum M. Sarna, *Genesis: The Traditional Hebrew Text with New JPS Translation/Commentary by Nahum M. Sarna* (Philadelpha, PA: The Jewish Publication Society, 1989), p. 17.

12. Though it does not fall trippingly off the tongue, [Breath-Taking⇔Model of Divinity], for want of a better English term at this point, is the best I can do, though I admit I do like the overtones. From this point on, I will use [*Tzelem*⇔*N'shamah*] (see note 14). the brackets indicate the interrelated unity of these two elements; the double arrow signifies reciprocal relationship.

13. Literally, a good soul.

N'shamah is the breathing/somatic/corporeal part of each of us. The *Tzelem* is still understood as it was by Maimonides to be humankind's cognitive intellect, since the creating God was, and is, incorporeal, and any other understanding is, or borders on, idolatry.[14] Cognitive intellect is not all we are, however, nor is it independent of our [Breath-Taking] being, our *N'shamah*.

This religious "fact," that humankind is modeled after and molded by Divinity, and whose resulting inalienable core is the functioning, interacting, reciprocal [*Tzelem ⇔ N'shamah*], undergirds our entire Jewish religious structure. This "fact" accounts for who we are and how we are. We ignore it at our peril. All are created this way. If only one of us is not so created, then we are all and each of us in trouble.

One could well assert that it is more important how we are created and function than even who created us. The [*Tzelem ⇔ N'shamah*], and how one lives so as to fulfill the covenant of that relationship, is what is being explored, expounded on, and expanded in rabbinic learning and teaching. How heterodox Judaisms view these underpinnings, and understand them in today's world, is crucial to what an authentic Jewish position can be, and to how we function in the world.

This relationship model suggests that our repeated use *of Tzelem Elohim* (the image of God)[15] as a mantra is an inadequate half-truth. A well-intentioned distortion of our biblical underpinnings, it is simplistic and does not deal with the reality of how we are as human beings, how we are with those "independently" existing parts of us that seem clearly not "in the image." It has become a truism, widely accepted, that, though having served us well, is now less than adequate and has seen its day. In this book we will affirm that humankind is modeled after and molded by Divinity.

Though our tradition clearly maintains that God's words are spoken and heard in multiple ways,[16] suggesting and affirming a world of multiple truths, not all truths are equally useful and choices among them have to be

---

14. Maimonides, in Hebrew **RaMbaM** (Rabbi Moshe ben Maimon), 1135-1204. Arguably the greatest Jewish commentator and philosopher, he was also physician to the court of Sultan Saladin of Egypt. See *Guide of the Perplexed*, trans. M. Friedlander (New York: Hebrew Publishing Co., 1881), Chapter 1: "In man the 'form' 'Tzelem' is that constituent which gives him human perception: and on account of this intellectual perception the term 'Tzelem' is employed."

15. Used in the King James Bible of 1611. "Image" according to *Merriam-Webster's Collegiate Dictionary* (Eleventh Edition, 2003), is a Middle English word that means "a reproduction or imitation of the form of a person or thing: *esp.*: an imitation in solid form," or, alternatively, "exact likeness; SEMBLANCE," as in God created man in His image. Certainly in modern usage "image" has much more of a visual sense to it. It does not mean what *Tzelem* meant, then or now. An Italian saying puts it best: *Traduttore traditore*—"The translator is a traitor." The only question is degree.

16. Babylonian Talmud: Eruvin 13b, Gittin 6b, and others.

made. In the light of this [*Tzelem*⇔*N'shamah*] model, we do well to re-write, and thus update, some of the "in the image" language that pervades our speech and writings and underlies descriptions of what we are about. To illustrate, I will rewrite a statement of "Reform Jewish Sexual Values" as one example of a myriad of locations where the writer, though meaning well, uses "image" and which requires reformulation. The original reads:

> *B'tzelem Elohim* ("in the image of God"). This fundamental Jewish idea, articulated in Genesis 1:27: "And God created humankind in the Divine image—male and female," is at the core of all Jewish values. *B'tzelem Elohim* underscores the inherent dignity of every person, woman and man, with the equal honor and respect due to each individual's integrity and sexual identity. *B'tzelem Elohim* requires each of us to value one's self and one's sexual partner and to be sensitive to his/her needs. Thus do we affirm that consentuality and mutuality are among the values necessary to validate a sexual relationship as spiritual and ethical and, therefore, "in the image of God."[17]

In the [*Tzelem*⇔*N'shamah*] relational model, the aforementioned would read as follows:

> Humankind is modeled after and molded by Divinity and created [*Tzelem*⇔*N'shamah*]. This fundamental Jewish idea, articulated in Genesis 1:27 and Genesis 2:7; that humankind—male and female—is endowed by their creator with the interacting [*Tzelem*⇔*N'shamah*], is at the core of all Jewish values. [*Tzelem*⇔*N'shamah*] underscores that we are, first of all, a relationship between *"selves,"* each *"self"* with its inherent dignity and its corollary: that all others who themselves are relationships between *"selves"* possess inherent dignity and the respect due to each one's worth and identity. Each of us is a "relationship," not a self. Being created [*Tzelem*⇔*N'shamah*] requires each of us to value all of our *"selves,"* without striving to rid ourselves of one or another. We start with our *"selves"* because that's where we live, and even when focused outward, we do it from the position of our own self-identity, which includes all of our *"selves."* Sustaining the [*Tzelem*⇔*N'shamah*] relationship requires each of us to value all of our *"selves,"* and those of our relational partners, so as to be sensitive to their needs. Before we can deal effectively with others, our own internal [*Tzelem*⇔*N'shamah*] has to be in a love-respect,

---

17. *CCAR Journal*, Fall 2001, p. 3, quoting Rabbi Selig Salkowitz from 1981.

[I–You][18] relationship. When that relationship within us is present, we can work with and begin to care for others. When this happens, consentuality and mutuality can happen, and the resultant relationship brings *kedushah*[19] to the world and glory to God.

The different presupposition makes a profound difference.

Another profound difference: The pursuit of oneness often based on the *Sh'ma's*[20] proclamation of the "oneness" of God is antiquated, a less than futile pursuit. In "Reform Jewish Sexual Values" we read:

> Jewish religious values are predicated upon the unity of God and the integrity[21] of the world and its inhabitants as Divine creations. These values identify "shleimut" as a fundamental goal of human experience. The Hebrew root sh-l-m expresses the ideal of wholeness, completeness, unity and peace.[22]

We can no longer assume that *"sh'leimut"* is the fundamental goal of human experience. The people we deal with are not Selves, as we have previously known that they are, each of them, a relationship between and among *"selves."* [Both/And] thinking is crucial. Life is all about relationship. Wholeness, or *sh'leimut,* is an impossibility and is undergirded by either/or fundamentalist thinking. We are not fruitlessly pursuing *sh'leimut,* whether that means wholeness, completeness, unity, or integration. Dvorah Simon points out that

> wholeness is temporary; fluid, the self will always find new dialogue, new ways to be two, not one. This is not a problem: it is precisely in the gap between the two descriptions, the two players in the game as it were, that dimension, meaning, and connection are made.[23]

---

18. After Walter Kaufmann, and in consultation with my wife, Ingrid, a native speaker and teacher of German, who affirms that "you" is a better expression of what Buber meant by the German intimate "Du." Kaufmann, "I and You: A Prologue," in Martin Buber, *I and Thou: A New Translation* (New York: Simon and Schuster, 1970); also see in this book "A Guide for the Reader," p. 2, n. 3.

19. Holiness/sanctity.

20. Deuteronomy 6:5, "Hearken O Israel: YHWH our God YHWH (is) One." Fox, *The Five Books of Moses,* p. 880.

21. According to *Merriam-Webster's Collegiate Dictionary* (Eleventh Edition, 2003), "an unimpaired condition : SOUNDNESS . . . the quality or state of being complete or undivided."

22. "Reform Jewish Sexual Values," *CCAR Journal,* Fall 2001, p. 9.

23. Gilligan and Simon, *Walking in Two Worlds,* from the preface, p. x.

Amos Oz, in his brilliant essay, "Like a Gangster on the Night of the Long Knives, but Somewhat in a Dream," puts it this way:

> People always ask if a story is written "on purpose," or "consciously." What is "consciousness"? There is nothing whatever perhaps that anyone does while "being of sound mind," as they say in the law courts: whatever one is doing, even if it is only mending a dripping tap, one's sound mind is mixed up with something which is not "mind" and not even exactly "sound." It is obviously the same if one is making a picture or a statue or a master plan for a new town, or making a story. If a man sits down to write, let us say, music, he has to be, on the one hand, alert and sharp-witted like a gangster on the night of the long knives, when any split second could be vital, and on the other hand he also has to be somewhat in a dream. If he is alert and nothing more, he cannot write music. But if he is entirely in a dream he cannot write music either.[24]

Peace may be worth going for if we lovingly acknowledge and accept the reality that we are more than one *"self"* and that [Both/And] thinking is essential. This book is about relations between those multiple *"selves"* and relational care, working within these [*Tzelem⇔N'shamah*] premises.

The [*Tzelem⇔N'shamah*] is **not** negotiable. It is a given, ever present in us and in all others. The [*Tzelem⇔N'shamah*] is **not** contingent on our thinking and feeling correctly, on our behaving one way or another, on our accomplishments or the lack thereof, on our perceived goodness or experienced badness. Each of us—do what we will or won't—cannot be rid of it. It is our original **essence.**

The [*Tzelem⇔N'shamah*] Self does not exist in glorious isolation. It is exquisitely vulnerable to influential others and to random events. Each of us is not a Self; each of us is a relationship between and among *"selves."* These *"selves"* are often wounded by the exigencies of life; few escape unscathed.[25] The [*Tzelem⇔N'shamah*] Self exists in relation to these. All are in relation. This is where problems begin, and bad things happen.

Often obscured in the fog of compromised living, the [*Tzelem⇔N'shamah*] is **always** waiting to be seen and heard, attended to, and returned to.

---

24. Amos Oz, *Under This Blazing Light* (New York: Cambridge University Press, 1979), pp. 185-189; quote appears on pp. 188-189.

25. See Jack H Bloom, *The Rabbi As Symbolic Exemplar: By the Power Vested in Me* (Binghamton, NY: The Haworth Press, 2002), Chapter 7, "The Silenced Modim—*Modim d'Rabanan:* Tending Our Wounded Selves," pp. 169-171.

When we and/or others turn away from the [*Tzelem*⇔*N'shamah*], neglecting it in ourselves, ignoring and disregarding it in others, harm is done, commitments are broken, intimacies are violated, sexual violations occur, children are hurt, trusts are betrayed, and great evil is perpetrated. Blame and contempt, anger and condemnation, violence of all sorts, directed toward ourselves but even more dangerously at others, increase our sense of alienation and isolation, turning us ever more away from the [*Tzelem*⇔ *N'shamah*] with which we are blessed, blocking any chance of experiencing it in others.

As we are not a Self, each of us being a relationship, the charge each Jewish relational caregiver is faced with is to search out, tune in to, stay focused on, respect, nourish, sustain, and sponsor the [*Tzelem*⇔*N'shamah*], first, in all of our *"selves,"* and then in others.

That is a daunting challenge! It is, after all, in our inner life where we are most vulnerable to ruptures in our relationship with our own [*Tzelem*⇔ *N'shamah*]. When we lose contact with our [*Tzelem*⇔*N'shamah*], we, without fail, lose contact with others, and losing contact with theirs is a sure sign that we have lost contact with ours. That these relationships break down time and again goes with being human. What do we do when in our inner life thoughts and feelings appear that, despite our best efforts, imply that our [*Tzelem*⇔*N'shamah*] relationship is out of kilter? How do we reconcile our experience of these "negative *selves*," which do not seem compatible with the [*Tzelem*⇔*N'shamah*], with what our creation proclaims is our core and being? No matter the public persona we present, we consider these "negative *selves*" to be "persona non grata." *"They"* distance us from the [*Tzelem*⇔*N'shamah*] and leave us feeling diminished. We struggle valiantly against these "negative *selves*," hoping that they disappear, or at least have the good sense and common courtesy to stay out of public view.

Repairing the breach by turning to our [*Tzelem*⇔*N'shamah*] is a supremely important undertaking. It requires an inner dialogue of mutual respect, leading to a loving, personal human relationship between each and all of our *"selves"*—those we value and those we distance; the "positive" and the "negative"; the "acceptable" and "unacceptable." To do this we must value and bless all of our *"selves"* and bring each and all back, particularly those *"selves"* previously rejected, into relationship within the [*Tzelem*⇔ *N'shamah*].

We rabbis dare not abandon the field to the world of psychotherapy and pop culture. As symbolic exemplars of God, we can, given proper training, be especially effective in caregiving.

So it is true! ***One finds God in relationship.*** For God, it is a welcome home to God's own creation. For us, it is coming home to all we are. For those we care for, it is a priceless blessing.

2

Language As a Relational Tool:
Using Your Mouth with Your Head?

Jack H Bloom

Language—the relational tool par excellence—pervades everything we do. It is a major tool in the work of all clergy who provide Jewish relational care. Be it the communal language relating to text or prayer, or the caregiving language we use, it is imperative that rabbis and other clergy be, first and foremost, professional relational communicators. Viewing ourselves this way unifies the disparate aspects of the vital work we do and helps prevent burnout. This chapter is about using your mouth as a relational tool to get results worth having and to amplify your caregiving ability.

Learned at an early age, language became for most of us one of our first relational tools. Adults listened eagerly for our first sounds that resembled words, and though there was little similarity between what we uttered and words that meant something, they rewarded us enthusiastically. *It was magic!* "Ma-Ma" came out of our mouths and mother came to attend to our needs; "Da-Da," and we got a big smile from the tall man who was picking us up. We said "wa-wa" and water appeared. Soon adults were repeating our sounds, and in the effort to *relate* to us, *they* learned to talk baby talk. As toddlers, we were praised for our first coherent words. *It was magic all over again!* Sometimes when we didn't get what we wanted, we would talk more or louder or throw a screaming tantrum. That sometimes worked. We didn't know a better way. Even as adults, we at times still resort to those childhood tactics. We assume that others are supposed to understand us and immediately grasp what we want them to do. We've been acting on that principle all of our lives because it feels natural and right. But when the old ways don't work so magically anymore, we wonder why we don't get what we want, why others don't seem to understand us. "Perhaps if I just say it louder or . . ."

Despite times when you're disappointed, you *are* incredibly adept at using language. You use it to order a cup of coffee, ask instructions on how to get someplace, tell others where you hurt or how you feel about them and so on. Your frustration in using language lies in the desire to achieve better results from communications with others. Now that you're a fully grown dedicated caregiver, you need tools that will give you new ways to think and plan and to pay attention to what works and what doesn't. You need to develop new ways of using language to get the job done. You need to be able to change tools if what you're using isn't doing the job. You'll need tools that give you flexibility and will stop you from doing the same thing over again, only louder. Getting messages through, and having a lot of ways of doing that, so that your ideas are received, related to, and acted upon in a meaningful way, is the focus of this chapter.

You will not be learning all of the ways in which we relate and communicate with others,[1] but instead exploring one of the most powerful relational tools: spoken language. How you use language can change your Jewish relational caregiving. This chapter can help you exercise your mouth with your head in new ways, for your own learning and pleasure, and for the benefit of those you encounter. You can do it your old "natural" way—you're pretty expert already at doing that, and it has gotten you a long way—but if you want to learn new ways of relating, and have some fun doing it, read on and sample these new ideas in small bits or mouthfuls.

What Is Language Anyhow? What Does It Do?

Language, as with the air we breathe, surrounds us totally; we're usually not aware it is there, though it affects everything we do, and life without it would be most difficult. Until we feel the wind against our bodies or hear it rustling in the trees or, worse, see it or smell it, we pay little attention to the air around us. Language, too, is so much a part of our environment that we're often not consciously aware of it. It just is. Yet, language determines

---

1. The special uses of music, location, smell, and touch, though extremely important, will be touched upon only briefly in this chapter. An example: On June 12, 1993, on a Sabbath morning, I was sitting in synagogue chanting the service, thinking about nothing in particular, when the cantor used as a melody for one of the prayers "Erev Shel Shoshanim," the processional chosen by my bride at my first wedding. In a flash, I was transported back to June 12, 1960, thirty-three years earlier—that wedding and marriage, its good and bad times, intruded into my thoughts and feelings. Returning to a place where you had a good experience; hearing a song that evokes good times; employing a particular touch or look; wearing an article of clothing; playing with your wedding ring while doing marital counseling—all communicate.

much of what we consider to be reality: what we experience, how we experience it, and even if we experience it.[2]

Ever since the Tower of Babel,[3] when God recognized the awesome power of everyone having the same language and decided to limit humankind's power and arrogance by making us unable to understand one another, language has often confused us. Still, language remains a major source of our power. It molds and determines the world in which we live. Without it, we would get on only with great difficulty. Its variations broaden and limit us. Its wise use can change more than we can imagine.

The most prevalent way that sound is created is by air passing over an opening—in the case of language, the mouth. The particular sound is determined by the size of the opening, the air pressure, and any interference with the airflow, be it tongue, teeth, or whatever. This interaction produces a series of "sound symbols" (words) to which our mind, both conscious and unconscious, gives meaning. Hearing the sound *chair* evokes inside us certain pictures and experiences that give this arbitrary sound meaning. *Chair,* as processed inside, is a four-legged thing to sit on, and not an animal we pet. such as a cat. When we hear *cat,* we make sense of that sound differently, evoking in our minds the image of a four-legged animal, perhaps accompanied by nostalgic memories of childhood, or the faint beginning itch of a sneeze. If I use the word *table,* without specifying which table, your mind will come up with something out of your unique history to make sense of that word (sound). If I use such words as *love* and *affection, truth* and *good,*

---

2. Compare Jurgen Ruesch, MD, and Gregory Bateson, *Communication: The Social Matrix of Psychiatry* (New York: W.W. Norton and Company, 1987), pp. 204-205, n. 2:

   The late Doctor Stutterheim, Government Archeologist in Java, used to tell the following story: Somewhat before the advent of the white man, there was a storm on the Javanese coast in the neighborhood of one of the capitals. After the storm the people went down to the beach and found, washed up by the waves and almost dead, a large white monkey of unknown species. The religious experts explained that this monkey had been a member of the court of Beroena, the God of the Sea, and that for some offense the monkey had been cast out by the god whose anger was expressed in the storm. The Rajah gave orders that the white monkey from the sea should be kept alive, chained to a certain stone. This was done. Doctor Stutterheim told me that he had seen that stone and that, roughly scratched on it in Latin, Dutch, and English were the name of a man and a statement of his shipwreck. Apparently this trilingual sailor never established verbal communication with his captors. He was surely unaware of the premises in their minds, which labeled him as a white monkey and therefore not a potential recipient of verbal messages: it probably never occurred to him that they could doubt his humanity. He may have doubted theirs.

3. Genesis 11:1-9.

your mind will tap your personal experience to make sense out of these sounds. One person may hear the word *love* and see in the mind's eye a famous painting, another may see a mother's smiling face, and yet another may recall walking on the beach hand in hand with his or her first love. Each will understand the word *love* differently. Each one's experience will be unique.

Though produced by the physical process of vibrating airwaves bouncing off our eardrums, language has the power to tap our intangible emotions; it can make us laugh or cry, enlighten or confuse us, cause us to go to war or to extend a hand in friendship, excite us with new possibilities or bore us to tears. Language shapes how we think, how we feel, what we see, what we don't see, and even how the hormones flow through our bodies. Our problems are defined by language, as are our solutions. Take *midlife crisis,* for example. Though humans have always struggled with life cycle transitions, there was no such thing as "midlife crisis" until it was named. Now everyone is expected to go through it and deal with it. Another example of language's ability to mold our reality involves perceived social roles for males and females. "Boys will be boys" is very different from "sexual harassment."

What you say and how you say it influences, and can often determine, other people's responses, whether they agree or disagree, how they feel about themselves and you, and even their small muscle movements and blood flow. Spoken language, though in and of itself nothing but air, is extremely powerful. The meanings we attach to these sounds give language its power to define our experience. That is no small thing.

Language Creates and Describes Experience

When we talk, the sounds (words) we produce can be heard, the air we move and shape can be felt, and, if one reads lips, the words we speak can be seen. What comes to us externally is processed inside to make sense of the sounds: the relationship between the two creates our experience.

Words and language are ways of accessing and transmitting experiences of all sorts (the taste of a hamburger, the mood of last night's movie, the feeling we think is love, etc.) to other members of our species, though the *words* used to describe experience are at least once removed from the *actual* experience. In this way, words become codes for experience, but they do not only describe experience. Words, spoken and heard, are expreience itself, and codes for experience. They point the way to and evoke experience that is not in the room as they are spoken.

Language in Relationship Can Create and Change
Others' Experience

Because words are codes for experience, when we use language to describe experience, we can create and evoke experience in others. We decipher the word codes by accessing in our own memory bank both cognitive and somatic experiences that seem to fit the codes, but these codes are not deciphered in the same way by all people. For example: You are sitting comfortably with a friend, and both of you feel just fine. You start talking about your friend's mother's death or a love affair that just ended or the time he or she had to repeat kindergarten, and as you talk, the person's face contorts and his or her breathing becomes constricted. Using language, just a bunch of sounds from your voice box, you have relationally changed your friend's experience. Though Mother may have died ten years ago, and the breakup is long over, and the friend has succeeded in many things since being six, with language you have effected a change in your friend, who walked in feeling wonderful and now may leave feeling awful. You did all of this with words—noises from your mouth, unwisely used, that brought changes not worth having. A more positive example: Some friends are feeling down in the dumps, worthless, and useless, and you tell them how much you appreciate everything they have done for you, and they may soon feel better.

Your use of language creates experience and evokes the memory of experience in others. Though it happens all the time, we don't pay too much attention to the power of words to create and re-create experience, to effect changes in people's feelings. These changes are, as we all know, not just inside our heads. If you think as you read this of going to the refrigerator to get a snack, something ordinary, yet remarkable, happens. Before you even leave your seat you may start to salivate and your muscles, with very minor, almost unnoticeable movements, will prepare for you to stand up and then walk to and open the refrigerator. If you start to think about the time in high school when you played basketball and you turned to shoot over your head, not only your mind but also your body recalls the experience, and what happens is that your muscles start to prepare for that activity. You may recall vividly the first time a date kissed you, and thinking of this affects blood flow in your body. Similarly, recalling an argument from years ago can cause your body to tense. Using words in a relationally meaningful way can create changes in others as well as in yourself.

We take this everyday phenomenon for granted, often not recognizing the almost miraculous nature of it. We don't give much thought to those automatic responses to words until we're in a place where the language is different and what we say makes absolutely no sense. Imagine being in a foreign country at a restaurant and ordering one thing, assuming the server understands, but ending up with something else. You wonder why no one seems to understand what you want when you have been perfectly clear. Why is your server being so difficult?

Miscommunication in a relationship frustrates both parties, but it does not have to be this way. You *can* learn "new" language skills to communicate relationally, to change others' experience and their responses to you, if you're willing to practice. As with all new skills, you'll be a little awkward at first, but with practice you *can* learn to use your mouth with your head.

You may protest: "I don't want to manipulate anyone." *Manipulation* is usually taken to mean exploiting others against their best interests, getting them, through deception and cunning, to do what you want, most often for your benefit and without them having full knowledge about what you and they are doing. That said, it's no wonder *manipulation* carries a distinctly negative relational meaning. Yet, *manipulation* can be more neutral, even benign, depending on the user's intent and the steps taken to realize that intent. In fact, to achieve anything in our environment, *we have to manipulate it*. Walking around in deerskin, spreading wheat seed to get bread, using flint to make an arrow—each is a manipulation of the environment. Without manipulation, there can be no successful interaction between two people. When you tell your server what kind of sandwich you want, you are manipulating the server's next move. When you approach your spouse to scratch your back, to make love, to ask if supper is ready, or to suggest going to a movie, you are manipulating. The nature of the manipulation depends upon your integrity, openness, and intentions in the relationship—whether you think that you and your relational partner can both be winners, or whether one of you has to win and the other lose. Manipulation is inevitable. How we manipulate is the question. To change an individual's "Jewish" life or a patient's experience, you will have to manipulate that person, but keep in mind that this should be done with integrity and has to work for both of you in relationship.

You may demur: "I am how I am! I just want to be myself and talk naturally!" Know that *acting naturally* means doing what you are used to doing over and over again, i.e., following a well-practiced routine. If you're getting the outcomes you want, turn to another chapter in this book, but if your outcomes are not satisfactory, then read on. Learning new ways to use language will take some time and practice. As with using any tool competently, using language elegantly in relationship requires practice, practice, and more practice. Employing a new skill may seem overwhelming because you are trying to do many things at one time. Take walking, for example. You don't think about walking. You just walk. You are doing a lot of different things, all at once: you're keeping one foot on the ground all the time; you're maintaining a balance of tension and relaxation in your legs; you're supporting your hips; you're keeping your balance; you're holding your head straight. You don't think about all of these different things as you're doing them. You just think, "Hey, I'm hungry. I think I'll go get a snack," and then you walk to where the snack is hiding from you.

Practice makes the unnatural natural. Do something often enough and at some point you won't have to think about it consciously. Practice removes a new skill from the realm of conscious effort and helps it to become an un-conscious—smooth and easy—action.

Years ago, when driving, I used to get angry when the passenger in the other seat suddenly yelled, "Watch out!" or "Stop sign!" or whatever, and I would yell back: "Don't startle me!" or "I saw it [whatever it was]!" or "I know what I'm doing!" or "Your yelling only created a danger by scaring me!" Over time I learned that this behavior didn't make much sense because my passenger was not trying to hurt me and was, in fact, trying to help. I de-cided to learn to say, "Thanks." The first thousand times, saying "Thanks" when startled was decidedly unnatural, and I bent my jaw out of line getting the words out. With practice this gradually became easier and easier and has since become my natural response. I now automatically respond to a pas-senger's scream with a grateful "Thanks—I appreciate your help."

Along with all of the aforementioned, however, we must remember this: *Language is not reality.*

Then What Is Reality?

Whether building a house or baking a cake, you had better know some-thing about the lay of the land, or that sugar is different from jalapeno pep-pers. When using language you need to know something about language's relation to "reality." A limitation each of us has in using language is deeply ingrained: we think that language describes *reality.* We all have our own ideas about what is real and imagine that what we "know" what is *reality.* If we didn't believe this, then we couldn't function. We don't go into a grocery store to ask, "Where does this bus go to?" We don't expect to fly somewhere on vacation by flapping our arms in the air. Because we understand *"real-ity"* in our head, we think that the way we experience things and talk about them is the way they *are.* However, as the old Gershwin song puts it, "It ain't necessarily so." So let's talk about what's real, so that you won't get stuck by what you *think* is "real."

What you consider real is mostly inside your head. **Reality** is a construct that you create and sustain between your ears.[4] Everything you see, you see inside your head. There is no color out there, only waves. A beautiful meadow is what your brain makes of the waves. Everything you hear, you hear inside your head. There is no sound out there, only waves. Beethoven's Ninth is what your auditory system produces from that set of waves. ***It is your own construct.*** It can be no other way. Talk to the blind about Monet's *Water Lilies,* or to the deaf about Mozart's *Eine Kleine Nachtmusik,* and you'll understand what I mean. Others *seem* to share reality with you because they are organized similarly. This is especially so with those who "speak the same language." They are taught by language to see and hear things as you do. Yet things being similar does not mean that they are identical. You produce your own "reality." Another's reality will be different from yours, and therefore your ***"reality"*** is unique. And if your reality is unique, so are you. And so are they, every last one of them.

Paul Watzlawick,[5] a philosopher, has pointed out that our construct of reality is composed of different parts:

1. First-order reality (which I will shortly explain)
2. Second-order reality (which I will also shortly explain)
3. How people organize and use those two realities

First-order reality includes those elements of life on which language has little influence. The sun rises in the east (though what we call east is a matter of mutual agreement defined by language, and, as a matter of fact, the sun doesn't actually rise . . .), gravity gives us weight, we need air to breathe or we will die, and so on. There are animals classified as mammals, similar to us humans, even though some (e.g., whales) live in the water (as with amphibians) and others (e.g., platypuses) birth their young by laying and hatching eggs (as with reptiles and birds). Yet, all life depends on oxygen to live. These things are first-order reality.

Second-order reality concerns itself with the meanings we attribute to the first-order reality. Is it important to save the whales? Should we limit polluting the atmosphere even if that means giving up vacation travel? How do we greet one another in a way that indicates we have good intentions? Do we bow, as do the Japanese? Do we shake hands or give a high-five, as do Americans? Do we hold our hands together in the prayer position, as is done

---

4. Paul Watzlawick, "The Construction of Therapeutic Realities" [workshop]. 1994 Ericksonian Congress, Phoenix, Arizona.

5. Paul Watzlawick, ed., *The Invented Reality: How Do We Know What We Believe We Know?* (Contributions to Constructivism) (New York: W.W. Norton, 1984).

in other parts of the world? The first-order reality of these greetings involves the movements themselves. The second-order reality is what we say the movements mean, and it matters greatly what our second-order reality is. Some are kinder, gentler, and more useful than others (a second-order reality judgment). Our religious constructs are almost wholly second-order reality. They are quintessentially statements about meaning. Where we often get stuck in the world of meanings is when we mistake second-order reality for first-order reality and insist that there's only one right or true way. There may be more than one way, but some *are* better than others.

A screwdriver (the name is a second-order meaning/description of the first-order reality, which is the wood or plastic or metal of which the tool is composed) is no more real, or better, than a hammer. Each is given a different "meaning" in keeping with the purpose it serves. How you use them (which is a derivative of the meaning you give them) will determine the results you get. You can hammer with a screwdriver or try to install a screw with a hammer, but you won't get the best results. You can use a screwdriver or the other end of a hammer to open a can of paint and either will do the job. Your choice of second-order reality makes a difference.

Language has first-order reality elements—the sound and moving air of which words are composed—yet the words themselves make sense of and give meaning to the first-order reality. *What things mean counts more in relationship than what things are.* Thus, language is crucial in creating and sustaining the meanings that are essential to second-order reality. Language is a primary tool that has a profound influence in shaping, changing, and creating the maps we use to get around in what we call **reality.**

The world out there is the world. Whether it was created by a God who makes demands on us is a second-order reality question. Meanings are *second order,* not *first,* and thus malleable; they can be moved around, changed or adjusted, and framed in new ways to help you achieve better, more worthy outcomes as a relational caregiver. Your understanding of second-order reality as flexible, arbitrary, and created by humankind allows you to play around with it to make good things happen, avoiding the crucial mistake of thinking that second-order reality (language) *is* first-order reality (what things *really* are). Fundamentalists of all stripes confuse second-order reality with first-order reality, often reaching the point at which they have to either convert everybody or kill them (for their own good, of course; the poor benighted don't know what is "really so"). *You* don't want to do that. It will not only leave you with many fewer relational partners, including scaring off those you really care about, but also certainly diminish your life experience. You will be living only with people you *think* are like-minded. The schisms and breaks in all fundamentalist groups are indications that like-mindedness is a fiction. As a Jewish relational caregiver, you are dealing with second-order reality—what things *mean*, not what they *"are."*

Changing second-order reality is no small thing because this is the reality in which most of us live most of the time. Second-order reality determines happiness, longing, love, work, ambition, marital satisfaction, fights, etc. Judaism, as we know it, is second-order reality, containing meanings that as committed Jews we think are crucial to us, and for which many of us have died "for the sanctification of God's name"—a second-order reality statement if ever there was one. Using your mouth with your head can lead to second-order changes that can alter your life, your relationships, the experience of your fellow Jews, and the lives of others around you.

How to Build Rapport: An Essential for Jewish Relational Care

Respect Others' Thoughts and Feelings

Whether you want to paint, sculpt, plant a flower, play an instrument, or exercise your body, you've got to get ready first. You've got to prepare the canvas, shape the clay, prepare the soil, tune the instrument, or warm up your muscles. If communicating as a Jewish relational caregiver is what you want to do, the preparation phase is called building rapport: being in the same "space" comfortably with your relational partner, experiencing a sense of mutual trust, emotional affinity, and alliance with the other. You'll know it when you have it.

Rapport is absolutely crucial for effective relational caregiving. Without rapport, you won't be able to do much of anything. If you lose it, you need to get it back pronto. To achieve and sustain rapport, it is vital that the tools you employ be carefully chosen and worthy of the job. Some ways of communicating, though well meant and persistently used despite their disastrous track record, are still in use, though they seriously impede rapport. You would do well to be rid of them, so let's examine the more common rapport breakers.

Cease and desist telling people that they shouldn't think or feel the way they think or feel. Stop trying to cheer them up by saying, "Don't feel that way—it's a sunny day" or "Count your blessings: other people are worse off than you are" or "How can you feel that way when you have a lovely spouse, good children, live in such a nice place, or . . . [fill in the blank]." Be particularly careful with such phrasing as "You have so much to be thankful for." These work so seldom that you would do better not to use them at all. Telling people that they ought to be thinking or feeling differently implies that something is wrong with them. That serves to reduce their confidence. Most people don't learn and change from a position of low self-esteem. It also demonstrates to them that you simply don't "get it." It is a mode of subtle torture and will only undermine the rapport you need to build with them. *People think or feel the way they think or feel.* You need to respect that.

Each of us sees, hears, and feels in a unique way. That's how it is. We naturally assume that experience impinges on others the way it does on us. This "one size fits all" design hinders achieving rapport. The "my size fits me and yours is appropriate to you" design is very useful here. If you can comprehend, be curious about, respectful, or even in awe of how others think and feel, you will do better at building rapport. Having a lot of life experience will make this way of thinking more available to you. If you are still perplexed, wondering how others could possibly feel and think the way they do, you can experiment by saying (even though you may not fully understand), "I understand that you *can* feel that way." By doing this you start to build the rapport frame where *they are,* not where you think they *ought to be.* If after further life experience, you feel more confident, you can offer, "Of course you feel that way." "Naturally" works just fine as well; "Me too" does the job if you've been there yourself.

For successful rapport you need to normalize other people's experience. You need to let them know that they are not bad, foolish, or just plain stupid to think or feel the way they do. They are quite convinced, given their model of the world, that how they feel or think is quite right and appropriate. Their model of the world (their second-order reality construct) is the only one of which they are aware. Consequently, whatever they're thinking or feeling is experienced as "real." A useful approach is to let them know that you accept their frame, respect how they see and experience the world, and can even speak their language (more about that anon).

Throw Out Your Obsolete "Blamer"

This is not as easy as it sounds because blaming is often the first relational tool we learned how to use. Blaming others is a time-honored way to deal with not getting what we want. If you are not getting the response you want from those you care for, you may seek to blame them, their family, their upbringing, their religion, their ethnic heritage, their genes, or whatever. There is something wrong with *them.* Reasonable people would respond the way I want them to, so they must be mad or bad. Blaming others may provide some brief satisfaction, but it does not do much that is useful in the long run. More important, by blaming others, you put yourself in a spot where *they* have to change for *you* to feel better. Lo and behold, you've made yourself helpless. A tool that leaves you helpless, waiting for others to change, isn't worth much.

Cleaning up the "blamer's debris" is arduous. Blaming is a veritable family heirloom, a venerable old tool that has been in the family and honed by parents, grandparents, and ancestors over countless generations. It is difficult simply to *stop blaming others,* but you might try this audacious experiment: Reach deep into the innards of your tendency to blame and grab what is there, and with one quick, deft motion turn your old, antiquated, ineffective "blamer" inside out. When you succeed in doing that, your tendency to blame turns into a three-in-one tool of infinite value. You will find yourself recycling blame and giving credit, appreciation, and praise in liberal doses. Along with Rav Kook, you are on the lookout for the holy sparks[6] present in all that others have done. You become aware of the worthwhile outcomes and positive intentions that your partners in relationship have had. You note the resources that they have demonstrated. You surprise yourself by suggesting that whatever success takes place in your relationships, with those you care for, results from their efforts and not from what you may have done. You find yourself saying, "How did you get that to happen? What did you do to get things back on track? What did you do to control yourself while you were angry with me?" In my psychotherapeutic role, when patients give me credit for the changes in them, I automatically respond, "I couldn't have done it without you." Granted, turning that tendency to blame others inside out/upside down is not easy. If throwing out your "blamer" requires a level of effort that you cannot muster quite yet, if it's an old treasured tool you've used for years and are nostalgic about, put it in a safe deposit box and give the key to someone you won't ever see again. This will at least make getting to it difficult.

Nullify Negatives

To achieve rapport it helps to become especially sensitive to black holes in experience. Sometimes what is taking place is so bad, or hurts so much, we, or those we care for, just want it to *stop*—to *not* be there. If only we'd stop fighting, or that pain would go away, or they would stop nagging me about something so trivial, or they would not criticize me perpetually, or they wouldn't be so obsessed with me. We want it to *stop!* The trouble is that the unconscious cannot process the absence of something, what we call

---

6. *Abraham Isaac Kook: The Lights of Penitence, The Moral Principles, Lights of Holiness, Essays, Letters, and Poems* (The Classics of Western Spirituality), trans. B. Z. Bokser (Mahwah, NJ: Paulist Press, 1978).

here a "negative." Telling a child, "Don't spill the milk," or a lover, "Don't feel jealous," or a congregant, "Don't always criticize every little thing I do," or, to use the classic example, "Don't under any circumstances think of the color green" will only help spill the milk, arouse jealousy, incite criticism, and get someone to think of green. "Negative" here has nothing to do with good or bad; it has to do with black holes in experience. By emphasizing that there is "something" that we want to *not* be there, an experience we want to negate, we are left with a black hole in experience and no replacement for it. The unconscious fills that hole by dropping the negative. A patient may want the pain to stop, but something *has* to take its place. Simply wanting a congregant to stop nagging does not offer an alternative. What do you want this person to do instead? Wanting your spouse not to yell is okay, but not sufficient. What do you want your spouse to do instead? There is no way that "nothing" can happen. Learn to spot black holes in experience and then to nullify the negative with what you want to happen. That's a positive worth pursuing.

Positive language gives you a direction in which to go. You say what you want, instead of what you don't want. By nullifying the negative you encourage others to let you know what they want, rather than what they don't want or what they want to have stop. You find yourself asking repeatedly, "If *x* stops happening, what will happen instead?" Most people start with nonverifiable synonyms. Saying, "I want you to be 'nice' to me instead of 'nagging' me" is something, but "nice" is not verifiable. You may be tempted by vague synonyms, but as a "negative nullifier" you need specific verifiable, sensory-grounded descriptions—something you can see, hear, or touch—of what you want to happen and how you'll know when it is happening. A camcorder can't record "nice." A hand can't grasp the emptiness: it can be held by another hand. An eye can't see the invisible: it can take in a smile. An ear can't hear the silence: it can respond to a change in another's voice. You need the "know-how" to negate the negative so you can, as an old song suggests, "accentuate the positive" and, thereby, have a direction in which to go. Being sensitive and developing skill as a negative nullifier, an expert in identifying black holes and filling those holes in experience, will help you do this job in a positive, useful fashion.

Express Good Intentions

To achieve rapport, hone all the ways you have to let others know that you mean well for them. Dispensing credit instead of blame is a wonderful technique for letting others know that you are not there to hurt them, or do them in, or put them down in any way. Merely saying this has only limited use.

Assuming others' good intentions is most useful. Sometimes this is done through memories of times when it was crystal clear that they cared deeply about you or others and acted for your or their well-being; when they selected you as a companion; in recalling acts of friendship; in their welcoming you when you first came to the congregation; or in their response when you visited the hospital. Staying focused on their good intentions will keep you in a place where you can use your own new learnings competently and effectively. You need to respect that they are doing the best they can do, and in some ways that isn't bad. It would be naive to assume that everyone means well for you. If they *don't* mean well for you and are really out to get you, the tools presented here don't apply and you need to take care of yourself. Most people are *not* out to get you, so working on the initial assumption that their intentions are benign is a useful place to begin. If you assume that, then their intentions will most often turn out to be benign, and that will help you do your caregiving work.

Be Multilingual

Understanding and speaking others' language—how they choose the words they use and how they talk their talk—will build rapport. Everyone you encounter, though they say they talk your language, actually speaks a different one. It is useful to consider what their background is—how they came to think as they do, talk as they do, and act as they do. Imagine how, under different circumstances, you might have grown to think, feel, and experience the world as they do. Men and women generally talk differently about sex, power, work, and children. Talking itself means something quite different to men and women. People, depending on their background, culture, ethnicity, family history, and the rules, overt and covert, by which they grew up, and even their genetic endowment, are different. They process and express difference differently.

Attend to how others process information inside their heads by noting what they say and how they say it. Attend to the tone, pace, and volume of their voice; attend to the words they choose. Being aware of these elements can be extraordinarily useful, as they are clues to how others interpret their experience. Remember that others are different from you and their experience is not yours. Using your mouth intelligently means recognizing these facts and pacing your communication to match theirs. Embracing their model of the world and speaking their language will allow you to gain the rapport you need to help move them to a better place for you and them.

Consider the example of three people—A, B, and C—who have gone for a walk together. Each describes the experience:

A: Wow! That was a terrific walk—a sight for sore eyes. The air was so brilliantly clear; as I moved along, my internal fog seemed to lift and I saw things in a new way. It's true that on a clear day you can see forever. I was aware of seeing a bird in the distance. The bright color of that bird's plumage was just wonderful.

B: Wow! That was a terrific walk—a really moving experience. Feeling the brisk air on my face, I just warmed up as I moved along. I felt energized. Getting my body going at a quick pace, I felt alive and tingly all over. The crunching of leaves under my feet was invigorating. I haven't had such an exciting walk in a long time.

C: Wow! That was a terrific walk—a hymn to nature. As I moved along, I tuned in to the rhythms of the world. There's such harmony out there, if we only listen for it. I could hear the birds chirping, the wind whistling through the trees, and the sound of the leaves crunching under my feet. It is a day made for singing.

Three people went on the exact same walk and described a seemingly identical experience, yet each person processed the experience of the walk differently, and we thus have three rather different descriptions. By paying careful attention to their words, you can diagram their experience—what each one attends to, processes, and says about what has happened.[7] Listening carefully you note that Mr. A used visual words, Ms. B used feeling words, and Mrs. C used auditory words. To achieve rapport, it helps to talk their language. If you want Mr. A to do something, you get him to envision it. If you want Ms. B to do the same thing, you tell her about the good feelings she will have. If you want to get Mrs. C on board, you explain how sound an idea it is and how attuned she is to what needs to be done.

These examples *are* oversimplified. Most people use more than one system, both to process incoming experience and to express that experience in language. Most people, though, seem to have a preferred system for overall experience and a preferred one for specific activities. Take your time in learning this. You've had little or no practice in listening for these differences in others or even in yourself. You, most likely, have your own preferred system of which you're probably unaware. You may not be in touch

---

7. Robert B. Dilts, John Grinder, Richard Bandler, Judith DeLozier, and Leslie Cameron-Bandler, *Neuro-Linguistic Programming 1* (Cupertino, CA: Meta Publications, 1979).

with what you do, or you don't see yourself in that special way, or you don't listen to how you express yourself. You also have not learned to adjust your own response to others in a practiced way. You need to learn this, but do it in small bits.

Knowing how others process and represent experience and then talking the way they are talking are helpful when seeking to establish rapport. You can also breathe at the same rate they are breathing, adopt their body position, and change your body position when they do. Doing this will help teach you how they view their world, an important first step toward gaining rapport. For example, a loving couple, the epitome of rapport in relationship, are sitting across from each other in a restaurant. You may notice that each one's body position mirrors the other's. Then, a curious thing happens: one of them moves and, lo and behold, the other one moves—what one might call a rapport dance. We see and experience this phenomenon all the time. As a relational caregiver, it is your task to attend more actively to how others are and to use the information in building rapport, which is crucial to your work.

The previous five skills are minimum requirements for achieving rapport and they bear repeating, as well as practice, practice, and more practice:

1. Affirm others' experience. It *is* what is going on with them.
2. Drop blame. Give credit instead.
3. Fill empty holes in experience immediately.
4. Assume and convey positive intent.
5. Learn others' language and use it.

Framing

Whether we are aware of it, and most of the time we are not, one tool, fully operational in all of us, determines our day-to-day "being" in this world. This factory-installed, original equipment is not an add-on, and it operates far beyond the level of any computer. This tool is our *framer.* We just cannot get around without one, because there is always more "reality" out there than we can process. For each of us to get around in the world, we have to make sensory input meaningful and manageable. Our framer does that for us and is shaped and honed by our genes, our experience, our innate knowledge, and what we have been carefully taught or learned quite by accident. Our framer selects what we attend to; what we ignore; what we see, hear, and feel; and, more important, what we think it all means *and* what we think our choices are. Our ability to frame experience makes survival possible.

If your framer goes totally on the blink, your world becomes chaos— nothing makes sense and nothing works! You *could* think that coffee is heated blood, that you can drive against traffic safely, that red lights mean go and green lights stop, and that loaded guns are back scratchers, but such thinking does not reflect "reality." Framing organizes what is out there and determines what *your* "reality" is. Framing lets you know that the blinking lights on the car ahead of you are *not* in observance of Chanukah, and that it would be wise not to pass the car to wish that driver "Happy Chanukah."

Our framing always limits us, though, and it cannot be otherwise. There's just too much going on out there to handle. In some ways framing functions similar to taking a picture. To snap a photo, we frame the scene and focus the camera. The frame and focus determine what we see and how we see it—what is clear, what is fuzzy, what is included in the picture, and what is left out. To get prints, we take our photos to a lab or use our own or others' computer skills, knowing that we can adjust the picture, the lighting, the composition, the contrast, and the frame, and that any and all of these can vary startlingly. For example, I have on my wall a picture I took of the Statue of Liberty. The five prints made from my negative are startlingly different—so different that they appear to have been taken at different times. I chose one I liked, ordered an enlarged matching print, and was surprised when what I got back looked different from all of the others. I surrendered, knowing that it was as close as I was going to get to the reality my camera had framed.

Being married to a painter, I hear much about the importance of frames. A painting is just dabs of color on canvas. Change the frame and you change the way the painting looks. Some frames bring you into the picture, and some frames keep you out. A darker, more ornate frame can make a medio- cre painting look important, or just pretentious. A wide frame can accent a painting or overpower it. Some frames complement colors in the painting and thereby become part of the scenery, and some frames, such as gold, seem to match any setting. A renowned art critic notes: "Great frames bind, border, emphasize and generally aid in the display of a painting. They can also be works of art in and of themselves."[8]

We judge others' actions with the frame we put around what they do. For example, I was working on this chapter while on vacation with friends in a foreign country. One evening we were waited on by an exceedingly brusque waitress who threw our food down in front of us and gave curt, often obnox- ious answers to our questions. It became clear to me that the frame we put around her behavior would determine the amount of her tip. Was she just

---

8. Bess Liebenson, *The New York Times*, Connecticut Section, May 8, 1994.

overworked, having trouble with her husband, just plain ornery, physically uncomfortable, or expressing her antipathy toward men with receding hairlines being out with beautiful women (such as my wife, Ingrid)? How we framed her behavior would dictate our response.

When we are absorbed in an activity, we don't hear the "background noises" outside the frame. For example, my cousins, who lived in a house next to an elevated subway line, could sleep through the racket of the subway passing their bedroom window and still wake up at the slightest whimpering of their baby. Frames have a built-in, automatic quality to them. Once we establish a frame for a particular situation, we are able to overlook anything outside that frame, yet many factors create, influence, and hone these frames which seem so involuntary.

Language is a frame. It determines what we see, experience, and choose as reality. English is different from German, and each determines how we think and what we attend to in the world. Eskimos use language to communicate the slightest nuances of different kinds of snow, an important aspect of their lives that has no meaning for Australian Aborigines.

Culture determines our frames. What we see and hear, eat and drink, experience and imagine, and think is important, as well as how we behave, is often culturally determined. Take shaking hands, for example. We shake hands after not seeing a friend for a long period of time, but how do we "instinctively" know it's time for another handshake? If you are attending an all-day meeting, you shake hands first thing in the morning. Following the two-hour lunch break you wouldn't shake hands again, though you might conclude the day by shaking hands, this time in parting. The time span is built in culturally and the frame is learned without any formal instruction. Cultures have entire contexts that other cultures don't. Cultures determine what it means to be a man, a woman, a husband/father, or a wife/mother and dictates who does the dishes and how they do them.

Family inculcates frames. My father taught me that if I wanted to see a museum properly, I should move around to the right. I was with my wife in Denmark and I was about to utter that injunction when I realized that this was not the only frame for seeing the museum. Families have their own sets of rules about what constitutes proper behavior—what is appropriate table talk, how a marriage should be conducted, whether children should be seen and not heard, and on and on.

Some Common Frames and Their Possible Limitations

> If your frame is organized to notice only how difficult the world is and
> attends to all the obstacles and not the opportunities, life will be all

about struggling and overcoming, and you may not feel like getting up in the morning.

If your frame is constructed to notice what is missing, you will tell friends about those who did not show up to your party, instead of the wonderful time had by those who came.

If your frame dictates that only one person can be right, you'll get into a lot of fights with your spouse, co-workers, congregants, patients, and anyone who experiences the world differently than you do.

If your frame dictates that for you to feel good about yourself, you have to earn a certain amount of money or have a packed synagogue every week, you'll be vulnerable to the vagaries of the stock market, salary negotiations, and spending lots of time counting who showed up that week.

If your frame insists that everyone has to love you, you will have difficulty saying to people what you really mean for fear that they won't love you, and you'll most likely find it difficult to get what you want and need.

If your frame says that only Mozart knew how to write music, you probably won't enjoy yourself at a New Orleans jazz festival.

If your frame constantly asks the question "Am I doing enough so that others will appreciate me?" you will not only work too hard but also expend a lot of energy checking the "mail" for thank-you notes.

If your frame anticipates that the person you're scheduled to meet is a bore, your time waiting and the meeting itself will be tiresome and you'll end up being doubly bored.

We need to ask these questions: How well does my framing serve me? How elegant is my framing? Do my frames enhance my living and my work, or do they narrow my possibilities and choices for the work I do with those in my care?

You create frames no matter what you do. How you frame determines what you attend to and gives that meaning, and from those meanings you take action. You would do well to hone your skills so as to produce ever more useful frames that make life easier, not harder. That may not come too easily initially, but it is a worthwhile investment of time and effort. Practice using the following frames until they become second nature to you, and you will be well on your way to maximizing your experience and your ability to relate meaningfully to the world around you.

Some Useful Frames

1. **The "outcome trumps intention" frame.** The meaning of your communication is in the outcome, irrespective of your intentions.[9] This is a distortion of the truth, a lie, but a most useful one. Acting *as if you* produced the result by what *you* did can change the way you communicate and open the world of choice. "You have made it all happen" is not a *true* statement. It is *not* first-order reality. It is *not* the way the world *really* is, but it is a *very useful frame*. What happened may not have been what you intended, but in this frame your intentions *are irrelevant*. Your communication is measured by the outcome, not by what your intentions may or may not have been. This frame can get you to focus differently, to see things in a new way, and to open the gateway to choice. If you are the cause of the outcome, you can do something different. By acting differently you have a chance of getting outcomes worth having.

That is tough for all of us. Few of us easily act as if we have produced the results we have gotten. Proclaiming good intentions as an excuse is built into our framing from childhood. We learned as children that good intentions made a difference. We could be excused based on our intentions: "I didn't mean to spill the milk; I was just reaching for the butter." "I didn't mean to break the window; I was just trying to hit the ball." "I didn't mean to hit my sister; I was just trying to . . . [fill in the blank]." A million childhood excuses were based on good intentions, and sometimes they worked. We were, after all, cute. We often did not know what we were doing, and we truly did not intend to "spill the milk," or whatever.

The "outcome trumps intention" frame precludes blaming others for your behavior. You take full responsibility for the outcome. If someone is grossly insulted by your behavior, it is not enough to say, "I meant well" or "I didn't mean to do it," unless of course that happens to work. Don't count on it, though. Experiment with something more useful.

Another response to not achieving what we want, and the stress that often ensues, is being castigated by an internal "other"[10] who, having gotten a foothold in our being, attacks and alienates us from ourselves, telling us, "You are not worthwhile, never have been and never will be." Internally we hear: "You do that to yourself." "You're just incompetent." "You *never* get what you want." "You're just not adequate." "You never measure up." Though this may sound similar to a "no excuse" frame, it is in fact *very* dif-

---

9. R. Bandler and J. Grinder, *Frogs into Princes* (Moab, UT: Real People Press, 1979).

10. Compare Stephen Gilligan, *The Courage to Love* (New York: W.W. Norton and Company, 1997).

ferent, in that a no-excuse frame holds no blame, either for others or for you. The absence of "self"-alienating blame does not mean having no responsibility. You are responsible for what you do and, in this frame, even for the outcome you achieve.

Spending time and energy blaming yourself—experiencing what a friend and teacher of mine[11] calls an "alien" attack—alienates you from your own "being." That attack is disrespectful of the essential you, who is modeled after and molded by Divinity and created [*Tzelem*⟺*N'shamah*],[12] and it impedes your ability to change.

The "outcome trumps intention" frame omits any blame for others, or for yourself. Though new, and none too easy to learn, it is of crucial importance. If you practice and use this frame, you *will* change. Kicking yourself in the rump and hopping around on the other leg, besides being uncomfortable, doesn't allow for much movement or flexibility. A first sign of your changing will be exhibiting greater flexibility and perceiving more choices. More choices in communicating relationally will lead you to getting more and better outcomes in the caregiving relationships that mean so much to you.

Remember:
    Good intentions are a poor excuse.
    Alienating self-attacks cripple you.
    Taking ownership of whatever happens gives you a chance
        and a choice, allowing relationship to happen.

2. **"Nobody is quite like me" frame. I am who I am.** This frame keeps you on your toes, alert to the fact that *nobody else in the world is organized quite like you are. You are unique and they are unique.* This frame returns you to your unique inner core, and it helps make all of the other frames possible because it allows you to be all you can be, with a minimum of interference from yourself or others. It is a return to your natural self, to your inner gifts. And though this may sound similar to New Age philosophy, it has deeply rooted antecedents in the biblical story of creation[13] and is a core audacious assertion of the Mishnah:[14]

> To demonstrate God's greatness, only one person was created in the beginning.

---

11. Stephen Gilligan, PhD, in multiple contexts.
12. See Jack H Bloom, *The Rabbi As Symbolic Exemplar: By the Power Vested in Me* (Binghamton, NY: The Haworth Press, 2002), especially Chapters 6 and 8.
13. See in this book Chapter 1, "Premises of Jewish Relational Care," pp. 10-11.
14. Babylonian Talmud: Mishnah Sanhedrin 4:5, Second Century CE.

A human being mints many coins from a single mold and all are duplicates, interchangeable with one another.

Yet, God creates everyone in the mold of the first person and there are no duplicates; each human being is unique.

Therefore, each and every one of us is obliged to affirm;

For my sake, the world was created.

This frame is one of the toughest to sustain. It is counterintuitive and, thereby, in a sense, unnatural. Most often *natural* is taken to mean "well practiced"—"I've done it a million times like that before"—having done something so many times it has become second nature. We think of it as natural, but it is actually the result of much practice.

This frame contradicts the only source of experience you have, and have ever had. What you know of "reality" in the world is what goes on inside your head. All of your life you have organized and experienced the world around you through the senses of your own body: Your eyes take in light rays and your mind produces images; your ears absorb sound waves and your mind recognizes noise; your fingers brush against an object and your mind lets you know how it feels; you put food in your mouth and your mind identifies the morsel by taste. Your mind processes sensory stimuli of your body; it is the interpreter between what you encounter outside of yourself and what you know in your mind from experience. All of your experience is created in your mind, so new experience is based upon the old, and so on; thus, your own experience of the world is all that you know of reality.

Even reading, witnessing, or hearing of someone else's experience is made sense of in your own head, so it is difficult to understand that others are organized differently; all we really know is how the world is organized for us. You have not had anyone else's experience. How could anyone else be different? Yet they are. Having only your own experience to go by, you will be tempted to make a big mistake in assuming that since you are organized in a certain way and walk and talk and get along a certain way, and have been taught right from wrong, good from bad, etc., then therefore everyone must be organized the way you are.

The "nobody is quite like me" frame reminds you constantly that people are put together in odd ways. Everyone is different from you. We bump up against this all of our lives and wonder: "How could they be different?" Out of this we make all kinds of judgments: "How could they think the way they think; say what they say; be sad on a sunny day; enjoy that weird music; eat spicy food? How could they be like they are; like what they like? They really should know better." Yet they are different. It is useful to think of the person you are caring for as being an ***alien reality.*** Your task, should you choose to undertake it, is to get that unfamiliar yet somehow familar being to respond in ways that are good for you both, to influence and relate to the "other" in a way that provides mutual benefits.

You have to learn to question what seems self-evident to you. The "nobody is quite like me" frame requires doing that. What might be love for you might have no meaning for your partner, though it might be love for someone else. But if you want to demonstrate love to your partner, you do best to find out what love means to your partner and then see that your partner gets a dose of it. My wife loves Impressionist paintings, so when courting her I gave her coffee-table books on the Impressionists. That didn't do much for me, but it meant a lot to her because of her model of the world. You have to be flexible. It is useless to say, "They should have liked what I like." That will get you stuck. As it is said, you have to learn to talk their talk, to walk their walk. We mostly love others the way *we* need to be loved, not the way *they* need to be loved.

3. **The "boundless resources and flexibility" frame.** You and they have all the resources needed, and you have the flexibility to access them. You can get any outcome you set your mind to as long as you are flexible enough. Framing the world this way, focusing on resources, rather than impediments, will take you a long way. Awareness of potential resources in your repertoire and in others will help you be flexible in accessing and using them.

That doesn't include playing quarterback in the Super Bowl if you are a forty-five-year-old woman—although there once was a one-armed major league baseball player who devised a way to catch the ball, tuck the glove under his stump, and throw the ball back to the infield in one fluid motion.[15] That's more flexibility than we usually allow ourselves to imagine is possible, but learning to access the resources you do have will provide the flexibility to achieve outcomes that you, until now, have hesitated to envision.

This frame does not apply to you alone. Those you are caring for are also created [*Tzelem*⇔*N'shamah*]. The task as Jewish relational caregiver is to use your resources to access theirs. Though there may be a lot of roadblocks, your flexibility is supported when you have this frame in place. You can do it. You have all of the resources that you need. You just need to be flexible enough to access and develop those resources. You also need to recognize that there are things you can't do—*yet!*

---

15. Pete Gray, who played in seventy-seven games and batted 218 with the St. Louis Browns in 1945.

Reframing

There's *framing,* and there's *reframing.*[16] Using and practicing the frames previously recommended gives you a head start toward improving your caregiving, yet some challenges remain. What do you do about those venerable frames, relics of the past, that keep popping up untouched by what you have just learned? What do you do when your tender, budding frames are inundated and overwhelmed by others' less than useful frames? Simply put, their frames can engulf yours. Your new frames get knocked out and stop functioning adequately. Imagine being yelled at, the object of anger or rage felt by someone in your care; imagine being rejected for a job you dearly wanted and knew you could handle; imagine being nagged by a spouse and told that you are mad or bad or that your intentions are evil. The best of frames can crumble under such assaults, leaving you defenseless. *It happens to all of us.* Changing your frames does not mean that others will share your new ones.

    I. **Reframing** *is* a way of handling these situations.

   II. **Reframing** *is* a method of coping when your own less than useful, old frames grab hold of you.

 III. **Reframing** *is* a way of dealing with others who come at you with their less than useful frames, provoking you to adopt theirs and thus relate to them in ways not useful for either of you.

 IV. **Reframing** *is* a composite that is fabricated from parts of what we have learned thus far. Like many composites, it can be extremely flexible, resilient, and useful. Bad composites can be fragile and dangerous.

    A. Behavior is an event (first-order reality) that has no meaning in and of itself, except for the meaning (second-order reality) that we attach to it.

    B. Second-order reality is flexible and most meanings are arbitrary. Therefore,

       1. the frame will determine what a situation means and how it is experienced, and

       2. meanings are malleable.

    C. The composite that is reframing is made up of a judicious mixture of the following skills:

       1. Knowing what's important to others

       2. Being able to use their language

       3. Assuming their good intentions

---

16. For more, see R. Bandler, J. Grinder, S. Andreas, and C. Andreas, eds., *Reframing: Neuro-Linguistic Programming and the Transformation of Meaning* (Moab, UT: Real People Press, 1982).

Every communication has at least two parts: a behavior or event and the intention or meaning that is applied to that behavior or event. One might put it as such: every interaction is composed of what happens and what "what happens" means. The behavior or event is first-order reality. The intention or meaning is second-order reality. Saying "I am annoyed with you" in a loud voice is a behavior or event. Whether the person's tone of voice means that the person has acid indigestion, has for the first time taken a stand, or thinks you are totally detestable is a question of intention/meaning. Reframing splits the intention/meaning from the behavior/event. Reframing opens up the possibility that the behavior could have a different meaning, which gives you some room to maneuver.

Reframing's first task is to split the intention from the behavior by signifying that the meaning of the event happening could be quite different from the first experience of it. Reframing can be used to *split others' behavior (event)* from what it signifies; it can also be used to split one's own intention from one's own behavior.

When that split is completed, reframing enters that divide by substituting an alternate, albeit appropriate, *intention/meaning* to explain the behavior. The alternate intention/meaning should fit the facts of the situation and seem reasonable, thus acceptable, to those engaging in the behavior (yourself or others). To be successful a reframe will have to meet some of the criteria valued by those who are doing the behavior, but that may not be evident while they are engaged in the behavior. Reframing needs to be done in keeping with the others' needs, and it's useful to start by accepting and affirming their behavior as presented so as to gain rapport, before then delivering the reframe.

A helpful hint: Humans, more often than not, want their intentions to reflect what they consider the best in themselves. A grown man who is crying would rather have that behavior described as sensitive than as weak or frightened. Reframing, by crediting others with good intentions, can make the situation better for you and for them. *Since behavior has no meaning in and of itself,* the problem is almost always in the perceived interpretation of the intention/meaning. Reframing allows the possibility of giving the behavior a new and different intention/meaning. Be watchful, however, of crossing the border between reframing and *rationalization,* which involves making excuses for ourselves. The skillful application of the frames learned earlier will help to rule out excuses.

> **Reframing** changes what an experience means, by molding new meaning around the communication/event/behavior, while not changing what has happened (the content of the experience) at all.

Reframing can powerfully change your experience, when you use it on yourself.

Reframing can powerfully change the experience of those others who are the source of the pressure on your frame.

Reframing can move relations with others to a place that's better for you and, hopefully, for them as well.

Reframing is a mighty tool.

Examples of Reframing's Multiple Uses

1. **Crediting others with benign intentions toward me, I reframed and changed my own experience.** They did not even know that they were being reframed, and whatever frames they did or didn't have made very little difference to the positive outcome.[17]

I have always enjoyed bicycling, and I once owned an expensive bike of which I was *very* protective. One Labor Day, while riding with my future wife and her father on an eight-mile trek to a lovely lighthouse, my bike's front tire went flat. I said to my lady: "I'll ride *your* bike back into town, to find someone who repairs bike tires. I'll put your bike on my car (parked in town), come back here, take my bike back into town, have it repaired, load both bikes on the car, return here, and we can go on. You and your dad can wait here." They nodded, so I thought I had a clear agreement to my elegant arrangements. I found an open bicycle shop, got my car, and headed back to pick up my wounded bike. As I approached, I saw my bike lying on its side with its front wheel off, its tire being unceremoniously stripped from the rim. My lady's father, formerly an efficiency expert in a factory that made high-precision lenses, knew how to do these things. I was feeling violated and becoming *angry*.

My frame about agreements and borders being honored, and my word being attended to, was "under attack." This could well lead to a fight: "Why did you take the wheel off my beloved bike? Nobody listens even when I'm crystal clear." I needed to reframe what was happening, pronto, to create a benign intention in the minds of those who were "violating" my bike. I needed to think that their intention was to help fix the bike and not prove that I was untrustworthy. They meant well toward me. I did not know what their intentions were, but it did not matter. The reframe enabled the ensuing fight to last for about three minutes instead of three days. I had reframed others' intentions to change my own response. They had no idea what was

---

17. Rav Abraham Kook's use of *nitzotzot k'dushah* is a superb ongoing example of reframing.

going on in my head, nor I in theirs. The behavior (stripping the tire off the wheel) could have had any kind of meaning because meanings are malleable. The meaning you give a behavior will determine your response, and your response will influence others' responses.

2. Reframing with others preemptively, as a caregiving/educational/ religious tool. A specific behavior/event/outcome may commonly lead to feeling bad/sad/diminished. Reframing the probable inner/outer experience of others is a major caregiving task.

Having graduated from Columbia College, I made it an annual ritual to take my kids to an afternoon of "torture" known as the Columbia-Yale game. In the Ivy League, Columbia is too well acquainted with last place and Yale regularly contends for first place. My kids wondered why we would bother to go, since the scores over the years totaled something like 4,836 to 9. They said, and others concurred, that we must be masochists or suffering from some other obscure personality disorder. I **reframed** our attendance as ***character building,*** which is infinitely more worthwhile than merely ***winning.*** That the reframe seemed to take is testified to by the response of my youngest at another unequal match. With Columbia down by only one touchdown at halftime, my daughter Rebecca offered that she would allow her character to be built by staying for the second half. Unfortunately, or fortunately, depending on the frame, the final score was something like 48 to 6. We built a lot of character that day!

If you have children, you've done that reframe a million times: you say that something does not mean what your children, or someone else, may think it means, but something else entirely. Another classic reframe is the expression "growing pains," which reframes discomfort into a positive experience, such as growing or maturing. Crying children might be considered crybabies, or in touch with their feelings and free about expressing them. That *is* a good thing, isn't it?

3. Reframing to change others' frames, not preemptively. This, for Jewish relational caregivers, is a crucial use of reframing, one that is much more daring and interesting than any of the previous uses. You will be splitting others' behaviors/actions from their intentions/meanings. You will, by reframing, show others that what they are doing means something quite different from what they think it means. Crafting different positive/constructive/worthwhile meanings for their behaviors, you help them to think differently about their intentions. By reframing their behaviors, you are able to respond to the good intentions *you* have placed there (the reframe), and not to what was originally there (whatever their intentions seemed to be).

This is the most sophisticated use of reframing, and though it requires practice to be proficient in its use, you'll be surprised by how much experience you've already had with it. Whenever you attach a meaning to a behavior that's different from the one that seems to come with the behavior, you are, in the language of communication skills, reframing. Reframing, used with precision, is one of the most powerful tools that you have at your disposal.

Examples of Reframing with Others

BEHAVIOR: A friend comes charging over to you in a public place and at the top of her voice says, "You always claimed to be, and encouraged me to be, a caring, considerate person, and now when I was going through a difficult illness, you didn't bother to call or to write. You just let me go through it totally alone. You had no contact with me at all. You are a hypocrite and a phony."

REFRAME: "I'm sorry you're angry. I wasn't in touch with how much I mean to you." The behavior (loud words) is split from the intention (angry accusations of hypocrisy and phoniness) and a new intention is placed on the behavior. This is now a message about "how much I mean to you." What might that do? That may well stop the anger. What you might be dealing with at that point instead of anger is how much you mean to each other—a totally different discussion.

BEHAVIOR: A friend says, hesitatingly, in a low tearful voice, "You can't imagine how frightened I've been about discussing this with you."

REFRAME: "It takes great courage [different meaning for same behavior] for you to open up to me given all that's happened." That might change the friend's self-perception, and the experience can shift usefully.

BEHAVIOR: "I am really very angry with you. We arranged to meet yesterday afternoon at two o'clock, at the beginning of the hiking trail, so you could lead us to where we needed to go. All we knew is that it was a five-mile hike, but we didn't know what route to take. We waited and waited for you, and you didn't show up. We waited until three o'clock and then we finally set out to find the route ourselves. It took a long time, but we managed without you."

REFRAME: "I appreciate how upset you are because I know you count on and trust me. If you didn't, you would not be so angry [getting rapport]. Yet you did demonstrate terrific resourcefulness [different meaning] in getting where you needed to go, despite being angry about my letting you down." The different meaning crafted here (on the same behavior) is a message, first and foremost, about the other's resourcefulness in reaching a goal, while respecting the anger.

REFRAME (alternate): "I can imagine how furious you are and I deserve it. I appreciate your letting me know the full extent of your anger. I need to learn not to do that ever again." What was an angry outburst is now given a new and different meaning. The outburst (behavior) is now a lesson and a favor to a friend. If the behavior is such that it posits divisiveness and disagreement, saying "I agree" or "I'm sorry" can be a powerful reframe.

Reframing by "Going Meta": The Outcome of the Outcome

You can reframe head-on, as in the previous examples, by splitting others' behaviors/actions from their intentions/meanings, and offering new/different intentions/meanings that will both account for the behavior and leave them and you with a better frame in which to operate. You can also do it another way. You can start the process of splitting their intentions from their behaviors by moving to a "meta level." *Meta* means, according to the dictionary, "what is situated behind," "beyond," "transcending," "more comprehensive," "at a higher state of development."[18] In other words, this means moving them to "the outcome of the outcome."

Let's say that a couple wants to divorce. Accepting their apparent intention at first blush, you ask, "What will divorcing do for you?" You are asking about the intent of the intent, the outcome of the outcome. You are automatically putting one frame inside another larger, more comprehensive frame.

As you move to a meta level, the frames tend to be more general and, for most people, more benign. By enlarging the frame, moving up the logical levels, you can reframe intentions, and behaviors will signify something other than their original meaning. Moving to a meta level is a reframe because it focuses on the intention and keeps altering the intention until you have a positive one with which to work.

"Going meta" can be used as an agreement frame with couples and groups, moving people from disagreement to agreement. You start by ascertaining what each of the parties desires—"What I understand you want is . . ."—and then get their agreement that that is indeed what they want, even as you do not ascribe any motives to each one's desire. Then you ask them a question as to what their specific outcomes will do for them: "How will [attaining the outcome] change your life?" or "What will [attaining the outcome] do for you?" You keep going—meta-meta, intent of the intent, outcome of the outcome—until you sense that they have reached a common outcome. Then, you can say, "So what you both want is . . ." If at first you don't succeed, continue the "going meta" process.

---

18. *American Heritage Dictionary,* Version 3.0, 1993.

You can also "go meta" on yourself when you're about to do something incredibly absurd. Ask yourself, "What's the more comprehensive frame for what I am doing? How would my life change? What would it do for me?" An example:

BEHAVIOR: A congregant is in a rage over your not visiting during a brief illness and lets you know, in no uncertain terms, that "you are the most inconsiderate, selfish person in the history of humanity."

REFRAME: You gently inquire, "What will letting me know how angry you are do for you?"

RESPONSE: "I need to get it off my chest."

REFRAME: Knowing you need to reframe it further, you dauntlessly continue: "And if you get it off your chest, what will that do for you?"

RESPONSE: "I'll feel better."

REFRAME: At this point you can go on: "And if you feel better, what will that do for you?"

RESPONSE: "I'll be . . ." (You name it.)

The reframe is successful once you can sense that you've moved to a level where you and your congregant can have a calm discussion about how to feel better.

You can also use meta-level reframing with others who are disagreeing among themselves. Take your kids, for example. When they are fighting and want you to mediate, you can ask each in turn what will happen and how things will be different if each is allowed to have his or her own way. You can move the discussion from disagreement to agreement by employing meta-level questions.

Skillful Reframing

Reframing frame 1: *As the recipient of a communication, you have the power to mold the meaning of that communication.* Since meanings are arbitrary and nothing means anything in and of itself, the message *can* have the meaning you give it, if your response is not off the wall. One of the things that prevents us from responding adequately is that we have had programmed into us from childhood standard responses to certain words, certain tones of voice, certain expectations, etc. If your spouse offers to help you with the groceries, and you respond by saying, "That's kind of you," you have framed your spouse's act as kind. The intention might have been to show you what a wimp you are or how much more capable your spouse is compared to you, or it might have been an act of love or consideration. Whatever you decide the intention to be will determine your response and can influence your spouse's experience. The multitude of options is limited only by your flexibility and persuasiveness.

A relational partner berates you with loud, angry, negative words, accusing you of something terrible. Your life experience tells you this is an attack because that tone of voice and decibel level always accompanied being attacked when you were a child. You have, at that moment, a choice: You can respond on the basis of your past training, or you can choose a different way of responding. You can defend yourself, thus defining the behavior as an attack, or since attack and defend may not be the most useful approach with that person, you can mold the meaning into, for example, one of the following:

> Integrity—This person wants to let you know how he or she feels even though it risks hurting you.
>
> Courage—This person wants to confront you, even though afraid of risking your love.
>
> Concern for your well-being—This person cares about you and is willing to get upset to let you know that.
>
> Constructive criticism—Again, because this person cares.

If it's one of these and you respond with appreciation, you will have defined the person's behavior as different from the original intention, and different from your well-practiced response. You can conclude that this person is suffering from lack of sleep or indigestion, show concern, and offer an aspirin. You will have defined the person's communication as a call for help and put a useful frame around it.

Think of this reframe as a TV set, with lots of signals coming in and many channels to choose from. The split-screen option demonstrates that the channel you choose determines your experience. The more channels you subscribe to, the more varied your reception, and the greater the likelihood of a positive channel-surfing experience. Even knowing that there are more signals out there than anyone can handle, reframing with expertise means that you are expert at molding incoming signals. It is not easy. It takes practice. You are used to responding just one way. You have learned to call that one way "natural." It's not "natural." It's only one choice among many.

Reframing frame 2: *When reframing, go with positive intention.* Generally people appreciate and do have positive intentions. It is useful to assume the best about the other and, in most cases, to slap a positive intention on whatever is coming at you. This is difficult to do but also very powerful. It is a great way to reframe. Others will find the spot where you tend to respond automatically. To the degree that you can attribute to them that they mean well, that the intention is good, positive, noble, and so on, you will have started to split the behavior from the intention, and then you will be able to mold a new meaning around their behavior. An example: A wife tells her husband for the thousandth time to go for an annual medical checkup. He says to a buddy, "She's a blasted nag!" His buddy (an expert reframer) responds, "She must love you a lot to try so hard to get you to take good care of yourself." Through reframing the situation using positive intention, he has changed the meaning of the behavior. The next time she "nags," he may hear love behind it instead.

Agreement can be a potent reframe. Sometimes your communication partner is just plain correct. Your partner may come at you with what sounds like an attack, expecting that you will defend yourself. When you agree with your partner, you will have reframed the situation, from attack/defense (or counterattack) to something much more benign, and created a situation in which you may be able to work together.

Another way of changing meaning is by judicious relabeling. You can frame something positively simply by relabeling it. Being selfish can be described as treating oneself with respect; a time of crisis can be referred to as a transitional period; arguing can become lively discussion; pain can be reduced by calling it discomfort; yelling can be expressing your feelings; nagging is caring; and so forth.

Reframing frame 3: *Almost all behavior is appropriate and useful— someway, somewhere, somehow.* This frame gives you another choice beyond changing the meaning. If the problem is that someone always does thus-and-so, or that someone else is doing thus-and-so, you can reframe the meaning as we've been doing, or you can reframe their behavior by affirming that there are places where it's very appropriate to do whatever it is that they are doing. Some examples: If a mother complains that her son is stubborn, you can point out that being persistent is really useful when trying to get ahead in the world. If a father was strict with his teenage daughter, you can praise him for teaching her to get by in a tough world. Behavior has different meanings in different situations. Sometimes a behavior that is inappropriate in one context is expected in another. If you're playing volleyball and break down crying in the middle of the game, your behavior might well seem inappropriate, but the same behavior at a funeral would seem perfectly appropriate. You can change both the *content* and the *context* directly by recognizing that the behavior, whatever it is and no matter how annoying it is, might be useful in some other situation.

I offer here an example from the world of psychotherapy that I have found to be eminently useful in clergy encounters:

> A man comes to a therapist: "I am having trouble with my wife."
> "What is the trouble?"
> The man explains that his wife is blonde and that, periodically, on alternate Tuesdays when the moon is full, "I find myself enraged with her and criticizing her mercilessly."
> "Tell me about your mother?" Among other things, it turns out that the mother, with whom he has had a tumultuous relationship, is also blonde. After a long stretch of "meaningful" silence, the therapist says, "Your problem is not with your wife; your problem is with your mother."

An interesting reframe, it suggests that the behavior is understandable in another time and place. This can make a powerful difference. The man goes home and tells his wife what he has learned in his session, that when he criticizes her, it has nothing to do with her but, rather, with his mother. This reframe starts to shift their relationship. His behavior begins to change because he realizes it may have been appropriate in a different setting. His wife also may experience it differently, thinking it has nothing to do with her, and say to him when it starts, "Hey, I'm not your mother. Don't yell at me."

Good therapists are expert at reframing. Good Jewish relational caregivers need to be as well. **Molding meaning by reframing is a most power-ful tool.** You need to learn how to do it. You need to practice, practice, and practice, until it feels not just well-practiced but natural. Changing your own and others' frames can make life easier for you *and* them. Reframing is a powerful way of using your mouth with your head. **Reframing is to be used with integrity and respect for both you and your relational part-ner.**

These are a few of the tools you need to use in communicating relationally in your caregiving. Others I have written about elsewhere.[19] You will have many occasions to use your mouth with your head in your work as a relational caregiver, and in the greater world around you. It is a fascinating and powerful skill to have. Go forth and learn.

---

19. See Bloom, *The Rabbi As Symbolic Exemplar,* Chapter 11, "Curing and Heal-ing."

CARING FOR THE CAREGIVER'S RELATIONAL "SELF"

– 3 –

Taking Care of Ourselves: It's About Time!

David J. Zucker

This chapter is about time management. Traditional time management books address how to make more *efficient* use of your time. Rabbis, cantors, chaplains and clergy live in a world where constituents (perhaps unreasonably, but nonetheless) consider their spiritual leaders to be available at any time that they are needed.

Consequently, given these constraints, this chapter, written by clergy for clergy, considers how we manage that "time on" as well as that "time off." For example, when we are "on," we need really to "be on" and to make better use of that time. As someone remarked, "You can always buy more things; you cannot buy more time." Then, conversely, we need periods when we really are in time-off mode, to the extent that this is realistically possible.

The work of the rabbinate, cantorate, chaplaincy, or other clergy can seem without limit. How do people often gauge your effectiveness within a community? Ideally it would not be by the number of meetings one can, and is expected to, attend in a given week. Nonetheless, in the words of one rabbi,

Author's Note: The author thanks Sandra L. Mayer for reading an earlier version of this and offering insightful comments.

> I know of no other profession or skill . . . where one man is called upon
> to be so many things to so many different people. Success in the rab-
> binate will often depend upon the number of meetings a rabbi can at-
> tend . . . the number of people he can see . . . the number of phone calls
> he can make . . . and the number of congregational activities he can
> juggle in one week. Such frenzied activity can only tend in the direc-
> tion of shallowness.[1]

Though this "complaint" appeared in a journal several decades ago, there is
little reason to believe that much has changed in the intervening years.

Then consider this fictional account found in the novel *A Place of Light*.
It reflects well the reality of today's insistent world. Rabbi Lynda Klein had
just skipped her lunch.

> She'd missed breakfast too, for there had been no time. The Religious
> School board had scheduled a coffee meeting in the morning. . . . Af-
> ter it broke up, the singles-group president came in, and it took her
> half an hour to talk him out of resigning. Then . . . she'd dashed off to
> the hospital, where Nita Gold was undergoing emergency surgery.
> She'd gotten back in time for Abe Katz's funeral . . . [but] she still had
> correspondence to do, not to mention the two boys coming in for bar
> mitzvah training.[2]

There were so many calls on her time and energy. In the early days she had
found time to pray, even if it was late at night in the synagogue. Yet the real
demands of the rabbinate have interfered with her plans. As the novel relates, "there was no time. The congregation waited, a jealous lover. Hundreds of people wanted her to inspire them, to lead them to God, or prayer,
or to their own souls."[3]

Does that sound familiar? These congregants, in real life no less than in
the fictional depiction, desire the rabbi's time because, rabbis (as all clergy)
are symbolic exemplars. "It is the symbolic exemplarhood which distin-
guishes the rabbi [cantor, chaplain, clergyperson] from the social worker,
psychological counselor, or federation executive."[4] For congregants (and

---

1. Albert M. Lewis, quoted in Maurice M. Shudofsky, "Portrait of the Inauthentic
Rabbi," *Reconstructionist* 20:5 (April 23, 1954), p. 24. See also Paul Wilkes, *And They
Shall Be My People: An American Rabbi and His Congregation* (New York: Atlantic
Monthly, 1994), pp. 18, 17.

2. Rhonda Shapiro-Rieser, *A Place of Light* (New York: Pocket, 1983), p. 271.

3. Ibid., p. 243.

4. Jack H Bloom, *The Rabbi As Symbolic Exemplar: By the Power Vested in Me*
(Binghamton, NY: The Haworth Press, 2002), p. 136. See David J. Zucker, *American
Rabbis: Facts and Fiction* (Northvale, NJ: Jason Aronson, 1998), p. 77 ff, ad loc.

these can be congregants in a pulpit or a nursing home or a hospital), the rabbi is a symbol of something other than herself or himself. The

> rabbi is a symbolic leader who is set apart to function within the community as a symbol of that community and as an exemplar of their desire for moral perfection. The rabbi is thus a walking, talking, living symbol . . . the embodiment of what people ought to do, but have no intention of doing.[5]

Being a symbolic exemplar means you possess great moral authority, but it also is time-consuming and emotionally demanding.

The public perception of rabbis, cantors, chaplains, or clergy is that although *in principle* they have a private life, when they are "needed," these selfsame rabbis, cantors, chaplains, or clergy are available. It does not matter if that conflicts with a rabbi's personal life. Crises come when they do, and, likewise, funerals need to be attended to in a timely fashion. Claiming it is your day off, and therefore you will not conduct the service on that day, is not an acceptable option for most rabbis. Therefore, since time is limited, one of the challenges you face is how to make more purposeful use of your time.

One paradigm for reevaluating how to use your time is found in the book of Exodus, the incident in Chapter 18 when Jethro, Moses' father-in-law, tells Moses what he surely does not want to hear. Jethro explains to Moses that despite his son-in-law's best efforts, and the long hours of his day, Moses is not being effective in his work. Day in and day out, from morning to evening, Moses has been meeting with people. Not surprisingly, Moses is mentally and physically exhausted. The people likewise are frustrated, impatient, and exhausted. With an experienced caregiver's clarity, Jethro tells Moses, "This task is too heavy for you; you cannot do it alone. You will surely wear yourself out, and these people as well."[6]

The most basic interpretation of this verse is that Moses needs to delegate some of his responsibilities. That undoubtedly is correct. There are, however, other important meanings contained in Jethro's words. One is that Moses is not using his own time wisely. Second, he is wearying the people as well.[7]

---

5. Bloom, *The Rabbi As Symbolic Exemplar*, p. 140.

6. Exodus 18:18. Note the number of the chapter and verse in which these life-giving words are found: double *ḥai*.

7. Some of these concepts were discussed in a different form in David J. Zucker, "When Do the Best Rest—and Why? A Work in Progress," *Journal of Jewish Communal Service,* Fall 2001, pp. 56-59.

Time On: Using That Time More Effectively and Finding Resources

Moses had high expectations and high standards. In his mind, he wanted to, and thought that he could, do it all. He wanted to be the ideal leader: guide the people, hear their human needs, address their affairs, and do so as a caring, compassionate counselor. The reality was that Moses had no, or a very limited, concept of setting priorities. Not everything has, nor can it have, the same value, the same call on our time. As that was true for Moses, so it is true for us today.

Fortunately, resources are available in our world to help us sort through the time-demands dilemma. Support and possible solutions are there if we choose to seek them out. Whether from our local library or the local bookstore, many books suggest ways for us to make better and more efficient use of our time. Some people reading this will think, "Oh I can save some time. I will check out books on the Internet." Perhaps. In my experience, this needs to be a literal hands-on endeavor. You will want to thumb through these volumes and see if they truly appeal to you. It is likely that only parts will be applicable to your situation. Alternately, you might simply relate to certain sections or suggestions, and not others. Find a book or two, and then when you locate something that suits your temperament, you will want to hunker down and commit yourself to meaningful change.

A book that contains some sage advice is Barbara Hemphill's *Taming the Office Tiger*.[8] She begins by asking rhetorically, "What is organization?" (followed by a small section, "Why do we resist it?"). Among her common-sense observations are these:

> "Organizing is NOT a moral issue (No matter what your mother told you!)."
> "Organization is not necessarily 'neatness.'"
> "Organization is not a final decision."
> "Organization does not always equal efficiency."
> "There is no right or wrong way to organize."

Then, under this last rubric she writes, "It doesn't matter *what* you do, but that you do it *consistently*. [Further, you need to ask yourself . . .] Does it work, and do you like it?" (italics in original), recognizing that what works

---

8. Barbara Hemphill, *Taming the Office Tiger* (Washington, DC: Kiplinger Washington Editors, 1996).

for you may not work for others.[9] She suggests that five elements or components to implementing and maintaining organization are

1. positive attitude,
2. sufficient time,
3. adequate skills,
4. proper tools, and
5. ongoing practice.

Following some other management gurus, such as Steven Covey, Hemphill explains that one way to think of your time is to classify it into four quadrants:

1. Urgent and Important
2. Important but Not Urgent
3. Urgent but Not Important
4. Not Urgent and Not Important

She explains that "Urgent" is usually determined by outside circumstances—such as Yom Tov[10] is coming (though she does not use that specific example)—and "Important" is connected to our own personal values, what really matters to us and what we desire to accomplish, be that in our professional or personal lives. As follow-up points she notes, "Just because I choose not to do something now doesn't mean I can't do it later" and "Sometimes I can get satisfaction by doing something less than perfect."[11]

Another book to consider is Jan Jasper's *Take Back Your Time*.[12] Chapter titles in her book include "Setting Priorities"; "How Do You Want to Spend Your Time?"; and "Time Mastery." Jasper offers some cogent advice:

> "Notice what gives you energy and what drains you."
> "Positive selfishness—getting your reasonable needs met—is necessary for healthy relationships. . . . Learn to say no and hold your ground. . . . Start with saying no to small things. . . . Then build to bigger no's."[13]

---

9. Ibid., pp. 3-5.
10. A holiday.
11. Hemphill, *Taming the Office Tiger*, pp. 66-67.
12. Jan Jasper, *Take Back Your Time: How to Regain Control of Work, Information, and Technology* (New York: Griffin, 1999).
13. Ibid., pp. 16, 24.

Elsewhere, echoing Jethro's advice to Moses, she writes that

> having to pass on some worthwhile activities makes us feel sad. But
> there's something far worse—continuing to delude yourself that it's
> possible to do everything and becoming more exhausted and frus-
> trated. You won't get it done because you won't live forever.[14]

In the chapter on time mastery, Jaspers suggests:

> "You can always get more stuff, but can never get more time."
> "Diagnose your disruptions. Start writing down what sidetracks you
>   each day. After a week or two, analyze your record and look for
>   patterns . . . [and] learn to say, 'No'"
> "Do things early rather than later. Do the most important thing first."
> "Leave a cushion of time in case things go wrong."
> "You can do a lot in five minutes. Much of our time is in small bits.
>   Use it!"

She urges the reader to make time to exercise: "Sometimes you may not
make it on the assigned days, but if you don't make appointments you won't
get there at all!"[15]

Being Fully at Work

Doing God's work, serving as a rabbi, cantor, chaplain, or clergyperson
of any kind, is demanding in terms of time, energy, emotion, and commitment. When you are "on," you need to be fully on. You need to keep your
appointments on time, you need to be attentive to what you are doing and
sincere in what you are saying and doing, but then you need to leave that appointment behind you. For rabbis, cantors, chaplains, or other clergy, to do
less is to miss opportunities to be true to our sacred work.

One way to monitor your behavior is to think of your "time on" in terms
of the four B's: Be there. Be present. Be honest. Be gone.[16]

---

14. Ibid., p. 28.

15. Ibid., pp. 68, 70, 71, 74, 80. Regular exercise is not for everyone, but on a personal note, I find this an essential ingredient in my life. It gives me "time off" during
which I simply cannot be reached, and, indeed, oftentimes I find that as I exercise new
ideas come to me.

16. Some of these concepts were discussed in a different form in David J. Zucker
" 'Bless Me': An Opportunity Missed?" *Ministry,* March 2004, p. 26.

Be There

Time is a precious commodity. Your time is valuable, and so is that of other people. Just as you have made time in your day to see them, in many cases, they have rearranged their schedules to meet with you. When you schedule an appointment to visit with someone at a specific time (be that person a congregant/client/resident/patient), it is vital to keep that promise. Not to do so conveys the message that, for you, the person is not important or lacks value in your eyes. Conversely, simply by honoring your commitment, by being on time, *where* you said you would be *when* you said you would be there, tells people that you hold them in high esteem. You care about them. You have taken the time to be there. Your word is good.

Be Present

When you are with your appointments, it is imperative to be fully focused and aware. Look at them and both establish and keep eye contact with people. Listen carefully to what people before you are saying, and perhaps to what they are *not* saying. Take notice of their body language and gestures. Be with them, compassionately, emotionally, and mindfully. Be involved in the conversation. Be an active listener. Offer an empathetic ear even as you interact with them. Do not have half of your mind thinking of what you need to do next. Yes, you need to monitor your time, but stay focused on those before you.

Be Honest

Never promise something that you are unable to deliver. You are in a position of trust. Remember, you are a *symbolic exemplar,*[17] and in that role you carry enormous power. Do not overstep the limits of your authority. You do not, you cannot possibly, have all the answers. Know when you need to say, "No," and know when to say, "I do not know." Another aspect of being honest is to admit that this is not in your field of expertise. You cannot be all things to all people. All of us have limits. Know when you need to refer. Know the deeper meaning of truth and the limits of truth.[18]

---

17. Bloom, *The Rabbi As Symbolic Exemplar,* pp. 177-178.
18. Honesty can be honesty in the moment. Honesty can mean something other than absolute, unbending, unwavering truth. If the person before you is suffering from dementia, literal truth may be counterproductive to the health and well-being of that person. Should you be working with people you know or suspect may be somewhat demented, even if they are

Be Gone

Rabbis, cantors, chaplains, and clergy in general work with the public day in and day out. They sincerely care about the members of their communities. That is why one of the hardest acts to internalize is knowing when to disengage. When is it time truly to be gone? Yet the answer can be quite simple. How? Leave the appointment at the appointment. Leave the office at the office. Leave the meeting at the meeting. Leave the residents at the long-term care center. Leave the patients at the clinic, hospice, or hospital. Leave work at work. Know when it is time to leave the office and refrain from "just" sending one more e-mail, making one more phone call, or checking out one more site on the Internet. Modern Hebrew offers the expression *yesh g'vul*—there is a limit!

An adjunct of making a division, a clear border between work time and nonwork time, between "being on" and "being off," is in respect to the issue of privacy. Often you may hear privileged information. After all, you are a figure of trust. Always be respectful of confidences. Do not share professional experiences in an unprofessional manner. Do not share privileged information with family or friends. Further, be circumspect in open spaces, such as hallways, foyers, public bathrooms, or elevators, where information may be overheard and transmitted inappropriately. Keep private confidences private and privileged. If you err, do so on the side of caution.

Using Technology

Another aspect of time management can be a good use of modern technology. The "blessing" of electronic gadgetry found in the marketplace can be a wonderful thing, or it can be a *b'rachah l'vatalah.*[19] Many, if not most, colleagues whom I know are "wired." Whether it is a palm pilot, a cell phone, or simply a pager, with rare exceptions, they (we) are but an electronic signal away. On the negative side of the equation, these electronic

---

close acquaintances, congregants/clients/residents/patients, know when you need to "cross over the street" to meet them where they are. Be honest, even if that means being honest with them where they are in their dementia. For example, when speaking to an octogenarian in a nursing home, truth needs to be contextual. When eighty-five-year-old Bessie tells you that she needs to leave now because her mother is expecting her home, the "honest" answer is, "Yes, I understand that you want to meet up with Mom." That is a form of honesty. If Bessie then says to you, "Do you know where my mother is? Have you seen her?" the "honest" answer is, "No, I have not." It is not "honest" in this situation—and certainly not helpful—to say, "Actually, Bessie, your mother died many years ago, and, no, you cannot go out."

19. An empty blessing.

leashes can restrict us. They can function as our merciless masters; we then become their passive, submissive servants. This electronic wizardry can prevent us from taking care of ourselves by making it harder for us to say, "No."

On the other hand, the world of technology is here. To close our eyes to that fact would make us modern-day Luddites.[20] The more important issue is how do we make the best use of this technology. Pagers and palm pilots provide us with a freedom unknown in the past. We can be accessible, and we are expected to be accessible, but we should monitor the reasonable use of this technology. Not every claim on our time has equal value. As we make choices in other areas of our lives, choosing this over that, so a more considered and careful use of our electronic devices will give us back time, instead of taking time from us. Too often, we forget that we ourselves are making this decision. We are opting to be connected continuously in the way that we are. It is a conscious choice on our part to choose to be always "on." We have internalized the newest mantra: wired 24/7.

Not so long ago National Public Radio aired a story about how modern technology can intrude into our "off time." Some professionals had planned to spend a couple weeks in the wilds of northern Canada, to get away from it all. They were looking forward to this adventure, and the joy of seeing such pristine beauty without any interference from the outside world. Before they left, one of the families prevailed upon them "just" to take along a cell phone "in case" they were in imminent danger. It was the beginning of the slippery slope. In the end, they took along not only a cell phone but also other electronic gear, so that they were in principle—and in actual practice—connected to their offices and families back home. They did not set and commit to clear and reasonable limits. "I will only use the technology if I am in dire straits." Likewise, "Do not contact me unless it is a true life-or-death emergency." Instead of allowing themselves to let go, they were mentally and emotionally tied to their homes and their workplaces. On some level, they never "got away" at all.

Wearying the People

Jethro made it clear to Moses that this great leader was not using his time effectively.[21] Yet worse than that, he was wearying the people as well. In re-

---

20. Defined as "1. somebody who opposes technological or industrial innovation; 2. a worker involved in protests in Britain in the 1810s against new factory methods of production and in favor of traditional methods of work." *Encarta® World English Dictionary* © 1999, Microsoft Corporation.

21. Exodus 18:18.

ality, by creating a situation where he presented himself as indispensable, Moses was infantilizing the people. He was encouraging them to depend solely on him. The spoken message Moses was articulating was, "Turn to me. I have the answers." The unspoken (and maybe unrealized) message to the people was, "I am crucial. You need me. You need me because you cannot do it by yourselves. You need me to solve all of your problems." A "true" caregiver, by contrast, would empower the people to take care of themselves.

When we make ourselves available without reasonable, professional limitations, we are saying to those with whom we interact (be they congregants/clients/residents/patients), be it at the office or elsewhere, "Here I am, your trusty support. Lean on me. Depend on me. You do not have to be independent in your own right. You do not have to develop and rely upon your own inner resources."

We need to set reasonable limits on our own behavior. We then must take responsibility for our choices, to be "on" or to be "off." Trying always to be there, to be responsible and responsive, and to be the perfect caregiver is arrogance on our part. It is also intellectually dishonest. We can rationalize that we are so committed because "we care deeply and sincerely" about our congregants/clients/residents/patients, but truly we are there because it is our paid job or because it makes us feel good about who we are.

If, or when, conditions changed and we took another position, especially in another location, we would not commit to weekly visits to those people. No matter that they are precious in our lives today, under new conditions we would leave them behind. We would transfer our affections and find new congregants/clients/residents/patients to make weary with our continuous compassion and love.

Like Moses, we enjoy feeling needed. It is a tremendous boost to our egos. We are indispensable! We enjoy it so much that we want to sustain the fantasy. We end up more committed to sustaining that false notion than to committing ourselves to what we should: the *mitzvah*[22] of self-care. In actuality, attempting to be indispensable hurts us—and likewise it hurts those we are purporting to help.

Taking Care of Ourselves

The relationship between clergy and congregants is a sacred covenant. A significant part of that contract revolves around the use of our time. Though in both cases they were not addressing time management directly, nonetheless we can learn a lot from the advice of two figures: the sage Hillel and

---

22. In Hebrew, fulfilling God's command; in Yiddish, a good deed.

Nancy Reagan. On the face of it, they make an odd couple. To be sure, for some they may both be heroes, but in many clergy circles, at least, even the juxtaposition of these names seems inappropriate and incongruent. The former is a revered teacher and *Tanna*[23] of the first century BCE, the latter the wife of a politician, albeit a successful politician and a president to boot. Yet, each person offered many pieces of advice, and their particular wisdom here is directly applicable to the subject of time management.

Hillel's dictum is well known: "If I am not for myself, who will be?" Nancy Reagan's advice is equally terse and true: "Just say no!"[24]

As rabbis, as cantors, as chaplains, as clergy, we want to do it all. We want to be there for our people. We want to offer advice, care, comfort, compassion, spiritual guidance, goodness, help, leadership, wisdom, and the list can go on nigh endlessly. Our hearts are large, and our intent is pure and praiseworthy. Yet, when we try to translate those ideas into reality, we soon find that they often are impossible and unrealistic fantasies. We cannot be there for people all the time. We cannot solve all the problems with which we are faced.

If I am not for myself, who will be? If I do not take care of myself, if I do not monitor wisely what I do, when I do it, and how I do it, what kind of a leader am I?

Just say no. Likewise, if I do not set reasonable limits, if I cannot say this far, and no further, what is the worth and measure of my leadership?

To put it another way, if I am going to be my other person's true and healthy keeper, I need to begin the process within myself. The early Zionist leadership rule said it well: *hadrachah b'dugma.*[25]

To paraphrase Hillel, if we do not make time for our own souls, who will? The answer is no one will. We need to stand up and claim our own time and space. *If I am not for myself, who will be?* How does one do so, how does one say, *"Yesh g'vul"*?[26] Rabbi Susan Grossman explains that the congregation benefits from the rabbi setting time boundaries:

> When I set limits on what my congregants can reasonably ask of my time, I explain to them that if I can't do it [i.e., make time for my own family], how can I ask them as doctors, lawyers, executives, busy people to make time for their families as well.[27]

---

23. Rabbinic teachers mentioned in the Mishnah (second century CE).
24. Hillel: Mishnah Avot 1:14; Nancy Reagan's dictum was within the context of saying no to drug use. Her advice nonetheless is apposite here.
25. Leadership by example.
26. "There is a limit."
27. Susan Grossman, "The Dual Nature of Rabbinic Leadership," *Conservative Judaism* 48:1 (Fall 1995), p. 46.

In other words, we need to take responsibility for our own actions/behavior.

Sometimes we just need time simply "to be," and not "to do." As Rabbi Bonita E Taylor wisely has asked:

> What makes it so hard to consider that God wants us to be human BE-ings, not human DO-ings? Why always measure yourself by what you do? Why can't you just be? God has entitled you from time to time to just BE![28]

To be truly effective, we do need time off. This is difficult for caring, compassionate caregiving clergy. Jack H Bloom suggests that being a rabbi brings special tensions. He writes that being a rabbi (and the word *rabbi* in this context should be understood as rabbi, cantor, chaplain, clergyperson)

> means being set apart, lonely, and subject to unreasonable expectations and demands from all sides. Being a rabbi means belonging to one's own family, the congregational family, and beyond that, being a parafamilial member of many different families. Being a rabbi means dealing with the inevitable conflict between the rabbi's life cycle and congregants' life cycles; having to decide what to do when an event in the congregational family coincides with one in the rabbi's family.[29]

Time Off

To manage time for ourselves, to make time for ourselves, we need to internalize Nancy Reagan's words of wisdom. We need to "Just say no!" *No* is not a four-letter word, even though many of us think—or act—as if it is. We need forcibly and absolutely to commit ourselves to having sufficient personal time.

In many cases we can work out an arrangement with a colleague. I will cover for you when you take your personal time—be it for a "date" or for a vacation or to attend a conference—and you will cover for me. Our congregants want us to be "on" 24/7, but, generally, they comprehend that if we are "away," then someone is covering for us.

One recent book, *Turn It Off* by Gil E. Gordon,[30] contains valuable suggestions for how to restructure our lives. He takes a very basic approach. Gordon begins by asking, "How did we become so attached to our offices?"

---

28. Personal communication to the author.

29. Bloom, *The Rabbi As Symbolic Exemplar,* p. 135; Zucker, *American Rabbis,* p. 184.

30. Gill E. Gordon, *Turn It Off* (New York: Three Rivers, 2001).

And for the word *offices,* you can substitute *cell phones, pagers, e-mail,* or *daily schedules.* Then, he raises a series of questions that help us to think through whether we have lost control, whether we have "gone over the line." Having determined that answer, and assuming we have done so, he offers thoughts how we can once again get control over our lives.[31]

Gordon's image is simple. He provides us a tripartite model for balancing life and work: 100/60/0. When you are officially "on," you are in the 100 percent zone. Clients, colleagues, congregants, residents, and patients can expect that you will either be on the job or reachable. The way that you are available, whether by telephone, cell phone, or pager is a matter of style and personal taste. Yet when you are in that 100 percent zone, you need to give your full attention to the demands of your professional life.

When you are in the 0 percent zone, you are officially off, and off in reality. Those days you have designated as your days off, or the middle of the night. It is, so to say, a real Shabbat.[32] While on is on, and off is off, what turns out to be the most difficult zone to define is that middle one, the 60 percent zone, when you are neither *fleishig* nor *milchig*[33] (though Gordon does not use these terms). To help us to think through that dilemma, he poses questions for us to consider, for example:

> To what extent are we required to be available and accessible during off-hours, holidays and vacations?
> To what extent do we feel obligated or expected to be available and accessible then?
> To what extent do we want to be totally inaccessible or unavailable then?[34]

As I commented earlier, it is probable that no one book will address all of *your* particular issues. You will find answers in various works, and you will need to thumb through these volumes to see if, how, and to what degree they truly apply to you.

It is not a question of [Either/Or]: *Either* I am there for them all the time, *or* not. Rather, it is a matter of [Both/And].[35] It is inevitable that days off will be trampled upon, or promises to family unmet. In those cases, whenever possible, do try to take compensatory time. If working on your day off

---

31. Ibid., p. v.

32. The Sabbath—a day for rest and renewal.

33. Literally, meat or dairy; colloquially, "neither here nor there" or "neither one nor another."

34. Gordon, *Turn It Off,* pp. 110-111.

35. Bloom, *The Rabbi As Symbolic Exemplar,* Chapter 6, "The Inner Life of the Rabbi."

decreased your family's time together, make an extra effort to find that comp time, whether it is official or unofficial. You will never really catch up, but something is better than nothing. Sometimes the best you can do is a balancing act. [Both/And] sometimes means "Yes, but . . ." A rabbi's child offered this observation about what he thought a parent needs to do:

> He must be honest about himself and his job. He must . . . be able to explain why he attended the board meeting instead of the basketball game. He must assure his children and his congregation that his roles of parent and rabbi are not mutually exclusive. He must be able to say to his disappointed child that "he is a rabbi, too," and to his disappointed congregant that "he is a daddy, too." He must assure both constituencies that although he may occasionally disappoint them, he never deserts them.[36]

Realistically, no one will take care of us, unless we do so. To frame this in the language formulated by Jack H Bloom, we need to attend to our own [*Tzelem*⇔*N'shamah*] relationship.[37] We need to notice what gives us energy and what drains us. We need time off and time away. As we take better care of our *"selves"* we will be more effective as human beings and as caregivers. That, however, should be secondary in our thinking. We should take care of ourselves first and foremost because we are modeled after, and molded by, Divinity, and to do God's work we need to honor our being so created by being healthy humans, who have a working reciprocal relationship between the different parts of us. In Mishnah Avot[38] (3:14) we learn that humans are loved because, quoting Genesis 9:6, we are modeled after God. That is partially true. Again reflecting Bloom's language, the *Tzelem* is our cognitive being, what we might call today *our mindfulness,* for saying that we are physical icons of God borders on idolatry.[39] Yet we are more

---

36. David Eli Stern, "Today's Rabbinate: the Personal Equation" [symposium], *Central Conference of American Rabbis Yearbook: 90* (New York: Central Conference of American Rabbis), 1981, p. 147.

37. [Breath-Taking⇔Model of Divinity]. See *ABC's of Jewish Relational Care* in this book; for further explication, see Bloom, *The Rabbi As Symbolic Exemplar,* especially Chapters 6 and 8.

38. Teachings of the sages; aphorisms and moral sayings attributed to the early rabbis (300 BCE-200 CE).

39. Compare Maimonides, *Guide of the Perplexed,* trans. M. Friedlander (New York: Hebrew Publishing Co., 1881), Chapter 1, p. 30. "In man the 'form' 'Tzelem' is that constituent which gives him human perception: and on account of this intellectual perception the term 'Tzelem' is employed."

than *Tzelem.* We live corporeally because God has given us breath. The *N'shamah* that God has breathed into us, giving life to the clay from which we are created (Daily Prayer Book), is in itself holy. The one cannot work without an interacting reciprocal relationship with the other. Daring to anthropomorphize, we can say that God, as any good teacher, leads by example. At the end of creation, God rested on the seventh day. God rested, not because God needed to take time off, but because we need to take time off, and God wanted us to follow in the divine example. Exodus 31:17 says it well: "For in six days the Eternal made heaven and earth, and on the seventh day [God] ceased from work and was refreshed." The well-known Hebrew phrase is *shavat vayinafash.*[40] As symbolic exemplars, following in the footsteps of God, we need to lead by example and we need *shavat vayinafash.* We need to be healthy humans; our personal goals need to include true wellness—a time for *nafash,*[41] time for doing things that absorb us deeply, a *nafash* that will refresh our *nefesh.*[42]

In the end, it's all about time. There will never be enough time, and on top of that, we do need time away. Yet there are ways we can help ourselves. Be mindful when you are "on" and pay attention to the four B's: Be there. Be present. Be honest. Be gone. We need to adopt an organizational structure that works for us. To implement and maintain it requires a positive attitude, sufficient time, adequate skills, proper tools, and ongoing practice. Some of our most important work will be to empower congregants, clients, patients, and residents to find strength within themselves. For their own health, it is not wise for us to be there for them at all times. In addition, as we make conscious choices about how we use, and respond to the possibilities of, modern technology, so will we make better use of our time. We have to decide how best to use these electronic devices and need to accept responsibility for our choices. It is possible to "get away" and have "time off." Using Gil Gordon's image, it is up to us to think through the 100/60/0 time zones. Arranging coverage is part of that solution. As symbolic exemplars we can set good examples and lead through our wise behavior. Time management done well is sacred work in action.

---

40. Rest and fresehment for our whole being.
41. Rest.
42. Physical and mental spirits.

– 4 –

Managing Compassion Fatigue

David J. Stern

Rabbis have as their job being intimate participants in all the major life cycle events of their congregants. They are expected to, and they will want to, be openhearted and open-minded in the presence of many births, life challenges, and deaths. In addition, they must constantly wrestle with the conflicting wishes of congregants as, together, they try to cocreate a community that sustains and nourishes people's spiritual lives.

When their job brings them face-to-face with large quantities or great intensities of common and not so common brands of human struggling and strife, they will be liable to suffer from what has come to be called "compassion fatigue."[1] Clergy and others in the helping professions are familiar with the term *burnout. Secondary,* or *vicarious, trauma* is a term that describes symptoms which sometimes arise when people are exposed to another person's trauma.

Although the phenomena that the term describes do exist, and need to be addressed, I suggest that *compassion fatigue* is based upon a limited understanding of compassion. This chapter will explore the deeper meaning of this term, beginning with an examination of the several reasons why compassion fatigue develops.

First, when we fail to place ourselves high on the list of those for whom we care, when we neglect our basic needs, we become fatigued. It is not uncommon for caregivers and clergy to be skillful at caring for others and not so skillful at self-care.

Second, the nervous systems of caregivers are exposed to so much pathos, it can be difficult to metabolize all the intensity. It can simply be exhausting to live in the midst of so much human drama. Clergy (and other healers as well) need skillful support and self-healing practices to help

---

1. Eric Gentry, Anna Baranowsky, and Kathleen Dunning, "ARP: The Accelerated Recovery Program (ARP) for Compassion Fatigue," in *Treating Compassion Fatigue,* ed. Charles R. Figley (New York: Brunner-Routledge, 2002).

cleanse their nervous systems and strengthen their capacities to process, or digest, all that confronts them. Failing to care for their own physical, emotional, interpersonal, and spiritual needs, they become depleted.

Third, when we are presented with problems, complaints, and strong emotions, we naturally feel called upon to solve the problem, answer the complaint, and ease the emotional upset. That is what compassionate people, and particularly compassionate people who are in the helping professions, feel expected to do. The impulse to "fix" problems is understandable, and mostly misguided. This impulse is usually driven, not by compassion, but by fear, anxiety, and a kind of self-hatred, and it is a neurotic form of compassion. Most of us are in the habit of hating or rejecting these feelings, these aspects of ourselves. We think of them as interruptions or distractions. Consequently, we are prone to switch into fix-it mode.

One of the purposes of our anxiety and fear is to call us to be compassionate with ourselves. Having established a compassionate self-relation, we can begin to look at the problems with which we are faced with greater equanimity. If we fail to first bring compassion to ourselves, we will tend to respond instead from our self-hatred. We will short-circuit the life of compassion and the almost effortless wisdom that flows from that ground.

When we are not connected with ourselves, our compassion cannot be true compassion. It may be sympathy imbued with a genuine wish to be helpful, but when we are not connected with ourselves, our motivations and methods will always be somewhat askew, effortful, and less than effective. The relational field will register our disconnection, and compassion will not flow. The fatigue that will inevitably develop from this way of working is commonly called compassion fatigue. This fatigue comes from another kind of failure to heed compassion's call.

We live at the intersection of the "temporal and the eternal," of matter and spirit. Kierkegaard states: "What is it that really binds the temporal and the eternal? What is it other than love, which therefore is before everything else and remains when all else is past."[2] From the vantage point of our finite everyday life of "matter," we must include ourselves among those for whom we show compassion. Stephen Covey tells us that we must take care of our physical, emotional, intellectual, and spiritual needs. He calls this "sharpening the saw."[3] No matter how skillful we are at accessing the spiritual center of our work world, if, as an expression of our spiritual life, we do not "sharpen the saw," it will become dull and useless.

---

2. Soren Kierkegaard, *Works of Love,* trans. Howard and Edna Hong (New York: Harper and Row, 1962), p. 24; originally published in 1847.

3. Stephen Covey, *The Seven Habits of Highly Effective People* (New York: Fireside, 1989), p. 287.

From the vantage point of spirit, there are endless reservoirs of energy. When we practice *t'shuvah,*[4] when we turn, again and again, to the source of life, we will find, in every corner of every situation, ample resources to get the job done. Turning to God and looking past our limited resources, we open ourselves to receiving the boundless creative energies of the universe, which animate every inch of that universe. This is not a theoretical statement. It is a deeply practical one.

This exploration of compassion will offer ways to think about the relationship between everyday rabbinical work and the palpable dimension of God's presence that we call compassion. Remembering that we, ourselves, and the people we serve are already in God's hands, we can relax into and draw upon the vital energies that animate all existence. It becomes easier to know when and how to step back and take better care of ourselves.

Compassion Described

The word *compassion* can be broken down into two parts: "com-" and "passion," the latter of which is defined as "strong emotion"[5] and "suffering and endurance of ill."[6] Passion describes a fullness of feeling. It describes our total immersion in the river of life and the intense feelings that are an expression of this immersion. The river of life is an expression of God's boundless and ongoing creativity. When immersed in the river of life, we do not always feel that we are in the presence of a compassionate God. When we are in the river of life, there can be no question about the fullness and bounty and endless ongoing-ness of creation.

If passion describes our immersion in the river of life, then "com-"—meaning "with"—describes our place on the banks of that river. We can think of this "with-ness" as that part of self which stands apart from, or alongside, experience, so that we can be *with* and not just *in* the experience that we are having.

A river without bounds is a problem. Unbounded love without discernment, without a sense of boundary, is likewise a mess. The opposite is also true. Critical distance without any felt sense for the flow of the river is desiccated.

---

4. Repentance; return to the good way, regret, abandoning sin; a return to God and to the right path. See Chapter 22, "*T'shuvah* in Sexual Violations with Direct Implications for Other Situations," in this book, for further explanation.

5. *The Concise Oxford English Dictionary* (Sixth Edition) (Oxford: Oxford University Press, 1976), sv "passion."

6. Eric Partridge, *Origins: A Short Etymological Dictionary of Modern English* (Fourth Edition) (New York: Macmillan Publishing Co., Inc., 1966), sv "passion."

As children, we initially find ourselves totally immersed in the river of life and we require our adult caregivers to be the banks of that river. As we grow, we learn how to step out of that river with a discerning intelligence that can travel alongside the flow of the river without being totally immersed, or even lost, in the flow of that river. While some *"self"* in us is able to stand back from the river of life, the whole Self can never really leave the river. As long as we are alive, our home is always both in and beyond the river.

Our capacity to step back, even as we are immersed, is a defining feature of what it means to be human. It is a blessing and great danger. Because a *"self"* in us can live alongside the river, we are perpetually in danger of forgetting our place in the river of life and the laws that govern the flow. Because life is so intense, unpredictable, and experienced as all-encompassing, there is a profound tendency to want to secure a place that is free from the wilds of the river. From this nominally separate vantage point, we don't really live life. We just watch it from a safe distance. Think of the ways in which we avoid conflict or confronting someone we love with a difficult matter. We are afraid to stir things up and face the storm of emotions and other consequences that may follow.

An opposite danger exists as well. We can refuse to own our capacity to be a discerning Self-presence. We can refuse to grow up and instead require others to watch over us while we remain lost in the river. For example, in writing this chapter, I was at times overwhelmed by the challenges of ordering my thoughts, of presenting them in an intelligible fashion. At times I was paralyzed with conflicting emotions about this work. I felt as though I were drowning. No one could take over for me and write this chapter. I could get support and help, but, in the end, I had to climb out of the river, stand on the bank, and survey the situation. Only then could I jump back in, bringing with me a fresh perspective. I had to do this again and again. We all have to. It is only when we are willing to develop a *"self"* that dwells *in and alongside* the river of life that the fullness of Self emerges. Gilligan describes this form of *"self"* as the "relational *'self'*." The relational *"self"* is that *"self"* which spontaneously arises when we relax into a felt experience of multiple dimensions of Self. When we are able to feel our place both alongside and in the river, this relational sense between multiple *"selves"* emerges.[7]

Our experience of the river of life includes all of life. It includes others who have their own experiences of the river. The human community is part

---

7. Stephen Gilligan, *The Courage to Love: Principles and Practices of Self-Relations Psychotherapy* (New York: W.W. Norton and Company, 1997).

of that river. The common understanding of compassion refers to our capacity to be "with" the "suffering" of others. The question is, How it is possible to be with others at all? How can we really be with others and their suffering?

In a very real sense, this is impossible. When someone steps on a nail, the nail pierces that person's flesh and not our own. That person experiences the particular kind of pain that is associated with this insult to bodily integrity. We do not, and we cannot, experience it for him or her. When someone is dying, that person's death is, strictly speaking, his or her own. There is a very real gap between us and the world around us.

At the same time, when we see someone step on a nail, our body-mind cannot help but respond. We may flinch, flush, or feel a flash of nausea. Like a finely tuned piano, when a note is struck on a neighboring instrument, our own strings cannot help but vibrate in sympathy. When we see someone in pain, our body-mind cannot help but remember our own experiences of pain. When we are with someone who is dying, we cannot help but feel our own anticipatory knowing of that death, which is, in a mysteriously latent manner, always already with us too. We are both separate and, at the same time, at one with him or her.

Spiritually, there are many ways to understand our fundamental separateness and togetherness. We can simply say that we share a common relationship with unfathomable mystery.[8] We are both related and separated by divine mystery. Our lives arise from the same mysterious source and will be returned to that same ground. This mystery marks our beginnings and endings and permeates all we do. We are made up of mystery and share this in common. This is more than just a neat idea. In and through this strange and wondrous connective tissue, we *feel* the presence of fecund mystery that links us to one another. However, even as we feel the connection to all of life, we feel this across a gap. This divine connective tissue both separates and connects. We are joined in mystery, and in mystery our unique and somehow separate existence is preserved.

We can think of compassion as one dimension of God and of this divine connective tissue. To understand some of the ways that compassion is a part of that mysterious connective tissue of life, we need first to understand something about the different dimensions of existence and of all experience. This will help us recognize the different ways that compassion makes itself known and even calls to us through the different dimensions of experience.

---

8. One of God's qualities is described as "mystery."

Levels of Reality and Dimensions of Compassion

Life reveals itself through different modes of being and knowing. Different modes of knowing are called into being by, and correspond to, different dimensions of reality. With clarity about the phenomenology of these dimensions of reality, we have a map to orient ourselves within our experience of the world and ourselves. Compassion reveals itself through distinct and knowable dimensions of our experiences and connects us not only with one another but also with the source of life.

In the kabbalistic texts of Jewish mystical tradition, four dimensions of reality correspond to the four universes and to the four levels and kinds of soul that are described. Here we will simply speak of the dimensions of reality that relate to the body, psychology, mind, and spirit. These four levels are a "nested hierarchy"; that is, each next level transcends and includes the preceding level. Ken Wilber speaks at great length about nested hierarchies or "holarchies."[9] Developmentally speaking, we can say that these levels of reality unfold from the most concrete and dense to the most ethereal. At certain stages of our development, we may not be able to identify, distinguish, or access the dimension of spirit. It is, however, always present and ontologically foundational.

In the example of a friend stepping on a nail, we witness how compassion operates within the material and everyday level of reality. That we feel a rush of adrenaline, a wave of nausea, and the visceral memories of times when our skin was pierced allows us to feel connected with another human being across the impossible gap of our separate lives. When my daughter, May, witnesses her brother getting hurt, she cannot stop her hand from automatically reaching out to touch, caress, or comfort him. His pain has transmitted a message to May's nervous system, and her nervous system cannot help but respond. His nervous system receives her touch and expresses some physical sign of release, evidence that his cry of pain accomplished its mission. Her response and his release complete the circuit. This organic circuit is a preconscious and physiological substrate of what we call compassion. It is evidence that compassion occurs naturally. It is an impulse that arises effortlessly from the ground of experience and from within the deep structures of our being. This is a way compassion reveals itself at the level of body, action, and matter, and of prepsychological reality.

In addition to the physiological response to the intrusive nail, we experience a rush of emotion, recall affective and imagined memories from our own similar experiences, and feel an impulse to speak with our injured friend, for whom we cannot help but feel empathy. We may find ourselves

---

9. Ken Wilber, *A Brief History of Everything* (Boston/New York: Shambhala, 1996).

saying, silently or aloud, "Ouch! Are you okay? . . . Here, let me help you." This flood of sensory input reveals the dimension of experience that is about psychology, narrative, and emotion. A simple injury activates a flood of dialogical intra- and interpersonal relational circuitry. This circuitry illuminates both the inescapable separateness and connectedness of the person stepping on the nail and the witness.

As we look at our friend who has just stepped on the nail, our friend looks back at us, and our eyes meet—a timeless moment of connection across the gap of our separateness. For a moment we experience a shared sense of mind, when all of the sensations are present, and all of the memories, feelings, and impulses to speak are active. In the midst of this—a still point—time slows or even stops. Everything happens in slow motion. Everything is still going on, yet there is a time and place for everything. We are somehow beyond the physical and the psychological/emotional dimensions of the experience. We feel called to look at one another, and from this vantage point we feel seen and known. That we know and see is an expression of the life and call of compassion within the context of that dimension of existence which we call "mind."

As our eyes meet, we may share the question "Why did this happen?" We can handle this almost rhetorical question in many ways. We may turn to that implacable source of life and genuinely ask this question. Some small thread of understanding may arise from the silent depths, and maybe not. Together and separately, we know that these kinds of small mishaps, as with everything else in life, finally rest in the hands of an intelligence that is greater than our own. We are joined in our ignorance and our searching for answers. The context of spirit calls to question, gives itself as a question. Again, in the context of spirit, we are forced to bear the questions on our own. We are also joined in the common call of spirit that brings us as a community of human beings to "sit on the rim of darkness and fish far fallen light with patience."[10]

Compassion arises from, and is an expression of, the connection that we experience across the impossible gap. The gap that preserves our identity in the face of our radical connectedness is another manifestation of our being human.

Sometimes Life Hurts Like Hell: To Be or Not to Be

If compassion is such a nourishing, natural, and almost effortless dimension of our lives, why do we become fatigued? Because of our profound

---

10. Pablo Neruda, "If Each Day Falls Into Night," in *The Sea and The Bells,* trans. William O'Daly (Port Townsend, WA: Copper Canyon Press, 2002), p. 83.

connectedness with the world, because the very fabric of Self is the world, we feel not only our own pain and joy, but also the pain and joy of the world. Our home is both in and beyond the river of life. We cannot escape the part of our home that is in the river. The relational nature of self affirms that our pain and the world's pain are only nominally separable. I may not be able to feel your pain, but I cannot escape pain, and your pain cannot help but remind me of this.

Because life hurts, it is at times difficult to be present to life. In difficult times, it is hard to be human. We find ourselves trying to avoid pain. Some pain is avoidable and should be avoided. When we have accidentally placed our hand into scalding water we immediately remove our hand. However, many kinds of pain simply cannot be avoided. When a friend is terminally ill, we feel many kinds of pain. We feel the pain of our anticipated loss of this friend. We feel our own mortality. We may be reminded of another loved one who has died. We feel the pain of our helplessness to stop the illness from claiming someone we love. We also feel the sympathetic resonances of the pain of our friend as it courses through our nervous system. We may simply not know how to be in this situation. With all we feel it may be hard not to flee, and there are so many ways to flee.

We may find ourselves losing touch with this friend or avoiding visiting. Perhaps we fall back upon our professional identity, choosing to act as the rabbi instead of being a friend, or, as a rabbi, we may enact the ritual forms but leave out our *kishkes*,[11] performing the rituals without *kavanah*.[12] We may choose to do our business from the banks of the river and never admit to what we are experiencing from our place in the river.

Fleeing from necessary pain, we disconnect from a piece of God's creation. We flee and, explicitly or implicitly, say to this little piece of reality, "You are not welcome." We step back, creating our own little world apart from the rest of the world. We reject a portion of God's creation and therefore exile ourselves from God's world and from reality. *This is when trouble begins and when fatigue begins to develop.*

Sometimes we step back and don't know that we are doing it or forget that we have done it. Glad to have some distance between ourselves and the current external source of pain, we may simply fall into a relieved forgetfulness. Sometimes we step back because we are afraid and angry and tired. We are unable to face the pain that lies before us and the pain that this can

---

11. Literally, our guts, our belly, and our heart. When we are connected with, and include, our *kishkes,* the physical and emotional dimensions of our *"selves"* become a vital part of our interactions.

12. Literally, direction or intention. As Jews, when we pray or perform rituals we are enjoined to do so with focused and directed attention and clear intention.

awaken in us. Getting lost happens all the time. Stepping back, or even running away, is something we do time and again, sometimes more and sometimes less consciously. We are not God, who is omnipresent. Our presence to ourselves, and to life, is touch and go. Being modeled after and molded by God means, in part, that we are free to choose to be or not to be present to life. This choice is not made once and for all. We are called to choose again and again. This is how we exercise our free will and claim our relative freedom. Our freedom is a structural dimension of our being. Therefore, we must choose life and reality over and over again.

Please understand, we cannot help fleeing. We will do so many times a day and many times over the course of life. That is not the problem. We constantly move in and out of resonant connection with various aspects of life. It is natural to step back, to reclaim our sense of a boundaried and protected *"self."* To develop a sturdy *"self"* that can relax in the world even when there is much pain, we need to practice coming and going. As long as we keep returning, we are doing okay. The problem is not that we get lost. The problem, and greater danger, is that we forget that we are lost. When we are gone too long, when we are not adequately present to life, life will simply not work as well. Because there is this constant danger that we might forget, we draw upon traditional and nontraditional practices to help us remember our place alongside and in the river of life.

Practice

To foster and enjoy a more natural flow of compassion, one that is more effortless and mutually nourishing, rabbis need to be able to do several things. First, they and others in the helping professions need to be able to ride the often intense waves of their sensations, emotions, and thoughts. They need to become skillful at remaining openhearted and open-minded in the face of life's ongoing surprises and challenges. Everything that arises is a flower in God's garden. Everything arises from the same source and is, therefore, a source of blessing. Rabbis must learn to model the kinds of self-presence that are an embodiment of this reverence for all the dimensions of existence.

Second, rabbis need to develop skill at harmonizing mind and body. They need to learn and practice some form of mindfulness or self-presence. Self-presence is a basic skill that helps us develop a capacity to be both in and alongside the river of life even when that river rages intensely. To serve life as it unfolds, rabbis need to stabilize consciousness and for the riverbank to be solid and alive to the river. One goal of contemplative practices is to train the body-mind to serve life by welcoming all that arises with an ever more skillful, rich, and transparent presence. Through skillful self-presence, we become more present to the world. We establish the circuitry through which the many qualities of life energy may flow, and, accordingly, our lives and the lives of those around us are enriched by that flow.

Finally, rabbis need to actively cultivate a relationship with God. As a part of any contemplative practice, we must not only be present to the material and psychological dimensions of reality but also include a contemplative engagement with the mystery of mysteries, with the source of life. The more that we are able to dwell in relation to and with this larger, pre- and postrational dimension of reality, the more at home we will be in our lives, and the more we will truly be able to ride the waves of life with openhearted and open-minded joy, equanimity, loving-kindness, and compassion. When mind and body are harmonized, these qualities emerge in a natural way. By establishing attentional circuits with the ground of being, our lives come to be infused with the primordial and unfathomable wisdom that cannot help but arise from those mysterious depths.

The exercise that follows uses one piece of a practice that I call *structured self-presence* (SSP). It is designed to foster mind-body harmonization. It helps establish intrapersonal circuitry so that life energies can flow more freely.

STEP 1: Take a moment to simply tune into your breathing. . . . Follow the rhythm of your breath. . . . There is no need to change anything. As you ride the waves of your breath, . . . follow these waves more and more deeply into a felt relationship with your body. . . . Take your time. . . . Begin to notice how your body is feeling. . . . Gently scan your body and notice any tensions, any softnesses or flutters or emptinesses . . . anything at all. You are simply noticing how your body is holding itself.

STEP 2: Now, allow anything that is troubling you, or that is on your mind, to come into your awareness. . . . Take your time and allow that situation to make itself known as vividly as you can. . . . Notice all the details. . . . Be specific and concrete.

STEP 3: Notice what this situation awakens in your body. Simply pay attention to any physical sensations that arise and track these. . . . Notice the shape, size, and quality of these sensations. . . . Do the sensations move around? Are they static? Stay with these sensations. . . . Do not try to change or get rid of whatever is happening. Treat it like a flower that has just bloomed in God's garden. . . . Stay with the situation, let it work on you, and let your body-mind work on it.

STEP 4: As you continue to focus on the difficult situation, or whatever else was calling for attention, notice your mood and any emotions that seem to be moving through your body. . . . Find words to describe what you are feeling and sensing. Do not interpret, explain, or look for reasons why. . . . Let your emotions and mood show themselves to you. Let yourself receive these.

STEP 5: Now begin to wonder where all of this is coming from. . . . Feel your way into the darkness and the ground from which all of this is arising. . . . Remaining attuned to sensations and emotions and the situation that you have been paying attention to, sense the relationship between the mysterious ground and that which is arising from that ground. . . . Allow your curiosity to remain open to that darkness to see what arises.

STEP 6: When you are ready to bring closure, return to the original situation that was the object of your attentions. Notice any changes in how you view the situation. Then, return to your breathing and ride the waves for a few minutes.

Practice this exercise for twenty to forty minutes. It is a great way to begin building the circuitry that links the front of your brain with your emotional and more primitive autonomic brain. It helps build connections between mind and body. It also teaches ways to ride the waves of difficult experiences. Our body and mind can and do metabolize and transform our difficult experiences. Practicing self-presence, we allow our body-mind to act as the bridge between Creator and created.

Once you have developed some facility with this exercise, practice it with friends or family. As you are with someone, turn over 60 percent of your attention to your breathing and then to your sensations and emotions. You will find that your body and your emotions are always already in tune with what is going on in and around you, providing lots of information about the reality at hand. Though you are giving more attention to yourself than you may be used to, you will actually feel more connected with others. As you practice, you may get feedback from others telling you that you seem more present. With practice you will notice that you feel a tad more tender and vulnerable and, at the same time, more grounded. More and more compassion will permeate the field of your interactions. Having developed mastery at doing this with others, try doing it when you are leading services or giving a sermon, or even when you are running a difficult administrative meeting.

Rabbis need to take care of themselves and find ways to nurture their own spiritual and psychological development. Developing a contemplative practice relies on many contemplative traditions and many fine teachers. Within Judaism, there has been a return to our own rich contemplative traditions. Many Jews are now studying and practicing contemplative practices that derive from the Jewish mystical tradition.[13]

Self-presence involves learning to work with different dimensions of experience. We must all learn to be at home in our bodies and to ride the waves of sensation that move through our bodies.

To learn how to ride the waves of emotions, and patterns of personality, we need the help of skillful guides and partners. To incorporate our own God wrestling into all areas of our lives, we need companionship as we wrestle with, explore, and deepen our relationship with the source of life. Individual and group therapies can be great ways to become familiar with the psychological dimension of our lives. Mindfulness is also an essential tool to developing the capacity to sit alongside yourself as emotions and patterns of personality come roaring through.

The Jewish community has begun to develop its own version of "spiritual direction." Rabbis need peers with whom they can share their spiritual seeking ways. We cannot do this alone.

As a rabbi, when you bring attention and kindness to your body, with all of its intense physical sensations of struggle, of pleasure and pain, you make it all right for your congregants to find God in their own embodied struggles. You model for and make it all right for your congregants to find God in their neuroses, their personal fears, pain, and confusion.

Physics applies to this kind of modeling. When we make room for all of the dimensions of the sometimes intense flow of the river of life, and when we hold this river within a skillful loving presence, others who are near us will find it easier to make more room for that flow. This happens naturally. Like attracts like. The depths call forth the depths. Soul calls forth soul. This physics is an expression of the life of compassion. This call is the call of compassion. When we are able to practice skillful self-presence, compassion becomes the ground and the medium on and within which all human interactions operate. Compassion becomes a kind of loving energy that flows, from the source, through all of our interactions and back again, and it calls all of us into God's loving embrace.

Compassion is, in a palpable and knowable way, one dimension of God's love. It makes up a strand of the mysterious spiritual connective tissue that preserves and helps to realize the identity of all life, and it is the basis for the connectedness of all life. We experience the life of compassion in our bod-

---

13. *Sefer Yetzirah; The Book of Creation in Theory and Practice,* trans. Aryeh Kaplan (York Beach, ME: Samuel Weiser, Inc., 1997); Aryeh Kaplan, *Jewish Meditation* (New York: Shocken Books, Inc., 1985). Kaplan expounds the Jewish history of contemplative practice.

ies, our emotions, and our minds. Compassion is a ground state of being that relates human beings not only to one another but also to the source of life.

Compassion fatigue develops, not from being too connected with one another, but, rather, from breaking our relationships with ourselves, with one another, and with life. Properly understood, compassion can help us to find our way into the heart of God's creation. Compassion makes it possible for us to rest in a profound and balanced intimacy with the world and to feel sustained and nourished by that world.

Maintaining Balance: The Kabbalah As a Resource

Susan Gulack

CLIMBING THE TREE

I step out on the very narrow bridge.
It stretches ahead of me over the chasm of my life.
I try to let go of fear and to learn balance.
I breathe in and center.
I control only the infinitesimal space of the present moment—
This breath, that is all.
I am the servant of the limitless One,
Attempting to follow the will of the limitless One in this
    moment and place.
I hold the first balance and attempt to find my center.
I am but dust and ashes,
A cracked vessel unable to change anything,
But for my sake the world was created.
The small mote of dust lands in the still pond
And causes endless ripples.
My breath moves the world.
I breathe in to the balance point of my body, my *kishkes,* my womb,
And try to find a way to live both of these realities.
Next, I center on the second balance point, my heart.
I desire rules and limits,
Imposing order on the chaos of my life.
At the same time I want to love fearlessly, boundlessly,
Leaping off into the void of possibility.
Again I struggle for balance,
Giving in and forgiving.
I breathe into my heart and breathe out love to the world.
I center on my thoughts, the third balance,

Wrestling always with seeing things as they are
And as I want them to be.
Wringing out meaning by combining hard-won facts
    with the flash of insight
That comes from letting ideas compost.
I breathe in for this wisdom and let it go into my life.
Now I breathe in the presence of the One, the fourth balance,
From which all the others are suspended.
Knowing that all the other breaths are filled with this as well
And my struggle to balance is holy,
I am not afraid.

Life is a series of balances that are all interrelated. The system of the
s'firot[1] is a beautiful way of describing these relational balances that we
seek in our own lives and in our interactions with others. The *s'firot* are related to the four worlds: the physical, the emotional, the mental, and the
spiritual. This system, which is also known as the Kabbalistic Tree of Life,
also balances vertically, with the question of how much of us is physical and
how much of us is spiritual. Let us examine each of these relational balances
to see how they work, both intrapersonally and interpersonally.

Olam Ha'asiyah—*The Physical World*

Let us start at the bottom of the tree, with the physical world. The physical is not less important than the others, as it is the base on which they all
balance. The tree would topple without its roots. The tree stands on *malchut*.[2] Rather than being in charge of everything, *malchut* can be seen as the
absolute servant. I am the subject of the *Kadosh Baruch Hu*.[3] The only thing
I control is this moment, this breath. How am I going to use this moment in
time, which is unique and unrepeatable? So much of our work, and our
lives, depends on the prioritization of people and tasks that this first *s'firah*
represents. This is the tightrope on which everything else balances. Our
lives are made up of the choices we make about how we will use each moment.
    The first balance, which can be seen as a tightrope walker balancing on
the tightrope of this moment, centers on *y'sod*.[4] This balance has two sides

---

1. The ten or eleven spheres that represent different ways the Divine is expressed in
us and in the world.
2. Kingdom or reign.
3. The Holy and Bountiful One.
4. Foundation; our core identity.

in relationship: *netzach*[5] and *hod.*[6] *Netzach* says that the world was created for my sake; I am the center of the universe. On the other side, *hod* says I am but dust and ashes, unable to effect any change. An individual must balance both of these realities in relationship. One cannot live at either extreme without having major problems. Many of the men whom I meet in my work as a prison chaplain live in *netzach.* They can't understand the impact that their actions have on others, or even that it should make a difference. My older son, who has a minor form of autism, also falls on this side of the balance. He literally is not able to understand that other people have needs and desires outside of his own. I am sure that we can all call to mind examples of people who fall on this side of the balance, as well as times in our lives that we have felt this way.

The other side of the balance is *hod.* People who live on this side of the balance can be described, in part, by the typical, long-suffering Jewish mother line: "Never mind me. I'll just sit in the dark." For them, the world is about everyone's needs except their own. Does this sound familiar to you? As caregivers, we inevitably struggle with maintaining this balance all the time. How can I take time to care for my own needs? Everyone else needs *me!* When we allow ourselves to live too far on this side of the balance, we lose our sense of self and can burn out and become bitter because our needs are never met. It is only from finding the relationship in *y'sod,* a healthy foundation, that we can live out the truth of both *netzach* and *hod.* The balanced truth is that the world was created for our sake *and* we were created to serve others.

Olam Hay'tzirah—*The Emotional World*

The love relational balance is centered on *tiferet,*[7] balanced abundant love. The two extremes are *chesed*[8] and *g'vurah.*[9] Interestingly, in the sexual imagery of the Kabbalah, *chesed* is seen as the male outpouring, while *g'vurah* is seen as the receiving vessel of the womb. *Chesed,* love without limits, is sometimes our preferred way of functioning. We think we should be able to deal with everyone, to give people what they need. We want *chesed* for ourselves. We want to be loved for who we are, without having to do anything for it. When dealing with people who live in *hod, chesed* is

---

5. Victory.
6. Humility.
7. Balanced and abundant love.
8. Flowing, endless, giving love.
9. Strength and boundaries.

what they need from us to help tilt the balance into understanding that the world was created for their sakes. They are worthwhile. Sometimes, though, the reality of life calls for *g'vurah*. If I give my son everything, I reinforce his living in *netzach,* his belief that he is the center of the universe. I have to draw the line with the people I work with, only doing for them what really is my job, and having them do their part.

One of my priest colleagues taught me what he calls the "poop in a pouch" theory. When we walk the galleries of cells, inmates will want whatever it may be that we are handing out. If we had a bag of junk, they would take it. When we say instead, "If you want a bible or note cards or a calendar, drop us a note with your name and cell," the demand decreases perceptively. It is important for us to set this boundary; otherwise the inmates don't value what is being given. How true this is in all of our work, where often we enable helplessness instead of taking the extra step to empower others to learn to lead the service, read Torah,[10] teach adult education, and so forth. The congregation to which I belong is a pleasure to be in because the whole culture of the congregation encourages every member to participate fully. I am not saying that my rabbi never feels the need to do it all, but he is working on the relational balance.

I came to the understanding, for myself, that when I am having difficulty staying in *g'vurah,* setting the limits with my children or with others, what I need at that moment is *chesed.* That may come in my prayer life and in the experience of the Divine washing over me, or it may come from the acknowledgment and support of family and friends, something I am learning to reach out for and accept. The relational balance may not come easily internally, or in one specific relationship, or in one "world"; we need to look at the whole system, at life as a whole and holy unit.

Olam Hab'riyah—*The Mental World*

In the mental world, the central balance is not found on every chart of the tree. In the *Chabad*[11] system, *daat* forms the relational balance point for *chochmah* and *binah* (thus *CHa, Ba,* and *D* for *chochmah, binah,* and *daat*). *Chochmah* is flash insight, the understanding that comes to us without our knowing how or where it originated. *Binah* is hard-earned wisdom, taking the time to memorize the multiplication tables, read the books, and learn the lessons. A person who lives in *chochmah* can be the dreamer, the idea per-

---

10. The scroll containing the Five Books of Moses, read publicly in the synagogue.
11. Acronym for the Hebrew: *chochmah* (wisdom), *binah* (understanding), and *daat* (knowledge). This term has been appropriated by the Lubavitch movement.

son, the one who experiences *mo'achin d'gadlut*.[12] One who lives in *binah* is the detail person, the bean counter, *mo'achin d'katnut*.[13] We know that one cannot exist without the other. Every organization, every relationship needs both: one who can dream the big dreams and one who can pin down the nitty-gritty details that will make them work. All writing needs both. We need to nourish in ourselves the expanded mind, the ability to see the big ideas and dream the big dreams, but then we need to translate them into words and grammar that actually communicate them clearly to others. *Daat*, enlightened understanding, is the relational balance that lets us do that.

Olam Ha'atzilut—*The Spiritual World*

Keter,[14] relating to *Ein Sof,*[15] sits by itself at the top of the tree. Rather than seeing it as without a relational balance, I see it as the vertical balance with *malchut,* both true at the same time. In every *b'rachah,*[16] we go from *Baruch Atah*—Blessed are You in the first person, right here with me—to *Melech haolam*—Ruler of all time and all space. God is eternal and universal, yet present here and now. That is true externally and internally. I am the servant of the Holy One, but I am also the Holy One made manifest in this world, and so are you. This can also be seen as *yesh*[17] and *ayin,*[18] the balance between the physical and the spiritual that makes up the world. What makes a bowl? Is it the sides or the empty space in the middle? They are both the bowl; we are both body and spirit.

This relational balance plays out for me in how I see myself as a rabbi. At times I am where I need to be in ways that appear to me to be divinely planned. By my own sense of direction, I should not have been where I was, and yet I was there, and there was someone who needed my presence or what I had to offer. Sometimes I give the One all the credit. Other times I look at my skills and abilities and think that I am the one doing all the work. If I stay on that side of the relational balance too long, I get overwhelmed. I can't be responsible for it all; that is not my job. It is beyond me to understand how much of my work gets done because I am me, and how much of it happens because the Holy One uses me. I don't have one answer because the tree, like any good mobile, is constantly swaying and dancing. Change is the constant.

---

12. Expanded mind.
13. Small mind.
14. Crown.
15. That which has no limits.
16. Blessing.
17. Being.
18. Nothingness.

PERCENTAGES

A friend of mine, a mathematician, says,
I am 80 percent American and 70 percent Israeli.
There are times when numbers are not enough.
This helps me understand
A problem I have been meditating on:
How do I nullify my self in You
And still bring the gift of my self to You?
Can I be all Yours?
Dare I even think I can be 100 percent Yours?
And still be me?
With my gifts,
My will,
My self?
Yesh—being in this world—
and *ayin*—the nullification of the self in the One—
Don't have to add up to 100 percent.

HEALING MUSES FOR JEWISH RELATIONAL CARE

– 6 –

The Muse of Visiting

David J. Zucker
Bonita E Taylor

When people we know, respect, or love are unwell, or they are suffering from the inevitable consequences of aging, it is natural for us to want to do something to help them return to a place of good health and spiritual wholeness. Often these desires, although praiseworthy, are unrealistic. Since, in most instances, visitors, including clergy, cannot bring "help as curing," we need to redefine what "being of help" means. This chapter addresses what actions we can take to make life better for compromised individuals.

The Blessings of Visiting

In the biblical narrative in the book named after him, Job's health declines precipitously. When Job's friends hear about his calamities, they visit him. During their time together, Job laments his losses, and his friends offer their thoughts by way of support. Although their words do not bring him the comfort that his friends had intended, they do at least stay with him.

Unlike our ancestor Job, most people who are physically and/or spiritually bereft, have a very different experience. They find to their dismay that increasingly the world goes on without them. Initially, family and friends are attentive. When, despite their best efforts, this support group does not see improvement in loved ones, they start to feel helpless. These feelings are intensified when their loved ones face progressive degeneration or death. Everyone's sense of powerlessness, including the medical staff, makes it increasingly harder even for loving visitors to continue what too often becomes an unspoken burden of which they are ashamed. If those who are ill do not recover within a "reasonable" period, eventually, most visitors need to return to the normalcy of their own lives.

Despite this phenomenon, in Judaism, *bikur cholim*[1] remains a sacred task, *a mitzvah*.[2] All Jews, whether they are professional clergy or nonprofessional laity, share the same obligation to partner with God in being attentive to those who are unwell.[3] The prayer book used for our daily morning service includes a Talmudic passage which reminds us that we are to act in kindly ways toward one another. Among the activities that further define what it means to be kind is visiting with those who are unwell. This is so important that we earn rewards for it in the World-to-Come.[4]

Of course, God is the quintessential visitor. Yet we, as God's representatives, facilitate God's kindness here on earth. We present God to those who may not be aware that God is there for them. We *re*-present God to those who have forgotten that God is everywhere. We represent God to those who feel abandoned. As God's representatives here on earth, we have a responsibility to one another. We also have the response-*ability* to one another to define, and sometimes to redefine, what it means to care for someone during the times when they feel isolated, in hospitals, nursing homes, hospices, and home care facilities. The significance of "being there" for people in their time of infirmity is also addressed in a series of vignettes recorded in the Talmud:

> This was an age where pain was thought by some to be "precious," and where the pious were expected to accept suffering willingly because they would receive their reward in the World-to-Come. One day Rabbi Chiya bar Abba fell ill. His colleague, the famous Rabbi Yochanan, visited him and said: "Are these sufferings acceptable to you?" Rabbi Chiya replied to his colleague: "Neither they nor their re-

---

1. Visting individuals in their time of vulnerability and apprehension.
2. In Hebrew, fulfilling God's command; in Yiddish, a good deed.
3. Solomon Ganzfried, *Code of Jewish Law/Kitzur Shulchan Aruch* (Revised Edition) (New York: Hebrew Publishing, 1961), Volume 4, 193.1. The *Code of Jewish Law/Kitzur Shulchan Aruch* (Abridged *Shulchan Aruch*) is a handbook that lists standard Jewish practices from a traditional viewpoint.
4. Babylonian Talmud: Shabbat 127a.

ward." Rabbi Yochanan then said to his ill colleague: "Give me your hand." Rabbi Chiya gave Rabbi Yochanan his hand and Rabbi Yochanan cured him.

In the next vignette, we learn that the same Rabbi Yochanan, the man who had contributed to his colleague's cure, fell ill. A third colleague, Rabbi Chanina, visited him. Rabbi Chanina asked Rabbi Yochanan the same question: "Are these sufferings acceptable to you?" Rabbi Yochanan replied to Rabbi Chanina: "Neither they nor their reward." Rabbi Chanina then said to his ill colleague: "Give me your hand." Rabbi Yochanan gave Rabbi Chanina his hand and Rabbi Chanina cured him.[5]

This Talmudic story makes us wonder why the healer, Rabbi Yochanan, could not cure himself. In response, the Talmud reminds us that prisoners cannot free themselves; similarly, those imprisoned in compromised bodies, demoralized spirits, and disheartened souls cannot "free" themselves from their situations by themselves. If even the healer, Rabbi Yochanan, needed another person to contribute to his healing, so do we.

We need one another. No one of us is knowledgeable enough, resilient enough, or objective enough to engage various stages of infirmity without some assistance from at least one other person. We may not be able to heal others simply by touching them, but we can offer compassionate caring, an empathetic ear, a hearing heart, a gentle gesture of concern, a wise word, and a helpful hand. And while it may not be possible for one person to make everyone's life better, each of us can help one compromised person feel more comfortable. For nonprofessional visitors, this means attending to people's needs, cheering them, and, for all visitors, praying for mercy on their behalf.[6]

Planning a Purposeful Visit

Earning the *mitzvah* of a blessed visit is not easy, but it is extremely rewarding, both in this world and in the World-to-Come. The following seven guidelines will assist you as you seek to partner with God in deeds of *g'milut chasadim*:[7]

---

5. Babylonian Talmud: B'rachot 5b.
6. Ganzfried, *Code of Jewish Law/Kitzur Shulchan Aruch,* 4, 193.3.
7. Loving-kindness to others. A different version of these ideas is discussed in this book in Chapter 3, "Taking Care of Ourselves: It's About Time!"

1. The Blessing of Planning
2. The Blessing of Being There
3. The Blessing of Being Present
4. The Blessing of Being Respectful
5. The Blessing of Brevity
6. The Blessing of Referral
7. The Blessing of Bestowing a Blessing

The Blessing of Planning

To maximize the healing effect of your visit, plan ahead to be intentional before, during, and after the visit. Before you visit, think it through and ask yourself these questions: Why are you there? What do you hope to accomplish?

Before you visit, take the time to familiarize yourself with institutional routines, such as visiting hours, mealtimes, and rehab schedules, as well as local regulations, for example, restrictions on lighting candles. Consider the medical needs of the person you are visiting. If visiting on Shabbat[8] or another Jewish holiday that is traditionally celebrated with sweets and wine, consider first whether this person should be ingesting sugar. Even Shabbat grape juice and *challah*[9] may be too much for a diabetic. Before you visit, think of nonfood and non-fire-related ways to celebrate Shabbat, Chanukah,[10] Purim,[11] Passover,[12] and other holy days.

Just before you enter the room, take the time to center yourself. In a moment, you may see something for which you are unprepared: someone who does not resemble his or her usual self but, instead, may be gaunt, pale, unkempt, connected to machines, distracted or disoriented, anxious, medicated, and dressed in a skimpy hospital gown or senior center casuals. People who normally wear a wig or toupee, false teeth, or makeup may be missing "the face" they normally show to the world. Visits can take their toll upon you emotionally because people who are not well or are aging often will have changed from the way you hold them in your memory. It can be upsetting and draining to see someone with whom you have a relationship looking so poorly. Find out if there is a chapel in the hospital or nursing

---

8. Sabbath.
9. Braided loaf of bread used especially on the Sabbath and holidays.
10. Eight-day festival commemorating the rededication of the Temple in Jerusalem by Judah Maccabee and followers (165 BCE).
11. Holiday commemorating the biblical story of Esther and the saving of the Jews in Persia.
12. Festival of freedom commemorating the exodus from Egypt.

home and take a few minutes there to center yourself—before and after the visit. If no chapel exists, take a few moments in the nearest family lounge.

The Blessing of Being There

Having decided to visit, make a date and schedule a specific time with the person you will visit. Keep that promise to be there at that time. If you don't show up on time because you think that this person has all the time in the world, while your schedule is so very busy, you may find that the person's available time is more limited than you anticipated. Healing consumes both time and energy. If you don't arrive on time, or arrive while the person is sleeping, in rehab, taking tests, exhausted from the day's "wellness" schedule, or otherwise distracted, you may disappoint someone who was looking forward to your visit. Worse, your absence may convey the message that you do not consider this person's time to be as important as your own, when, in fact, this person's time may be extremely precious. You tell people that you value them when you are on time.

Most of the people who visit compromised individuals are doctors, nurses, social workers, technicians, therapists, housekeepers, and others who are paid to be there. Only you visit freely. Only you do not have to be there.

> Sometimes [a visitor] does not want to visit a particularly difficult patient. Sometimes [a visitor] only inadvertently does his or her duty. What matters in the end is that you get there. Your motives for visiting are not all that important. Your presence at the bedside is what counts.[13]

The Blessing of Being Present

Those who are unwell and/or aging often feel cut off from their society—because they are. When you visit and are fully "present," you can connect them with people and events in the world at large in ways that even television or radio cannot. When you are visiting people, look at them directly and listen closely to what they say, not only in words, but also through gestures and body language. Watch out for signs of fatigue. Be sensitive to their physical medical realities. If they offer you something from their dinner tray, consider that their food and drink intake may be monitored, and by tak-

---

13. Burton L. Visotsky, "Presence, Study and Prayer," *Jewish Spiritual Care* 6:2 (Winter 2005), pp. 4-5.

ing a simple cup of tea, you may be sending the wrong message to the medical staff about how much they are drinking.

When visiting those who are aging or seriously unwell, encourage them and help them to talk about their lives—no matter how many times you have heard their stories. After all, how many times have we heard stories from the Torah,[14] and how many more times will we hear these stories? Think about each person as a living human Torah with stories, lamentations, and lessons from which we can learn. As with Torah study, much of what we learn depends upon the heart and spirit that we bring to the story. During these visits, you have the additional blessing of truly listening to people and helping them feel that their time on earth mattered, that they made a difference to someone, somewhere.

If other friends are there, visit with them later. Your purpose is to be with, and to give full attention to, the compromised individuals you are visiting. Your object is to make them feel "seen" and "heard" in an environment that too often makes people feel invisible. Let your responses be attentive, compassionate, and emotionally empathetic.

The Blessing of Being Respectful

Visiting people who are aging or unwell can be challenging because you do not want to offer false hope or cause them to be despondent.[15] Your conversation requires judgment and tact as you encourage them to talk about their lives, sometimes in the valley of the shadow of possible death.

This sometimes means suspending your version of the "facts." Part of your responsibility is to "cross the street" to where the compromised individuals are and to let their "truth" be your own—even when it differs from your objective "reality." It is not appropriate to argue with people or to label them "in denial." In fact, the line between being in denial and wanting a second (or third) opinion can be slim, and not for you to determine.

This also is true for compromised individuals who, suffering from dementia, believe themselves in a past that is decades old. That may be their truth *as they understand it.* It is harmful to tell them that, in reality, their spouses (parents, siblings) died decades ago. It is also not uncommon for such individuals to move back and forth between "old time" and "current time," alternately engaging you in one or the other.

---

14. In the narrow sense, the Five Books of Moses; more broadly, all of Jewish learning.

15. Ganzfried, *Code of Jewish Law/Kitzur Shulchan Aruch,* 4, 193.5.

Another aspect of being respectful is your conscious effort to guard all information and to treat it as privileged. As titillating as it might be, you don't need to share what you know and who you saw, whether it was a synagogue member or a celebrity. Also, do not speak even to authorized personnel about your visit while in public areas, such as elevators, the nurse's desk, the bathroom, or any other place where information may be overheard and transmitted. If something bad happened to you or your loved ones, how much information would you want broadcast? In any event, this is now not only an issue of respect but also the law of the land, specifically the Health Insurance Portability and Accountability Act (HIPAA).[16]

Visiting vulnerable individuals is a sacred task. To sustain this holiness, visitors must be religiously and spiritually respectful of the person before them. This may require self-compromise by visitors, who may have to withhold personal religious beliefs when these beliefs differ from those of the person visited. It is blatantly inappropriate, indeed spiritually harmful, for someone from a liberal religious background to ignore religious traditions of a more orthodox nature when these traditions are meaningful to the orthodox person visited. It is equally inappropriate and spiritually harmful for an orthodox religious visitor to suggest to a religiously liberal person that God offers "but one way" for the person to go forward. It is never appropriate for non-Jewish visitors to impose their religious beliefs upon Jewish individuals who are compromised or for Jewish visitors to question or challenge the religious beliefs of non-Jewish individuals who are emotionally vulnerable.

Finally, your literal human touch—if it is welcome—can make a difference to those who are homebound or in hospitals, hospices, or nursing homes. Compromised individuals are not often touched, except by staff during medical procedures, and then it is not pleasant. If you want to touch others, first think about whether it is your need or their need. Then ask if you may hold their hand or touch their shoulder or forehead during a prayer. Your touch may be frightening to those who have had unfortunate experiences, or it may provide an important gift: the warm and caring connection of one human to another.[17] You won't know unless you ask.

---

16. In 1996, Congress enacted the massive Health Insurance Portability and Accountability Act (HIPAA) to improve "portability" and continuity of health insurance coverage. See www.hipaa.org for further details.

17. Myriam Klotz, "End of Life Care," in *Bechoref Hayamim—In the Winter of Life* (Wyncote, PA: Reconstructionist Rabbinical College, Center for Jewish Ethics, 2002), p. 109.

The Blessing of Brevity

By definition, people who are compromised by unwellness or aging are challenged. Often, they have limited amounts of physical, emotional, or psychic energy. That you have made time for them is commendable, but because of their condition, plan to keep your visit relatively brief—even if your travel time was lengthy. Remember that they are not there for you; you are there for them.

The Blessing of Referral

If, for whatever reason, you cannot attend to the compromised person personally, or if you and/or the person you are visiting is uncomfortable seeing you in the role of a pray*er*, see if the facility has a chaplain, or if your synagogue has someone available to make hospital or home visits. Even if you do pray, *ask* whether the compromised person would like you to request a chaplain. It is not uncommon, nor is it inexplicable, that those who are challenged by aging or illness might prefer to unburden themselves to a stranger who is trained to work with individuals facing life-and-death issues.

In Jewish tradition, visits by such "strangers" symbolize a visit by God's representative, as our patriarch Abraham was visited by God when he was unwell.[18] Board-certified chaplains are trained to pray with sensitivity and respect, using spiritual language appropriate to those whose belief systems differ from their own. Increasingly, hospitals, nursing homes, hospices, and other institutions are requiring their chaplains to enhance and refine their professional caregiving skills to ensure that individuals who are compromised receive the spiritual care that they need. Professional chaplains are engaged in learning how best to treat those who are compromised in their own or in another's denomination or faith. This extensive education is known as clinical pastoral education (CPE).

The Blessing of Bestowing a Blessing

Praying for someone who is vulnerable is deemed a *mitzvah*.[19] In this case, it is both an obligation and a blessing, no matter where you are along the Jewish denominational spectrum. When you pray in the presence of a compromised person, you are also praying before the Divine Presence who is at the person's bedside.

---

18. Genesis 18:1.
19. Ganzfried, *Code of Jewish Law/Kitzur Shulchan Aruch*, 4, 193.3.

At the beginning of this chapter, we wrote that it is natural to want to do something to help when individuals that we care about are unwell or are suffering from the inevitable consequences of aging. We noted that, although these desires are praiseworthy, often they are unrealistic. During this chapter, we discussed our responsibility to those we care about and have offered suggestions for appropriate responses in difficult circumstances. We all know too well that loved ones can do little in the direct sense of *curing;* certainly, there is no "cure" for aging. We also know that there is much that we *can* do in the direct sense of *caring.*

At the center of the book of Leviticus, God tells us: *K'doshim tihiyu, ki kadosh ani Adonai elohecha.*[20] By being a blessed visitor, we can choose both to bestow a blessing and to be a blessing.

---

20. Leviticus 19:2. "Holy are you to be, for holy am I, YHWH your God!" Translation of Torah text by Everett Fox, *The Five Books of Moses: A New Translation with Introductions, Commentary, and Notes* (New York: Schocken Books, 1995), p. 601.

7

The Muse of Silence

Jeffery M. Silberman

Silence in spiritual care has great power as a tool for healing. Silence can create space, convey openness, or demonstrate patience and acceptance. It can also be a powerful means for mistreatment. Silence can cause fear and anxiety, convey rejection or abandonment, demonstrate apathy or neglect.

It seems somewhat absurd to write about silence. Although some have suggested that God dwells in silence, it is really simply a matter of pointing toward the ineffable. This defies the logical means of ordinary communication. Yet, religious traditions have long utilized silence, as in silent prayer, meditation, and reflection. Many religious traditions consider silence as a pathway to connect with the Divine. Silence, thus understood, can reflect a personal—rather than the Jewish communal—connection to the Divine.

The use of silence in counseling is rooted in the psychoanalytic techniques of Sigmund Freud. Freud sat silently behind the couch on which his patients lay. His patients could not see him, and often they also did not hear him, as Freud allowed the process of projection to unfold during the therapeutic session. Thus, his patients would express to the analyst, for example, their negative feelings about their absent fathers. It has been suggested that Freud's own discomfort with being seen by his patients contributed to this modality that he pioneered. Yet, until recently, most classically trained psychoanalysts have essentially continued this practice. More and more, psychoanalysts, as well as most psychotherapists and counselors today, have moved to a visible position and engage the patient with greater verbal interaction. Silence is obviously used in therapy, but not to the degree it once was.

In spiritual care, we attempt to establish relationships with other people, who are coping with illness or crisis, by helping them to access their own spiritual or religious resources. In building this connection, we try to enter into their stories at the level of real meaning for them. The task of spiritual care providers is to invite others to share their immediate concerns, what is in their hearts, and the stories of their current lives that weigh upon them at this time. Part of this sharing of others' concerns is facilitated by the symbolic presence of the rabbi. People perceive the rabbi as one who cares and as one who represents the presence of the Divine. Whatever the level of religious observance, whatever the particular affiliation or lack of formal connection to the Jewish religious community, the opportunity to tell one's story is often compelling. My assumption is that every person wants, at a very basic level, to tell his or her story. The barriers to this telling can come from the person, rooted in his or her fear of trusting another, or from the spiritual care provider, whose agenda, lack of patience, or obvious emotional distance conveys a message of disinterest. One common way spiritual caregivers build such a barrier is by refusing to stay with, and sit in, the silence. We hope to transcend these barriers, as well as the environment of the hospital, to establish a meaningful level of interpersonal communication. Silence is one tool to accomplish this connection.

This task is complicated by the nature of health care institutions. Be it the drone of biomechanical devices, the constant chatter of medical and nursing personnel, or the intense blaring of commercial television in every room, an extraordinary level of noise pervades the atmosphere of most hospitals. As the rabbi or chaplain visits, silence is a rare phenomenon. In fact, for many people in their daily experience, silence is a strange and unfamiliar state of affairs, more feared than sought. Their ordinary world is more often filled with a range of mindless noise, rather than quiet and stillness. Even so, the aura of sanctity created by silence is something that most people recognize. The special feeling generated by quiet surrounds and compels one.

Silence is not something with which I have always been ease. I remember as a beginning chaplain how uncomfortable I felt when faced with a period of silence in the middle of a patient visit. I would wait, hoping that the patient would say something. I assumed that it was my responsibility to offer some profound wisdom in those moments, so if no one said anything after a few awkward moments, I was compelled to say something, even if I didn't have anything especially meaningful to say.

It took a while before I was able to appreciate the power of silence in spiritual care. I began to see how silence was a unique opportunity, similar to a time-out. Moments of silence became a time when people could reflect upon and hopefully comprehend an issue. Silence allowed for connection to and expression of one's feelings, generally an unspoken dialect. Silence also marked a time when a topic was completed and provided a natural shift to move on to another issue. Sometimes silence denoted that the visit was over.

Silence in the work of the rabbi has a dual nature. It can be the silence of complete trust or the silence of suspicion. It can represent the calm feelings of peace and comfort or the terrifying feelings of devastation. Silence can be the response when words are inadequate or inappropriate, and silence may be the appropriate response to the oft-uttered question "Why?"

In using silence as a tool in spiritual care, touch may serve as a complementary instrument. Holding a patient's hand, offering a gentle pat on the shoulder, or calmly stroking the arm may communicate care and concern. I have often used these gestures to care for patients, family members, and hospital staff who were faced with tragic circumstances. When words fail, touch expresses love, sympathy, and understanding. While we must be always mindful of Jewish religious sensibilities, as well as the current social and legal environment regarding interpersonal boundaries, spiritual care providers must also read the unspoken emotional needs of the people for whom we care. Certainly, caregivers must know their inner self well in order to understand and convey the proper meaning of both touch and silence.

Theologically, silence can be creative and powerful. Silent prayer allows for the personal expression of pain and suffering. Silent communion with another may allow the spirit of the Divine to dwell between two people. Silence in the Jewish mystical tradition suggests unique possibilities to connect with the Divine.

In the end, silence is a challenge to our normal way of encountering the world. It allows us to touch feelings and thoughts that otherwise might go unrealized. It opens us up to the unknown in our experience, and in that of others. Silence can feel like a vast uncharted wilderness of uncertainty and helplessness, thus challenging the Jewish relational caregivers' work of spiritual care. It is essential that we monitor the nature and meaning of any silence, discerning its import in each instance when it occurs. We can learn from silence and we can teach in silence. We can care with silence and we can communicate in silence. How we do this depends on our ability to remain silent ourselves, in the face of strong cultural urges to the contrary.

8

The Muse of Relational Listening

Samuel Chiel

Sometime after his death, a friend said of the Chasidic Rabbi Moshe of Kobryn, "If there had been someone to whom he could have talked, he would still be alive."[1] Rabbi Moshe must have listened to the problems of his Chasidim for many years and was likely very helpful to them. When it came to his own problems, however, he had nobody to whom he could pour out his heart. His friend was convinced that if he had had such a person to talk to, he might not have died so prematurely.

Each of us needs somebody to listen to us, but very few people know how to listen well. Most people are too preoccupied with their own needs and concerns to be able to focus on the needs of others. If we clergy can't listen well, people will be discouraged from speaking to us about serious problems. They may exchange pleasantries with us, but they will soon realize that we are not the "listening" type. If that happens, we are effectively closing off a vital channel of communication that can make a profound difference in the lives of those for whom we are charged to care.

Some people are hesitant to seek help from psychiatrists, psychologists, and social workers. They fear that such a relationship will mark them as being mentally ill. Meeting with their clergy, though, does not carry a stigma and may help those people who will not turn to other professionals. If we "listen" well, we can make a major change in their lives and give them the hope and strength they need to be able to cope with life's challenges.

What are the guideposts for good listening? First, we have to avoid distractions. When we are listening to somebody, we must not accept any phone calls or permit any other interruptions. These distractions not only break our train of thought, as well as that of our counselee, but also bespeak a lack of seriousness in our concern for the other person. We have to work hard to banish any intrusive thoughts of our own as we listen to another. We

---

1. Martin Buber, *Tales of the Hasidim: The Later Masters,* trans. Olga Marx (New York: Schocken Books, 1948), p. 172.

may have a number of urgent commitments following this appointment, but if we think about them for even a moment or two, we may miss the urgent tone of the message that is being expressed by the other.

We have to listen to the other person as if his or her life depends on those words because, at times, the person's life may indeed depend on our hearing and feeling what the person is really saying. Philosopher and mystic Martin Buber tells the story of a young man who came to see him.[2] Buber had been immersed in a deep, mystical reverie, and instead of listening fully to the man, he was distracted by his own mystical experience and never fully heard the man's anguish and his deepest feelings. Later he learned that this man had been so troubled by his imminent entry into the army that he subsequently committed suicide. Buber could never forgive himself for not listening as if the man's life depended on it. Indeed, it did.

To listen well, we have to learn to listen with empathy. Empathy is far more than sympathy. Empathy means to identify fully with the other person so that you feel his or her pain. Even if you are unable to provide all of the answers, just listening well to that person is a great comfort. It means that at least one person in the world understands his or her pain, thereby helping the burden to become less oppressive.

Rabbi Moshe Leib of Sasov believed that you could learn from every person. He once related how he had learned from a peasant how to love his fellow human beings. He was sitting in an inn and listening to some peasants talking to one another. One of the men was silent for a long time, but when he had imbibed a considerable amount of wine, he turned to the man sitting next to him and asked him, "Tell me. Do you love me?" The man answered, "I love you very much." The first man declared, "You say you love me, but you don't know what I need. If you really loved me, you would know." The other man didn't know what to say and fell silent. Rabbi Moshe Leib concluded, "I understood. What he was saying was that to know the needs of people and to bear the burden of their sorrow is the true love of human beings."[3]

We clergy give people additional clues as to whether we are good listeners by the sermons we give. The kinds of themes that we deal with in our sermons will tell people if we are good listeners. If we speak about themes that deal with people's personal problems, such as relationships between husbands and wives or parents and children, and other family dilemmas, and we do this with tenderness and sensitivity, people will look to us when they are facing these same kinds of problems themselves.

---

2. Martin Buber, *Between Man and Man,* trans. Ronald Gregor Smith (London: Routledge and Kegan Paul, 1947; New York: Macmillan, 1948).

3. Buber, *Tales of the Hasidim,* p. 86.

If our sermons bespeak an understanding of the human situation and are delivered with a certain amount of humility, people will look upon us as kindred spirits and will come to us to seek our help. We don't have to know all of the answers, but we have to be seen as people who, while struggling with our own problems, are still able to understand their hurts and feelings because we, too, face the kinds of problems with which all mortals contend.

As clergy, we bring to the counseling session a unique dimension in our understanding of people. We see each human being as having been created by God and therefore infinitely precious and unique. We can offer our people the hope and strength that comes from a compassionate and loving God who helps to sustain us in our time of greatest need.

And should you ask, "What happens if many of our congregants begin to come to us for counseling—won't that take a major part of our time and add greatly to our already overburdened schedule?" The answer is that it will definitely take some of your time but is well worth every moment because you will be touching peoples' lives in a most profound and lasting way, and you will help them to live with much less pain and far greater feelings of fulfillment.

9

The Muse of Music and Song

Shira Stern

Music has always been considered a bridge to God. From the earliest chants of religious systems in both East and West, the sacred power of word and voice has been recognized as the communion between humans and the Divine.

Don G. Campbell[1]

Hear, kings; listen, princes; I will sing to Adonai! I will sing praise to Adonai, the God of Israel.

Judges 5:3[2]

For human beings, the first sounds we hear are the gentle whooshing of our mother's womb, and the rhythmic beat of her heart. We respond—with or without being slapped—with a primitive cry at birth, and so music begins. Long before we respond to Mozart or "Mary Had a Little Lamb" or a grandmother's lullaby, we can feel the beat in nature's undulation. We do not even have to "hear" the sound—the vibrations are powerful enough, as a hearing-impaired colleague has told me.

So it is natural, and part of our nature, to bring wholeness and healing through the medium of music. As a pulpit rabbi and as a rabbi in a hospital setting, I have learned a number of key lessons, at first, by accident, but then with some revisions, with intentionality.

---

1. Don G. Campbell, *Music Physician for Times to Come* (Wheaton, IL: Quest Books, 1991), p. 330.
2. All translations of biblical text are by the author.

Lesson 1: Music Enhances and Highlights Words

> Sing to God a new song, make music at your best among shouts of joy.
>
> Psalm 33:3

Simple message, powerful medium. When a rabbi or cantor enters a hospital room, invading the public/private sanctity of a patient's temporary home, that patient can respond in one of two ways: the first is to welcome the visiting clergy, seeing this encounter as an opportunity to talk, to be comforted, and to be spiritually soothed. The second response, and more common, is a tendency to be wary—wondering why this person has come to visit at this particular time. Sometimes, once I identify myself as a rabbi/chaplain, the patient or the family responds, "But *we're* not religious—we don't belong—who sent you?" The corollary, unspoken, but clearly the elephant in the room, is, "Is she going to ask me to *do* something Jewish?" If I ask them whether I can say a prayer for them, the answer is invariably no, but if I ask permission to sing them something, they often welcome the *b'rachah.*[3] Some even ask for more. I invite them to close their eyes, find a comfortable position, and let the melody—sung quietly and never at full voice—create a healing moment.

Lesson 2: Music Connects Us to Places We Thought Our Minds Had Long Forgotten

> Then after many calamities and troubles have come upon them, this song will testify before them as a witness, because their descendants will still be reciting it and will not have forgotten it.
>
> Deuteronomy 31:21

For several years as the community rabbi in suburbia, I would visit area hospital, assisted-living, and long-term care facilities. Once a month, at one nursing home in particular, I would visit late enough on Friday so that one could legitimately call it *Kabbalat Shabbat.*[4] The attendants would wheel twenty-five to thirty residents into a large room, gather them around a makeshift ritual table, set out the grape juice in tiny medicine cups, cut *challah*[5] in small, manageable pieces, and leave me alone with the resi-

---

3. Blessing.
4. Friday evening service welcoming the Sabbath.
5. Ceremonial braided loaf used at the Sabbath meal.

dents. I would look around the arts and crafts room, call out to people by name, trying to muster some energy in our makeshift *shul* [6] before I started. A few people actually looked forward to this event, but most residents would sit quietly in a semisleep, unresponsive and mute—until I began to sing familiar melodies. Eyes would fly open, heads would lift, and, all of a sudden, we were singing in three-part harmony. Where I struggled with verses, they could fill in words without hesitation. They belted out the chorus of *L'chah Dodi* and *Shalom Aleichem,* [7] and would teach me special versions of songs in Yiddish I had never heard. And when I was inspired to learn a song of my own to share with them, they cried and held my hands and kissed them. When we were done and *kiddush* [8] sung, they retreated back into their shells, with a little more color in their cheeks, and a vigor that had not been there before.

I never truly understood the staying power of what we teach in the early Hebrew School years, until I began to visit one young woman of forty-three, a resident in a rehabilitation facility for a number of years whose advanced multiple sclerosis made speaking difficult, clearly almost impossible, but she could sing the *sh'ma,* [9] with a strong, comprehensible voice. So we chanted together, over and over and over again. The impact of what she could do was not lost on her, and each time I left, May[10] would pound her closed fist on her chest, nodding and repeating just *sh'ma.* It had become her very identity once she could no longer say her own name.

Lesson 3: Music Is Universal and for Everyone

A song: A Psalm of David: "My heart is firm, O God; I will sing and chant a hymn with all my soul."

Psalm 108:1-2 ff

Ignore grade school bans on singing in public: if you can sing in the shower, you can sing, with permission from the patient, at the bedside. What you lack in tone and pitch and musical sophistication will be amply balanced and gratefully appreciated because of your intent. Perhaps the family present or the patient, if he or she is so inclined, will be tempted to join in. This leads me to the fourth lesson.

---

6. Affectionate diminutive for synagogue.
7. Hymns welcoming the Sabbath Queen.
8. Prayer said over wine sanctifying the Sabbath or holiday.
9. Central prayer of Jewish liturgy.
10. No real names are used.

Lesson 4: Music Releases Endorphins

God is my strength and my song, and God has become my salvation.

Psalm 118:14

Music is good medicine.[11] Just as Norman Cousins discovered alternative therapies to help him overcome a seriously debilitating, near fatal disease,[12] recent studies indicate that, indeed, music can increase endorphin levels. In Don Campbell's *The Mozart Effect*, "the healing chemical; created by the joy and emotional richness in music . . . enable[s] the body to create its own anesthetic and enhance the immune system."[13] Furthermore, a growing number of health care institutions around the world are finding significant benefits from music for patients and for staff:

- A 1995 study found that surgeons who listened to the music of their choice while operating had lower blood pressure and a slower heart rate and could perform mental tasks more quickly and accurately.[14]
- A professor of music and psychiatry, Dr. Paul Robertson of Ontario has run studies which show that patients exposed to fifteen minutes of soothing music require only half the recommended doses of sedatives and anesthetic drugs for painful operations.[15]
- At the University of Massachusetts Medical Center, harp music has been prescribed instead of tranquilizers and painkillers for cancer patients.[16]

Chemotherapy and dialysis patients use music to make it through the procedures with greater ease and comfort; people undergoing root canal and MRIs turn up the headphones to compensate for the grating, violent

---

11. See Robert F. Unkefer, ed., *Music Therapy in the Treatment of Adults with Mental Disorders: Theoretical Bases and Clinical Interventions* (New York: Schirmer Books, 1990).

12. Norman Cousins, *Anatomy of an Illness As Perceived by the Patient* (New York: Bantam Books, 1979).

13. Don G. Campbell, *The Mozart Effect* (New York: Avon Books, 1997), p. 71.

14. Ibid., p. 132, citing K. Allen and J. Blascovitch, "Effects of Music on Cardiovascular Reactivity Among Surgeons," *Journal of the American Medical Association* 272 (1994):882-884.

15. Ibid., p. 133, citing Paul Robertson, "Music and the Mind," *Caduceus* 31 (Spring 1995):17-20.

16. Ibid., citing "Music Facilitates Healing, Bodymind Coordination," *Brain/Mind Bulletin* 8 (December 13, 1982):1-2.

machinery noises, and New Yorkers listen to music as protective gear when they ride the subway. In each instance, music—often something one can sing along with—becomes the balm that promotes well-being. "Without a doubt," states Raymond Bahr, MD,[17] "music therapy ranks high on the list of modern-day management of critical care patients. Its relaxing properties enable patients to get well faster by allowing them to accept their condition and treatment without excessive anxiety."[18]

Lesson 5: Music Frames Our Time and Space

> David appointed them to be in charge of the service of song in the house of Adonai, after the ark had found a permanent resting place.
>
> 1 Chronicles 6:31

If you have ever turned on the radio and caught a song playing that reminds you of events past, you have experienced time travel. Suddenly, you are no longer on the highway commuting to work, but at this wonderful concert the summer you were sixteen, or you are sitting alone once again in your room thinking about a broken relationship you have long forgotten.

We mark the Jewish seasons with different melodies for similar liturgy and demarcate Shabbat from the rest of the week with the singing of *z'mirot*.[19] We teach young ones about the holidays through songs to which they can relate. We bring new music and new texts to the circles of our healing services, which have multiplied fantastically in the past ten years, not because we are sicker, but because we are looking for ways back to health and need other people to be with us on our journey.

Lesson 6: Music Is a Traditional Jewish Response

> I will be glad and exult in you. I will sing praise to Your name, forever.
>
> Psalm 9:2

Collectively as Jews and individually, we have sung to show joy, sorrow, longing, and gratitude to God. Singing is part of our textual and experiential

---

17. Director of Coronary Care at St. Agnes Hospital in Baltimore, Maryland.

18. Mitchell L. Gaynor, *The Healing Power of Sound: Recovery from Life-Threatening Illness Using Sound, Voice and Music* (Boston: Shambhala Publications, Inc., 2002), p. 83.

19. Festive Sabbath and holiday songs, sung around the dinner table.

memory. At the most dramatic times, our ancestors used music to articulate important events:

- Moses sang in *Shirat Hayam,*[20] "I will sing to *Adonai,* for God is highly exalted: horse and rider God threw in the sea." (Exodus 15:1)
- Miriam picked up her timbrel, gathered the people around her and sang: "Sing to *Adonai,* for God is exalted! Horse and rider God has thrown in the sea." (Exodus 15:21)
- Israel sang, "Spring up, O well—sing to it, the well which the chieftains dug." (Numbers 21:17-18)

In fact, the Bible attributes three entire songs to Moses: the Song at the Sea in Exodus 15, the final poem at the end of Deuteronomy (32:1-52), and Psalm 90, which is also attributed to Moses due to word similarities and construction.[21] The Bible also includes nearly 100 instances of Israelites singing, the majority of which can be found in Psalms, most of which were penned by King David. But even before he composed these moving compendia of verses, accompanying himself on the lyre, he used his harp to heal King Saul: "David took a harp, and played with his hand: and Saul was refreshed, and was well, and the evil spirit departed from him" (1 Samuel 16:23).

While David healed bodies, later generations of Jews, both Ashkenazim and Sephardim,[22] wrote *piyutim*—lyrical poetry set to music—to heal their souls, describing their hopes, their dreams, and their visions for the future.

Even our books contain music: because our past began as oral history, when Bible redactors in the first millennium of the Common Era set the books of the Bible in order, they also recorded the intricate Torah *trope* marks we had used as fathers sang texts to sons, who sang the texts to their sons. By doing so, these early rabbis made it possible for all following generations to chant the holy text in some unified fashion.

If music—the human voice especially—has been so integral a part of our survival mechanisms in the past, then it has the ability to continue to do so. We should have music in every spiritual toolbox we carry around with us, as rabbis, cantors and all clergy as caregivers who recognize this gift as one that must be shared.

---

20. Song of redemption sung following the parting of the Sea of Reeds.

21. Gunther Plaut, *The Torah: A Modern Commentary* (New York: Union of American Hebrew Congregations, 1980), p. 1555.

22. Literally, German and Spanish Jews—actually Jews from Northern Europe and Jews from Southern Europe and the Mediterranean Basin.

10

The Muse of Chanting

Bonita E Taylor

Chanting is like breathing. . . . The chant is a numinous ribbon anchoring the person to the universe, linking the human and divine, an intimate expression of the soul. . . . To hear a . . . chant in its depth and power is haunting. It's as if the sound comes from a place in the body that is like an internal seashell that floats in the cosmic tides long after the physical body is gone. It is the primal human cry for meaning. [1]

Most—if not all—spiritual traditions chant. I started to chant five years ago as part of a rhythmic deep-breathing program that was designed to help my body detoxify from severe mercury and lead poisoning and heal from their wounding of my neurological system. Today, I continue to infuse my daily spiritual practice with a combination of chanting and breath work for both health and spiritual benefits.

I have learned from the Reverend Joan Witkowski:[2]

Regular intentional breath work develops and strengthens our diaphragms to help our bodies inhale greater quantities of oxygen and exhale greater quantities of waste. Chanting simultaneously, because it requires extra effort from our diaphragms, has an effect that is similar to adding weights during physical exercises. It further strengthens our diaphragms and helps us to better use the oxygen that we are inhaling. In addition, when vibrations of elongated sounds resonate

---

1. Rita Ariyoshi, "A Culture Speaks," *Hawaii Magazine,* January/February 2004, pp. 45-46.
2. From personal communications with Reverend Joan Witkowski, a Minister of The Church of the Movement of Spiritual Inner Awareness and a specialist in breath work.

throughout our bodies in overtones, they synchronize and balance our brain waves. This assists our bodies in opening up and becoming freer. Together, intentional breath work and chanting revitalizes our cells, relaxes our bodies, and helps us to heal.

In the book of Numbers,[3] Miriam and Aaron challenge Moses' leadership. Miriam then is struck with an undefined skin disease and is quarantined for a week outside of the camp. Generally, during this kind of occurrence, the camp moved on, leaving the ailing person to catch up when—and if—he or she became well. According to Jewish tradition, however, Miriam is so highly regarded by the Israelite people that they refuse to move forward until she is able to go with them. At that point, at Aaron's behest, Moses prays these words: *El na, r'fa na lah*—Please God, please heal her.[4] When I approached this passage, Moses' sincere, yet fervent prayer touched my spirit and I began to chant it spontaneously, first in Hebrew and then in English, for I, too, was feeling shut out of the camp, as do many individuals that I have cared for who suffer from ongoing conditions of medical distress.

In sharing this chant with many others, first as a sitting chant indoors and then as a walking chant outdoors, an overwhelming majority reported experiencing extraordinary spiritual sensations, especially during the outdoor chanting walk. Rabbi David J. Zucker[5] reports:

> We chant this during Shabbat services and the congregation has become very attached to it. It evokes deep spiritual meaning for us.

The Reverend Patrick Bradley[6] reports:

> I believe that any prayer chant would work—however, the prayer for healing is easier to use because it meets people where they are. . . . The link to healing is important. Psychologically, it hooks the patients and they are more likely to do it.

---

3. Numbers 12:1-13.
4. Numbers 12:13. Translation is the author's.
5. Rabbi David J. Zucker, PhD, BCC, is the Director of Pastoral/Spiritual Care and Recreation, Shalom Park, Aurora, Colorado, a senior continuum-of-care center.
6. The Reverend Patrick Bradley, MA, BCC, is Director of Pastoral Care for United Medical Center, Cheyenne, Wyoming.

Retired Colonel Lawrence Schneider[7] shared the following:

> I think you've hit upon something, although I don't necessarily associate it with religion, albeit many religions chant. The voice and rhythmical breathing together cause me to feel what I enjoy when I am running. . . . I think it is very helpful.

In these pages I invite you to experiment with it. If you are shy about chanting, take the deep breaths, hum, and think the prayer. While breathing and chanting—or humming—visualize specific body parts and/or particular individuals who could use an infusion of healing and energy from the Source of Healing.

I have adapted this prayer in several ways:

1. The first set (in either language) is an adaptation that beseeches the Divine Source of Healing to heal the chanter.
2. The second set retains the original entreaty to heal "her" (*"la"* in Hebrew). However, in this chant, "her" refers to our soul. In Hebrew, one of the words for soul—*N'shamah*—is feminine, whether we are female or male. Judaism encourages us to advocate for ourselves. The sage Hillel teaches: "If I am not for myself, who will be?" and "If I am only for myself, what am I?"[8]
3. The third set asks the Divine Source of Healing to heal all of us, wherever we may be.
4. In Judaism, the number *3* is a potent symbol of holiness, balance, reconciliation, and completeness, and the number *5* is associated with healing.[9] As you close the chant, I invite you to invoke these five sacred qualities by repeating three times the fifth line of the very end of the third set: *El Na R'fa Na Lanu* ("Please Divine One Please Heal Us").

In time, the Divine One healed Miriam and brought her back within the camp. May the Eternal Source of Life allow each of us to live within the camp.

---

7. Colonel (Retired) Lawrence Schneider is Director of Land Forces, Defense Mission Systems, Northrop Grumman, Washington, DC.

8. Mishnah Avot (Ethics of the Ancestors) 1.14.

9. According to the author, the numerical associations come from Jewish folklore that she has known since childhood.

Chant Outline

EL NA R'FA NA LAH (Numbers 12:13)
PLEASE DIVINE ONE PLEASE HEAL HER (Miriam)
Take one deep breath, and with that one breath,
say each line and *hold the final sound* for as long as you can. . . .

1. *El*	hold final sound . . .
2. *El Na*	hold final sound . . .
3. *El Na R'Fa*	hold final sound . . .
4. *El Na R'Fa Na*	hold final sound . . .
5. *El Na R'Fa Na Li*[10]	hold final sound . . .
a. *El*	hold final sound . . .
b. *El Na*	hold final sound . . .
c. *El Na R'Fa*	hold final sound . . .
d. *El Na R'Fa Na*	hold final sound . . .
e. *El Na R'Fa Na Lah*[11]	hold final sound . . .
1. *El*	hold final sound . . .
2. *El Na*	hold final sound . . .
3. *El Na R'Fa*	hold final sound . . .
4. *El Na R'Fa Na*	hold final sound . . .
5. *El Na R'Fa Na Lanu*[12]	hold final sound . . .
[repeat three times[13]]	

PLEASE DIVINE ONE PLEASE HEAL (Numbers 12:13)
Take one deep breath, and with that one breath,
say each line and *hold the final sound* for as long as you can. . . .

1. **Please**	hold final sound . . .
2. **Please Divine One**	hold final sound . . .
3. **Please Divine One Please**	hold final sound . . .

---

10. This is an adaptation. In Numbers, the final Hebrew word of this prayer is *lah* or "her," referring to Miriam. Here, we use the Hebrew word *li* for "me."

11. We use the original *lah,* but referring here to our *N'shamah*—our soul; that is feminine in Hebrew, whether we are female or male. Think of specific body parts and/or particular individuals who could use a healing prayer.

12. This is an adaptation. We use the Hebrew word *lanu* for "us." Think of all in your heart who could use healing prayers—whether present or not.

13. In mystical Judaism, the number 5 is associated with healing, as with the five "fingers" of a *chamsa,* a popular amulet for good luck and well-being in the Middle East, most often seen in the form of a hand.

4. **Please Divine One Please Heal**   hold final sound . . .
5. **Please Divine One Please Heal Me**   hold final sound . . .
   a. **Please**   hold final sound . . .
   b. **Please Divine One**   hold final sound . . .
   c. **Please Divine One Please**   hold final sound . . .
   d. **Please Divine One Please Heal**   hold final sound . . .
   e. **Please Divine One Please Heal Her** hold final sound . . .
1. **Please**   hold final sound . . .
2. **Please Divine One**   hold final sound . . .
3. **Please Divine One Please**   hold final sound . . .
4. **Please Divine One Please Heal**   hold final sound . . .
5. **Please Divine One Please Heal Us**   hold final sound . . .
   [repeat three times]

11

The Muse of Creative Ritual
for Relational Healing

Marcia Cohn Spiegel

At moments in our lives we become aware that we are not alone. We long for a spiritual connection in a moment of crisis or sorrow, of joy or celebration. We may turn to Judaism for the appropriate prayer or ritual to meet this need, only to find that it does not exist. As Jewish relational caregivers we are called upon as the experts. When others turn to us for help, we may feel unprepared to step into this void. The truth is that we can turn to tradition to help us create something new that feels rooted in our past while meeting the needs of the present.

The purpose of a personal ritual is to enable an individual to acknowledge a change of status so that they will be transformed by the ceremony. We recognize this change of status at ceremonies of *b'rit*,[1] *bar* and *bat mitzvah*,[2] confirmation, and marriage. In the past twenty-five years we have become increasingly aware of events in our lives for which there are no rituals. We turn to our leaders and community to help us find ways to acknowledge these events. Many of the new rituals have originated from the Jewish feminist movement to enable women to participate more fully in Jewish life. They include ceremonies initiating newborn daughters into the covenant of the Jewish people and ceremonies for miscarriage or abortion, weaning a child, coping with aging, and healing from sexual abuse.[3] The creation of new rituals for women has allowed men to look at their own unmet needs.

---

1. Ceremony welcoming a child into the covenant between God and Israel.

2. At age thirteen, a young person is obligated for the fulfillment of God's commands. The occasion is marked by being called to the reading of the Torah, and participating as an "adult" in the service.

3. Debra Orenstein, ed., *Lifecycles I: Jewish Women on Life Passages and Personal Milestones* (Woodstock, VT: Jewish Lights Publishing, 1994).

Creating a unique ritual is most effective when grounded in our tradition, which is extremely rich in these matters. Ritual acts can be seen as metaphors that can be adapted to create new ceremonies for those occasions for which we do not as yet have formulas. We have a compendium of familiar rituals to draw upon. We recite blessings at special moments to set them apart from the routines of life, to acknowledge the presence of God in our lives. We say the *shehecheyanu*[4] at very special moments of celebration. *Havdalah*[5] uses our senses of taste, scent, and vision to separate Shabbat from the coming week. We light candles at Chanukah[6] to bring light during the darkest time of the year. We cleanse our homes of unwanted *chameitz*[7] at Passover. The *Mi Shebeirach*[8] prayer is recited for those in need of healing. We recite *gomel*[9] when we survive an accident or other traumatic event. During mourning we cut or tear our garments. During acute illness we may change our name to fool the angel of death. We wash our hands before a meal and say grace afterward; we eat and bless special foods at various seasons, give or pledge gifts of charity, study Torah[10] or other texts, plant trees, and wear special garments. Using personal or family ritual objects helps this new ritual have powerful resonance for those involved. A grandfather's *tallit*[11] or a grandmother's hand-crocheted tablecloth can become a *chuppah*[12] for a marriage ceremony or be used to wrap new parents and their child for a special blessing. These components can be combined in new ways for special occasions.

Whether this new ritual is as informal as a special blessing for a patient in the hospital, or as elaborate as a *Simchat Chochmah*[13] in a large synagogue, certain factors need to be included. First, the ceremony must be separated from the mundane world. This transition can be accomplished as easily by a

---

4. Thanking God for enabling us to reach this day.

5. Service of differentiation between sacred and the secular.

6. Eight-day festival commemorating the rededication of the Temple in Jerusalem by Judah Maccabee and his followers (165 BCE).

7. Leaven, not permitted on Passover.

8. A specialized prayer in the synagogue liturgy often, but not exclusively, used for healing: "May the God of our Ancestors bless (and heal) So-and-So, the child of So-and-So."

9. Prayer thanking God for saving us in a life-threatening situation.

10. In the narrow sense, the Five Books of Moses; more broadly, all of Jewish learning.

11. Fringed shawl worn by worshipers in synagogue.

12. Canopy that the wedding couple stands under during the ceremony, symbolic of the Jewish home the couple will establish together.

13. "Celebration of Wisdom," a new ceremony of aging. Savina J. Teubal, "Simchat Hochmah," in Ellen Umansky and Dianne Ashton, eds., *Four Centuries of Jewish Women's Spirituality: A Sourcebook* (Boston: Beacon Press, 1992), pp. 257-265.

few seconds of silence as by a full orchestra playing the wedding march. If you are blessed with the ability to carry a tune, humming a *niggun*[14] can bring the voices of others together for a special beginning. Lighting candles, reciting *kiddush,*[15] and joining hands are other ways of saying, "This is a special moment that we are sharing together." Next is the body of the ritual itself, which can be a blessing of healing for one person while we are alone with a patient, or a complex service involving many people and new liturgy. Finally, a transition needs to take place back to the world from which we started. This can be as simple as a squeeze of the hand to recognize what has taken place or, in a more formal setting, music that is sung or played.

Many of us feel uncomfortable when we stray from traditional practices. Those who are requesting our help to create a new ritual may also be uncomfortable asking for help for their own needs, being the center of attention, or trying something new. Grounding ourselves by using familiar elements helps us to feel more at ease. It is important that we fully explore what is wanted and whether other people will be involved, so that no one will have any surprises. We should be careful not to make assumptions about what we think others would like but thoroughly examine together their desires and our suggestions. Don't be afraid to try something new: sing new songs, recite new prayers, and create new rituals. We have now resources to help us create or adapt rituals for many occasions.[16] We may need courage to try something new, but taking the first step will enrich our own lives as well as those with whom we create these rituals.

Mikveh, *a Ritual of Purification*

Mikveh, the ritual bath, is described as a cleansing bath in living water performed as an act of purification.[17] Traditionally observant women go to the *mikveh* following the conclusion of menstruation preparatory to resuming marital relations. Men often go to prepare themselves for the Sabbath or festivals. A bride may go to prepare herself for marriage. Ruins near the old city of Jerusalem remind us that visitors to the Temple went to a *mikveh* before ascending the Temple mount. The ritual of immersion as a spiritual act of purification has been adapted by contemporary women recovering from sexual abuse, violence, or even a difficult divorce. Rabbis codified the con-

---

14. Melody without words.
15. Prayer said over wine sanctifying the Sabbath or holiday.
16. www.ritual.org.
17. Leviticus 15:13.

struction of the ritual bath, but for purposes of these new rituals, hot tubs, rivers, streams, lakes, and swimming pools are made holy by the spiritual activities that take place in them. Women who have been raised in a liberal or secular environment may find this a profoundly transformative ritual of rebirth and purification, whereas women who have been raised in orthodox settings in which the laws of family purity are observed may not be comfortable using the *mikveh* in such a nontraditional way.

Although some women might prefer to do the ritual alone for reasons of modesty or privacy, I have usually participated with at least three other women, in a hot tub or pool. The loving support of friends is important to women who want to transform themselves from victims to survivors. As in the traditional ritual, the participant immerses herself three times. During the first immersion, she concentrates on feeling the water cleansing her while she lets the traumatic memories of abuse be washed away. As her supporters join hands around her, she immerses herself a second time, savoring the love and comfort of this community. Finally she immerses herself for a third time, envisioning her future, taking her first steps into a better and more peaceful life.[18]

Some women prefer to use the ancient blessings for immersion; others find this an opportunity to write their own blessings or guided visualizations. Music can play an important role in enhancing the experience. Start with a *niggun* or familiar song, sing Debbie Friedman's *Mi Shebeirach* or another of the new versions of this prayer of healing,[19] and conclude with a song of joy and celebration.

This *mikveh* ritual was adapted by a gay man who was mourning the death of his partner from AIDS. At the end of a year of mourning, he gathered together a few of his closest friends who had supported him during his time of sorrow. He did the three immersions just described, but added another element. At the conclusion of his ritual he changed his name to represent his new status. He now goes by this new name. He used Marcia Falk's beautiful new blessing for changing one's name: "Let us sing the soul in every name and the name of every soul."[20]

---

18. This ceremony was created by a group of women who call themselves "The *Mikveh* Ladies." A variation of it can be found in Jane Litman, "Meditation for the *Mikveh*," in Orenstein, *Lifecycles I*, pp. 253-254.

19. Synagogue 2000, *R'fuah Sh'leimah: Songs of Jewish Healing* (New York: Transcontinental Music Publications, 2002). Synagogue 2000 is a national, not-for- profit institute dedicated to revitalizing and reenergizing synagogue life in North America. It is a cross-denominational Jewish organization (see www.s2k.org).

20. Marcia Lee Falk, *The Book of Blessings: A Feminist Jewish Reconstruction of Prayer* (San Francisco: Harper, 1996), p. 205.

It is not difficult to imagine using this ritual with someone recovering from cancer, undergoing chemotherapy, moving beyond a difficult family relationship, or grieving the death of a beloved partner or spouse.

Simchat Chochmah, *a Celebration of Wisdom*

In 1986, when she turned sixty, Savina Teubal wanted to create a rite of passage that would establish her presence as an elder in her community, Beth Chaim Chadashim. She wanted to read publicly from the Torah for the first time, particularly the story of Sarah.[21] For that occasion, she designed a very special ritual, *Simchat Chochmah,* which took place at a Saturday morning service.[22] As I participated in this extraordinary event, I began to plan my own ritual for the following year when I turned sixty. Although using the same elements that Savina had spelled out, I chose a different format. I had already had the honor of reading publicly from the Torah and was concluding a period of mourning for many of my closest family members, including my parents and husband. I chose to celebrate my *Simchat Chochmah* as part of a *Havdalah* ceremony in my own synagogue, Congregation Ner Tamid.[23] Since then many others have adapted the ritual as their own. Some of these rituals have taken place in synagogues as part of a regular or a special service, at a dinner at home, or at a banquet in a hotel. Many participants celebrated a sixtieth birthday, some celebrated at sixty-five, and still others at seventy-five or eighty. Because these women grew up in an age when girls were not *bat mitzvahed,* these elders felt that they had never appropriately celebrated a passage of aging. Each service was unique to the individual who had created it.[24]

Savina chose to incorporate familiar symbols in her service, and these have become the core of the ritual:

1. *Changing or donning a new garment.* Both Savina and I chose to recognize our mortality by putting on a *kittel,*[25] which we would wear for services and celebrations and which would eventually become our

---

21. Genesis 12 ff.

22. Savina Teubal, "Have You Seen Sarah?" in Susan Berrin, ed., *A Heart of Wisdom: The Jewish Journey from Midlife Through the Elder Years* (Woodstock, VT: Jewish Lights, 1997), pp. 183-188.

23. Marcia Cohn Spiegel, "Moving On: Celebrating 60 and Beyond," in Berrin, *A Heart of Wisdom,* pp. 275-278.

24. See the video *Timbrels and Torahs: Celebrating Women's Wisdom,* produced and directed by Miriam Chaya and Judith Montell (www.timbrelsandtorahs.com), 2000.

25. A simple white garment first worn by a bridegroom at his wedding.

shroud. Other celebrants were uncomfortable with the idea of putting on a shroud and chose rather to put on a *tallit* for the first time, or a special piece of jewelry or an amulet.

2. *Reading from a text or expounding upon a text.* Savina read publicly the story of Sarah. I spoke about the qualities that made Miriam a leader.

3. *Changing or validating your name.* Savina took the Hebrew name Sarah, and I became Miriam. Some use their new names for only ritual purposes; others change their names in English as well to confirm their transformation.

4. *Planting a tree.* Our sages remind us that when we plant a tree in our old age, it will bear fruit for future generations. Both of us are fortunate to enjoy the fruits from the trees that we planted many years ago.

5. *Making a gift to charity.* I pledged to continue to support the women's spiritual community to which I belong and also made a vow to continue my work in the field of sexual and domestic violence. The songs composed by Debbie Friedman and Drorah Setel that were sung at our rituals have now become contemporary classics in the Jewish community.[26] The *Havdalah* blessings that Marcia Falk led appear in her *Book of Blessings.*

At the conclusion of my service, an old friend told me that he didn't remember participating in this ritual before, although he was sure that he had. It affirmed for me that when we use familiar elements, even in innovative ways, the ritual seems grounded. This same man added, "It's too bad it's only for women." I have been unable to convince him that, since we invented the ceremony to meet our own needs, he should feel free to adapt it to celebrate his life. As individuals we can set the appropriate time in our lives to recognize aging, honor what we have done in the world, celebrate our lives, and look forward to the future. In a recent conversation Savina and I realized that, although we thought our major work had finished as we turned sixty, we have both gone on to do new things, and rather than an ending, *Simchat Hochmah* was the beginning of our "eldering."

A Ritual for Rage

Miriam Gladys came to me in a state of fury and anxiety. She had just learned that her late husband had betrayed her in a viciously cruel way. She needed to express this anger but was terrified of her feelings. She felt that

---

once she started she would not be able to stop. We explored what she felt she needed to do. Her first need was to do something physical to release her rage before she could move on to find peace. At first she didn't want any witnesses to her pain but then decided to include her closest and most trusted friend.

We performed this ritual in her backyard, starting by holding hands silently. First, she brought out her wedding photographs and smashed the frames, broke the glass, and ripped the photographs to shreds while she screamed curses. I had prepared a hole for the wood and glass and paper. When she had finished ripping and tearing, we lit a fire in the hole so the pictures and frames would burn into a fine ash. While the small fire burned, we sang Debbie Friedman's *Mi Shebeirach*. Finally, Miriam planted a small lemon tree in the hole, transforming the pain from the past into the flowers and fruit of the future. In conclusion we read Psalm 121.[27] We chose a lemon tree because, although the skin may be bitter, the fruit is tart and the flowers are sweet. She tells me that she feels joy when she picks the lemons, as they are a reminder that she doesn't need to continue to carry the anger and rage.

Sometimes unbearable pain can be made bearable by creating ritual. Sharing our private angst with other people creates a circle of intimacy. We can scream and smash and curse but know that our actions will be contained. We know that someone else is facilitating and will keep things moving toward a transformative conclusion. We acknowledge that we need the help of that Power which is greater than ourselves to survive and thrive.

Creating a Group Prayer

Many of us reach out for help, comfort, and inspiration from others who share our situations. Myriad support groups offer environments for addressing an infinite variety of issues: people living in nursing homes; cancer patients attending wellness centers; patients staying in hospices; individuals and their families participating in recovery from drug addiction and alcoholism; infertile couples contemplating adoption; patients and survivors dealing with illness or trauma. Sharing our thoughts, feelings, and problems with like-minded people can provide comfort and awareness that we are not alone.

Support meetings assume some aspects of ritual. Often they open with a d'var[28] Torah, a prayer, or a format created by the group. The close of the

---

27. "I turn my eyes to the mountains; from where will my help come? My help will come from the Lord, Maker of Heaven and Earth."
28. A short commentary on a text.

session may feature another moment of prayer, a song, or a closing circle. I have found that creating a group prayer can be a powerful way to close such a meeting. It takes only a few minutes and requires, at most, a card or paper to write on and a pen or pencil. The blessing we create together is based on the traditional blessing formula, but personalized for this occasion.

In creating a prayer or blessing, we first address by name the one to whom we are praying. Because it is wise when requesting a favor to praise that individual, we consider positive attributes. Then we are ready to ask for what we need. In conclusion, we again praise the one whom we have asked. Looking at prayer in this way allows all of us to express our unique voices. The group may need to be reminded that we are each expressing our individual thoughts, and that we should not judge or try to correct what someone else is saying.

As I explain each step, I give the group a moment to think about what they want to write. We begin by naming God in whatever way we feel comfortable. Our first line then is to write, "Blessed are You . . ."; some may prefer "Lord, God, King of the Universe," whereas others may choose *Shechinah,*[29] *Rachamim,*[30] healer, or unknown power. Writing is done in silence.

For the second line, we consider the quality or attribute of deity that speaks to us at this moment in time. This statement can begin with the word *who,* for example: "Who nurtures and protects us" or "Who brings joy." Again we write in silence.

On the third line, we state our desire or blessing, for example: "Be with me in this hour of need"; "Bless this special child I am carrying"; "Help my mother to find peace."

Finally, on the fourth line, we describe God's ability to act in the world, for example: "Blessed are you who binds up our wounds"; "Praised are you who makes all things possible"; "Holy is the one who accompanies us on our journey."

When each person has finished writing, we form a tight circle. I prefer not to have people touch one another in any way at this time because some group members may have suffered physical abuse and will be uncomfortable having strangers embrace or touch them. We instead stand as close together as is comfortable.

Before we begin, I explain that no one is required to read and may quietly say, "Pass," if they are not ready to share. I also ask that they not explain or comment on what they have written but save any explanations for after the

---

29. Divine Presence, often represented as the feminine, caring aspect of the Divinity.
30. Merciful One.

exercise. First, the leader starts by reading his or her first statement; then each person in turn reads his or her first statement. Next, each of us reads the second statement, then the third, and finally the conclusion. As our voices travel around the circle expressing our own thoughts and needs, they become one voice. The individual prayer now belongs to the group. We each are empowered. As our voices create a circle, all can feel the spirit of *Shechinah* dwelling among us.

Caveats

In closing, I offer here a few reminders when creating rituals:

1. Be aware of those in the group who may not be able to participate fully because they cannot stand, see, or hear. You might want to say, "Will those who choose (or are able to) rise . . ." If deaf people who use sign language will be present, you may be able to arrange for a qualified signer by contacting your local organization for the deaf.
2. Be careful of using scents. Rose petals in the spice box may set off an allergy. Many people find strong scents or perfumes disturbing.
3. Make sure that you know who is bringing any ritual objects that will be used. Matches, wine, candles, and spices are often forgotten. If planning a ritual fire, prepare some tinder to ensure the flames catch.
4. Agree beforehand whether recordings, photographs, or videos can or cannot be made.
5. Don't assume that everyone present can drink alcoholic beverages. Provide nonalcoholic options for *kiddush*. One way to handle this is to use white grape juice and red wine so people can tell which is nonalcoholic. An alternative is to use only grape juice so no one needs to make a choice.
6. Some individuals do not like to be touched or hugged. Don't suggest that the congregants put their arms around one another's waists or shoulders for certain songs or prayers.
7. If you distribute a printed program or prayer book, be sure to credit your sources. You may need to get permission to use copyrighted materials.

12

The Muse of Spontaneous Prayer for All the [*Tzelem*⇔*N'shamah*] Relationships

Charles P. Rabinowitz

In Nedarim 39a, we are taught that "an individual who visits the sick removes 1/60th of their suffering or illness when they depart." This occurs only when the individual becomes a *ben* or *bat gil*.[1] The idea is to find a common life story piece and, for me as the chaplain, to have integrated it successfully so that in revisiting the experience I am not overwhelmed.[2] Only then will that fraction of the suffering or illness be removed. It is a great challenge and responsibility.

Rabbi Margaret Holub teaches that *hitlavut ruchanit*[3] is the essence of our rabbinic role. Rabbi Friedman explains this eloquently:

We walk along with those we serve in the course of their journeys through suffering, illness, change, and joy. Like Miriam, who stood and watched as a baby Moses sat in his basket on the banks of the Nile, our greatest gift is sometimes simply being alongside our peo-

---

1. A true peer to the patient.

2. My summary of Rabbi Kestenbaum's definition; see Rabbi Israel Kestenbaum, "The Gift of Healing Relationship: A Theology of Jewish Pastoral Care," in *Jewish Pastoral Care: A Practical Handbook from Traditional and Contemporary Sources,* ed. Rabbi Dayle A. Friedman (Woodstock, VT: Jewish Lights Publishing, 2001), pp. 6-7, 12-13.

3. Spiritual accompanying. We all owe a debt to the writings of Rabbis Israel Kestenbaum, Margaret Holub, and Dayle A. Friedman, who have taught us how to bring ourselves into the holy space at the bedside. Their work on how we become a *ben* or *bat gil* and how we create a sense of *hitlavut ruchanit* is an important foundation stone. See Rabbi Dayle A. Friedman, "Hitlavut Ruchanit: Spiritual Accompanying" and "Letting Their Faces Shine: Accompanying Aging People and Their Families," in *Jewish Pastoral Care: A Practical Handbook from Traditional and Contemporary Sources,* ed. Rabbi Dayle A. Friedman (Woodstock, VT: Jewish Lights Publishing, 2001), pp. xi-xiii, 3-15; Kestenbaum, "The Gift of Healing Relationship," pp. 286-316 (specifically, 301-302).

ple. We join them, at times offering encouragement or concrete help, at other times simply witnessing their endurance, their pain, and with God's help, their resiliency.[4]

We need to be open to these moments whenever and wherever they may occur. We need to sit in the patient's moment, to be available and to listen actively to what this human being shares with us from his or her life story.

From these foundation stones, we can delve more deeply into an understanding of the relationship with the [*Tzelem*⇔*N'shamah*] in both the patient and the chaplain. In essence, the *ben* or *bat gil* is the individual who can find a way to reframe his or her life story pieces with the patient's own through empathic listening and genuine interest in the person in the bed. Through the rabbi's conscious effort, we can use these relationships to engender the creation of prayer in this setting.

I use three *midrashic*[5] images in rediscovering my own [*Tzelem*⇔ *N'shamah*] self each new hospital morning. These images allow me to discover afresh each day how my triangular relationship relating self, others, and the Divine is functioning on a given day.

The first is a marvelous *midrash,* taught to me by Reverend Joan Hemenway, about the relationship between rabbi/chaplain[6] and patient:[7]

> I, the rabbi, see the patient and the bedside as a beautiful tropical island. The island's beauty is breathless. From the crystal clear blue water, I can see a path from the dock to the patient's bedside. When I dock, the patient will serve as my tour guide, taking me from one wonderful setting to the next. Each path through the island has trees

---

4. Friedman, "Hitlavut Ruchanit," p. xi. Her biblical allusion is to Exodus 2:4.

5. *Midrash* is not just discovering nonliteral meanings for the TANAKH and other Jewish texts. We are reinterpreting text and adding new metaphors and story pieces to the sea of Jewish knowledge. In some ways, *midrash* to me is more metaphor than is the Jewish method of writing parable.

6. Please understand that my work *"self"* has a number of relational roles as a rabbi, a dayan, a Reform Jewish educator and a certified Jewish chaplain, who is different from who I was as a Congregational rabbi/educator and an intermittent chaplain. My own [*Tzelem*⇔*N'shamah*] is different now that I'm just in the hospital. In some way, rabbi and chaplain are interchangeable. To my non-Jewish readers, please remember that I serve as a multifaith chaplain. To make things easier for all my Jewish readers, I will use only rabbi from here forward.

7. Reverend Joan Hemenway, my CPE supervisor at Greenwich Hospital, Greenwich, Connecticut, Didactic, September 2000. She called it a parable and explained that the original metaphor came from the classic work *The Art of Pastoral Conversation,* by Heije Faber and Ebel Van derShoot (Nashville, TN: Abingdon, 1980; originally published in 1965), pp. 42, 46.

and flowers that represent different threads of the patient's life story pieces, relationships, and emotions. There are peaceful places and some ugly, hurtful places as well. Some paths are choked with vines. The patient needs to cut through them and might ask me for help. . . . In this beautiful setting, the patient is waiting for me to dock. I am a boat circling the island that is attempting to dock so that I can walk paths around the island with the patient. Some days, I am a battleship or an aircraft carrier, ready to barrel over anything that gets in the way of accomplishing clinical relational care that day. Some days, I am a frigate, darting in and out quickly. Some days, I am a submarine that takes a peek but never lands. On the best of days, I am a sailboat gliding into dock so I can stroll the island with the patient.

Now a second *midrashic* image is helpful. As the rabbi, I need to be like Robert Louis Stevenson, who sketched a map of Treasure Island before writing his book. He wrote:

The map was the chief part of my plot. It is my contention—my superstition, if you like—that he who is faithful to his map, and consults it, and draws from its inspiration, daily and hourly, gains positive support . . . [and] as he studies [the map], relations will appear that he had not thought upon.[8]

When I am aware of who I am as I approach the patient's island that day, I can mobilize the process of self-supervision that helps me function fully as a rabbi. As I sit in the moment, allowing my [*Tzelem*⇔*N'shamah*] relationship to meet my patient's [*Tzelem*⇔*N'shamah*] relationship, self-supervision activates my sense of these relationships and allows me to be aware of why I am reacting in the way that I am to what the patient is saying. What is triggering this reaction? Why is the conversation developing in this direction? What should I ask next? Why am I fleeing from this particular subject on this particular day? With these and other questions floating in my head, I reflect on what I am hearing and make the necessary adjustments as I continue my empathic listening. I reframe afterward through my own mind, and with the help of my supervisor, why and how this conversation took place. I reflect on what I could have done differently, and on what I might want to take with me into the next visit. This self-supervision better allows me to accompany the patient spiritually, and to transform myself into a *ben* or *bat*

---

8. Quoted by Miles Harvey in *The Island of Lost Maps* (New York: Random House, 2000), p. 39.

gil. In this way, my wounded places are less likely to get in the way of my empathic listening. This ensures that I can sit in the moment with the patient and walk with the patient throughout his or her island.

In my own mind, a third *midrashic* image provides another, more mystical way to activate [*Tzelem*⇔*N'shamah*] relationships. The middle point of every human being's chest features a slight indentation. I believe this to be where the Eternal One places a piece of the Divine Essence. Most important for the [*Tzelem*⇔*N'shamah*], however, is how each member of that person's "moralnet"[9] gives a little piece of his or her own Divine Spark to that other individual. What this means for the patient (or the family member) with whom I am engaging in a clinical caregiving conversation is that no one is ever alone. Through this connectedness of sparks, each individual is always part of a caring and concerned covenant community. For the patient, who feels a loss of control in a world that has shrunk to the size of a hospital bed, this sense of community relieves the pain of negative thoughts and feelings of hopelessness. For the family member, who cannot be physically present 24/7, it lessens the intensity of raw emotions (guilt, anger, fear, and the sense of being overwhelmed) that flood any individual maintaining a bedside vigil. Thus, a hospital bed becomes a tropical island full of life story pieces and healing relationships.

Use these *midrashic* images I can find a new way to listen empathically. By docking on the island, I hear the story of what brought this patient to the hospital, as well as story pieces from earlier life chapters that relate to the current situation. I hear about family members and how the patient relates to each of them. By sitting in the patient's moment, I experience his or her raw feelings of the moment and concerns about tomorrow and what shape the future will take.

What Is Spontaneous Prayer? How Do We Use It?

I ask myself internally a series of questions to clarify the two triangular relationships that are focused on the sense of *k'dushah*[10] present at the bedside. These are some of the ones that I find to be most useful:[11]

---

9. The *moralnet* is a psychosocial term for all the individuals with whom we form our closest relationships—our immediate family members and other relatives, our teachers, our friends, and our colleagues. This means that even my grandparents and my best teachers, who are long gone, are still a part of that net.

10. Holiness.

11. This is in addition to whatever spiritual assessment tool a chaplain uses to develop a spiritual care plan.

What is this patient trying to tell me?
Is any emotional thread or story piece repetitive?
What raw feelings has the patient shared with me?
Besides the patient and me, who else is in the room, and how does this
    shape clinical relational care?

In relating the [*Tzelem⇔N'shamah*] of the patient to my own, what I gather up, reflect, and reframe back to the patient is of paramount importance. The response is not just an empathic one. My [*Tzelem⇔N'shamah*] yearns to connect with the patient's. I want to create a holy space in which God is present as a partner in creating meaning and growth for the patient. My response takes the form of a spontaneous prayer that utilizes the answers to the previous questions. In essence, if this spontaneous prayer works, then it is a gift of connection between the people present in the room and God. It creates a *chatimah*[12] on the pastoral visit. By placing my seal through spontaneous prayer, I'm raising up respectfully, for the patient, the sublime beauty of having been given the gift of accompanying this human being for a moment. I want to convey clearly through this *chatimah* that the relational conversation ends with a blessing that values the life story pieces, the emotions, and the precious moments that we have shared together.

Different Ways to Create Spontaneous Prayer

Unleash the Power of Music

One way to create spontaneous prayer I learned from Mr. P, an African-American Episcopalian in his eighties:

Mr. P had been the director of his church choir for fifty years. He had also sung for over thirty of those years in a Reform Synagogue, which he called "his personal warm-up for every Sunday morning." He was DNR (do not resuscitate), CHF (chronic or congestive heart failure), and weary.

The first time that I visited him he said, "You have a nice speaking voice, Rabbi. I bet your singing voice is a sweet tenor. Could you sing me something?"

"What would you like to hear?"

"*Shalom Aleichem.*"[13]

So I began to sing quietly to him. After a moment, he joined me in his weak, but sweet, baritone voice as well.

---

12. A seal.
13. A Friday night hymn welcoming the Sabbath.

He smiled deeply and said, "That feels good, Rabbi. Do you have time to sing me something else?"

"What would you like, Mr. P?"

"That 'O Guide My Steps *Hashkiveinu*.'"[14]

"Wouldn't you like something from your house of worship or a folk song? You could give me the words . . ."

"No, no. Your soul is wide open to me when you sing. It fills my soul with hope and strength. It brings hope to my mind as well. Sing that song for me. Now don't whisper it. Can't hurt my roommate to feel it touch his soul too."

His roommate piped up, "Please, Rabbi. I agree with Mr. P. Your voice touches my soul."

Sighing, I took his hand in mine and began to sing:

"O guide my steps / And help me find my way / I need Your Shelter now / Rock me in Your arms / And guide my steps . . ."

Suddenly, Mr. P sighed and his voice, now rich in timbre and strength, continued with me: "And help me make this day / A Song of Praise to You / Rock me in Your arms / And guide my steps . . ."

Mr. P squeezed my hand and beamed at me. He asked, "Will you come again and sing it with me?"

"Yes, sir."

Over the next two weeks, we sang that song together every other day at the end of each clinical relational conversation. In some sense, this became our spontaneous prayer. It filled each of us with hope, patience, and strength. It had form. It had repetition. But each time when he had spoken enough, he would urge me to begin and he would join in.

A few months later, his daughter called me to tell me that her father made her sing that song with him every day. As he was dying, he said, "Sing it one more time so I can feel connected to that chaplain." He died peacefully in his own bed surrounded by his large family. With tears in their eyes, they sang it one more time together. His daughter told me, "It connected our souls with his. In our raw feelings of loss, we did what our father had done with us all our lives. We sang and we lifted those good feelings up to God."

Nothing compares to song when opening a window into my [*Tzelem* ⇔ *N'shamah*] relationship with another. Part of my own personal makeup is that I love to sing—and it helps that I have a good tenor voice. I use song when patients tell me of their great love for singing and how music serves as a necessary coping skill for them. I ask patients if I may hold their hands because I want to create a safe physical connection. When patients are very anxious before surgery, I will sometimes sing to calm them down. If patients are immobilized by the waiting or the pain that is dragging them down into feelings of hopelessness, then I might sing to free them. If patients are

---

14. Hymn from the evening liturgy.

facing end-of-life care, then I will sing something following a life review, some major decision, or recitation of a *vidui,*[15] to take the edge off the moment for the family members in attendance, or for the individual who is still alert and oriented.

As I listen to the life story pieces and relationships that patients are verbalizing, I search for an appropriate melody. Sometimes I ask patients to sing me a little something and then respond with a tune of my own. Sometimes patients ask for specific Jewish prayers or songs. If nothing particular comes to mind, then I fall back on the wordless melodies that we call *niggun.* Singing American folk, folk rock, holiday, or healing songs can open my [*Tzelem⇔N'shamah*] to patients or family members.[16] You need to find the songs that fit you.

Encourage Meditation and Guided Imagery

A second way to create spontaneous prayer is through meditation and guided imagery, as the following example demonstrates:

Mrs. T, an elderly Swedish and Lutheran patient, would leave for rehabilitation or to go home, only to end up back in the hospital a few days or a week or a month later.

During her second hospital stay, she looked at me and said, "What about that guided imagery stuff I've heard about? Do you think that you can think of something that will help me when all the bed thoughts[17] start to bite when my family isn't here? I told my nurse this morning that I feel like I'm slipping away. My nurse told me that she was present one day when you used guided imagery with another patient. The patient described something to you instead of you describing something to him. The patient felt better and so did she."

I took the hand that she offered to me and said, "We can try it if you like, but it will work better if you think of the right image. In your first hospital visit, your face lit up when you described to me the little church of your birthplace, and how it has brought you comfort to think about it. Or maybe you want to think of one of those special moments that you described to me about your

---

15. Prayer said when death is imminent.

16. For example: from Jewish folk rock, "Modeh Ani" or "Ma Yafeh HaYom"; from Kol B' Seder, "Walk with Me"; "Shir Chadash" by Julie Silver; "M'Shebayrakh," "Holy Place," "Tilfilat HaDerekh" from Debbie Friedman; a number by Steve Dropkin, such as "The World Yet to Come," "Let Us Rejoice," "We Share a Task," and "Light to the Nations."

17. The thoughts that occur from feeling isolated and hopeless when one is in a hospital bed for too long.

husband. Or maybe you want to remember a moment when you learned a new coping skill. What do you think will work?"

"Hmmm. How do I do it?"

"Put your feet firmly on the ground. Close your eyes. Lift up your shoulders, breathing in, and lower them, breathing out three times. Listen to your breathing for a moment. Then describe to me in short declarative sentences a picture of a life story piece. Just tell it to me like you told me the last time. Try to think of the little details and what your eyes see and what you are feeling. Don't forget to breathe in and out through your nose and your mouth."

"I'm a little girl. I'm going to church one Sunday morning. I can see the flowers in our front yard. I can feel the gentle breeze and hear it as it touches the leaves of the trees. How's that?"

"It's wonderful. Just keep on describing the walk. What did that path from the road to the church look like again? Just breathe in and out and continue."

"Let me see. We walk up a stone path made up of different sizes and shapes. They all fit together. The church is a very small and simple place. I can see the short straight steeple. I can see the whitewashed walls. I can see the simple colored windows that my grandfather placed in there with his own hands. Getting down on his knees so he can look me directly in the eye, the pastor smiles at me. . . . I'm not sure where to go next."

"Tell me what it was like to sit inside during the service."

"As I sit in there, I look around at the people and my mother tells me to sit straight. I feel safe. There are no strangers. There are only family and friends. Most of the time, everyone is kind to each other. The church is full of love and strength. I can feel the prayers moving gently upward. I can hear the music. I try to stay awake during the sermon. I try not to fidget. I feel my parents squeezing my hand, and smiling at me . . ."

Mrs. T paused for a moment and continued to breathe in and out. She had a smile on her face. Suddenly, she stopped and said, "This feels so good to remember. It feels like I'm praying with them. I don't feel so afraid. I feel content. I think that I'm going to open my eyes now."

For Mrs. T, it was enough to help her to talk to me more about what was happening to her. Every once in awhile, as the conversation continued, she would stop and smile. The remembering was not a formal prayer, but it served as one, having just flowed out of her mind and her heart.

It is not just my patients of Eastern religious paths who use this technique to pray spontaneously. I have also found that a picture of a labyrinth or a particular saint for a Christian patient, or a mandala[18] for a Hindu patient, that can be traced with a finger while breathing gently in and out, is an appropriate response. Sometimes I use a family picture as a guided imagery tool. Sometimes I ask patients to close their eyes and visualize a particular

---

18. A mandala has various designs, usually circular, and is a symbol of the universe.

person's spark piece that is attached to them. With Jewish patients, I use the breathing in and out of such words as *shalom, r'fuah, ahavah,* and *mishpachah.*[19] With other faiths, I suggest words that fit their spiritual paths. I encourage patients to choose a short prayer from their faith. With particularly anxious patients, I encourage them to visualize the Divine Breath traveling throughout their bodies, touching the places of pain or dealing with particular feelings that are causing patients to freeze or flee from their situations. Sometimes I use the "multiple spiritual paths" image—all roads leading up to God at the top of the mountain—developed by my tenth-century rabbinic forefather, Rabbi Baruch ben Meir of Barcelona,[20] to help patients feel more comfortable receiving a blessing from me. All of these active breathing meditations and guided images stimulate the relaxation response. Because they are individualized, and chosen at that moment, they become spontaneous prayers as well.

Fall Back on Tradition

Most of the time, to create spontaneous prayers, I simply try to find the right words as I sit in the patient's moment, as in the following example:

Mrs. D was a Holocaust survivor in her nineties. Her husband had died a few months earlier of congestive heart failure, and she had lost her children at Auschwitz. She found herself in the same room, and bed, as her husband had been in four months before. His presence was very strong and comforting, yet disconcerting at the same time. She was about to undergo surgery to repair a leaky heart valve and was feeling anxious, scared, and very alone. This is the spontaneous prayer that I spoke to her:

May God bless you and keep you.
May God fill you with grace and healing strength.
May God look deep into your mind and your heart
    and take the edge off your pain and your anxiousness.
    Because they prove that you are a human being and not a robot,
    may you be grateful for these deep and real feelings.

---

19. *Shalom* means "hello, good-bye, peace, wholeness"; *r'fuah* means "healing"; *ahavah* means "love"; *mishpachah* means "family."

20. This is an oral teaching passed down from rabbinic father to rabbinic son in my family. Rabbi Baruch ben Meir of Barcelona is the founding member of my continuous rabbinic line. The idea is that each faith has its own path. Each path has similarities with and differences from the others. No path is more valid than another. Each path is a good one for the individuals on it. Each individual walks differently up the mountain path. Some stop and smell the flowers. Some sprint. Some start up, go down a little, and then continue. Everyone ends up at the top of the mountain with the Divine.

Your husband's presence is very much present with you. As you
    remember your sixty-one years together, may it be more
    comforting than disconcerting.
May Dr. ———'s hands be quick, steady, and sure as he takes
    you through this surgery and back onto the path of healing.
Be grateful for your care.
Be grateful for your life partner whose calm presence beats so
    strongly inside of you and for your niece and nephew who will
    sit here and shower you with love and strength.
In the names of our fathers and mothers, praised are You who heals
    the sick, takes you safely through surgery, and from there back
    into the fullness of your life path.
Amen.

I compose my spontaneous pieces using formulaic phrases such as these:

May God bless you and keep you.
May God fill you with grace and healing strength.
May God look deep into your mind and your heart.
May Dr. ———'s hands be quick, steady, and sure.

Be grateful for your care.
Be grateful for your family member(s).
In the names of our fathers and mothers, praised are You who heals the
    sick, takes you safely through surgery, and from there back
    into the fullness of your life path.
Amen.

These formulaic phrases reflect and reframe some of the patient's presuppositions: that the hospital has an excellent reputation; that the surgery or procedure will be successful; that the postsurgery time will follow a pattern
from intensive care, to step-down, to regular rooms, to home or rehabilitation. The spontaneous prayer reinforces the patient's thoughts on these issues. I remind the patient that "I will pray over you tomorrow although you
might be asleep." Simple words, such as *after*—"after your test or procedure or surgery"—or *when*—"when you go home or to rehabilitation"—fill
the patient with hope and strength.

Then I add to these phrases what I've heard about the patient's life
story—his or her raw feelings and concerns—blending this into the prayer.
Following Rabbi Jack H Bloom's teachings about the process of curing and
healing for the spiritual exemplar in a pastoral care visit, I need to think
about what I hope to accomplish in this particular spontaneous prayer as I
accompany this patient:

What can I (the rabbi) do that will help this person heal, deal with pain, cope with permanent life changes, and even oncoming death? . . . To do this, rabbis need to learn as much as they can about the world their patients live in and how they structure reality. . . . How the people they are dealing with are organized; what maps they use to get around in life; how they think; how their belief systems work. To do this means knowing their "language," values, concerns, and resources. This means knowing their "history" as they perceive it and as others interpret it. . . . No two people respond the same way.[21]

These words are not meant to be all sweetness and light, but to bring up some issues that may need to be thought about more clearly. The patient may have expressed the need to cut through some of those vine-covered paths. Is there tension in the room between the patient and the family member by the bedside? Has the patient, in telling me life story pieces, brought up some wounded places that need to be included in the prayer? Have we touched a place that is too hot to handle?[22] How do I express, in this person's own language, some emotional knowledge that the patient has expressed but is not relating to usefully or fully?

I watch carefully both the body language of my patient and my own. I listen for the patient's quiet reactions to the words. I modulate the tone, rhythm, and pace of my voice as I speak the prayer as another means to convey the *chatimah* to this relational conversation. What other cultural and religious needs should I consider in developing this spontaneous prayer?

I need to remember that I am a spiritual accompanier and not a fixer. I respect the boundaries that the patient's [*Tzelem*⇔*N'shamah*] relationship has shared with me, and I use the patient's own language to reframe what was said to me. I am expressing what I have learned during our walk around the patient's island. Hopefully, we have explored far enough to track down something of meaning.

Finally, at times, I need to stop in the middle of a prayer to check in with the patient because clearly the patient is having difficulty following along or seems puzzled. Sometimes a patient interrupts, and I find myself asking these questions: Is the patient telling me that I've said enough? Did the prayer begin to trigger something else that the patient wants to talk about?

---

21. Jack H Bloom, *The Rabbi As Symbolic Exemplar: By the Power Vested in Me* (Binghamton, NY: The Haworth Press, 2002), p. 238. Within this chapter, Rabbi Bloom teaches a number of tools for finding out this information (see pp. 244-267). They are more for assessing than for the *chatimah* at the end of the visit.

22. This is a point of self-supervision as well. Am I reflecting the patient's or my own hot spot here? I need to ensure that it is the patient's and not my own.

Have I forgotten anything? What else does the patient wish me to include in this prayer? These questions allow me to assess what is taking place, and to transform what could be a broken spontaneous prayer into a whole one.

It does not matter what path the patient walks up the mountain to God. When I find a way to connect the patient's [*Tzelem⇔N'shamah*] relationship with my own, the words will ring true, calling forth an emotional response from the patient and words of gratitude for whatever form the spontaneous prayer takes. At such a moment, it is not unusual for a Catholic patient to call me "Father" or a Muslim patient to call me "Imam," or for any patient to tear up. This is clear affirmation of my success in formulating a spontaneous prayer that enriches the *k'dushah* at the bedside.

Creating the holy space at the bedside is contingent on who I am on any given day, how my [*Tzelem⇔N'shamah*] relationship is working, and whether I am available to become a *ben gil* and a spiritual accompanier to this particular patient. Without this understanding of who I am today, I could not create a holy space wherein my [*Tzelem⇔N'shamah*] relationship is open to the patient's, and both of ours are open to the Divine. Creating spontaneous prayer through song, meditation, guided imagery, and words of blessing is crucial work for the rabbi doing Jewish relational care. Each will find his or her own way. It is not always easy, but it is perhaps the most fulfilling work one can perform.

> May your dreams soar on eagles' wings,
> As you continue to walk the path of service,
> From strength to strength, and blessing and blessing.
> Amen.

– 13 –

Caring for the Non-Jews
Within Our Community

Gordon M. Freeman
Stuart Kelman

Foundation Myths: The Role of Narrative
in Defining Community

Communities do not exist in a vacuum. Those who count themselves as members of the same community share a common myth that provides unity and coherence. These underlying stories have various names: operative ide-

---

Author's Note: This chapter is part of a larger work of the Tiferet Project and was underwritten by a grant from the Haas Foundation of San Francisco. It was originally intended to refer specifically to the Conservative congregations of the Greater East Bay of Northern California. The following people participated in the original study as members of the Tiferet team: Rabbi Mark Bloom, Rabbi Ted Feldman, Rabbi Gordon Freeman, Rabbi Stuart Kelman, Rabbi Harry Manhoff, Rabbi Mimi Weisel, Rose Levinson, and Glenn Massarano. The editor (Jack H Bloom), believing that it applied to all heterodox congregations, chose to include it here.

als,[1] value concepts,[2] or foundation myths.[3] These narratives form the basis for what is seen as essential to the community. Foundation myths set the course and destiny for those who count themselves as part of the group. They are a key factor in defining where and how boundaries are set, who is in and who is out, what is required and what is expected.

As times change, the myths are reinterpreted in the search for new meaning and application to current issues. In fact, at times, the foundation story becomes irrelevant. Then the framing mythic narrative must be radically reshaped in the light of overarching realities.

For example, after the destruction of the Second Temple in 70 CE, the rabbis discerned that a new source of hope for survival was needed. They then placed their emphasis on Torah[4] as the source for salvation. The path to redemption was to be assured through participation in the study and observance of Torah. Reshaping foundation myths is no easy task, and it is one that happens gradually. Those who articulate the framing stories for the Jewish community find themselves grappling with texts,[5] with interpretation as it is expressed in law and custom, and with the reality of life as it is lived by the community in a particular time and place.[6]

Law, practice and observance, communal norms and institutions, events and celebrations all flow from the foundation myth and from the ideals that apply that story to life.[7] As rabbis, intimately involved with the lives of the people who are part of our community, it is clear to us that significant changes have occurred in our Jewish world. One in particular is the reality that increasing numbers of Jews marry or partner with non-Jews who do not choose to convert. In seeking to find ways of keeping the Jewish story continuous, and not casting out intermarried Jews who are committed to our destiny, our foundation myths need to be reexamined.

Changing the narrative always encounters resistance. A fiction is accepted that the story and tradition does not change or even evolve over time.

---

1. Robert MacIver, *The Web of Government* (New York: Macmillan Company, 1947). See also Neil Gillman, "The Problematics of Myth," *Sh'ma,* January 2002.

2. Max Kaddushin, *The Rabbinic Mind* (New York: Blaisdell Publishing Company, 1965).

3. Gordon M. Freeman, "Israelite Society in Transition," *Etz Hayim* (Philadelphia, PA: The Jewish Publication Society, 2001), pp. 1348-1352.

4. In the narrow sense, the Five Books of Moses; more broadly, all of Jewish learning.

5. Gordon M. Freeman, *The Heavenly Kingdom* (Lantham, MD: University Press of America, 1986), p. 59.

6. Ibid., p. 144 ff.

7. Freeman, "Israelite Society in Transition."

This is understandable, as much is at stake. Because communities are deeply invested in creating stability and preventing chaos, strategies are chosen to assert order. Often, such strategies include the denial of change. Mechanisms for overcoming denial are to be found, for example, in Talmudic discussions.[8] Anything regarding innovation is clothed in discovering precedent in previous teaching or authority. Since transformation always destabilizes the social fabric, change is disguised by invoking precedent. This use of precedent is a means of enabling the community to deal more comfortably with necessary change rather than to feel completely threatened by it.

To take one example: Rabbinic commentary on the revelation at Sinai abounds, yet little is found in the Bible itself that reflects this event. The book of Psalms constantly refers back to the events of the Exodus story and hardly even touches upon Sinai, despite the rabbinic emphasis on the latter. This shift in emphasis—from a focus on Sinai to one concentrating on Exodus—illustrates a shift in the dominating foundation myth. The significance of the Sinai myth is not challenged, nor is it discarded. Rather, the Exodus story comes to predominate.

Earlier Layers of the Myth

For the long term, another myth is chosen as the prevailing foundation myth. It is set atop the previous myth, forming a palimpsest,[9] one layer added to another. Previous layers (myths) are not discarded, but they shift under the preponderance of a new meaning structure. One foundation myth does not eliminate or replace an earlier narrative. The additional narrative augments what has gone before.

Another example of these kinds of changes is to be found after the destruction of the Temple and the abandonment of the sacrificial system. Texts describing prescribed offerings are still included in traditional liturgy. The mere mention of these offerings reminds readers of the Temple foundation myth. However, the context surrounding offerings has completely

---

8. Jacob Neusner, *Politics and Piety* (Englewood Cliffs, NJ: Prentice-Hall, 1973), p. 2 ff.

9. A palimpsest occurs when a manuscript inscription has been erased and another inscription is applied. The previous inscription(s) can still be detected and sometimes even recovered. An example is found in the language of the creation story, Genesis 1:2, where the word *t'hom* is used to refer to an abyss, whereas the word actually echoes the Babylonian *Enuma Elish* myth, which features the goddess Tiamat. The previous reference (Tiamat in Babylonian lore) has been erased and replaced by *t'hom*. We can still detect the original reference.

changed. Not only are sacrifices no longer offered, but the text describing
them is now embedded within the wider context of the Torah foundation
myth.

To repeat, ample precedence exists for such shifts.[10] In the past, events
occurred that were so catastrophic they completely changed the foundation
story of our people and radically transformed Jewish operative ideals, law,
observance, and practice. Cessation of offerings and the fact that prayer instead of the sacrifices became the central feature of Shabbat[11] and holiday
celebrations is but one significant example of a major shift. We are at such a
transition at the present time.

The Next Layer

Rabbi Yitzhak Greenberg, in his *Perspectives: The Third Great Cycle of
Jewish History,* posits that the Jewish People has experienced two previous
global changes to its myth.[12] He proposes that after the events of the Holocaust and the establishment of the State of Israel, we are at the beginning of
a Third Era.

Yet beyond the issue of the cycles he identifies, the central question remains the same for all three eras. It is the thread informing all narrative response. That question is, "What is the means to redemption?" or "How do
we create a redeeming world?" In response, we look to the foundation stories and how they have been interpreted. We also examine the possibility of
an altered narrative.

The first foundation myth is the Exodus, the ur-story of redemption (not
only for the Jewish People, but also for peoples throughout the globe). This
story is still told and included in liturgy and celebration, most notably Passover. Yet during the biblical period, this story became subsumed in yet another powerful narrative: the building of the Mishkan.[13] The answer to the
question regarding the road to redemption made a subtle turn from Exodus
to Temple. In fact, Passover was forgotten until King Josiah (640-609 BCE)
reinstituted its practice in dealing with the spiritual crisis of his day.[14]
While Temple narrative became a central myth line, it never eclipsed the
Exodus myth to the extent that it could be called a foundation myth. Rather,
it served to bridge the two myths.

---

10. Neusner, *Politics and Piety,* p. 3.

11. The Sabbath—a day for rest and renewal.

12. Yitzhak Greenberg, *Perspectives: Third Great Cycle of Jewish History* (New
York: The National Jewish Center for Learning and Leadership [CLAL], 1982).

13. The original portable Sanctuary.

14. II Kings 23:22.

Sinai framed the second major narrative of the Jewish people. Sinai began to take center stage after the destruction of the First Temple (586 BCE). Flowing from this story was the institution of Torah reading and study created by Ezra (500 BCE).[15] By the time of the destruction of the Second Temple, Sinai was the major foundation myth. Exodus was understood as the beginning of a process that led to Sinai. Shavuot was reinterpreted as a Torah-giving holiday, with the harvest aspect taking a secondary place. The road to redemption was now to be realized through the study of Torah and the observance of its teachings. *Halachah*[16] became the means of redemption.[17] The Sinai myth now coexisted with the Exodus foundation myth.

Greenberg suggests that the Third Era began with the Holocaust and Israel.[18] Some would argue, however, that the roots of change began with the destruction of ghetto life in Western Europe as a consequence of Napoleonic conquests. Jews now had another means of redemption: citizenship in the nation-state.[19] Judaism began to emphasize rituals and liturgy, much like Christianity.[20] The battle for meaning, for religionists in both traditions, was lost to the nation-state, which now became the operative ideal. Although the nation-state began the process of change, the Holocaust, as Greenberg dramatically proclaims, was the definitive crisis in meaning. A growing crisis in competing myths in the secular realm existed as well. Communism lost out to Capitalism as the prevailing ideology for developed nation-states.

For the Jewish People, the establishment of the State of Israel became the central focus of Jewish life. Political considerations overpowered the development of any other significant elements in communal life. All communal energy was devoted to supporting Israel and vulnerable Jewish communities throughout the world. Concern about individual spirituality was not on the communal agenda until recently. Given the breakdown of meaning climaxing with the Holocaust, and the rearrangement of meaning concomitant with secular shifts, the miracle is that, for the most part, Jews have chosen to remain Jews! Greenberg says that the Holocaust broke the covenant with God. At that point, he asserts, the Jewish People could have chosen to cease to exist.[21]

---

15. Nehemiah 8.

16. Jewish law; literally, the "way to go."

17. Jacob Neusner, *There We Sat Down* (Nashville, TN: Abingdon Press, 1972), p. 55 ff.

18. Irving Greenberg, *Voluntary Covenant* (New York: CLAL), p. 14 ff.

19. Howard Sachar, *The Course of Modern Jewish History* (New York: Dell Publishing Company, 1958), pp. 66 ff, 139.

20. Ibid., p. 147 ff.

21. Greenberg, *Voluntary Covenant.*

Greenberg goes on to argue that the establishment of the State of Israel became the new core of meaning, the framing narrative myth, for the Jewish people.[22] Some[23] would argue, however, that while the State of Israel has dramatically transformed Jewish life and holds deep reserves of meaning for Jews, it is problematic to identify it as the core of the Third Era's foundation myth. For one thing, Israel itself is a nation-state and struggles with powerful inner contradictions: how to maintain a Jewish state while dealing with a significant and growing non-Jewish population and how to function as a democracy without any appeal to non-Jews to join the Jewish people.

We look to different antecedents for our revised myth, rooting ours in the emergence of modernism in the eighteenth century. The increase of secularization and the breakdown of ghetto walls saw Jews shifting from traditional authority to one grounded more on the state and less on Jewish obligations. The increasing secularization of the world opened new possibilities for Jews, providing access to hitherto undreamed-of ways of joining a world not bounded by particularistic ties.

The changes that began in the eighteenth century are amplified and expanded for us in the twenty-first century. Jews live in a time when individualism dictates modes of behavior far more than does communalism. Greater participation in the context of our pluralistic world continues to be accompanied with a break from both tradition and rabbinic authority.

The New Reality

These factors present difficulties as well as opportunities. Within this pluralistic world, Jews are part of a mass society in which the individual loses significance. The notion of community is diminished as well. Goods and even services, for example, automated telephone responses, are mass-produced. Handcrafted articles and the works of artisans are in the realm of art rather than everyday utility. Polls, statistics, and mass culture all diminish the individual, making people an easy target for marketing and political manipulation.

The tension between upholding the communal aspect of Judaism, with its network of obligations and ethical demands, struggles with the competing call of a secular world that offers apparently limitless means for self-expression. Also, as Greenberg points out, the events of the Holocaust broke the covenant Jews had with God and gave further impetus to the need to understand that we all became Jews by choice.[24]

---

22. Ibid.
23. Ibid., p. 18.
24. Ibid., p. 14 ff.

In this Third Era, people command. God becomes manifest in human acts of justice, righteousness, and compassion. Like the rabbis, we are engaged in negotiating a new covenant. Those rabbis insisted that revelation, God's intrusion into communal matters, must cease. Responsibility for determining Jewish life must be completely within the human realm.[25]

But unlike the rabbis then, who saw *themselves* as determining how matters in the human realm were to be handled, we have now opened this process up to the Jewish community at large. The current process of decision making takes into account a great number of determinants, many of them stemming from the attitudes and outlooks of those who make up the *kahal*.[26] The covenant has been transformed from obligatory to voluntary. This represents a profound change, with a consequent need to reframe our guiding story.

Integrating the New Reality into the Jewish Myth

We propose that the foundation myth for this Third Era is the Creation narrative. From it flows the potential to shape communal decisions based on the value of the individual. Individual worth comes from personal uniqueness and a system that is based on equality. Franz Rosenzweig posits that God's creating is the beginning of self-expression, that creation is the granting by God of the opportunity for everyone to find his or her own way in making a unique contribution to the process of redemption.[27] The Creation story is based on the concept that every individual, Jew and non-Jew, modeled after and molded by Divinity has intrinsic worth.[28] Choosing the Creation myth as the foundation story for our era does not obviate revelation.[29] Creation values are counterintuitive in our mass society, obscured by a pervasive attempt to reduce people and ideas to the lowest common denominator. Rabbis, therefore, must rely upon revelation as the basis for authority in implementing creation values. Revelation provides the footing upon which the efficacy of creation values rests.

---

25. Talmud Bavli: Bava M'tzia 59a.

26. Jewish community.

27. Franz Rosenzweig, *The Star of Redemption,* trans. William Hallo (Oxford, England: The Littman Library of Jewish Civilization, 1984), p. 113.

28. Genesis 1:26-27 and Genesis 2:7.

29. See Jon Levinson, *Exodus and Sinai* (Minneapolis, MN: Winston Seabury, 1985). He explains that the Sinai story had little impact in the Bible itself. For example, it is hardly mentioned in the Book of Psalms, which constantly refers to the events surrounding the Exodus.

Divine revelation in our time, however, cannot be the same as our first reading of Sinai in Exodus 19-20. The sense of revelation for us is to be found in the Aleph of Anochi.[30] It is the divine spark within each one of us. In the resultant claims and counterclaims, covenant becomes an agreement-making process to create a beneficial community based on pluralism and mutual respect.

During this era, redemption is to be transformed to a process, a verb. Redeeming the world is an everyday process of keeping promises and thereby building trust. Redeeming the world means that the values of Creation will lead us to understand that the divine spark inhabits everyone and every aspect of creation. It is the foundation for a Judaism open to participation, to an acceptance of pluralism as both real and another part of the divine plan.

The question of the role and place of non-Jews in the context of the Jewish community is not a new one.[31] Under changing circumstances, however, the response to the question changes. Biblical literature reflects the self-confidence of a majority culture, one not threatened by its non-Jewish inhabitants. Israelites were taught to protect the *ger toshav*,[32] with the added reminder to remember that we ourselves were once resident aliens (in Egypt).[33] Israelites were enjoined to treat this vulnerable population with justice and compassion.

We know of two distinct groups of non-Israelites. The *ger toshav* chose to live among Israelites, taking upon themselves the obligations of taxation and obedience to the law as resident aliens. Their relationship to the government assumed consent to Israelite government. Their relationship to the culture was based on mutual obligations.[34] The second group of non-Jews was not part of the culture and did not live among the Israelites. These non-Jews sent delegations when the Temple was dedicated and offered sacrifices. Their voluntary participation in Temple ritual was accepted.[35]

---

30. Gordon M. Freeman, "On Translating Our Heritage into Contemporary Language," *Proceedings of the Rabbinical Assembly* (New York: Rabbinical Assembly, 1994), pp. 167-171. One Chasidic master taught that the Israelites heard only the first letter of the first word (the *alef* in *anokhi*, which is a silent letter) and intuitively understood the rest (Menahem Mendl of Rymanov). The Rabbinical Assembly and the United Synagogue of Conservative Judaism, *Etz Hayim: Torah and Commentary* (Philadelphia, PA: The Jewish Publication Society, 2001), p. 441.

31. The issue of the relation to non-Israelites begins in the Bible. See Joel Rembaum, "Dealing with Strangers: Relations with Gentiles at Home and Abroad," in *Etz Hayim*, pp. 1377-1382. See also Shaye J. D. Cohen, *The Beginnings of Jewishness: Boundaries, Varieties, Uncertainties* (Berkeley, CA: University of California Press, 1999).

32. Resident alien.

33. Leviticus 24:22.

34. Rembaum, "Dealing with Strangers," p. 1379.

35. I Kings 8:41-43.

Even though those who were classified as *ger toshav* were under no communal obligation to do so, they could voluntarily offer sacrifices.[36] The exception to this voluntary offering was the Passover celebration.[37] Because the Passover redemptive stories of the Exodus and Temple were not part of the *ger toshav*'s experience, the communal obligations stemming from these stories made sacrificial offerings inappropriate.

This entire situation changed when Jews lost their majority status at the time of the first exile and became a minority, often living under hostile conditions. Mutual distrust and antagonism arose between Jews and non-Jews during difficult times. Even in the best of situations, Jews were often merely tolerated. The dominant culture's attitude toward Jews was contemptuous. Jewish attitudes in turn were marked by feelings of superiority.[38]

In summary, the redemptive story changed from the Exodus tale to the Sinai narrative. This master narrative emphasized the exclusive relationship between the Jewish People and God, mirroring a social reality in which Jews were set apart from the dominant culture and forced to look more intensely inward for meaning and validity. In light of both social circumstances and theology, the question of the role of the non-Jew in the Jewish community was moot. In fact, one could say that it remained a silent part of the story until the events of the mid-1900s, with the explosion of a Jewish presence in the diaspora, especially in the United States.

Obligation and Community

With the secularization of the state and loss of regnant power of religious institutions at the end of the eighteenth and nineteenth centuries came the universalization of communal obligations. Both Jews and non-Jews were citizens of the state. Religious affiliation was secondary. Concomitantly, interpersonal contact between Jews and non-Jews increased. Attitudes toward Jews and Judaism became more respectful. Intermarriage increased.

Placing the Creation narrative on the top layer of our palimpsest ushers in a framework for a world allowing pluralism and participation to coexist—to the enhancement and enrichment of Judaism. Embracing this as our current, primary narrative makes it possible to acknowledge that a Jew married to a non-Jew and a non-Jew married to a Jew can both have a place in the community. It opens a way to validate the commitments made by intermarried families to the history of our people. The alternative is to cast out those

---

36. Exodus 12:48.
37. Numbers 15:14-16.
38. Sachar, *Course of Modern Jewish History,* p. 223.

who would join their destiny to ours were they permitted to do so. We are guided by a narrative that honors the God of Israel and finds ways to permit God's manifold creatures to dwell inside the Jewish tent.

Both the Exodus and the Sinai foundation myths are exclusive, permitting only certain of God's people to be part of the narrative. The Creation myth maintains that we all are God's creatures. It allows us to enlarge the narrative and to find a place for those who are "other."

The Creation myth also makes room for us to acknowledge that, in this Third Era, any community is based on the obligations that people choose to accept. The choice is voluntary, but once inside the community, obligations can be negotiated within the system. Thus, we can still define and maintain those boundaries which we recognize as crucial to maintaining Jewish integrity. With Creation as the key paradigm, redeeming the world means that the values of creation lead us to understand that the divine spark inhabits everyone and every aspect of creation. It is open to both participation and to pluralism, while not negating boundary maintenance.

To flourish, we must recognize that non-Jews married to Jews are linked to our community but not commanded to honor our obligations. In validating their place among us, we need to define what linkages do obtain and propose a means by which non-Jews can participate in nonobligatory areas of communal existence.

More to the point, we must recognize that Jews are the ones who experience most intensely a sense of alienation and rejection when their non-Jewish life partners have no standing within communal walls. For many Jews, the attempt to remain part of the community while also negotiating a successful life partnership sets up unbearable tensions. Often the Jew chooses to leave the community altogether rather than try to navigate within a sea of contradictions and perceived scorn.

Including the Other: Karov Yisrael

Redefining our guiding foundation story enables us to find valid ways to include our intermarried person, Jew and non-Jew, within the synagogue walls and community. By so doing we do not dilute our tradition. What we do is increase our numbers, finding a place for those non-Jews who dwell among us, and help to ensure that their children take their place as Jews.

However, designating people as "non-Jews" is exclusionary because it makes them nonpersons. One of the key concepts that we learn from the Creation narrative is that each person is modeled after and molded by Divinity and is therefore special and unique, like God. Hence, it is not right to treat the "other" as a nonentity. The Jewish community can also provide recognition to supportive non-Jews in our midst as a means of applying the inclusive values of the Creation myth without imposing obligations on them. One term, *Karov Yisrael,* created by the Tiferet team, has the double meaning of "relative" and someone who is close. It also reflects the sense of offering because it shares the same root with the word *korban.*[39]

We believe that *Karov Yisrael* is the best designation for those non-Jews who dwell among the Jewish people as the spouses, partners, and children of Jews. People studying for the purpose of conversion would also be considered a *Karov Yisrael. K'rovei Yisrael* are non-Jews who, while not under the jurisdiction of Jewish law *(Halachah)* and hence not obligated to observe the law, have drawn near to the Jewish community by affiliating with and participating in the life of the synagogue.

An analogy with the notion of the Latin phrase *amicus curiae*[40] is helpful. In legal terms, this is someone who is not a party to a lawsuit but who petitions the court or is requested by the court to file a brief on the basis of having a strong interest in the subject matter at hand. A *Karov Yisrael,* like an *amicus curiae,* has no legal standing because he or she is not bound or under the jurisdiction of Jewish law, but he or she does have a strong interest in the matter at hand—Jewish law and custom as it pertains to being intermarried.

As in much of Hebrew translation, the term can be rendered in a number of ways. We take it to mean "relative of the Jews" or "close to the Jews." This gives the designation maximum utility for our intent: naming and acknowledging the non-Jews who are an intimate part of our story.

In most cases, *K'rovei Yisrael* have no immediate intention of converting to Judaism. In some cases the *K'rovei Yisrael* practice no religion, and in other cases, they personally practice another religion outside the context of the synagogue. Still, they want to be recognized as partners with the Jewish people and as persons who have cast their lot in with the synagogue community by their presence and by their social, financial, and political support. They no longer wish to be ignored or treated as if they do not matter or, worse, as if they are a threat. They also wish to know what the parameters and boundaries are for their participation in the life of the synagogue, respecting the fact that not being Jewish forecloses certain possibilities.

The term *Karov Yisrael* is meant to be used internally, within the synagogue community. This term is meant to recognize the presence of allies and friends among us. The term is meant to apply to any non-Jew who is intermarried (or variously partnered) and affiliated with our synagogues. It

---

39. The sacrificial offerings presented in the ancient Temple.
40. Friend of the court.

also may apply to non-Jewish persons who are widowed or divorced and seek to remain part of the community to which they belonged while partnered. Giving them a "name" provides rabbis, lay leaders, and Jewish educators with a useful framework that facilitates their work with intermarried families.[41] Naming *K'rovei Yisrael* will strengthen efforts to have intermarried families make Jewish choices for their children, observe Jewish life more fully in their homes and synagogues, and identify with the ongoing narrative that is the life and history of the Jewish People. Giving a name will also retain and bring Jews into the synagogue by eliminating the need for them to choose between their partners and their community.

We must find some ways to honor those moments in a human life that are key markers in the human journey from birth to death. The intermarried who dwell among us give us many things—including their Jewish children. We can do no less than find a way not to rob them of the dignity of being a recognized part of our shared destiny.

Judaism is in a constant state of transformation, while maintaining core values. The Exodus/Temple myth provided the Jewish People with identity and purpose, origin, and destiny. The Sinai/Torah myth redefined the previous myth in terms of the exclusive, revelatory relationship with God in the context of a new reality, one of destruction of the center and exile from the land. Without the exclusive quality of this myth, the Jewish People would not have been able to survive. Persecution and oppression could be accepted only within a belief system that understood a dreadful reality: We were excluded from the world, and so we excluded the world. We became a community based on covenantal obligations, a constant reminder of our acceptance of the revelatory Torah. That sense of obligation became the meaning of participating in the Jewish community.

We are living in a world that no longer excludes us, for the most part. Social integration has been a blessing because it means that we are treated as individuals and the boundaries between Jews and non-Jews have become increasingly fluid. We need to maintain the sense of community based on obligation. The Creation myth is basically inclusive. Every person contains a unique divine spark. Justice demands that all people be treated based on their own merits. Accepting this core myth means that our obligations as a Jewish community must be founded on this concept of justice. Our challenge is to become an inclusive community while not abandoning the obligations that maintain the integrity of the Jewish People.

---

41. See Jack H Bloom, *The Rabbi As Symbolic Exemplar: By the Power Vested in Me* (Binghamton, NY: The Haworth Press, 2002), Chapter 10, "Witnessing, Naming, and Blessing."

We redefine our community by realizing that not everyone has the same obligations. The *K'rovei Yisrael* have chosen to participate in our community without converting to Judaism. We celebrate this choice by including them without imposing *Halachic* obligations on them. We treat the *K'rovei Yisrael* with respect and recognize their presence. That behavior is basic to the communal obligation that we learn from the Creation myth. By carefully examining Jewish law, we can determine areas of inclusion that do not impose Jewish obligations on persons who do not have them and do not abuse the sensitivity of Jewish practice.

14

Caring for Non-Jews Outside
Our Community

Judith B. Edelstein

A rabbi received a call at 12 a.m. just as she was going to sleep. It was a stormy night. The thunder was so loud that she could barely hear the muffled voice on the other end. "Rabbi, please come to me. I am dying, and I want to see you before I die." She jotted down the name and address, got dressed, ran out, and, after a long wait in the icy wind, eventually hailed a taxi. When she arrived at the caller's house, she was shocked to see crosses on the wall. "Why did you call me?" she gasped. "Why didn't you call a priest?" The person stared at her as if she were an imbecile. "Do you think I'm going to call a priest out in weather like this?"

Much about Jewish life has become common parlance to Americans at large: what we eat, Yiddishisms,[1] bar/bat mitzvah,[2] etc. As a result of our culture's dissemination through the media, and the high rate of intermarriage, most rabbis today work in an ever-expanding arena in which they come into contact with, and have the potential to influence, people who are not Jewish. In addition, many worthy institutions that serve anyone who comes through their doors bear the word *Jewish* in their name. Jewish Home and Hospital Lifecare System, Long Island Jewish Hospital, and Jewish Board of Family Services, which are all in New York, are three that come to mind immediately. Within institutional contexts as chaplains, teachers, heads of organizations, and professionals in the myriad other careers rabbis pursue, and as officiators at ceremonies for many life cycle events, rabbis

---

1. Yiddish expressions that have passed into English, such as *kosher, chutzpah,* or *kvetch.*

2. At age thirteen, a young person is obligated for the fulfillment of God's commands. The occasion is marked by being called to the reading of the Torah, and participating as an "adult" in the service.

find themselves ministering to Christians as well as to Jews. Our seminaries provide little preparation or training for this, which leaves many rabbis unprepared for, and uncomfortable with, the encounter.

Having had the blessing of many opportunities to work in an interfaith environment, I am pleased to offer a brief overview of some of my experiences that have greatly shaped my rabbinate. Being in a position where I am the Jewish representative in a multiethnic situation has not only sensitized me to the needs of those with whom I interact but also made me conscious of always wanting to be on my best behavior. This in itself is a reward. In addition, my life has been immeasurably enriched as a result of the diversity.

My first experience working as a rabbi with non-Jews occurred when I was a student on a chaplaincy rotation in a hospital. I chose to visit Christian as well as Jewish patients since, prior to seminary, I had worked in ecumenical settings and wanted to interact again with individuals from a variety of backgrounds. By and large the Christians whom I visited were eager for my presence. They greeted me warmly and were touched that a rabbi would come to visit them. Some were more enthusiastic than others, but they were all polite and most accepted and appreciated the ecumenical prayers and blessings I offered. In my first role in the world as "rabbi," I was amazed and touched to see non-Jews react so positively to a Jewish representative of God.

Another privilege I had as a student was teaching several courses to adults at a local Methodist church. It was among my most satisfying teaching/learning experiences. The group included retired ministers and Sunday school teachers. These students wanted to know as much as they could about Jewish perspectives on the Bible as well as basics about Jewish practices. They were eager to share their impressions with me and loved the interchange of our ideas, as did I. In fact, I believe that I learned more than they did because my exposure to Christianity prior to that point took place through only a Jewish lens.

Following ordination I worked as the rabbi of a Conservative synagogue where I learned that approximately 20 percent of the couples were intermarried. The board of trustees was shocked when I provided them with this information. In fact, the non-Jews were hiding. Very few of the members were aware of the high percentage of non-Jewish spouses, or even who they were. I must point out that these spouses were extremely respectful of me. The Catholics, in particular, expressed a preference for formality in relationship to me and to the services. Whereas I was attempting to introduce more English and to curtail the length of certain services to be more inclusive and to increase synagogue attendance, the Christian spouses sought sanctity, quietude, and the tradition of a church. They were happy with neither the din of children running around the sanctuary nor the requisite monthly Friday night Hebrew school class on the *bimah*[3] leading prayers.

Although these gentile spouses were not "official" congregation members, I interacted regularly with them, especially since many of their children were enrolled in the religious school. As a rule, these parents wanted to support their children at the temple without having to adopt Jewish practice themselves or introduce ritual into the home. In fact, they were not so different from many of the households composed of two Jews. Essentially they were asking the rabbi, "How can I get my child through *bar/bat mitzvah* without changing our family life?"

My approach to guiding these nonmembers, and wrestling with Jewish law, derived from my own desire to invite them in, if not to join us officially, then at least to feel comfortable while their families participated. I was always conscious of my obligation to treat them as I would want to be treated in their houses of worship. They needed me to cajole and to encourage them as I interpreted and stretched traditional Jewish practice so that they could participate in some way without feeling guilty. I did not learn any of these tactics in seminary.

A colleague of mine who had supervised the conversion of a woman marrying a Jew by choice referred the couple to me to officiate at their wedding, as she was not available. The *chatan*[4] had been married to, and divorced from, a born Jew. I was impressed that Judaism meant so much to him that he wanted his new wife to convert. During our counseling sessions prior to the wedding, I learned that the bride-to-be's family members, besides her parents, were unaware of her conversion. In fact, very few knew that it would be a Jewish wedding. The only Jews at the wedding would be the couple, the groom's two children, and two Jewish friends—just enough to sign the *ketubah*[5] and hold the *chuppah*[6] poles.

I was concerned about the secrecy and decided to invite the parents of the bride to meet with me before the ceremony. It was an act of intuition. When the mother came without the father, I knew the family had issues. After a superficial conversation in which she remonstrated that all she wanted was her daughter's happiness, she burst into tears. Eventually she admitted that "it" was not what she had envisioned for her daughter, but that she knew she had to accept "it." She also revealed that her husband had not come to terms with

---

3. The front of the synagogue where the rabbi and cantor officiate.
4. Groom.
5. Marriage contract outlining the duties and responsibilities of the couple to each other.
6. Canopy that the wedding couple stands under during the ceremony, symbolic of the Jewish home the couple will establish together.

"it." My heart ached for them. They were no different from most Jewish parents I know. This Catholic mother needed to talk to someone about her sorrow and disappointment over her daughter's choices, and she was ashamed to discuss this with her priest, so she consulted this rabbi instead. At the wedding the mother expressed her deep gratitude to me for our conversation.

Following my tenure in the synagogue I began working at the Jewish Home and Hospital Lifecare System in New York. As I mentioned earlier, despite its name, it actually caters to a mixed multitude. In fact, one aspect of working at the facility that pleased me when I began working there was the opportunity to minister to, and work with, a variety of people. Something about living and working with Jews exclusively during the previous years had begun to feel like my personal *mitzrayim*.[7] As a Jewish chaplain, however, I was charged with making pastoral visits to all who entered our doors, as well as with being the clergyperson for the staff.

My experiences during the past several years have been far more rewarding than I had ever anticipated. They have also heightened my awareness of some of the differences between Jews and non-Jews, while illuminating the commonalities between us. These new understandings continually challenge and motivate me to provide new sources of spiritual support for all our patients, residents, and staff, regardless of their religion.

During my first year at the nursing home, I walked the floors and visited with anyone who would let me in the room. Once I got through the door, most of those who could still communicate admitted me to the recesses of their hearts. I was, and continue to be, consistently greeted by staff as well as patients and residents, Jews and non-Jews, across racial lines. They were, and still are, eager to tell their stories and to be blessed. In a setting such as ours, where most people's days are numbered and so many are alone, the rabbi plays an extremely significant role.

We (a cantor and I share the job) set the tone as the spiritual and religious leaders for the institution and therefore are viewed as very important figures. Even though we are not Christian (the majority of our non-Jewish residents are Christian, with less than 10 percent being from other religious faiths or proclaimed atheists), residents still count on us to bring a feeling of Godliness into their sphere. We make a major difference in their lives as we listen attentively to their suffering and express support for their religious and life choices. We help them make sense of a world that, for many, has abandoned them.

For some, we are the only people with whom they can cry or express their innermost pain. We encourage them to let go of past assumptions about life

---

7. Colloquial for a place of servitude, as was Egypt *(Mitzrayim)* for the Jews.

and try to wean them off of a sense of pride that does not ask for help, or that bases itself on accomplishment. Simultaneously, we attempt to gently guide them toward a sense of self that communes with God. When they are actively dying, we are at their side with words of comfort, gentle song, and hand-holding. We do the same for their families and friends, as well as staff.

When I realized that many of the residents were physically unable to attend religious services in the assembly hall (we provide Jewish, Catholic and generic Protestant services led by Catholic and Protestant chaplains), I decided to hold an afternoon service (based on *minchah*[8]) on the residential floors. So many non-Jews wanted to pray that this *minchah* service evolved into what has become a spiritual support group for residents and patients of all faiths. It serves the dual function of enabling me to connect with a number of individuals whom I would not otherwise have the time to see as well as fostering a sense of community among them.

At our meetings, those capable of speaking raise some of the problems they confront on a daily basis and discuss their strategies for solving them. After each person has spoken briefly, I select a theme directly connected to their collective comments. A discussion evolves followed by prayers, songs, and a blessing. Those who are not able to speak because of medical problems or dementia simply listen. Although I may not hear their voices, I frequently see their lips move and their fingers tap as we sing such songs as *Kumbiya* and *Hinei Mah Tov.*[9]

Many of the residents look forward to our group, so much so that when I go onto the floor to visit someone, people ask if it is time for the prayer meeting. One day I had a private pastoral visit with Mabel, an eighty-six-year-old, African-American group participant. I am drawn to Mabel because of the incredibly kind expression in her eyes, though she rarely spoke during the group, as a result of a stroke that had affected her speech. I was moved to tears as she slowly and painfully revealed herself to me, expressing her fear of going to hell because of her sins. Several weeks later, following one of our "prayer meetings," as I was saying good-bye to her, she pointed to the staff member who was coleader of the group with me and, slowly, quietly, yet emphatically, said, "Tell her to take me to your church. I want to pray in your church. Wherever you preach, I want to be there."

From Mabel I have learned that Christians who are part of our ministries want rabbis to care about them just as much as our Jewish congregants desire it. And when we are in a Jewish setting, they especially need for us to be sincere about our concern for the health of their physical and spiritual lives. If they cannot express their spiritual needs to us, we are useless to them.

---

8. The Jewish afternoon service.
9. Hebrew folk songs.

It is not necessary for us to share their tenets, but we must validate their pain and joy. On the most obvious level, non-Jews want to be treated with respect for their religious beliefs. In the same way that Jews resent proselytization, so do non-Jews resent Jews asserting superiority. Although I also educate during group discussions by pointing out theological and ritual differences, I never assert that one approach is better than the other.

Similarly, non-Jews desire us to be informed about their religions. Since rabbis are viewed as teachers, it is incumbent upon us to reveal at least a superficial knowledge about other religions. As excellent teachers are cognizant about subjects tangential to their own specialties, good rabbis should know the basics about the other major religions. Most of the non-Jews I work with look up to rabbis. They seem to expect us to take leadership positions, particularly on issues of morality and social conscience.

Last, and probably most important, non-Jews seek compassion from rabbis. They desire our warmth, consideration, and empathy, just as their Jewish counterparts do. We could think of meeting their needs by calling upon our most religious inner resources, putting our best foot forward—as we would behave toward any Jew we encounter—while suspending ritual.

Rabbis interacting successfully with non-Jews requires no magic but, instead, awareness, sensitivity, honesty, an open mind, and the consciousness that we are all modeled after and molded by Divinity, each created [*Tzelem*⇔ *N'shamah*].[10] Seminaries would do well to add a course on this topic to their curricula, for it would go a long way toward better understanding among religions. Finally, on the most simplistic level, rabbis need to treat non-Jews in the same way that they would like to be treated. As R. Yohannan said:

> What is the meaning of "All faces are turned to paleness" (Jer. 30:6)? The words "all faces" refer to [the angels], God's household in heaven; and to [Israel], God's household on earth . . . the Holy One says, "These [the Gentiles] are My handiwork, and those [Israel] are My handiwork."[11]

---

10. See Chapter 1, "Premises of Jewish Relational Care," in this book.
11. Babylonian Talmud: Sanhedrin 98b.

15

What We Gentiles Need
in Jewish Relational Care:
A Minister's Perspective

Richard L. Rush

If we extend the [*Tzelem⇔N'shamah*] paradigm[1] that underlies this book into the realm of "what Gentiles need from rabbis," we must begin with rabbis themselves.

The degree to which rabbis are aware and accepting of this understanding of their *"selves,"* and the degree to which they are at peace with working to maintain their balance (albeit as a "work in process"), will inevitably shape their relationships with Gentiles, as well as with others.

Rabbis, ever laboring to be at peace with their [*Tzelem⇔N'shamah*] within, must ask themselves, "Why do I want to bother to take time away from personal or parochial matters, exposing myself to unrequired risks, by relating with the Gentile population other than in cursory or phatic modes?" Surely, part of the answer to this largely nonrhetorical query is, "That I may thereby encounter and come to recognize kindred human beings and be nourished in relationships with them." The [*Tzelem⇔N'shamah*] paradigm is not simply a *Jewish* construct; it is a "God-given" universal human condition. We Gentiles may not have mastered all the terminology of the construct, but many of us surely understand its significance.

If indeed rabbis, as [*Tzelem⇔N'shamah*] within themselves, are in stasis, then they recognize that, as exemplars, they model, portray, illustrate, reveal, and convey what is within them to those with whom they relate (or seek to relate), gradually moving from the shrouded, through the opaque, to the transparent. They become a conduit for the "teaching" to others of their

---

1. [Breath-Taking⇔Model of Divinity]. See *ABC's of Jewish Relational Care* in this book; for further explication, see Jack H Bloom, *The Rabbi As Symbolic Exemplar: By the Power Vested in Me* (Binghamton, NY: The Haworth Press, 2002), especially Chapters 6 and 8.

recognition and acceptance of the balance and tension of the *"selves"* within them (the [*Tzelem*⇔*N'shamah*] paradigm), thereby eliciting a recognition of the *"selves"* within by others, thus engendering a *"selves"*-fulfilling recognition.

In relationships with Gentiles, rabbis become light bearers, shapers (or reshapers) of language by which the [*Tzelem*⇔*N'shamah*] and its attendant awakenings can be recognized, owned, and applied—in this instance by non-Jews. If indeed "relationship is the basic religious and psychological unit," then both rabbis and Christian clergy are called by the same Holy One to find, share, and nourish (and be nourished by!) relationship and interaction that makes each of us whole. Thus connected, we share glimpses of what can be possible for us and for those for whom we each serve as symbolic exemplars. That, I believe, is a *mitzvah*[2] for us both.

Just as I cannot speak for all Gentiles, so I cannot pretend to speak for all Christians or Christian clergy. However, that in itself prompts an early caveat: Since Christians, their churches, clergy, beliefs, and practices, come in many different "flavors," my remarks need to be set in the context of my experience with local rabbis over my thirty-three years of ministry in First Church Congregational of Fairfield, Connecticut. Thus, my experience must not be read as an exact template for Jewish-Christian relationships in entirely different contexts, but merely as a recounting of what happened, what worked, and what might be adapted to other situations.

Huge differences exist between the Greek Orthodox Church, the Roman Catholic Church, and, say, a Methodist, Presbyterian, or Congregational church (United Church of Christ usually), let alone a local Pentecostal or Independent Evangelical/Fundamentalist congregation. Some of the differences are historic, some have to do with basic beliefs and theology, and some have to do with preferred focus and practice. We do not all believe the same things. We do not all practice our professed faith similarly. That fact alone may well vex and puzzle any rabbi. Who, then, speaks for us Christians? *No one individual.* Thus, answers to rabbis' queries about what works on an interfaith basis may receive varying responses, depending on the one to whom they are addressed.

Even more disconcerting is that individual clergy in the same denominations may differ widely in their theologies, practices, and focus. Some clergy are open and embracing of interfaith relationships and activity; others are fearful or couldn't care less about them. Saddest of all are the few who, for reasons of their own exclusive theologies, will not minister to anyone (Jew or Gentile) who does not subscribe to the same formulations.

---

2. In Hebrew, fulfilling God's command; in Yiddish, a good deed.

Finding out who among the local clergy are open, receptive, and even enthusiastic about interfaith issues is the starting point for building relationships that will eventually embrace more and more "others."

A beginning point is a local clergy group, if one exists. In my experience, we started from scratch by sending out a gentle generic invitation: "Is there anyone among us interested in some kind of occasional coming together as clergy to get to know each other and to share concerns?" The first positive response came the next day from a rabbi of a Conservative congregation. What evolved into a rich, and lasting, set of relationships had begun.

That may not always be true. I have witnessed other clergy associations that were insensitive to Judaism and to rabbis. Again and again their thrust was "Christian oriented," both in terms of topics (and language) and activity. The use of Christian "triune formulae"[3] publicly, or within the group itself, continued unabated. Their focus on planning communal events around Christian seasons (Advent, Lent, Holy Week, Pentecost) surely created roadblocks in the pathway to establishing levels of comfort, rapport, inclusiveness, and mutuality on a truly interfaith level.

What Do We Need from Rabbis?

The following qualities are necessary to establish beneficial interfaith relationships:

* A meaningful *presence* in the community: Rabbis should be recognizable, approachable, responsive, and involved (rather than distant, unresponsive, and disengaged) in our shared community.
* A sustained *willingness to reach out:* Rabbis should either respond to others' invitations or act on their own personal initiative to find common ground for participation in and contribution to the larger community we share.
* A *comfort with building bridges:* Rabbis should encourage understanding and appreciation among the religious communities, affirming their distinctiveness and celebrating their commonalities.
* A *desire to labor with others* in the community: Rabbis should be willing to work for the common weal of all, regardless of their circumstances.

The very last things we need from rabbis are their absence, noninvolvement, and silence.

---

3. "In the name of the Father, and the Son, and the Holy Spirit" or "Through Jesus Christ our Lord."

Building these interfaith bridges could begin with seminal encounters and appointments: a cup of coffee and a chat to share some life event that is current or especially meaningful at the time. Settings, symbols, and language are important and can be used to advantage in these early, founding stages of relationship building.

The following are low-risk early steps that rabbis can take:

- Write an op-ed piece explaining some of the background surrounding an upcoming celebration or poignant event, such as Succoth, High Holydays, Chanukah, or Passover.
- Attend a community event and offer to deliver a blessing before a meal or an invocation or benediction.

These steps can then follow the previous introductory efforts:

- Connect with the local group of clergy.
- Accept offers to be on panels/committees (religious and/or secular) that convene in the community and respond to presentations with constructive ideas and insights. The more poignant or controversial the reason for coming together and speaking, the greater the risk and opportunity. Upside? Increased exposure, comfort, and familiarity with the rabbi. Downside? In extreme instances, anonymous phone calls of criticism and disapproval and, upon occasion, hate mail.
- Extend an open invitation to pastors to bring a group of confirmation students or others to the Temple to attend a Friday Sabbath service. Offer and be open to giving a personal tour of the sanctuary to see and hear what holds so much meaning for the faithful of the congregation.
- Invite a local pastor to join (after consulting with lay leadership of both institutions) in proposing and instituting a series of "Living-Room Dialogues" in parishioners' homes, which convene congregants from both institutions to talk about issues that concern all. Testify that some of the most rich and lasting relationships between Jews and Gentiles are born right here!
- Propose to the clergy group that it sponsor at some location, not necessarily the rabbi's home synagogue, an adult education (lecture and discussion) series, with multiple local congregational clergy participating, and participate in that series as a lecturer and/or host. An example is the "Hammer on the Rock" series done in Fairfield, Con-

necticut, involving texts from the shared tradition taught and analyzed by multiple clergy from their own perspectives.[4]
- Teach a short course based on the Hebrew Bible (Torah,[5] Prophets,[6] or Wisdom Literature[7]) at one of the local churches or invite a trusted pastor to the temple to attend an in-house discussion group.
- Invite a local psychologist who understands what it is to be clergy to run a group of local clergy on a regular basis to explore what it means to be a spiritual exemplar and how to deal with situations in the congregation.

Hopefully, by now, other clergy are tuned in and responding to issues that embrace and engage the local Jewish community: events in Israel; the concerns about recurring anti-Semitism; the observance of the Holocaust. This will indicate a readiness to accept rabbis' suggestions and leadership in sharing their knowledge, perspectives, and resources. The following steps are now approproate:

- Establish an annual community-wide interfaith observance of the Holocaust.
- Put together an Interfaith Mission Trip to Israel.
- Reach out to the Christian community in times of hardship (e.g., the assassination of Yitzhak Rabin[8]) and offer one another understanding, support, and compassion.

The progression along this relationship-building continuum may not come about rapidly, but rather incrementally, as rabbis identify particular Gentiles (often clergy) with whom deeply nourishing relationships can be built, sustained, and shared. Such relationships are no longer a garnish on the plate, but the feast itself, nourising the spirit of and giving life to all communities. "One finds God in relationship," and these relationships are worth the effort, for their light shines beyond the rabbis/clergy to illuminate congregants as well.

Look within. Make the effort. Choose carefully. Take the risk. Commit. I know of no other way to succeed.

---

4. Series conducted annually by the Fairfield Interfaith Clergy (Fairfield, Connecticut), generally for the purpose of studying biblical texts.
5. The Five Books of Moses, Genesis through Deuteronomy.
6. Such as Isaiah, Jeremiah, Ezekiel, Amos, and others.
7. Such as Proverbs, Psalms, Ecclesiastes, and Job.
8. Israeli Prime Minister assassinated in 1995.

WHEN LIFE CHALLENGES OUR HUMAN "BEING"

– 16 –

Caring for and Supporting Those Going Through Divorce

Judith Levitan

If a person's heart is heavy with worry, let him unburden himself to other people.

Yoma 75A

Divorce is a life-shattering event. Every index used to measure life stressors lists divorce among the top three, along with bereavement and serious illness. It affects couples, children, extended families, friends, and the community in which one lives. Yet, in today's enlightened world, divorce is still a stigma. People who divorce often feel shunned by their friends and communities. They frequently report that their married friends drift away, as if divorce were "contagious." They also often describe feeling avoided or unwanted in their communities. It is a profoundly lonely time.

Divorce is hard for those who try to help as well. Although our tradition has definite rituals and prescribed ways for helping the bereaved, as well as organizations that are expert in comforting the ill, if you are divorcing, or if you are trying to comfort and counsel someone who is, spiritual solace and ritual comfort are not easy to access.

Another challenge exists. Divorce evokes ambivalence in those who wish to help and does so in ways that are different from other life traumas. The person who is suffering through divorce can be difficult to help. They may be angry, overly sensitive, or seeking someone—anyone will do—to take sides. These reactions are common, regularly accompanying the pain of divorce, but unless we are prepared, it is difficult to know what to do. This is especially true in communities because those who want to help often know both partners. Conflicts over divided loyalties make us uncomfortable, and we have precious few guidelines and structures to guide us. This often leaves suffering people feeling rejected by their community, and even more alone.

It is important to know that there are common reactions to divorce that most people experience. If you are prepared and can anticipate these reactions, you can make a tremendous contribution to someone's recovery. It is also true that having some guidelines about what you can and cannot do can give you the skill to become involved in an appropriate and constructive way.

It can be helpful and inspiring to know that people do recover from "divorce crisis." Though this is one of the most disorienting experiences of their lives, and they are truly not themselves, with time, their behavior stabilizes, emotions calm, and perspective is regained. Most people end up believing that although they never wanted the divorce to happen, they have become stronger, more reflective, and better people because of it. They also feel able to offer more to their communities. However, the process is a long one. Recovery can take between two and five years. Communal support is a powerful force for recovery and can speed the process along.

Common Reactions to Divorce Distress

Sara entered the room and immediately began talking about the ways in which she had been let down. She spoke quickly and angrily, describing how her husband had left her. She felt that friends were avoiding her. She was devastated when she sought her rabbi's counsel and he didn't seem to share her outrage. Her meeting with the rabbi had not been a source of comfort. Instead, she left feeling misunderstood, and convinced that her rabbi had taken her husband's side. I asked her how she knew that, and she quickly responded, "He would not agree that my husband was a terrible man. He even suggested that there could be two sides to the story. He seemed uncomfortable with me, and I felt that he wanted to end our meeting. The worst thing is that he never checked in with me after that day, and now I feel that he is avoiding me too."

Sara's rabbi is compassionate and cares very much about her and her family. His version of their interchange would be very different. He might speak of how sorry he was to see this good family coming apart in this way. He might express fondness for Sara and for her husband, Larry, as well. He might be surprised that Larry had decided to leave the marriage and done so in such an abrupt and uncaring way. He might also express surprise at the way Sara was talking and state that he had never seen her so angry and bitter. She revealed many terrible things about Larry during their interview, many of which made the rabbi uncomfortable. He didn't know what to say, so he stayed silent and listened. When he ended the discussion after an hour, he sensed that Sara still felt slighted. He had been thinking about the family since that appointment and had not yet decided how to proceed.

Elliott came to his rabbi after his wife, Karen, told him she was leaving. Elliott seemed despondent, depressed, and ashamed. His rabbi spoke with Elliott for over an hour about seeking counseling and also gave him the name of a lawyer. Elliott left the meeting feeling grateful to his rabbi but still bereft. He never asked for another meeting. Elliott attended services weekly but felt uncared for and empty. He couldn't really explain why.

Elliott's rabbi is concerned about him. During their time together, Elliott seemed somewhat lost and looked to his rabbi for guidance. His rabbi was glad that he was able to refer Elliott to both an excellent therapist and attorney. His rabbi encouraged Elliott to let him know if he needed anything, and he was glad to see Elliott at weekly services. When his rabbi approached him or shook his hand, Elliott said he was fine and didn't seem to want to say more. His rabbi wasn't sure how to proceed. He wanted to help Elliott but didn't want to be intrusive toward this sensitive man.

Sara's and Elliott's stories highlight many of the common reactions to divorce distress and illustrate how these reactions can make it difficult to help. In Sara's situation, she is talking and revealing too much, wants others to join her in blaming her spouse, and is very sensitive to slights. Her rabbi felt that none of these behaviors were characteristic of Sara before the separation. Elliott appears depressed and ashamed. He doesn't seem to know what he wants from his rabbi, so he could never let him know. Both Sara and Elliott are sensitive to rejection and are hoping that their rabbis can read their minds, perhaps better than they can themselves.

Identifying some of the emotions commonly experienced by those going through divorce can provide guideposts for caregivers. It is important to remember, however, that not everyone experiences any or all of the reactions described here or does so in a particular order. One person may never be able to forgive a spouse's cruel behavior, and another may recognize only one or two of the reactions listed here. Most important is to listen to each person's experience and understand that his or her experience is unique.

The following descriptions are best used as windows into the vast array of emotions one might face.

Sara suffered with several commonly seen reactions, such as these:

> *Excessive talking:* Sara cannot stop talking and revealing intimate or embarrassing details of her personal life.
>
> *Blame:* Sara has little ability to accept responsibility for any part of the breakup. Her partner is completely at fault.
>
> *Rejection sensitivity:* Being in the midst of divorce, Sara is sensitive to any slight or whiff of rejection. She tends to take everything personally and misunderstands or misinterprets the words and behavior of others.

Elliott, also highly sensitive to rejection, experienced the following feelings:

> *Depression:* Elliott feels hopeless and despairing. Everything, but everything, looks bleak. His life is at an end.
>
> *Shame:* Elliott is unable to tell family and friends about the breakup.
>
> *Loneliness:* Elliott is bereft, feels hollow, and craves physical comfort in any way he can.

The previous reactions and feelings are not limited to either sex; they run the gamut. Other emotions common to divorce include these:

> *Vacillation:* Highs and lows follow one another with astounding rapidity. Convinced one day that they have recovered, divorcing people may plunge into a depression or rage the following day. They can speak of their (soon-to-be) ex-spouses with hatred and contempt and then return to talk of possible reconciliation. They may be embarrassed by this vacillation.
>
> *Guilt:* Spouses who decide to leave can feel ashamed and subsequently withdraw from contact with those they believe will blame them—even their children.
>
> *Denial:* Often, the partners who are thinking of leaving will deny that this is so. Their spouses will try to convince themselves that everything is all right, even in the face of evidence to the contrary.
>
> *Shock:* People can feel ambushed by divorce if they had no indication that anything was wrong. This can make them feel stunned, foolish, or gullible.

Anger: Anger can be destructive, but it can also be a positive force to dispel depression.

Revenge: Some divorcing people may resort to using the children, taking mutually owned property, and even violence as means to get back at their spurning spouses.

Fear/terror: Many people fear not being able to survive on their own emotionally and/or financially.

Disenfranchised grief: People may experience feelings of grief that are not acknowledged by others as valid.

Rigidity: This manifests as repeating the same injustices, leading to an inability to move on in life.

Overcompensation: People may try too hard to prove that they are "just fine," for example, rushing into dating or a new relationship, or taking on major new projects or responsibilities.

An all too common feeling, as described by Rabbi Jack H Bloom, survivor and beneficiary of a difficult divorce, is "pervasive panic" at the "disintegration" of the "containers" within which we live and which sustain us. When one divorces, a number of the familiar life anchors, or "containers," disintegrate. The nuclear and extended family are both threatened with destruction; one's self-perception as partner in a marriage, one's role and position in the family as mother or father, and one's relationship to the world beyond are all suddenly up for grabs.[1] It is here that the rabbi's role is absolutely crucial. The rabbi, as symbolic exemplar of the community, is uniquely positioned to provide a sustaining "container" that supports the boundaries that enable a return from the "craziness" of divorce. It is crucial and vital for the greater community, with you as its symbol, to take a position of love, provide dependable boundaries, and offer sustained support for its member at this terrible time. Once this is in place and ongoing, the rabbi and the community can further help the divorcing person by suggesting and providing the very best psychotherapeutic help (individual or group) available. In divorcing situations, people need all the help they can get, and usually this requires the professional help of a psychiatrist, psychologist, or clinical social worker to address their anger and depression.

It is important to remind yourself, as you bring the community's affirmation to its hurting members, that you are most likely dealing with people who have been transformed by crisis, and who behave in ways neither you nor they could have imagined. Sometimes their behavior can be extreme and alienating. Treat people going through a divorce as people who have en-

---

1. From personal communication with Rabbi Jack H Bloom.

dured a terrible trauma and, as with other trauma victims, are experiencing feelings of shock, powerlessness, fear, and anger, all of which can wreak havoc on one's usual personality. In fact, divorcing people often describe feeling as though they are not quite "in their right mind." Your ongoing and persistent care and concern as the symbol of a caring community is vital. If you can resist the urge to withdraw, things will begin to change and you will have the good fortune to witness a transformation in which you will have played an indispensable part.

Practical Tips for Helping

Set clear but kind limits and let divorcing congregants know what you can and cannot do. If you know both parties, it is unlikely that you will be able to take sides. Your task it not to "fix" them or their marriage. You are not their therapist or their lawyer. Your helping role should include the following:

- Ask "How are you doing?"
- Offer spiritual solace.
- Acknowledge the person's bleakest feelings.
- Listen to anger with concern rather than condemnation.
- Understand the person's alternating hatred of the spouse and wish for reconciliation.
- Stay in equal and regular contact with each member of the divorcing couple.
- Make time to look in on the family.
- Remind the couple repeatedly that you want them to let you know how they are doing.
- Offer small, but important, comforting gestures, such as a warm hand-shake or pat on the shoulder, or a expression of greeting and welcome at the synagogue.

Rabbis do not have to face this difficult situation alone. They can call on the resources of their staff, congregation, and community to help. The clergy and a caring community can offer the following:

- Contact with another divorced congregant
- Accompanying them to a *beit din*[2]

---

2. A rabbinic court consisting of at least three people.

- Special attention for divorcing/newly divorced people going through a life cycle event, such as a *bar/bat mitzvah*[3] of their own children or the death of someone in their own or their spouse's family
- Support around the issues of their attending congregational events that are couple centered
- Help in composing a personal ritual[4]
- A spiritual partnership and relevant Jewish learning opportunities
- Shabbat[5] or holiday invitations
- Protection against unintended slights, particularly concerning billing or mailing issues
- Encouragement to find a counselor, therapist, or support group
- Ongoing contact and personal involvement
- Assistance with and support for the children, who may not want to talk about the divorce but will appreciate a concerned adult presence or the effort to include them in social events and congregational activities

The following behaviors can be hurtful and are to be avoided:

- Defending the other spouse
- Asking the person to see the other spouse's point of view
- Telling the person to move on
- Avoiding the person
- Sending letters and bills addressed to the estranged spouse
- Allowing the person to endure holidays and life cycle events without communal support

Returning to Sara and Elliott, we now know there is much more we can do to help. We might refer them to lawyers or therapists, but we would make other efforts as well. We could connect them to other community members. Perhaps Sara would feel comfortable talking to another divorced congregant, while Elliott might prefer to join a morning *minyan*.[6] We could let them know other ways we could help, such as creating a personal or group ritual for Sara or reading psalms with Elliott. Above all, we would mark our

---

3. At age thirteen, a young person is obligated for the fulfillment of God's commands. The occasion is marked by being called to the reading of the Torah, and participating as an "adult" in the service.

4. For more information, see Chapter 11, "The Muse of Creative Ritual for Relational Healing," in this book.

5. The Sabbath—a day for rest and renewal.

6. A quorum of ten Jews required for public prayer.

calendars so we would not forget to make a follow-up call or to send a note. We should also remember that, in the future, Sara and Elliott may want to help other congregants in crisis, and this will be a source of strength for them and the community.

The Healing Begins

In time, most people are able to accept and reflect with insight on what has happened. You will recognize this shift when you hear someone express the following types of feelings:

Reflection: "I am thinking of some of the signs I missed. I had my head in the sand."

Responsibility: "I did some terrible things to her and to the kids. I am determined to make it up to them."

Reassessment: "I think the marriage wasn't as good as I thought. I never would have made the move, but in some ways I think he did me a favor."

Forgiveness: "I played a part in this too. I think I have learned much about myself from this relationship, and once, a long time ago, we loved each other."

Moving forward: "I would never have believed I'd be able to say this, but now I am ready to imagine a future and put the past behind."

The Long Journey of Recovery

Beth's husband walked out on her the summer after their son graduated from high school. They had been drifting apart for two years, but Beth always imagined that things would improve. Her husband's abandonment was a shock. They were an observant Jewish couple—hardworking people and doting parents. Unimaginable things happened once they separated. Beth's husband broke into their house and took things that belonged to both of them. He cleared out their bank account and left Beth with no money. He brought his girlfriend along when he visited with his son.

Five years ago, Beth would have insisted that this was the only truthful side of the story, but now she knows better. During that awful time, Beth hurt her son by saying terrible things about his father. She revealed terrible things about her husband to her friends and to her rabbi. She was energized by rage and revenge. Beth's friend urged her to go for therapy. With the help of this friend, her therapist, and time, Beth began to let go. She made some new friends, got a new job, and started to date. Her synagogue reminded her of her former family life, so she finally joined a new one. She began to realize things about herself that she wanted to change. Beth would have never left her husband, but now she really believes she has the chance for a more honest, gratifying life.

When her son graduated from college, Beth and her ex-husband actually sat together during the ceremony. They shared pride in the wonderful son their love had created twenty-two years ago. Beth admits to thinking that her husband is still a jerk to have done what he did, but she doesn't hate him anymore. It's over. She is grateful to those who stood by and helped her through this awful time. They saved her life.

After divorce, it can be difficult for both partners to remain in the family synagogue, so one partner may decide to leave because the other spouse has the stronger connection, the synagogue now feels either too small or too large, or the family memories are simply too painful to revisit. It is often wise to suggest that the congregant not make a change immediately or impulsively, although there may be good reason to make a change. A rabbi can offer support and guidance in finding a new community for a congregant who is moving on in life. The congregant should have the chance to talk about the reasons for the change, and at this point, the rabbi can listen carefully to make sure the congregant is not leaving because he or she feels uncared for or rejected. This type of meeting offers the rabbi a chance to correct perceived rejections and wish the congregant well. Such a meeting can have a powerful, positive effect.

The Get

> There is something ancient and powerful about the *get*. All this work to create a perfect and beautiful document only to have it cut apart, like a marriage that began with hope and ended in pieces.
>
> Rabbi Laura Geller
> "Mourning a Marriage"
> www.ritualwell.org

The *get*[7] can engender a myriad of feelings in both partners of a divorcing couple. It may be helpful to clarify for them that the *get* is an item of Jewish law, but it is not a spiritual ceremony. It may also be helpful to describe in advance what will happen at the *get*, so participants can be emotionally prepared. They should know that they need to bring a copy of their *ketubah*[8] and other forms of identification. It may be helpful to know that three rabbis, one scribe, and two witnesses will be present. The rabbi will be

---

7. Jewish bill of divorce.
8. Marriage contract outlining the duties and responsibilities of the couple to each other.

asking many questions about names and nicknames. People may find comfort in knowing that all of these details and rules remain as they did in ancient times and tie us to our heritage.

Though they can feel tedious, they are endemic to a legal system where one must make sure the i's are dotted and the t's crossed, and the one to whom the document is addressed is that person specifically, and not someone by another name. Other important points you may want to explain about the *get:*

- Traditionally the *get* must be commissioned by the husband and presented to the wife.
- All of the details may be prepared ahead of time.
- You need not be present with your ex-spouse.
- It is wise to have a friend accompany you to the *get*.
- Someone else can represent you at the *beit din*.
- In Orthodox Judaism, a wife cannot marry Jewishly without a *get* even if she has a civil divorce.
- Conservative Judaism does require a *get* but has adopted procedures to ease the burden if you have a recalcitrant spouse.
- Reform Judaism does not require a *get* upon dissolution of a marriage.
- Your subsequent children can be affected if you do not have a *get*.
- A *get* can be authorized and delivered across international borders by officially appointed representatives.

We can do much to help those enduring the pain of divorce. There can be no better time for a caring community to encircle a family with concern, love, and spiritual strength. It will make a tremendous difference.

17

When a Pregnancy Is Unwelcome

Bonnie Margulis
Douglas Maben

The voice over the phone was tentative, full of pain. "Rabbi, I used to light the Shabbat[1] candles every Friday night. But last Friday night I couldn't, because I didn't feel clean enough." For me, as a rabbi working for the Religious Coalition for Reproductive Choice (RCRC),[2] no call is more disturbing than the one from a Jewish woman who is filled with pain and fear because she does not know that the weight of Jewish tradition supports her decision to end her pregnancy. If she had had the benefit of clergy counseling from a supportive rabbi prior to her abortion, she might not have had to endure the guilt and shame that was preventing her from feeling a full and worthy part of Jewish life.

All Options Clergy Counseling

No doubt, a welcomed, loved child is a gift from God and a blessing to a joyful family. Yet, not every pregnancy is welcomed (we do not confuse *unplanned* or *unintended* with *unwelcome*). That is why it is so important for rabbis to understand the many issues women and their families face in dealing with an unwelcome or problem pregnancy. Rabbis should also be able to counsel them appropriately, in a methodology known as "All Options Clergy Counseling."[3] This methodology allows rabbis to provide supportive and affirming clergy counseling for women facing a pregnancy that has

---

1. The Sabbath—a day of rest and renewal.
2. A national interfaith organization dedicated to preserving reproductive freedom. For more information, see www.rcrc.org.
3. This material is adapted from text written by the author for the RCRC Web site (www.rcrc.org). The RCRC offers training in All Options Clergy Counseling through its affiliates and its national office. For more information, contact the national office at 202-628-7700 or info@rcrc.org.

become problematic for them, for whatever reason. In this methodology, all options are explored, from parenting to adoption to abortion. This is a counseling methodology that we believe is the most appropriate response a rabbi can offer to those who seek out clergy for guidance and help in making their own decisions.

All Options Clergy Counseling is many things: It is emotional, relational, medical, financial, and legal in nature. It is also, at the core, spiritual. The conversations that take place during an All Options Clergy Counseling session are shaped by participants' various understandings of God. The unspoken questions of the counselees are, "Will God still love me?" and "Will God forgive me?" Therefore, how clergy speak about God is central to All Options Clergy Counseling, even when the woman cannot articulate her own anxieties.

The Three Options

When a rabbi counsels a woman on reproductive choice issues, it is important to explore all of the options available to her. Often, a woman, when facing a difficult situation and feeling in crisis, may feel she has no or only limited options. It is very helpful to talk her through the possibilities of parenting, making an adoption plan, or terminating the pregnancy. (Of course, for a woman facing medical problems, either maternal or fetal, the options are more limited.) All of these possibilities should be presented as equally valid and moral choices, each carrying both positive and negative aspects. Each choice can lead to feelings of pain and loss, as well as feelings of relief and resolution. None of these possible outcomes will solve all of her problems and life issues. The job of the rabbinic counselor is to accompany the woman on her journey, to explore with her all possible paths, and to offer her the wisdom of Jewish tradition. It is to help her to clarify her own values and beliefs so that she may come to a decision that is the best for her, with which she can most comfortably live.

In exploring the options with the woman, the rabbi should check in with her about her understanding of the medical, legal, and economic realities of her situation, and to help her identify whatever support system she may have to help her with her decision. The media present a great deal of misinformation and mythology about these issues, and a person in crisis is not always able to sort through all of this, to see her own life situation clearly. Each possible path has its own complexities and variations.

In considering parenting, the rabbi and the woman should discuss whether she would be parenting alone or in a relationship, with or without a support system of family and friends to help her. In considering abortion, if it is early in the pregnancy, she may have the option of medical or surgical abortion. There are a host of legal barriers to obtaining an abortion, ranging from waiting periods and "informed consent" laws to parental notification and parental consent laws. These vary from state to state. Practical barriers to locating an accessible abortion provider also exist, as 86 percent of counties in the United States have no abortion provider.[4] Later-term abortions involve possible legal and practical barriers that vary from state to state.[5] Adoption also involves many different possibilities, from varying degrees of open adoption to closed adoption, adoption through agencies, or private adoption. Informal guardianship is also a possible option. Adoption laws and procedures also vary from state to state. While a rabbi is not expected to be a medical or legal expert, he or she should be prepared to raise these questions with the woman, have some basic information available to share with her, and know where to refer her for more information.[6]

Issues Women Face

Stigma

Women face many issues when making a decision about an unwelcome pregnancy, in addition to the legal, financial, and medical considerations. The decision to terminate a pregnancy carries a considerable stigma in today's society, to the extent that many women feel it necessary to keep their decision secret. A recent study on the effects of stigma regarding abortion found that women who felt stigmatized by having had an abortion were less likely to disclose to anyone that they had had an abortion and were more likely to have negative emotional after-effects from the abortion. The conclusion of the study noted:

> Because women who have abortions are at risk for social censure and moral condemnation from others, they may find themselves caught in a bind between wanting to share their feelings about their abortion with others and fearing that they will be looked down on if their abor-

---

4. http://www.plannedparenthood.org/library/ABORTION/Training.htm.

5. For a state-by-state analysis of laws concerning abortion and emergency contraception, see http://naral.org/yourstate/whodecides/index.cfm.

6. For legal information, visit http://naral.org; for medical information, visit http://ppfa.org.

tion becomes known. . . . [A]as long as having an abortion is stigmatizing, the price of either disclosure or concealment can be high. [7]

A vicious cycle exists in our society, whereby stigma leads to silence, so women facing difficult decisions feel isolated and alone and, in turn, unable to talk about their situation. The ability to have a supportive clergy presence is tremendously helpful in alleviating both the stigma and the silence. In fact, if clergy counselors have any reservations or questions about their own feelings on this issue, such that the counselors are unclear as to whether they are able to extend to a woman anything other than warm, therapeutic regard, then they should certainly not engage in counseling that might further stigmatize the woman's situation.

Our society also stigmatizes women who choose adoption for their babies. Even the language we use says so much about how our culture views adoption. We talk about "giving a baby up" for adoption, or "putting a baby up" for adoption, as opposed to "keeping the baby." Clergy counselors who talk in terms of "making an adoption plan," "arranging for an adoption," or "finding a family to parent your child," and about the alternative of "deciding to parent your child," go a long way toward destigmatizing and legitimizing adoption as a viable option for a woman to consider.

Domestic Violence

Domestic violence is also a potential issue to consider when counseling a woman regarding an unwelcome pregnancy. According to a recent study, pregnant women are 60.6 percent more likely to be beaten by their partners than are women who are not pregnant. [8] Pregnant teens, ages thirteen to seventeen, are particularly at risk for violence from their partners. Women are four times more likely to be victims of abuse when experiencing an unwelcome or unplanned pregnancy. Indeed, the pregnancy itself could very well be the product of domestic violence through sexual abuse, marital rape, or denied access to birth control. Obviously, a woman who is coerced into pregnancy and is potentially at greater risk for violence during the pregnancy is going to feel restricted in her options.

---

7. Brenda Major and Richard H Gramzow, "Abortion As Stigma: Cognitive and Emotional Implications of Concealment," *Journal of Personality and Social Psychology* 77 (1999): 735-745.

8. *Fact Sheet of the Program of Women, Health, and Development,* Number 24 (November 2000) (Washington, DC: Pan American Health Organization).

For Jewish women, the stigma associated with domestic violence complicates the situation even further. For one thing, the myths that surround the Jewish family—that they are uniformly loving and stable; that Jewish men make the best husbands; that domestic violence only happens in low-income, undereducated households, combined with the myth that all Jewish households are upper income and well educated—lead to a belief that domestic violence does not occur in the Jewish community. This in turn leads to silence and stigma concerning the issue. Domestic violence actually occurs in Jewish families at about the same rate as in families of other religious communities, about 15 to 25 percent. One important difference, however, is that Jewish women tend to take longer to end an abusive marriage. One estimate is that Jewish women take seven to fifteen years to end an abusive marriage, compared to three to five years for non-Jewish women. Possible reasons for this might include the emphasis the Jewish community places on family and maintaining *shalom bayit*,[9] and the consequent fear of exposure and shame for being in such a relationship. Ironically, strong social and economic support might delay the feeling of crisis that might lead a woman to leave sooner.[10]

For the rabbi engaging in All Options Clergy Counseling, it is important to try to assess whether violence is a factor in the relationship and/or in the pregnancy, and to be able to refer the woman to a shelter, domestic violence agency, and counselor experienced in these issues. The rabbi may be able to help the woman deal with the immediate problem of an unwelcome pregnancy, but the other ongoing issues of her life will not be resolved when a decision is made regarding the pregnancy.

Fetal Health

Health issues in pregnancy, whether fetal or maternal, raise a host of issues for the one doing All Options Clergy Counseling. Adoption is usually not an option in these cases, so the counseling will focus on abortion and parenting. Ironically, advances in medical technology, including genetic testing and earlier and more sophisticated sonograms, mean that we have more information earlier in pregnancy than ever before. This in turn often means having to make decisions regarding what to do with the information

---

9. *Shalom bayit*, "domestic peace," is the value of keeping peace in the marriage and peace in the family. It is often seen as the wife's responsibility to maintain *shalom bayit*.

10. "Do Jewish Men Really Do That? Domestic Violence in the Jewish Community," *United Jewish Federation Online*, 2004; http://www.ujf.net/content_display.html?ArticleID=16958.

we are given. At the same time, medical science is not infallible, nor does it always answer all of the questions. Genetic testing can confirm the presence of Down's syndrome, for instance, but cannot predict how severe the effects will be. In fact, it is impossible to tell even at birth how severe the effects will be.[11]

Parents[12] receiving news of such genetic abnormalities will have many questions, fears, and issues, and each person or couple will deal with these questions in different ways. Some will try to find all the information they can regarding the medical facts of the syndrome, the financial implications of having a special-needs child, and practical information on the day-to-day realities of raising a special-needs child. Others will feel overwhelmed by too much information and need to step back to deal with their emotions, first and foremost. Many will question whether they are emotionally equipped to raise a child with physical or mental challenges: What will it mean for their relationship with their spouses/partners? What effect will it have on children they already have or may have in the future? If this is their first child, they may have fears about having subsequent children. If they are considering terminating the pregnancy, they may have feelings of guilt and inadequacy as parents: "If only I were a better/stronger person, then this wouldn't be a such a problem."

Parents who are people of faith will often be strongly inclined to believe at some level that the unhealthiness of their unborn child is a result of something they did wrong, or perhaps even that they are being "punished." Being called upon to listen to the torment that parents struggle with at such times can be both a great challenge and a great honor. Should rabbis be called upon to be present for these parents, it would be extremely helpful to have already thought through their own feelings about the issue, and what choices they might be willing to make in the same circumstances. The rabbinic counselors will have to balance providing practical information to answer the parents' questions with being able to engage in active listening, to understand what the parents are feeling.

Many thoughts will go through the parents' heads, and many conflicts will have to be wrestled with, some of which will be only their own, but others may involve transgenerational projections of guilt, remorse, and accusations. They will hear the voices of others who are part of their extended, per-

---

11. "New Parents," *Down's Syndrome Association Online,* 2004; http://www.downs-syndrome.org.uk/DSA_NewParents.aspx#yourbabyhas.

12. I speak of "parents" in this section because these are cases of wanted pregnancies, and the pregnant woman and her partner have been thinking of themselves as parents, or at least as parents-to-be, since the pregnancy first was confirmed.

haps older, families, who struggled through similar issues without the choices today's parents have. They will hear the voice of the life-yet-to-be asking why it is perhaps not to be. They will hear each other in ways they have not heard each other before. In this situation, rabbinic counselors cannot "fix" the situation, but they can help those involved to hear each other clearly and to clarify the voices to which their souls keep trying to respond. The rabbinic counselors in these cases can help the parents by leading them to discover for themselves that either decision, to parent or to terminate, takes love, strength, and courage. Whether the parents choose to continue or terminate the pregnancy, they will need ongoing support from their rabbi and their community.

In some cases of fetal abnormalities, the medical information clearly supports a decision to terminate, as there is no hope for a live birth or the baby will almost certainly die shortly after birth. Parenting is not an option and thus not a subject in counseling. However, even though medical authorities may be advocating for abortion, this does not mean the parents will not be feeling torn and ambivalent. They may wish to go through with the pregnancy, even if only to give their child a few hours of life, and to give them a chance to hold the child and be with the child when it dies. They may wish to terminate the pregnancy but still have feelings of grief, guilt, and loss. In either case, the care, concern, and support of their rabbi will be of invaluable help.

Maternal Health

Maternal health, as well as fetal health, can be a contraindication to continuing a pregnancy. For a woman with certain medical conditions (such as diabetes, high blood pressure, or heart disease), the pregnancy itself can prove life threatening. In these cases, Jewish law clearly supports a woman's right to terminate a pregnancy, as the fetus is considered a *rodeif,*[13] and, therefore, it is permissible, one might even say mandatory, to end the pregnancy in order to save the woman's life.[14]

In other situations, a woman might be facing a health problem not directly caused by the pregnancy, but treating the health problem might necessitate ending the pregnancy. For example, a pregnant woman diagnosed with breast cancer might be advised to terminate her pregnancy before beginning radiation and chemotherapy. What might a rabbi advise a woman in

---

13. A pursuer with intent to harm.

14. Mishnah Oholot 7.6; Yad Hil. Rotzeah Ushemirat Hanefesh 1.9; Shulhan Arukh Hoshen Mishpat 425.2.

this circumstance who is considering continuing the pregnancy against medical advice, essentially putting the life of the fetus above her own life? We know that people facing a life-threatening illness, or other threat to their own lives, can sometimes be inclined to want to do something magnanimous, something stoic, brave, and honorable, with their own lives. What could seem nobler than for a mother to give her life for her own child? It pulls at all our hearts, but such sentiments can also be tied to life's unfinished business, or the fear of being physically altered, or even the fear of death choosing us instead of us choosing the terms of our death.

As Jews, we believe the woman's love for her baby, for such it is to her, needs to be honored and respected. As rabbinic counselors, however, we should gently teach her Judaism's view that the life of the woman takes precedence over the potential life of the fetus.[15] "Now Choose Life"[16] means "Choose your own life." It means that it is not up to the woman to decide that her life is of lesser value than the life of the fetus, but, rather, that she must value and honor her own life and choose her own life above the potential life of the fetus.

Infertility

Infertility can be an issue in All Options Clergy Counseling. A particularly poignant and painful situation occurs when a woman has experienced miscarriage and/or other fertility issues and is then confronted with a problem pregnancy for which her doctors are recommending abortion. Her feelings of grief and loss are compounded by the fear that she may never be able to carry a pregnancy to term. In the Jewish community, infertility issues seem to be more and more prevalent, as young Jewish adults delay marriage and childbirth until after schooling is completed and careers are under way. Some estimate that up to 30 percent of Jewish couples have some experience with infertility (defined as inability to conceive within a year of having unprotected intercourse). About half of those will eventually conceive with medical intervention, and about half will never conceive.[17] The rabbi counseling a woman or couple dealing with these issues must be particularly sensitive to the cultural pressures the Jewish community places on couples to become parents, and the special pain of one who is physically unable to conform to those pressures.

---

15. Mishnah Oholot 7.6.

16. Deuteronomy 30:19. Translation of Torah text by Everett Fox, *The Five Books of Moses: A New Translation with Introductions, Commentary, and Notes* (New York: Schocken Books, 1995), p. 993.

17. Rabbi Elliot N. Dorff, "Bereshit," *Torah Aura Productions,* 2004; http://www.torahaura.com/Bible/hereat_/LTW_Breshit_5760?ltw_breshit_5760.html.

Religious Issues

The rhetoric of the religious right has saturated and permeated our society to the extent that it is nearly impossible to think of progressive causes and religion as going together. The idea of a "religious left" has become almost an oxymoron in the minds of most Americans. Media coverage today is replete with right-wing talking heads and right-wing language, so that the voice of the progressive religious community on a host of issues has been largely lost in the public arena. On social justice issues, ranging from reproductive rights to gay rights to issues of religious liberty and the separation of church and state, the media have presented the religious community as being uniformly "anti," with any presentation of the "pro" side being uniformly secular.[18]

The media have been generally uncritical of the actions and assertions of religiously conservative organizations and spokespeople, with the result that this segment of the population seems much larger and more powerful than they really are. For instance, when the Christian Coalition claimed millions of supporters, few media outlets reported that the actual mailing list of the Christian Coalition numbered 310,000. At the same time, right-wing organizations have been allowed to set the terminology for the abortion debate, with little or no challenge from the media. Indeed, these groups are ingenious at using and even inventing terminology that is deliberately intended to confuse, distort, and hide the truth. The following are just a few examples.

"Informed consent" laws have been passed in thirty-two states. Of course, who could argue that women should be asked to give informed consent before undergoing any medical or surgical procedure? That, however, is not the true nature of these laws. In reality, these laws mandate biased counseling and/or distribution of biased written materials designed to discourage women from seeking abortions.[19]

A piece of legislation that has come before Congress is called the Child Custody Protection Act. Again, who can be against protecting children? The true nature of this act, though, is to criminalize adults (relatives other than parents, friends, clergy, etc.) who transport a minor across state lines if she has not met the terms of her own state's parental involvement law. The use of the emotionally laden term *child* is designed to conjure up an image

---

18. Jeff Cohen, "Media Coverage of Religion: An Overview," *FAIR*, December 1999; http://www.fair.org/articles/media-religion.html.

19. NARAL Pro-Choice America, "2004 Who Decides? A State by State Report on the Status of Women's Reproductive Rights," p. 2.

of a small child in need of protection. Of course, the legislation really would affect teenagers, and the result of such a law would be more to endanger than to protect the teen, who may be forced to seek an illegal abortion to circumvent the consent laws.[20]

The most egregious example, of course, is the creation of the term *partial-birth abortion*. This is not a medical term, but a term created by the Christian Coalition and other anti-choice groups for the purpose of shifting the focus of the abortion debate away from the woman and onto the fetus. It was coined specifically to be inflammatory and emotional. The anti-choice organizations worked with legislators to get this language into legislation. The media picked up the term and brought it into public consciousness, where it has become firmly embedded.[21]

Couple this with the constant images in the media of protesters staging demonstrations against clinics in the name of religion, and the anti-choice efforts of the Roman Catholic Church, and it is no wonder that much of America thinks of religion as being inherently anti-choice. Jews are as susceptible to these influences as the rest of the population. The challenge, and the responsibility, of rabbis and Jewish leaders is to inform and educate the Jewish community on the long-standing support for choice among Jewish movements and organizations, as well as the long history of Jewish tradition supporting women's rights to abortion under certain circumstances.[22]

While the Reform, Conservative, Reconstructionist, and Humanist movements of Judaism all have pro-choice positions, as a matter of Jewish law and tradition, as well as a matter of public policy, many Jews are unaware of this reality. This ignorance can lead women to feel stigmatized, silenced, and alienated from their community just when they need communal support the most. Rather than reaching out to their rabbis for help, counsel, and support, they turn away from their synagogues. How great a service we would be providing for our congregants if we taught and preached about Judaism's views of abortion and presented ourselves as compassionate listeners, who are prepared to help women facing these difficult times. So much pain and isolation could be avoided if women and their families were aware of Jewish tradition and had their rabbis to turn to for help.

---

20. "The 'Child Custody Protection Act' Threatens Young Women's Health," Report from NARAL Pro-Choice America, July 19, 2004, pp. 1-8; http://www.prochoice america.org/facts/ccpa_womenshealth.cfm.

21. Religious Coalition for Reproductive Choice, "Words of Choice: Countering Anti-Choice Rhetoric," p. 2.

22. Rabbi Raymond Zwerin and Rabbi Richard Shapiro, "Abortion from Jewish Perspectives" (Educational Series #5), Religious Coalition for Reproductive Choice.

A woman once called the Religious Coalition for Reproductive Choice looking for such help. She was a Jewish woman, married, with two small children. Her husband had recently had to close his business and had not yet found other employment. They had no health insurance when she discovered she was pregnant. Her two earlier pregnancies had both been difficult, and she feared this pregnancy would be no different. We talked for a long time. She was torn apart by the choice she felt she had to make. Having had two children already, she knew the incredible love and joy a parent feels toward a child, and she did not want to say no to that love. However, she also did not want to put a further strain on her relationship with her husband, already stressed by their current situation, nor did she want to risk a potentially dangerous pregnancy with no health insurance. She already felt overwhelmed by taking care of her two children, one a toddler and one still a baby, and was uncertain about her ability to care for another baby. Finally, she asked me, "Rabbi, what does Judaism say about the fetus? Would I be committing murder?" I talked about Judaism's view of the fetus as potential life, sacred and honored, but not on the same level as the actual life of the woman. "I had no idea Judaism believed that," she said. We said good-bye soon after that. I will never know what she decided to do, but I did feel as I hung up the phone that she had found some comfort in the teachings of Judaism and was in a better position to make a decision that was right for her.

Upon occasion, a woman from an Orthodox background may come to a liberal rabbi for counseling, unable or unwilling to seek out an Orthodox rabbi to help her. For most Orthodox authorities, abortion is permissible, but only under sharply proscribed conditions. Many Orthodox rabbis would permit abortion only if the woman's life was under direct and immediate threat from the pregnancy. Some ultra-Orthodox rabbis may forbid abortion under any circumstance. For a liberal rabbi counseling a woman from such a background, a delicate dance must be performed to show her that other legitimate Jewish viewpoints exist, without alienating her from her community or beliefs. For an Orthodox woman, abortion might not even really be an option, if she feels it is not a choice she could live with and still remain in her community.

Stereotypes in the Jewish community can also present barriers to a woman trying to make the best decision she can for herself. When real life does not follow the stereotypes, a woman can experience feelings of inadequacy and failure. The Jewish ideal of the family and stereotypes of the nice Jewish girl or the Jewish mother can contribute to a woman's feelings of guilt if she is contemplating terminating an unwelcome pregnancy. As Jews, we are raised from birth with the idea that we will go to college, get married, and have children, in that order. A single Jewish woman who finds herself pregnant may feel embarrassed or ashamed, as "nice Jewish girls" don't find themselves in that situation.

At the *chuppah*,[23] we celebrate, not just the joining of two people, but the creation of a Jewish family. Friends and relatives often have little or no compunction about asking a couple when they intend on starting a family. The pressure put upon a couple to procreate, subtle and overt, is very real. For the woman, the picture of the "Jewish mother"—loving, nurturing, placing her children at the center of her universe (not always in the best sense, of course)—can make the prospect of terminating a pregnancy or placing a child for adoption unthinkable. Again, these are things a "nice Jewish girl" doesn't do. One of the tasks, then, before the rabbinic counselor is to ascertain to what extent, if any, these stereotypical images are in the woman's mind, and to help her see past them, to focus on her own real-life situation to determine what is the best course of action for her.

Ultimately, in every All Options Clergy Counseling situation, the rabbi must be with the woman where she is in her life. The rabbi must help her to clarify her own feelings and beliefs and present her with information to help her to explore paths she might not have been able to see on her own. Ultimately, however, the rabbi's task is to be with the woman on her journey, and not to make the journey for her.

A Suggested Model Counseling Session

The following annotated outline presents one possible model for a counseling session.[24] Of course, no counseling session ever really follows the model or includes all possible steps. The important thing is to allow the woman to be in the lead, and to be with her wherever she is in the moment. The model presupposes that this is a limited, one-time-only session, focusing on values clarification and decision making. For issues needing more intensive therapy, the rabbi is strongly encouraged to refer the woman to other resources for help. Some potential red flags that referral might be indicated include symptoms of depression, thoughts of suicide, other self-destructive thoughts or behaviors, alcoholism or drug abuse, or domestic violence.

---

23. Canopy that the wedding couple stands under during the ceremony, symbolic of the Jewish home the couple will establish together.

24. Adapted from "All Options Clergy Counseling for Women Facing Unwelcome or Problem Pregnancies," Religious Coalition for Reproductive Choice, 2002.

In all cases, it is imperative that you give preferential attention to the woman. Others—parents, partners—may be invited to join you *after* you've spent time with the counselee alone, and *only* if you and the counselee agree to allow them to participate. Keep in mind that you want to let the woman in crisis take the lead and rely more on the questions she asks than on getting answers to the questions you may have.

1. *Explore the presenting problem.* Let the woman define the problem. Encourage her to talk and explain her entire situation. Reflecting back her feelings and thoughts can help her clarify what the problem actually is and, perhaps, challenge her self-talk or the influence of others who may have been offering loads of unsolicited advice. Explore with her the issues related to her pregnancy. What are her feelings about being pregnant? About previous pregnancies? About her sexuality? About relationships with her partner and/or her parents? What are the social and financial situations? What were her plans before she became pregnant? What are they now?
2. *Explore her Jewish upbringing and her understanding of Judaism's positions on parenting, adoption, and abortion.*
3. *Explore her understanding of Jewish tradition on these issues.* Clarify any misconceptions she may have. Is she inclined to embrace or ignore Jewish law and tradition? Does talking with you as a rabbi make a difference to her?
4. *Examine her personal inclinations in this particular situation, and the positions taken by other loved ones involved in the decision.* Find out what options she has been considering, and what impact she believes each option would have on her future. Determine who else's life would be affected by the choices she's considering. Explore how she thinks other people in her life will react to her choices. In whom has she confided? What were their reactions? How did their reactions affect her? Is there anyone else she needs to take into her confidence to facilitate the decision making?
5. *Expand her knowledge of her options.* Share with her all of her options, if she has left any out. Review each option with her and allow her to verbalize the pros and cons of each as she sees them. Provide any factual information she needs that will help in the decision-making process. If you don't have a particular piece of information available, refer her to the resource(s) that can provide it. Empower her by giving her access to the information she needs to make her decision.

6. *Help her clarify her position, assist her in deciding on a course of action, and encourage her to set goals.* Reaffirm with her that it is her decision. Remember that you are helping her balance between time to consider her decision and time to act. Make sure she understands how the gestational age of her fetus affects her decision-making time frame. Be sure to have information on your state's restrictions on abortion after the first trimester. Reassure her that she has your permission to remain undecided or to vacillate in her decision, and that your task is to help her to find the direction that will lead to the decision that is the most fitting and appropriate for her, in keeping with her integrity and well-being. Discuss decision-making steps with her. Help her to reframe her situation and move toward a decision.[25]

7. *Support her decision.* Remind yourself that no single choice is best for all. You are accompanying a woman as she decides whether to bear a child in accordance with her own faith and belief. Offer any follow-up assistance necessary—other clergy, further counseling with you (at your discretion), support throughout the decision-making process and beyond. Tell her that you can supply her with any referrals she may need that will help her carry out her decision.

Rituals for Pregnancy Loss and for Healing After Abortion

Prayer and ritual can be great sources of comfort and healing to women and their families. During a counseling session, the woman may ask the rabbi to pray with or for her. Anne Brener suggests a variety of strategies and Jewish liturgical texts.[26] As she notes, prayer can be spontaneous, expressing the client's feelings, whether they be anger, fear, or a reaching out for comfort and strength. Prayer can also come from traditional Jewish liturgy, such as *Mi Shebeirach*[27] or *Birchat Hagomel*,[28] To encourage spontaneous prayer, she suggests asking the client, "What would you say if you found yourself face to face with God?" or inviting the client to write a letter to God.[29] Brener also suggests that the giving of spontaneous blessings can

---

25. For more information, see Chapter 2, "Language As a Relational Tool: Using Your Mouth with Your Head," in this book.

26. Anne Brener, "Prayer and Presence," *Jewish Pastoral Care: A Practical Handbook from Traditional and Contemporary Sources,* ed. Rabbi Dayle Friedman (Woodstock, VT: Jewish Lights Publications, 2001).

27. A specialized prayer in the synagogue liturgy often, but not exclusively, used for healing: "May the God of our Ancestors bless (and heal) So-and-So, the child of So-and-So."

28. A prayer said upon coming safely through a dangerous situation.

29. Brener, "Prayer and Presence," p. 142.

be an effective tool, noting that the person who receives a blessing from another is reminded that he or she is not alone.

The rabbi may also suggest that the woman take part in a ritual that might help her with the healing process. Such rituals can be conducted either on her own, with friends, or with the rabbi as officiant.[30]

---

30. Rabbi Dana Magat of Temple Emmanuel in San Jose, California, has created a ritual for miscarriage that he has graciously made available through the RCRC. To obtain a copy, please contact Bonnie Margulis at bmargulis@rcrc.org.

18

Caring for Those Whose Sexual Orientation and Gender Identity Vary

Nancy H. Wiener

A few years ago, a colleague shared this vignette with me:

Jon entered my office. I hadn't seen him in a few years, except for the High Holydays. I'd officiated at his *bar mitzvah*[1] and his confirmation; I'd seen him frequently when he'd been active in the youth group, but it had been three years since he'd last come into my office to talk. He'd grown a few inches and filled out considerably. Even the shape of his face had changed quite a bit. But there was no mistaking him. The broad grin and genuine warmth he'd always exuded entered the room with him. We made small talk for a few minutes, catching up on his college experience and his current interests. As he went into more detail, his demeanor changed. His eyes became downcast and he began to fidget. He stumbled over words. His normal ease disappeared. I couldn't imagine what he was getting close to telling me that evoked such a radical transformation. And then he said, "I never imagined coming home would be so hard." He paused; I waited. "It's painful being here. Everyone asks me how Amy is. They know we stayed together even after we went to college. We broke up this year . . ." I was tempted to say some words of consolation, but it was clear he wasn't finished. He was caught midthought. He eventually continued, saying the next words slowly and deliberately, ". . . because I'm gay." He took a deep breath. He visibly shuddered. "And nobody here knows. At least I don't think they do." He glanced at me briefly and then cast his eyes in the other direction. My mind was racing. I was filled with questions. I'd always been outspoken on gay and lesbian issues, encouraging our congregation to reach out and create a hospitable environment for our own gay and lesbian members. I'd officiated at religious ceremonies for gay and lesbian couples and their families. Jon knew this. So why his discomfort?

---

1. At age thirteen, a young person is obligated for the fulfillment of God's commands. The occasion is marked by being called to the reading of the Torah, and participating as an "adult" in the service.

My colleague was genuinely confounded by the interaction and was concerned that he hadn't been as helpful and responsive to his young congregant as he might have been. He, who had taken some time to educate himself and his congregation, still felt uncertain about how to respond.

He is not alone. We all struggle in every counseling situation to truly be there, to be responsive to the needs of those we counsel. We want to hear their concerns, their pains, and their joys and offer them our hearts, our souls, and our minds. Yet, as we know, we are anything but uncomplicated. We are all products of the families, religions, societies, and times in which we have lived. None of us is a blank slate.

We have no official estimates of how many members of our congregations have lesbian or gay family members. Statistically speaking, however, if approximately 10 percent of the population is gay or lesbian, then each family in each of our congregations is likely to have a family member—parent, child, grandparent, aunt/uncle, cousin—who is gay or lesbian. Yet we hear from very few of these people. If only this indicated that all of these lesbian or gay individuals and their extended families were comfortable. By and large, however, the truth is that our congregations, and we ourselves, still remain sources of anxiety and tension for people dealing with issues related to sexual orientation and gender identity.

Over the past few decades, in response to the lesbian, gay, bisexual, and transgender (LGBT) rights movement, all branches of Judaism have been forced to grapple with the emergence of LGBT Jews who affirm their sexual orientation or their gender identity *and* their identity as Jews. We all inherited a tradition replete with interpretations and laws that seem to condemn same-sex sexual contact. The notion that there could be a relationship—a relationship of meaning—that had a sexual component had never been entertained. For millennia, our tradition, even with its multitude of practitioners and interpreters, retained an assumption that all human beings were heterosexual, and that those who engaged in nonheterosexual *behaviors* were acting in an aberrant fashion, one that went against the very nature of what it is to be human. This belief was coupled with well-defined, socially enforced gender roles. The tradition maintained a strong emphasis on procreative marriage, the symbol of "a commitment to the future, a contribution to people-hood, and an existential concern around the passing on of a way of life into the next generation."[2] At the birth of a son[3] this perception

---

2. Irving N. Levitz, "The Impact of the Marriage Imperative on Jewish Life," *Journal of Psychology and Judaism,* 16 (Summer 1992): 110.

3. This prayer was originally said for males entering the covenant through the rite of circumcision. In liberal rabbinic manuals, the blessing is also offered during initiation rites for girls.

was expressed in the form of a blessing: As he has been entered into the covenant, so may he be introduced to the study of Torah, to the *chuppah,* and to *ma'asim tovim.*[4] Marriage in Judaism has thus been equated with continuity, both personal and collective. This heavy emphasis on marriage and procreation has fostered a belief that "one is not a fully responsible adult until one achieves these perceived milestones."[5]

As rabbis, we are seen by those who seek us out for counsel as the bearers and interpreters of this tradition, its representatives, and its defenders, despite anything we may have actually said or done to the contrary. The discomfort, confusion, and shame experienced internally by many of those who seek our counsel will often override their intellectual awareness of us. To be available, we must remain aware of this dynamic and not be surprised or put off by it.

Clergy and therapists are the two types of professionals most often consulted when people are dealing with issues related to sexual orientation.[6] With this reality, we owe it to ourselves and to them to prepare, in as many ways as possible, to hear what their actual needs, expectations, hopes, and fears are.

We must begin by looking at ourselves. We must search our own souls, honestly examining the ways we understand human sexuality and intimate human relationships. We must consider how we have been influenced by Judaism's and the broader culture's attitudes toward those who are not heterosexual and those whose gender identity doesn't conform to their anatomical sex. We must challenge our own assumptions about sexual orientation and meaningful, even potentially religiously celebrated or sanctified, relationships and families. We must take time to reflect on what markers we utilize to determine that someone has successfully entered adulthood, with its concomitant joys and responsibilities. We must take a look at our own ways of expressing ourselves sexually, and the ways in which our own sense of self is threatened or confirmed as a sexual being. If we are heterosexual, we must take an accounting of the ways in which we have benefited from living

---

4. *Chuppah*—nuptial canopy; *ma'asim tovim*—good deeds. This custom has ancient origins. Recently, some liberal rabbis have begun to use *ahavah* (achieving a loving relationship) in lieu of *chuppah,* to signal their inclusion of gay and lesbian relationships. Others who officiate at ceremonies for gay and lesbian couples under a *chuppah* utilize the traditional words, understanding that it is an inclusive term that can be applied to all relationships that are sanctified Jewishly.

5. Levitz, "Impact of the Marriage Imperative," p. 111.

6. Kelly D. Schuck and Becky J. Liddle, "Religious Conflicts Experienced by Lesbian, Gay and Bisexual Individuals," *Journal of Gay and Lesbian Psychotherapy*, 5(2) (2001): 72.

in a society that (legally as well as socially) rewards heterosexuality, as well as of the ways that we have not sufficiently challenged, or perhaps even contributed to, the persistence of this as the norm.

We can educate ourselves about the panoply of issues and concerns that arise when one's sexual orientation or gender identity is the cause of anxiety, discomfort, or discrimination. We can contact local and national organizations that help individuals and families negotiate the issues that arise during the process of "coming out."[7] At a minimum, we can stay abreast of the local, state, and national debates related to legalizing civil marriage for gay men and lesbians;[8] ideally, we can actively participate in bringing about change. We can speak with the therapists to whom we regularly refer, to discover appropriate referrals for people working on sexual orientation and gender issues. We can establish ongoing relationships with LGBT Jewish groups in our areas, helping individuals who are interested make personal contact with them and inviting their members to meet with and educate our congregants.

As rabbis, we understand how difficult it is to own all the different aspects of ourselves and to find ways to authentically and comfortably give expression to them.[9] We have intimate personal knowledge of what it is to be different from the norm, having chosen the lives we have or followed the path we believe we were meant to follow. We know what it is to perceive ourselves as "one of the guys," only to find that we are perceived by others as "odd man out." Even when we share the same likes and dislikes, we are often treated as "other," isolated from activities and topics of conversation because others assume we won't find them "appropriate." These realities can help us draw on a personal source of empathy when individuals come to us because of internal or external conflicts that have arisen due to sexual orientation or gender identity—theirs or a loved one's. Like us, they clearly perceive the innumerable similarities they share with their peers, while acknowledging the differences; all too often, however, for them as for us, their peers focus primarily on the differences and predicate their interactions on them. As we struggle to own all of our *"selves,"* and bring them to the

---

7. Many localities have gay and lesbian community and/or resource centers. Finding out what services and social activities they offer can help rabbis educate themselves and can provide a ready referral source. Also, local chapters of PFLAG (Parents and Friends of Lesbians and Gays) provide educational material and run support groups. Another important resource is the Lambda Legal Defense and Education Fund.

8. Lambda Legal Defense and Education Fund and the Human Rights Campaign are the best sources.

9. Jack H Bloom, *The Rabbi As Symbolic Exemplar: By the Power Vested in Me* (Binghamton, NY: The Haworth Press, 2002), Chapters 4-6.

world, so we can strive to help those whose sexual orientation or gender identity varies, or those who are concerned about the sexual orientation or gender identity of a loved one, to embrace their many *"selves"* and comfortably bring them to the world. Peggy Hanley-Hackenbruck describes a successful process of coming to terms with sexual orientation: "interpersonally, she or he has nurtured a rejected part of the self and elaborated a new ego ideal which leads to greater integration and integrity."[10]

What follows is a discussion of the most common issues related to sexual orientation and gender identity that we encounter in our work as *K'lei Kodesh,*[11] as well as suggested ways for us to help those who seek our support and counsel.

Coming Out

Coming out was originally used in reference to gay men and lesbians and the many transitions they went through, internally and externally, from the moment of first becoming aware of their sexual orientation, to identifying themselves as gay or lesbian, to taking on that identity, to accepting and expressing themselves authentically and sharing their identity with ever-widening circles of others, such as friends, relatives, and colleagues. Being "out" to oneself precedes "coming out" to others. Significantly, one can be "out" to people in one sphere of life and not in others. The process is often slow and, for some, it is never complete. Furthermore, those who are "out" in all spheres of their life still acknowledge that whenever they are in new circumstances they find that they are in the position of having to "come out" all over again, lest erroneous assumptions about them be made—by a new acquaintance, the florist, the new accountant, and so forth.

In time, the term has been expanded to encompass all individuals whose lives and identities are affected by an ongoing, personal relationship with someone whose sexual identity is not heterosexual or whose gender identity is not consistent with public perception based on physical appearance. Parents, siblings, close friends, and colleagues, as they are informed or become aware that someone's sexual orientation or gender identity is not what they had always assumed, must go through an internal and external process to assimilate this information and to act upon it. Family members, in particular, must go through their own coming-out process, and, more often than not, their process is not in sync with the LGBT family member who has come out to them.

---

10. Peggy Hanley-Hackenbruck, "Psychotherapy and the 'Coming Out' Process," *Journal of Gay and Lesbian Psychotherapy,* 1(1) (1989): 32.

11. Literally, Holy Vessel; colloquially, one who provides religious services to the community.

Over the past three decades, innumerable books and articles, including many personal accounts, have been written about the coming-out process. The classics in the Jewish world include Evelyn Torton Beck's (1982) *Nice Jewish Girls* and Balka and Rose's (1989) *Twice Blessed.* The more recent contributions include Alpert, Elwell, and Idelson's (2001) *Lesbian Rabbis;* Greenberg's (2001) *Wrestling with God and Men;* and Israel, Luz, and Avni's (2002) *Ima, Yesh Li Mashehu L'Saper Lakh.*[12] Striking among these are the numerous similarities among Jews of all different backgrounds, secular to Orthodox, American or Israeli. The common cultural and historical backdrop informs the concerns and fears, on the one hand, and the desire to proudly claim an identity not understood or accepted by the mainstream, on the other.

All born Jews know that their identity as a Jew defines them as a member of a minority, placing them on the periphery of the American mainstream. Some discover this as soon as they are old enough to establish friendships beyond the family. Others become aware of this more slowly and circuitously as they venture beyond a predominantly Jewish familial and friendship circle environment. As Jews come to terms with this reality, they can turn to relatives and friends who know the experience firsthand and who can offer support, wisdom, and encouragement for coping with its ramifications. Such is not the case for the overwhelming majority of LGBT individuals in our society. They find that they are "members of a stigmatized minority, whose minority status [is] . . . not shared with their families of origin (unlike ethnic and cultural minorities, where family membership is the entry point for minority status)."[13] While an increasing number of LGBT youths know individuals who are LGBT, from among family, friends or peers, they still must come to terms with being out of the mainstream because their sexual orientation or gender identity does not conform to societal norms.

The Coming-Out Process for Individuals

The "normal" developmental process for LGBT people moves from preconscious awareness through coming out (the various stages of acknowledgement)[14] to integration. In the earliest stages, individuals struggle with

---

12. "Mother, I Have Something to Tell You."

13. Laura Brown, "Lesbians, Gay Men and Their Families: Common Clinical Issues," *Journal of Gay and Lesbian Psychotherapy,* 1(1) (1989): 66.

14. David Scasta, "Issues in Helping People Come Out," *Journal of Gay and Lesbian Psychotherapy,* 2(4) (1998): 88.

their own fears, built and fostered by messages from the predominant culture, that there is something wrong or undesirable about this new identity with which they are beginning to associate. They fear that they will now suffer the same prejudices and hardships they have seen other LGBT people suffer. The threats of losing the love of family, the support of friends, and the range of professional opportunities they had once envisioned loom largest. The fears of never finding someone with whom to share a life and potentially create a family appear as well. Also, by and large, until individuals are certain within themselves about their identities, they harbor their suspicions and knowledge about themselves as a dangerous secret. They also must confront their own internalized homophobia, since they themselves are products of the same society as everyone else they know. Often this is the most insidious inhibitor of self-acceptance.

Whether the realization comes in childhood, adolescence, or adulthood, those who are struggling with a stigmatized gender identity or sexual orientation must learn to live in multiple environments simultaneously: those which are accepting/welcoming, those which are ambiguous/unclear, and those which are overtly hostile. For LGBT adolescents, in particular, accomplishing the normal psychological tasks of adolescence, which include establishing their own emotional identities, gaining self-knowledge, establishing independent identities, taking responsibility for their own lives, and learning to develop independent intimate relationships,[15] is exponentially more difficult. The process of dating encouraged by family and society promotes heterosexuality and fairly rigid gender expectations. Adolescents quickly learn they cannot publicly let on that they are attracted to or interested in a member of the same sex, or that they are more comfortable exhibiting traits associated with members of the opposite gender, unless they are emotionally ready to bear the stigma that is likely to come with doing so. Family members and friends discourage or actively interfere with relationships that are perceived as abnormally close to a member of the same sex and/or with behaviors that are not "gender-normative."[16] The possibility of actually dating someone of the same sex or behaving in a manner consistent with one's gender identity (when it isn't consonant with external physical attributes) exists for only a small minority of teenagers.

To get ahead, to be accepted, to fit in, to "prove" to themselves and others that they are "normal," most LGBT teenagers either deny or learn to hide

---

15. Patricia H. Meyer, "Between Families: The Unattached Young Adult," in Betty Carter and Monica McGoldrick, eds., *The Family Life Cycle: A Framework for Family Therapy* (New York: Gardner Press, 1980), pp. 73-74.
16. Warren J. Blumenfeld, *Homophobia* (Boston: Beacon, 1992), pp. 9-10.

their true identities. At a developmental stage when asserting one's own identity and acting on one's own desires, preferences, and viewpoints are crucial, an LGBT teen often finds instead that truth telling is exceedingly threatening and risky. At a time when peers are experiencing a process of integration, an LGBT youth is learning to split: "Passing for heterosexual offers a paradigmatic instance of [the] split between interior knowledge and superficial appearance perceived by others."[17]

The common belief, which arises from this socialization to heterosexuality, is expressed by an eighteen-year-old lesbian: "When I came out, I thought my life was over. I thought I'd never be happy now that I was gay. I thought I could never have a house, or children, or a relationship, or a good job."[18] For many, an essential part of coming out lies in discovering that their self-images and their future expectations are not at risk to the extent they had been socialized to believe. They need to learn to trust themselves and their feelings, and to believe in themselves, their abilities, and their self-worth. This is a process of relearning for some; for others, it is new. Some may never be able to achieve this level of self-acceptance. In essence, subsequent to coming out, LGBT individuals must (re)accomplish the psychological tasks associated with adolescence and early adulthood in light of their newfound sexual or gender identity.

As *K'lei Kodesh,* we will have individuals of all ages, professions, and marital statuses coming to us to discuss issues related to their coming out. They are seeking our understanding and support. They are hoping for our acceptance of them as they go through the confusing and disorienting transition of perceiving themselves and being perceived by others as fundamentally different. We can listen to their concerns, empathize with them, and share our knowledge of successful journeys similar to their own. We can help them identify obstacles and areas where resistance and rejection are likely to occur. We can help them recognize their own strengths and supports as they contemplate coming out to others. We can assure them of our constancy and of God's constancy. We can help them connect with other Jews who have found positive ways of expressing their LGBT and Jewish identities. The fears and concerns will vary from individual to individual. Whether it is the mother of two children in our religious school who worries about the repercussions for her children and husband within the synagogue once she comes out; or the fifteen-year-old who shares with us the hostility

---

17. Kath Weston, *Families We Choose: Lesbians, Gays, and Kinship* (New York: Columbia University Press, 1991), p. 49.

18. Diane Elze, "It Has Nothing to Do with Me," in Blumenfeld, *Homophobia,* p. 104.

her parents have expressed at her dressing as a male, the gender with which she clearly self-identifies; or the father who blames himself for his child's sexual orientation and is sure that he will be shunned by family, friends, and his peers in the Jewish community if they find out—in all of these and similar cases, we have a unique role to play as we offer a safe haven and a link to the broader world to those who are struggling to understand and find comfort.

All of us hold images of ourselves that stretch well into the future. From our youngest years, we anticipate certain things for ourselves, many of which are predicated on the dominant cultural assumption of heterosexuality and gender/biological identity. As LGBT individuals come out, or as family members go through the coming-out process, they often experience a period of mourning. They need to grieve those expectations which will not come to pass as they had once imagined, even those which might come to be in a different form. Readjusting hopes and dreams takes time.

We are all used to counseling people who are working on similar readjustments that have been necessitated by exigencies other than sexual orientation and gender identity. We can draw on the skills we have developed over time when working with people following other major life changes, such as divorce, death, diagnosis, and change of professional goals. We know how to provide people with an opportunity to identify what they feel they have lost and to grieve those losses. We know how to help people discover the resources and supports they have and work with them over time as they go through the stages of grieving, letting go, and moving on.

An ongoing source of tension for LGBT individuals and their families is how "out" they want to or need to be. Many families that are welcoming within the confines of their homes do not feel comfortable letting friends, acquaintances, or even other family members know. If their family members have partners, they have trouble finding ways to introduce the partners and typically dance around it when circumstances demand an introduction. This often causes conflict and resentment. Anxiety often heightens as families plan for life cycle gatherings. Be they happy or sad, family life cycle events will invariably reach beyond the smaller group to whom families have come out. As we work with families, we can raise pertinent questions: Who will be invited? How comfortable are they? Do they have any concerns, fears, or anxieties about sharing their family members, all of them, with those who will be attending? We can normalize their concerns and encourage them to explore the various possibilities that exist, so that well in advance a mutually acceptable approach can be adopted. In this way, these issues won't cloud or derail the focus of the gathering for which they are planning.

We also need to recognize that an ever-increasing number of young adults have grown up in metropolitan areas, where they could come out to themselves and family and friends fairly comfortably. (Of course, everyone is an individual and some will always need help, even in an accepting environment.) They have never lived a life of hiding and secrecy and have come of age at a time when discussions about gay/lesbian couples and marriages have entered the mainstream. These young adults present a challenge to us, as religious leaders, and to our communities, if we espouse acceptance— because they expect *real* acceptance. They assume that they are part of the larger Jewish community; our responses to their demands for full involvement, in all aspects of our communities, will be pivotal in determining their future commitments.

Same-Sex Ceremonies

With the ongoing national and local debates about civil marriage for same-sex couples and the increasing numbers of Jews seeking rabbis to officiate at their religious ceremonies, a few words about the particular issues related to premarital/preceremony counseling are in order. Although in many, many ways our counseling with same-sex couples who wish to celebrate their relationships by means of religious ceremony will resemble the counseling we do with heterosexual couples, some additional issues must be explored when counseling same-sex couples.

A couple seeking a rabbi to officiate at a ceremony already has negotiated the coming-out process well enough to want to affirm their commitment to each other publicly and to announce their desire to maintain a stable, intimate, interdependent relationship. We can provide meaningful recognition and affirmation of both the couple's status and the importance of their relationship. At the same time, we must be sensitive to the disparity that may exist between their private affirmations and the responses of those they care about. The degree to which each partner is "out" may differ; the responses of their nuclear families, friends, co-workers, and others may be quite varied. The ceremony for which they are planning is likely to be the most public statement they have ever made or will ever make of who they are and what they mean to each other. We ought to approach the counseling with an awareness that these issues are likely to (re)surface as the couple prepares to publicly affirm and celebrate their relationship.[19]

---

19. Betty Berzon, *Permanent Partners: Building Gay and Lesbian Relationships That Last* (New York: Plume, 1990), Chapter 12.

As we engage in preceremony counseling, we should prepare ourselves to hear of periods in the individuals' lives when they believed themselves to be heterosexual and engaged in heterosexual dating and long-term relationships, including marriage. We should prepare ourselves to hear about periods of experimentation and the coming-out process. We should also perhaps prepare ourselves for more candid reminiscences about past relationships and open marriage arrangements that have existed or may exist in the future.

For major life transitions to be successful and comfortable, they must be acknowledged by significant people and institutions. These second-order developments, as Terkelson refers to them,

> involve transformations of status and meaning, a need to be something new. The change is less in the performance than in the status of the performer, less in what is done and more in the meaning of the doings. In order to meet such needs, very basic attributes of the family unit must change. A member leaves or enters the family. Loyalties are realigned. Affections deepen or fade. Roles are reassigned. Ultimately the family's prior system of meaning gives way under the advance of the new shared reality. With the new system of meaning comes affirmation of the new status for the index member. . . . A second-order development calls for extensive revisions in consensual reality.[20]

Formal rituals help to facilitate these transitions and to revise consensual reality. As rabbis, we can be sensitive to the barriers that exist within the couples' families and the larger society that might impede their smooth transition. We can work with couples as they explore the ways that their families have recognized and responded to the realignment of allegiances that has occurred as their relationships have deepened. We can help them identify ways in which to express, prior to and through the ceremony, the nature of their commitment to being couples in ways meaningful for themselves and for their extended network of family and friends. Ideally, the ceremony can mitigate anxieties and tensions and increase acceptance of the couples' relationships. It can help to reframe[21] and normalize relationships that have hitherto been perceived as "foreign" or "unintelligible."

---

20. Kenneth G. Terkelson, "Toward a Theory of the Family Life Cycle," in Carter and McGoldrick, *The Family Life Cycle*, pp. 39-40.

21. See in this book Chapter 2, "Language As a Relational Tool: Using Your Mouth with Your Head?"

Many parents find that their fears for their children's happiness, well-being, safety, and acceptance are allayed by the participation in the ceremony of a representative from the established Jewish community. Their hope for a more accepting world for their children is increased. They can relate to the ceremony and its familiar symbols, gain a sense of validation, and even, perhaps, a sense that the community has a place for them and their children after all.[22]

Generations of gay men and lesbians never anticipated that their love might someday be ritually celebrated. As a result, many of them paid little or no attention to the mechanics and details when heterosexual family members and friends prepared for their weddings. This is but one example of the learning and socialization gay men and lesbians miss out on during their adolescent and early adult years. In recognition of this, we need to be prepared to sit down with couples whose knowledge of weddings generally, and Jewish rituals in particular, may be quite minimal, and to help them learn about the basics of these ceremonies.

The *ketubah*[23] is a tangible religious affirmation of a couple's status change. In fact, in the absence of legal civil recognition, this may be the only document that affirms the nature of the couple's relationship. (As laws change, civil documents that affirm the status change may need to be prepared and filed as well.) When a heterosexual couple marries, not only do their friends and families recognize their change of status, but also the government extends to them various rights and privileges, which will be in effect until death or legal divorce severs the relationship. These spousal rights recognize the spouse as next of kin, replacing parents, and govern inheritance and tax laws, pension benefits, powers of attorney, joint ownership, ability to file joint tax returns, options for family plan insurance, and so on. While no amount of legal documentation can replicate the myriad (more than 1,000) civil benefits that come with civil marriage, rabbis can encourage couples (some are making it a requirement for officiation) to draft legal documents with a lawyer conversant in issues specifically related to gay/lesbian couples, to ensure that they will benefit from as many legal protections as possible.[24]

---

22. Nancy H. Wiener, "*Kiddush Ahavah:* Counseling Same-Sex Couples As They Sanctify Their Love," unpublished doctoral project, Hebrew Union College and the Postgraduate Center for Mental Health, 1994.

23. Jewish marriage contract outlining the duties and responsibilities of the couple to each other; plural: *ketubot.*

24. A comprehensive resource for rabbis is now available on the Central Conference of American Rabbis Web site (CCARnet.org).

Where civil legal recognition of the ceremony is absent, we also have to discuss with couples the content of our final pronouncement. Without the "power vested in me by the state," with whose authority/power do we and they feel we are vested? Who is affirming and witnessing this significant life cycle transition? This may come naturally out of discussions we are likely to have with the couple about whether this is a *kiddushin,*[25] *b'rit ahuvim,*[26] or other nontraditional ritual. How we and the couple perceive their ceremony and refer to it is of great import and warrants focused discussion.

Many of the ceremonial variations, related to vows, *ketubot,* circling, rings, and so forth, that have long been the focus of premarital discussions conducted by liberal rabbis still have a central place in our discussions with gay/lesbian couples. We should, however, highlight and explore a few specific variations with same-sex couples. For example, the wording of the *ketubah* must be discussed and crafted, since even most liberal ones make reference to a heterosexual couple. A growing number of preprinted *ketubot* now exist for same-sex couples, and many calligraphers now create personalized *ketubot* with individual same-sex couples. Renderings of the *Sheva B'rachot*[27] and vow options that a same-sex couple may feel are more reflective of themselves and their relationship are now available.[28] We should make no assumptions about what rendition of prayers or vows will speak most directly and meaningfully to a couple. Some couples' natural inclination is to be as creative as possible; other couples think that including all of the elements of what they associate with a traditional Jewish wedding is what will make their ceremony feel authentic and real.

Finally, we have some choreographic and sartorial issues that we are less likely to discuss at length with heterosexual couples, but these may give rise to some conflicts or soul-searching for gay/lesbian couples. Jewish weddings have traditionally been gender-bound affairs. The clothes for bride and groom were clearly defined and different from each other. The groom arrived at the *chuppah* first. The groom veiled the bride. The groom gave a ring to the bride (prior to the introduction, in liberal circles, of a double ring ceremony). The groom broke the glass at the end of the ceremony. In a same-sex couple, what they will wear, how they will arrive at the *chuppah,*

---

25. A traditional Jewish marriage ceremony.

26. Commitment ceremony. Rachel Adler, *Engendering Judaism* (Philadelphia, PA: Jewish Publication Society, 1998), Chapter 5.

27. Seven blessings, which are the core of the marriage ceremony.

28. For vow variations, *Sheva B'rachot* variations, and *ketubah* options for same-sex couples, see Nancy H. Wiener, *Beyond Breaking the Glass* (New York: Central Conference of American Rabbis, 2000), Appendixes IV, V, VI.

whether there will be circling or veiling (or something to replace it), and who will break a glass or glasses, if any, are not simple decisions. Many couples are concerned that if one, but not both, engages in any of these activities or chooses certain clothing to wear, some of those in attendance will speculate or leap to conclusions about their roles within their relationship, thus creating an undesirable distraction. As rabbis, our patiently engaging in conversation, providing sufficient space for an airing of concerns, and confirming that they are not alone in having such concerns can go a long way toward eliminating problems in any of these areas.

Discussing the ceremony and the nature of the couples' relationships in specifically Jewish terms provides them with language and context in which to be grounded. It can affirm their identity as Jews and help them to see that there is a place for them in Judaism and in the Jewish community. The time we spend with gay/lesbian couples, affirming their relationships, acknowledging their past perceptions of and experiences within organized Jewish communities, and helping them find meaningful ways to (re)connect as Jewish gay men and lesbians can have a lifelong impact.

Ultimately, we serve as models for our communities. We can choose to model acceptance and recognition. We can choose to acknowledge the power of personal connection for the members of the couple and their family members with us, as their rabbis. Our positive attitude is essential to the success of our counseling. Our openness, empathy, and availability are invaluable. If we are prepared to assume many roles—teacher, counselor, guide, and officiant—we can help the couples and their families feel more connected to their Jewish selves and to the general Jewish world.

– 19 –

Relating to and Caring for Those
Who Don't Care About You

Steven Bayar

You shouldn't let that broken jaw influence you. . . . It was business, not personal. . . . Don't let anybody kid you. It's all personal, every bit of business. Every piece every man has to eat every day of his life is personal. They call it business. Okay, but it's personal as hell.

Michael Corleone
from *The Godfather*

What Is the Issue?

How do you care for someone who does not care about you?[1] This is not a question to be taken lightly. We are taught that each of us must care for each member of our congregations equally, a lesson easier learned than

---

1. This chapter is not intended to be an exhaustive study of the topic. Rather, I have written a suggestion of how being a symbolic exemplar offers a new orientation to this age-old problem. See also Jack H Bloom, *The Rabbi As Symbolic Exemplar: By the Power Vested in Me* (Binghamton, NY: The Haworth Press, 2002).

practiced. Try caring for someone who engages in character assassination of you and your family. How do you find words of comfort for someone who subtly implies you are a hypocrite at every board meeting or makes fun of you when you speak from the pulpit? How do you run to help someone who aggressively lobbies against your contract renewal?

It is not surprising, though, that most find ways to succeed. We learn to be there when we are needed. The pulpit is a short or very bumpy life for those who fail. Still, how do we learn to "care" for them? How do we learn to resolve our personal feelings so that they do not affect our ability to function? How do we learn to love them?

Our current model is not supportive. Professional lovers cannot "love" from a distance. Love requires not only proximity but vulnerability as well. Attempting to love people gives them a measure of control. They can reject that love. It is easy to see how this can lead to an unhealthy dynamic in which the rabbis are the suitors and the congregants constantly reject them. The situation can lead to abuse.

> The rabbi's contract was coming up for a vote. It was going to be close. The rabbi called each member of the board before the vote and personally assured them that he would still care for them no matter how they voted.

Symbolic Exemplar Redefines Our Role

Recognizing that we are symbolic exemplars[2] gives a structure to our profession that suggests different models for interaction and protection. Integrating this understanding should be a priority in our training. Our choice is to remain rabbis and accept being symbolic exemplars.

First, it means recognizing that we are different. There is a distance inherent in being "in, but not of, this world."[3] In the old model, this distance is alienating and ultimately self-defeating. Yet this same distance gives us room to redefine our role and build a new dynamic of congregational interaction.

The second step is to revisit our definition of success. If success comes from the respect and love we engender, we must fail, nor would we be doing our jobs if we tried. Our role requires us to make difficult decisions that affect people's lives—and beliefs.

---

2. See Bloom, *The Rabbi As Symbolic Exemplar,* Chapters 4, 5, and 6.
3. Ibid., Chapter 3, p. 115, n. 41.

As rabbis we need love. As symbolic exemplars we work for the betterment of the community, the Jewish People, and the world. We do not work for individuals. Bluntly, my definition of success is dependent upon the health of the community, not the caring of its constituents. Ideally, this change in dynamic should also redirect our "rabbinic egos." My ego is involved in how well I live up to my responsibilities and how effective I am as the adhesive that holds the community together. The new dynamic results in a new orientation: your personal opinion no longer has as much power over me. I work to make the community stronger. I can work with you to make the community stronger. I challenge you to work with me for the same purpose.

Training the Congregation Leadership in Triage Management Is One Key

Although symbolic exemplars are separated from their congregations, they need not work alone. Ideally, exemplars and lay leadership form teams to maintain healthy communities. The lay leadership provides administrative guidance and support for the rabbis. The rabbis provide leadership and direction.

We have ways to both minimize and deal with the destructive dynamics of a congregation. One important strategy involves "congregational triage," whereby the lay leadership provides information and feedback to the rabbis, but not all of the information and feedback. The leadership must distinguish what is constructive and necessary from what is spiteful and unnecessary.

Negative feedback must be dealt with immediately. When people are identified as hurt and angry, we must learn to separate their issues from their persons. Lay leadership and rabbis must reach out to these people. Dialogue, discussion, and response are all part of a healthy community. Within the new dynamic, rabbis reach out, not with the goal of recapturing the love of these congregants, but to resolve the situation and move forward. This helps remove the "personal" from the equation.

Obviously, this will not always suffice. However, the onus will always be placed upon members of the community to follow their rabbi's example. (Is that not what a symbolic exemplar is for?) Ironically, such a strategy eventually suggests that the congregants are human and conflicted.

Love?

Love is healthy when it is secure. Symbolic exemplars working for the betterment of communities must be able to interact with all manner of people who both like and dislike them. Yet, the common goal does not require affection. It requires an ability to work together. With such an orientation, rabbis become able to look at the "big picture" and not feel rejected by anger directed at them.

Each person contributes to the whole. Each person must be part of the whole for the community to function. Moreover, each person has value to the community, whether people like you or not. When we come to recognize the value of all people, it also becomes possible to love them, not because they love us and not because they are lovable, but because they are valuable to the community.

"Rabbi, what do I do with my son? He has left Judaism and practices nothing."

"Do you love him?" asked the rabbi.

"Of course."

"Then love him more."

20

Blessing Those We Have Trouble Blessing

Jack H Bloom

A rabbi's charge is, and remains, as was our father Avraham's:[1] *V'heyeh b'rachah,*[2] that having been blessed we, in turn, must bless others.

Being modeled after and molded by Divinity, with the Divine Breath pulsing through us,[3] we are each created [*Tzelem*⇔*N'shamah*], each a [Breath-Taking⇔Model of Divinity].[4] This is our blessing and our special charge as clergy covenanted in the footsteps of Avraham: to bless others.

The *Tzelem,*[5] following Maimonides, can perhaps best be understood to be humankind's cognitive being, since the creating God was and is incorporeal, and any other understanding is, or borders on, idolatry.[6] The biblical author, evidently unsatisfied with this partial truth in chapter 1, hastens to add the complementary truth in chapter 2: that beyond our cognitive essence, each of us is a **living** being because the Divine Breath, the *N'shamah,*[7] was breathed into us by the Living God.

Author's Note: An earlier version of this chapter appeared as "Being Blessed Is Not Enough: Things Our Father Yaaqov Could Not Teach Us," in *CCAR Journal: A Reform Jewish Quarterly,* Winter 2003, pp. 21-33.

1. Translation of Torah text by Everett Fox, except where the author takes some minor liberties. Everett Fox, *The Five Books of Moses: A New Translation with Introductions, Commentary, and Notes* (New York: Schocken Books, 1995).

2. Be a blessing. Genesis 12:2. Translation from Fox, *The Five Books of Moses,* p. 55.

3. Author's understanding and translation of Genesis 1:26-27 and Genesis 2:7, relating the two stories of humankind's creation.

4. The brackets indicate the interrelated unity of these two elements; the double arrow signifies reciprocal relationship.

5. Genesis 1:26-27. "God said: 'Let us model humankind after us, according to our likeness.' . . . God created humankind modeled after Himself, in the model of God He created it, male and female He created them." Translation from Fox, *The Five Books of Moses.*

6. Compare Maimonides, *Guide of the Perplexed,* trans. M. Friedlander (New York: Hebrew Publishing Co., 1881), chapter 1. "In man the 'form' צלם 'tzelem' is that constituent which gives him human perception: and on account of this intellectual perception the term צלם 'tzelem' is employed" (p. 30).

7. From the Hebrew root *N-Sh-M*—to breathe. Genesis 2:7.

The *N'shamah* can best be understood as our somatic being, marked by pulsation and throbbing, feelings of all sorts, pleasant and painful, and a sense of corporeal aliveness. We are blessed by the Living God [YHWH], who has infused in us the breath of life, saturating each with the precious gift of *N'shamah*.[8]

Blessing others is not easily done and certainly not done by the book. Blessing others requires a great deal of skill beyond the simple desire to do "it." Before adequately blessing others, a rabbi must develop significant skills in two other areas: **witnessing** and **naming.** Witnessing and properly naming evidences of the [*Tzelem*⇔*N'shamah*] must happen, and both are prerequisites for proper blessing.

Evidences of the [*Tzelem*⇔*N'shamah*] are often in flux, out of focus, flowing, moving at all times, and most often either too strident or too dormant. Our most stringent efforts are required to witness those difficult, irascible, unredeemed parts of ourselves, affirm their [*Tzelem*⇔*N'shamah*] relationship, and gracefully name them. When these two are done properly and with elegance, blessing can take place.

As blessed symbolic exemplars[9] of God *and* of those icons of God, humankind, every rabbi has taken a "solemn pledge" to bear witness to, properly name, and then bless the [*Tzelem*⇔*N'shamah*] always present and hopefully awakening in each person (our *"selves"* included) or community. That which is **unwitnessed, unnamed, and unblessed**[10] can never be fully human, and that which is not fully human detracts from God's presence in the world, thus, as it were, diminishing God. **Witnessing, naming, and blessing** the evidences of the [*Tzelem*⇔*N'shamah*] in us and in others is not easy or simple work. Yet, that is perhaps what the whole Jewish religious enterprise is all about.

Witnessing requires that at *all* times and in *every* encounter, we bring full awareness to the [*Tzelem*⇔*N'shamah*] always present and, especially in stress, almost always obscured. A rabbi is a sort of satellite dish, focused on picking up the distant, often scrambled transmissions and emanations coming from one's own and others' [*Tzelem*⇔*N'shamah*]. This tuning device recognizes that what is presented is not all that is there: behind anger may be fear; underneath a rigid, unyielding exterior may be a compassion-

---

8. See Chapter 1, "Premises of Jewish Relational Care," pp. 10-12, in this book.

9. The author coined this term years ago to best describe what it is to be a rabbi. A rabbi is a walking, talking, living symbol who stands for both God and the best in humankind. Symbolic exemplarhood is the major provider of rabbinic influence, potency, and power. It is also at the root of much rabbinic loneliness and isolation.

10. For a fuller exposition, see Jack H Bloom, "Witnessing, Naming, and Blessing," in *The Rabbi As Symbolic Exemplar: By the Power Vested in Me* (Binghamton, NY: The Haworth Press, 2002), pp. 201-221.

ate heart; hidden from view in the whining and suffering may be courage. Though the static may seem deafening, and the view murky at best, as rabbis, we are always checking for who else is in the room, for the light obscured by the shadow, the hidden parts that are evidence of the ongoing, never-ceasing presence of each human's idiosyncratic, and thus unique, [*Tzelem⇔N'shamah*]. **Witnessing** is incredibly harder to do when the [*Tzelem⇔N'shamah*] is obscured, often by our own inability to witness it in those whom we experience as "other." Witnessing requires a willingness to enter into an initially chaotic mess being curious about, alert to, delighted by, making room for, and being supportive of the signs and signals of the often hidden [*Tzelem⇔N'shamah*] in one's self, in the other, and in the greater community. *V'heyeh b'rachah*—to be a blessing, and to bless others, requires witnessing the [*Tzelem⇔N'shamah*].

Naming creates new realities. Naming takes the undifferentiated, underdeveloped, rudimentary evidence of the [*Tzelem⇔N'shamah*] and gives relational meaning to already existing, though inchoate, realities. "God said, Let there be light! And there was light. God saw the light: that it was good. God separated the light from the darkness. God called the light: Day! and the darkness he called: Night!"[11]

God not only creates the world but, by witnessing what has been created and naming it, moves the primeval chaos into a new reality. The light was light, but day is a new reality to which one can relate. This makes possible for His future creation, humankind, to be in relationship with it, and that makes it **good.**

Man himself is given the task of naming the animals, conferring order and meaning and relationship. The implication follows that, though the creatures exist, relationship with them can take place only when they are properly named.

When we [*Tzelem⇔N'shamah*] seekers witness constellations, ever present though long concealed; garner evidence of the [*Tzelem⇔N'shamah*] so often obscured and sometimes rejected; and, by proper naming, bring these into human "being," perception, experience, and discourse, we create, as it were, something new. Humans do not, and perhaps cannot, relate to that which has no name. Naming that which heretofore had no name makes relationship possible, and it is **only** in relationship that "things" attain human "being." Naming makes an [I–You][12] relationship possible. *V'heyeh b'rachah*—to be a blessing, and to bless others, requires proper naming.

---

11. Genesis 1:3-5. Translation from Fox, *The Five Books of Moses,* p. 13.

12. After Walter Kaufmann, and in consultation with my wife, Ingrid, a native speaker of German. Walter Kaufmann, "I and You: A Prologue," in Martin Buber, *I and Thou: A New Translation* (New York: Simon and Schuster, 1970). See also, in this book, "A Guide for the Reader," p. 2, n. 3.

Blessing others on God's behalf is an audacious act. Aware of our own relationship with God, whose bounty and being has made room in the world for us and our unique "being," and so knowing that our beingness is blessed, we, **in turn, can bestow blessing on others.** Blessing others with our personal presence and words is one of the ultimate acts of love a rabbi can do. Crucial to being a rabbi, it is a primary way of attending to the [*Tzelem*⇔*N'shamah*] in us and in others. As with Avraham, only one who receives the blessing can impart it. Rabbis, blessed by being God's exemplars, are duty bound to bless humankind.

To be a blessing requires blessing others. This blessing business, though, is no easy thing. Are we up to the task?

That the charge given to Avraham was no easy thing becomes evident in the life of his grandson, our paradigmatic progenitor Yaaqov, who was named and blessed and whose blessing name, Yisrael, we carry to this day. Yaaqov spends a lifetime stumbling around in the land of blessing. Astute in almost all things, witness to strengths and weaknesses in others, able to play on their hidden attributes, he is incredibly vulnerable in the area of blessing. He is vulnerable both in being blessed, as we have seen in the mess with Esav and their father, Yitzhak, and in blessing others, as we shall see when it comes to blessing his own sons. It is, one might say, following the text,[13] a wounded place in him. Whenever it is touched, he is close to being overwhelmed.

We know what happened with Esav. The contretemps began with the sordid business of trading some grub for the blessing "owned" by his overtired hunter sibling just back from a jaunt in the fields. Witnessed though he must have been by his mother in one of the first hunter-gatherer splits,[14] he surmises that he cannot be blessed as he is; he has to present as "other." To steal the blessing he had already bought, he clumsily makes himself appear as his older brother, whose heel he had entered the world holding. The deception is "successful" with the father who cannot "see" what is in front of him. Despite the text, which may reflect his mother's view of him, he had never really been the *ish tam,*[15] certainly not in respect to blessing. He had unfairly bargained for it and had received it under false pretenses. The blessing, bought and dissembled for, roused an understandable rage in his brother Esav and led to Yaaqov's being "cursed" with years of exile.

Though the inept blessing by his father led to pain and animosity, it taught Yaaqov little about blessing—its presence, its importance, its power,

---

13. Genesis 32:30-33.
14. Genesis 25:27.
15. Simple man. Genesis 25:27.

and its dangers. He did not learn that how one was blessed and what one was blessed for were crucial. The [*Tzelem* ⇔ *N'shamah*] present in others needs to be witnessed, properly named, and then blessed.

Perhaps we can forgive our errant forefather, understanding that Yaaqov's original blessing was tainted. Maybe it wasn't just nurture. Perhaps Yaaqov had inherited from Yitzhak a certain genetic predisposition toward "blindness" in the field of blessing. He, who was a shrewd assessor of what was going on in others and who saw the look in Lavan's face that indicated a subtle change in mood,[16] could not witness nor properly name the loyalty, love, and persistence resident in his wife Lea, and so he could not bless it even if he knew how. To him, she continued to carry the epithet "Dim Eyes"—this despite her seeing her husband and children with exquisite clarity. She wants what any of the matriarchs (namely, her mother and grandmother-in-law) want: to bear many children and have her children blessed by Yaaqov, who himself had been blessed, and whose task it is to bless. Yet, as we shall see, *none* of her children are blessed by their father. She does her best to get them blessed. She sees something special and unique in each of her "boys." She witnesses the nascent [*Tzelem* ⇔ *N'shamah*] present in each and quite properly names them, which, as we have seen, is a prerequisite for their being blessed. Her proper naming of them, she prays, will provoke not only his love and appreciation but more crucially their being blessed by their blessing-impaired father—her husband, who *had* been blessed.

Lea bears their first and proclaims: "Re'uven/See a Son!"[17] and when he is not seen, she persists and brings forth Shim'on/Hearing.[18] And if neither seeing nor hearing avails, then a third, Levi/Joining. He would join her husband to her[19] (as he was later to couple God and Israel with his service in the Temple), and so might blessing rub off on her and her progeny. When none of this bearing, witnessing, and naming brings blessing or even a hint of gratitude, she brings forth one who is destined to be one of the greatest of all, Yehuda/Giving thanks, for what God had provided.[20]

The text records a pause in bearing. With no newborn to suckle, her mind could well have been preoccupied with the ebbing hope that her four might still be blessed. It does not happen. With intensifying resentment, for she has truly merited more than she received, she bears Yissachar/There is

---

16. Genesis 31:2.
17. Genesis 29:32. Translation from Fox, *The Five Books of Moses,* p. 138.
18. Genesis 29:33. Ibid.
19. Genesis 29:34. Ibid.
20. Genesis 29:35. Ibid., p. 139.

hire—she has earned Yaaqov's blessing five times over.[21] Still nothing! She persistently follows with her sixth son, and since her husband will not/cannot bless, she ups the ante, attempts it herself, and, in one fell swoop, simultaneously names and blesses him Zevulun/Prince.[22] Then comes her daughter, Dina, for whom no explanation of naming is given. If the sons have not been blessed, what could one hope for a "mere" daughter, yet her fate will reverberate. Through all of this, Lea remains unseen, unheard, unwitnessed, unappreciated, and herself unblessed, and her progeny's special gifts, even when recognized, are unappreciated and unblessed. Perhaps her husband, Yaaqov, is the one with "dim eyes."

With his beloved Rahel's son, Yosef, it is different. Beyond the arrogant, insufferable, preening young man, Yaaqov must have witnessed something of the [*Tzelem*⇔*N'shamah*]. It is something very familiar, something very much like himself. There is greatness in the boy. Having been taught by his mother that "clothes make the man," always being taken with outward appearances ("and Rahel was fair of form and fair to look at"[23]), and having learned little about seeing beyond the surface, he gives Yosef a beautiful coat that marks him as "other." He knows well the part in himself that could put on a garment not his, present himself well, be clever beyond words, and use these artifices to be blessed by his own father, and later to achieve some of his God-given aims.

The coat is an awkward, inept attempt at blessing. It provokes anger for favoritism and infuriates the brothers whose very names testify to their own yearning to be blessed, and whose special gifts have gone unwitnessed and unblessed by their father. Time has not taught Yaaqov very much. He cannot name the greatness in Yosef appropriately and therefore cannot bless it in a way that is useful.

And upon reaching those generative years at the end of his life, when in the fullness of his life experience the task of blessing his progeny falls upon him full force, Yaaqov remains, as always, blessing impaired.

How Yaaqov dealt with that challenge has been unequivocally passed down to us as "Yaaqov's Blessings." The biblical editor, spin doctor extraordinaire, positioned the event for publication by repeating *three* times in one brief sentence that Yaaqov had "blessed" all of his sons.[24] As a matter of fact, Yaaqov had blessed only one, and the careful reader will nonetheless observe the degree of his impairment.

---

21. Genesis 30:18. Ibid., p. 142.
22. Genesis 30:20. Ibid.
23. Genesis 29:16. Ibid., p. 137.
24. Genesis 49:28.

Despite all of his brushes with blessing, Yaaqov has not learned that even though only he who receives blessing can impart it, that alone is not enough. To bless requires beyond the prerequisite[25] of being and feeling blessed, witnessing the essential [*Tzelem*⇔*N'shamah*] residing in each of his sons, then giving it a proper name so it can have "human existence," and, only then, blessing it.

Yaaqov continues to the end of his days the habits that have caused so much trouble and are destined to cause more. If it is true that *Ma'aseh Avot Siman l'banim*,[26] the acts of the patriarchs are an omen for their descendants, then maybe his habits (learned from Mom?!) engender the multitude of splits that have bedeviled our people. Those splits are foreshadowed when Yaaqov, unaware of the deeper implications of his words, says proudly to his brother Esav, now ready to reconcile over the stolen blessing: "For with only my rod did I cross this Jordan, and now I have become two camps."[27]

The text points in an unknowing allusion to all the splits, seeded so long ago, that are to have such great impact: the split between Yosef and his brothers; the split between Yehuda and the tribes who lived in the land named for Yosef's son Efrayim, later known as Israel, a split that was papered over in the reigns of David and Solomon,[28] only to resurface after Solomon's death;[29] the conflict between the sanctuary at Beth El in the Land of Efrayim and the Temple of Jerusalem; and on and on. The tendency implicit in the Genesis story of the twins is to think that there is blessing enough for only one. This leads inevitably to the insatiable craving to have it all. This split was passed over to our Christian and Muslim brothers and sisters, who claimed the blessing for themselves exclusively. This thinking is present in all of the splits between those who feel blessed and those who we think are not. It is a split implicit in all Fundamentalism, in all of the [Either/Or] splits that seem endemic in human nature and have wrought havoc with humankind.

Yaaqov's blessing his children commences when Yosef, fulfilling the *mitzvah*[30] of visiting his dying father, brings the grandchildren Efrayim and Menashe along. Despite the absence of the rest of his family, Yaaqov spontaneously decides to use the visit to bless his favorites. He starts appropri-

---

25. See Nahum Sarna, on Genesis 48:4, *The JPS Torah Commentary* (Philadelphia, PA: The Jewish Publication Society, 1989).
26. Talmud Bavli: Sotah 34A; others, Rambann Genesis 12:6.
27. Genesis 32:10. Translation from Fox, *The Five Books of Moses,* p. 152.
28. 1 Kings 4.
29. 1 Kings 12.
30. In Hebrew, fulfilling God's command; in Yiddish, a good deed.

ately enough by presenting his own credentials as one who has been blessed: "Yaaqov said to Yosef: God Shaddai was seen by me in Luz [and the reader will note that our blessing-impaired forefather uses the pre–Beth El, pre-blessing name of the place[31]] in the land of Canaan; *he **blessed**[32] me.*"[33]

In the presence of his favorites, he describes his own having been witnessed and properly named, as were Avraham (Avram) and Yitzhak ("for it is through Yitzhak that seed will be called by your [name]"[34]), but then he stumbles as he specifies the naming for only one set of grandchildren, Yosef's sons:

> Then he ***blessed*** Yosef and said: The God in whose presence my fathers walked, Avraham and Yitzhak, the God who has tended me ever since I was (born), until this day—the messenger who has redeemed me from all ill-fortune, may he ***bless*** the lads! May my name continue to be called through them and the name of my fathers, Avraham and Yitzhak![35]

Yaaqov has been adequate at witnessing the [*Tzelem*⇔*N'shamah*] in Yosef and Yosef's sons, Menashe and Efrayim, naming them in the line of his father and grandfather. Even this is done somewhat ineptly, for, no doubt, word of Dad's playing favorites again will get back to the other siblings, whose angry response we can presume.

Yaaqov then blesses Yosef's sons: "So he ***blessed*** them on that day, saying: By you shall Israel give-***blessings,*** saying: God make you like Efrayim and Menashe!"[36]

The words have become our Friday night way of blessing our children. And for those who serve Jews in the midst of "affluenza"[37] and secularism, it is a very topical and poignant blessing. It *is* crucial to bless those who, de-

---

31. Genesis 28:19.

32. Emphasis is mine. Here and in the following text, ***blessed*** is italicized and underlined and in bold to indicate the use in the text of the Hebrew root ברך *B-R-Ch*, "blessed."

33. Genesis 48:3. Translation from Fox, *The Five Books of Moses*, p. 226.

34. Genesis 21:12. Ibid., p. 89.

35. Genesis 48:15-16. Ibid., pp. 227 and 229.

36. Genesis 48:20. Ibid., p. 229.

37. Defined as "1. The bloated, sluggish and unfilfilled feeling that results from efforts to keep up with the Joneses. 2. An epidemic of stress, overwork, waste and indebtedness caused by dogged pursuit of the American Dream. 3. An unsustainable addiction to economic growth. 4. A television program that could save your life." John de Graf and Vivian Boe, PBS-KCTS/Seattle and Oregon Public Broadcasting, 1997.

spite their affluence and despite their being accepted, have heroically maintained their Jewishness in a foreign land.

Yet, not only Yosef and his foreign-born sons are Yaaqov's children; all twelve and unmentioned Dina are his. Now in his old age he must gather them together and bless them. This is the task he is not up to.

He himself summons them all to his bedside. They know what such a meeting portends. It is blessing time. They know the routine from what they have heard of the blessing of their father, their aggrieved uncle Esav, and their great-grandfather Avraham. They will hear about their future as their father has told them when he summoned them. Those predictions will be interspersed with words of blessing for each. That is the way it is done. Their expectancy rises as they gather to hear their father's blessing. One might think that having blessed Yosef and his progeny privately, Yaaqov would have the good grace, with his demise approaching, to this time, at least, not differentiate between them when all are present. The reader will note well a peculiar fact. Yaaqov has still not learned the lesson of the coat he had so long ago bestowed upon Yosef! Yaaqov uses the occasion, as he promised, to predict for them what would happen in their future. As he, one by one, calls the roll of the first ten sons (six of whom Lea of the "dim eyes" bore him and did the crucial work of preparation by witnessing and naming them for his blessing), the word ברך *B-R-Ch*[38] appears nowhere. *None* is blessed until Yosef's turn comes. Then, apparently unable to contain himself, Yaaqov erupts in an outpouring of blessing—**six times in just two verses:**

> By your father's God—may he help you, and Shaddai, may he give-you-**_blessing_**_: **Blessings**_ of the heavens, from above, **_blessings_** of Ocean crouching below, **_blessings_** of breasts and womb![39]

> May the **_blessings_** of your father transcend the **_blessings_** of mountains eternal, the bounds of hills without age. May they fall upon the head of Yosef, on the crown of the consecrated-one among his brothers.[40]

Yaaqov offers words of *b'racha,* blessing and abundance, only for one. For none of the others is there *b'racha.* Once again, only with Yosef and his sons Efrayim and Menashe is the Hebrew root ברך *B-R-Ch* used. Only Yosef's line is blessed.

---

38. Blessing.
39. Genesis 49:25. Translation from Fox, *The Five Books of Moses,* p. 233.
40. Genesis 49:26. Ibid.

Yaaqov isn't very good at witnessing and naming the [*Tzelem*⇔
N'shamah] in others, except for Yosef. His failing is that he cannot name
(though Lea has done her very best) and bless the [*Tzelem*⇔*N'shamah*] in
the others. There is not *one* word of blessing in the whole last testament for
them—cold, accurate, pungent descriptions, yes, but no blessing.

Yaaqov cannot witness the dedicated holiness resident behind Levi's anger that would one day mediate between God and God's people. Anger and
violence belongs to his brother Esav; it is not his. He lives by his wits and
his cunning; violence is not part of him. It is anger that he is most afraid of,
denying its presence in himself. And where is the creativity and music that
is to show up later despite Levi not being blessed? Yes, that happens too, despite not being blessed.

With Yehuda,[41] Yaaqov describes what will one day be recognized as
Yehuda's power and strength. Yehuda is lavishly praised, but contrary to the
party line commentary found in the Torah texts of both the Conservative
and Reform movements,[42] which list the words to him as being a blessing,
there is not *one* word of blessing for him. Blessing is reserved for only Yosef
and his progeny.

Yaaqov's failings are indeed an omen and a warning to us. We are reminded how crucial it is for us to "be a blessing"—to witness the [*Tzelem*⇔
N'shamah] in all, to give it proper naming, and to bless it.

Though crucial, doing this is no easy task. Witnessing and naming the
obvious, what we like and approve of, is not enough for blessing.

We are called to witness, name, and bless those different from Efrayim
and Menashe, who have not yet succeeded in creating Jewish lives in the
well-off Diaspora. We are called to ready for blessing those who are periph-
eral and struggling with who they are. Our task is to witness, name, and
bless those whose gifts are in hiding, those who need blessing to aid in the
discovery of who they really are.

Not too easy is this business of being witness to the blessing in us and in
others—alertness to, witnessing of, providing ongoing testimony for, advocating on behalf of, and naming and blessing the often obscured and sometimes rejected [*Tzelem*⇔*N'shamah*] in ourselves, in others, and in the
world at large. Yet being blessed, we are called to bless All.

None of us is fully up to the task—we can all do only a part of it. As Jewish relational caregivers we have no choice but to undertake it, knowing that
too often we will fail and spend a lifetime learning to do it better.

---

41. Genesis 49:8-12.
42. Etz Hayim, *Torah and Commentary;* The Rabbinical Assembly, *The Torah: A
Modern Commentary* (Philadelphia, PA: Jewish Publication Society, 2001), p. 300. "Judah is lavishly praised and blessed"; Plaut et al., *The Blessing of Judah* (New York: Union of American Hebrew Congregations, 1981), p. 312.

It is told of one of my teachers, the late Milton H. Erickson,[43] who was perhaps the greatest therapist of our era, that a patient, having heard of his healing prowess, traveled halfway around the world to see him. Entering Milton's somewhat shabby office, he was shocked as he took in its well-worn furniture, overused chairs, and ramshackle bookshelves—rather humble surroundings for such a great man. Erickson noticed him looking around in disbelief, fixed his intense gaze upon him, and said, "I know it's not much, **but I'M HERE!**"

I'M HERE! We can have no better motto. Each of us is more than enough. Each of us is all we've got. Each of us and all of us are blessed. We need to know and be assured that our blessedness is not in the doing; it is in the ***being.*** We are blessed through no choice of our own. Our being blessed is God's irrevocable gift. So when the going gets tough, and assuredly it will, each of us can do no better than to respond, ***"Hineni,* I'm Here,"** words that have reverberated down the ages. Each of us is more than enough. Each of us is a blessing.

---

43. Milton H. Erickson, MD (1901-1980), was a world-famous psychiatrist and psychologist specializing in medical hypnosis, utilizing unique approaches to the healing process, including metaphor and story to communicate with the client's unconscious.

21

A Story of Brokenness and Healing: The Relationship of Rabbi and Congregant

Rena Halpern Kieval
Dan Ornstein

Congregants look to their rabbis to help them feel God's love and presence—God's Self. What happens when rabbis' own struggles with their *"selves"* prevent them from being fully present with their congregants?

In 1994, a tragedy forced both of us to consider this question. Rena's ten-year-old son, Jonathan, died suddenly one week into Dan's tenure as the new rabbi of our congregation. The pain of this loss was exacerbated by a rabbi and congregant relationship that did not develop properly for either of us. Two years of personal and professional struggles eventually grew into healing and reconciliation. We learned much from this process about the nature of such relationships, grief, healing, and forgiveness.

Rabbis navigate a complicated network of demands between service to the congregant, to God, and to their own needs. In this chapter we present some of the insights we gained by examining our relationship following Jon's death. We explore the relationship between two aspects of the rabbi's life—being a reflection of God's Self and being a human being who is made up of many *"selves."*

Beginnings: Where We Came From

Rena

The day I gave birth to Jonathan, I also lost my innocence. My illusions of security and of life's predictability were shattered when the doctor told us, "Your baby has severe medical problems, and possible brain damage." Jonathan's life began with major surgeries, many weeks in the intensive care unit, and uncertainty about his survival and his future. Fortunately, his medical situation improved, and he developed well in many arenas. He was articulate and charming, and he learned to walk, talk, and read. But as he grew, neurological abnormalities affected his emotional development and social behavior, which did not conform to those of his peers. Jon never seemed to "fit," or to feel safe and at home in the world.

I was determined to help Jonathan overcome every one of his challenges. Part of me believed that if only I showed enough persistence and sheer willpower, then he would somehow "become normal" and behave like any other child. But as the years passed, reality began to sink in. I began to understand that there was only so much my love and my efforts could do to compensate for Jonathan's limitations, and that my task was to accept him for who he was. My helplessness came as a shock to me, as I was forced to apply to my own life a lesson I had learned as a professional social worker: some situations cannot be repaired.

The summer of 1994 was an important turning point. For the first time we planned two family trips during which Jonathan would stay at home with a babysitter. In addition to working toward acceptance, I began to forgive myself for not having the power to meet Jon's every need perfectly, and for wanting to have a life for myself, my husband, and my other children.

The shift in my attitude was accompanied by a renewal of my spiritual life. I had recently become more deeply involved in Judaism, appreciating anew some of the more profound aspects of my tradition. The rabbi of our synagogue was a significant mentor for me as I explored a new, more adult framework for my Jewish connection. In 1993, when he left for a congregation in another city, I mourned his departure. I hoped that the rabbi who succeeded him would be an important spiritual guide and religious resource for me, and I enthusiastically signed on as a member of the Search Committee to select him or her. By the spring of 1994, after a yearlong process, the committee had selected Dan, and he had accepted the position.

The week before Dan officially became the new rabbi, he and I met over lunch to discuss the synagogue's adult education programming, for which I was the chairperson. That weekend, my family was to leave for our second long trip without Jonathan. I mentioned our plans to Dan and commented that it was a big step for our family to go away without Jonathan. He asked about Jon, and I replied briefly, not inclined at that time to go into detail. There would be plenty of time, I thought, for Dan and me to get to know each other, and for him to get to know Jon. There was no hurry. Little did I know that Dan would never meet Jon, or that a few days later he would bury my little boy, officiating at the most terrible event of my life.

Dan

I recall from as early as the age of five accompanying my father, a nursing administrator, to the nursing homes in which he worked, visiting and talking with the residents. He and my mother, a public health nurse, exposed me and my siblings to experiences with the sick, frail, and elderly. They were not trying to scare or shock us, but rather they were teaching us to look for the humanity that resides in each person. As a result, I learned to focus on the whole person and to become engaged with that person. What I learned from my parents was, and continues to be, tremendously helpful to me in dealing with illness, death, and people's suffering. Yet I also learned to cope with the painful feelings arising from these encounters by distancing myself emotionally. This later became the "professional persona" that I would use to deal with painful circumstances, rather than acknowledge how sad, frightened, or angry I felt. Within limits, this mode of professional detachment is what allows clergy and all helping professionals to survive the storms of their work. However, my later experiences would show me what happens when that detachment becomes excessive. I carried this excessive detachment into my work as a congregational rabbi after I was ordained in 1989.

In 1994, my preparations to move to a new synagogue community were filled with the normal mix of excitement and anxiety. My first contact with what would become my new congregation in Albany, New York, was a telephone interview with members of the Search Committee. Rena, a member of the committee, asked me, "Rabbi, how would you explain to a mourner the meaning and importance of *kaddish*?"[1] I responded that a mourner is not looking for a lecture on the history or theology of *kaddish*, but for consolation. I explained that I would try to explore with the mourner how the regular repetition of *kaddish* in the embrace of community establishes a rhythm in the mourner's life, helping him or her to work through grief.

After several months of interviews and discussions, I was hired, and my family and I moved to Albany in July 1994. I arrogantly believed that, with five years of congregational experience under my belt, I was ready for anything, and yet I felt persistent anxiety as the demands and complexities of my new community became apparent to me. In addition, my wife, Marian, and I were expecting our second child, our three-year-old son was dealing poorly with the transition, and I had heard that a few people in my new community were unhappy with my selection as the new rabbi. I was also aware that my predecessor had developed a reputation which felt, to me, larger than life. Filling his shoes would be a daunting challenge. I arrived in my new community anxious and lonely. Whom could I turn to to sort through my feelings and concerns? My wife and I had no friends in our new community. We could barely keep pace with the demands placed upon us, and

---

1. Doxology recited often throughout the service and also said by mourners: "May God's name be hallowed and exalted throughout the world."

friends from out of town lacked the time and the energy to help us. I responded to these feelings by hiding behind a wall of tight-lipped restraint. Acting in "professional persona" became my strategy for fending off my feelings of dislocation and isolation. The more pain I felt, the more rigid, distant, and clinical I became. To complicate matters, by the time of the move, I had neglected my relationship with God for so long that I could not turn to it for guidance and strength. I tried to convince myself that I was strong, when in fact I was quite weak. I had lost my sense of how my work was actually a part of my relationship with God.

Lost

Rena

The Monday after our weekend in Lake Placid, I lay in bed contentedly. When we had returned the previous night, Jonathan had not been feeling well, and now Shalom went to his bedroom to check on him. Jonathan was not breathing. Next came a flurry of unbelievable events: the call to 911; the arrival of the emergency medical technicians (EMTs); their attempts to revive Jon; Shalom's departure by ambulance with him to the hospital; the stunned faces of our two other children as I stood in our kitchen receiving the phone call—Jonathan had been pronounced dead in the hospital emergency room.

I called Nancy, a close friend, to tell her what had happened and to ask her for a ride to the hospital. I was certain that I was sleepwalking in a nightmare. We arrived at the emergency room. A few friends had already heard the news and were waiting there for us. Shalom had asked the hospital to call Dan, our new rabbi, and he, too, was there when we arrived. As we began to contact family members, I was vaguely aware that Nancy and Dan had begun to discuss funeral arrangements. All I could feel was intense, suffocating pain, like nothing I had ever felt before.

Jonathan lay on a stretcher, looking peaceful and asleep. Could he really be dead? I was afraid to touch his skin and find it cold: that would mean that it was true. But needing desperately to touch him, I sat by his side and stroked his thick black hair over and over again. The sweet little boy who was a part of my being, the child on whom so much of my life had centered for the past ten years, suddenly was no more.

Arrangements were being made. Dan had been our rabbi for one week. The fact that he was virtually a stranger added to the unreal feeling of the situation, and to my feeling that everything familiar was being pulled out from under me. In the blink of an eye, I had lost control of everything. I was filled with panic as my child slipped through my fingers. We were surrounded by strangers—EMTs, nurses, doctors, the rabbi, funeral directors—one after another they were taking him away from us, his parents. Suddenly they seemed to have a claim on him, while we no longer did. I had lost Jonathan, for whom I had fought for so long. Now I was defeated. There was no more fighting back.

I did not know much about funerals. As we began to talk, I imagined Dan speaking publicly about my child, whom he had never met. I conjured an image of stilted, formulaic speeches. Desperate to hold on to Jonathan in whatever way I could, I decided that only Shalom and I would choose what words were said to sum up our child's life and to bid him good-bye. I asked Nancy to tell Dan that we did not want him to deliver the eulogy, that we would write one, and she relayed the message. The thought flashed through my mind at the time that Dan might hear this request as some kind of rejection, but I did not have the emotional energy to worry about that or to communicate directly with this person I hardly knew. I remembered Dan's professionalism during the Search Committee process and assumed that, under the circumstances, we did not have to be concerned about personal sensitivities.

The funeral took place the following day amid a sea of people and waves of overwhelming emotion. My son's body was lowered into the ground. Every minute that passed took me by surprise; it was hard to imagine that I could continue to live while enduring these events. The only relief was the numbness that came and went periodically, alternating with moments of agony.

Along with the sheer horror of that day, I experienced great comfort from the love of friends and family. In the back of my mind, however, I began to feel resentment toward Dan. The seeds of the alienation that was to plague us were planted at the funeral. Dan was physically present there and conducted himself with complete professionalism, but in some way he seemed absent. After he read the words Shalom and I had written about Jonathan, I waited for him to add some of his own thoughts. I wanted words of comfort from him, but I did not hear anything beyond formal prayers and formulaic words of condolence.

I experienced the same feeling during the week of *shivah*[2] at our house. Dan led the services and always spoke kindly and appropriately, but I kept sensing that something was missing. I began to question whether I or Sha-

---

2. The seven-day (hence, *shivah,* Hebrew for seven) period of mourning, following interment, spent at home receiving visiting consolers; called "sitting *shivah*"; one of the great inventions of Judaism.

lom had somehow unwittingly pushed him away, asked him to keep his distance, or whether he was standing back because we hardly knew one another. I wondered whether he was holding back because of the many rabbis in our family, afraid of intruding.

Sometime during the *shivah* week, I mustered my strength, approached him, and said, "Please don't think that because we come from rabbinic families, we don't need you. We do—we need you to be our rabbi." It felt like an open, honest moment, and he seemed to be listening, but nothing changed in our subsequent interactions. He seemed distant and closed off, strangely mirroring my own feelings of numbness and alienation. Nothing was connecting properly in my inner or outer world, and Dan became yet another component of that disconnection. Later I understood that Dan was also unwittingly one of the strangers who represented our loss, one of the interlopers who reflected the most frightening stranger of all, Death, the stranger who had claimed Jonathan from us forever.

Dan

The first Monday morning of my new position, I went to *minyan*[3] at the synagogue. August 8 was a pleasant summer day, typical of the Adirondack region of New York. Returning home in a good mood, I came home only to be told by Marian that she had received a call from a local hospital, asking me to come right away. I looked at the message pad: a son of Rena's had died. Fear seized me. Which son? Was it David, her eldest, whom I had just met? I got into the car and drove to the hospital, feeling the foreboding and anxiety of having to deal with a messy, ugly situation for which I was entirely unprepared. I gripped the steering wheel, thinking out loud about the right professional things to say and do when meeting the family.

I was led into a room in the rear of the emergency department. Rena, her husband, Shalom, and their friend Nancy stood around the examining table where Jonathan lay dead. I expected Jon's parents to be wild with grief, shrieking, as tears ran down their faces. Instead, both parents were silent, their faces contorted by a mixture of deep pain and shock. Rena continuously stroked Jon's hair, from time to time letting out a soft, muted cry.

I stood frozen, not knowing what to say or do. I felt a cold numbness and a dumbness about the whole scene. I felt I needed to say something, but only the right something, as if that could truly exist at that moment. We stood over Jon's lifeless body in excruciating silence. Then they asked, "What do we need to do to prepare for the funeral?" Nancy suggested that

---

3. A quorum of ten Jews required for public prayer.

we call one of the local Jewish funeral directors to handle the arrangements. When she broke the silence with a practical suggestion, it was a blessed relief for me. It gave me a chance to speak and to feel a sense of power in a situation over which none of us had any power. I could be useful; I could arrange for the rituals of burial to begin.

Unable to share myself in those moments—I was paralyzed by fear, horror, and confusion—I threw myself into the busywork of the preparations. I ran out to the phone booths in the waiting are of the emergency room to call a member of the synagogue staff who was on vacation at the time. The funeral director arrived and took Jon's body. We began arranging for the Jewish burial society to prepare his body, and I contacted the coroner and the pathologist's office to make sure that the dictates of Jewish law would be followed in the event of an autopsy. There seemed to be an almost otherworldly smoothness to all of the tasks, as if by their sheer orderliness they would dispel the chaos and horror of the situation.

I arranged to meet Rena, Shalom, and their other children, David and Daniel, at their home later that evening to finalize arrangements for the funeral, which would take place the next day. When I arrived, the house was mobbed with close friends, family, and neighbors. The family and I moved away from the noisy crowd into their living room. We spoke briefly about what would happen the next day, and I answered some of their more technical questions about the preparation of the body, the burial, and the *shivah.* Shalom and Rena kept the conversation rather matter-of-fact, despite the anguish that showed all over their faces and in their exhausted bodies.

I remember the scene vividly. I had never before dealt directly with the death of a child. I had counseled and prayed with families who had lost children in the past but had never confronted the lifeless body of a child in front of his grieving parents. Now I was sitting with a family I had known for one week, preparing with them for the funeral of their ten-year-old son. His death had ripped out the hearts, not only of his family, but of an entire community that had watched him grow up. Around me were strangers, people with whom I had yet to build relationships. Perhaps the "sin of humility" that I was about to commit during the week of *shivah,* and in the months that followed, was initially sparked by the family's request that they eulogize Jon, rather than I, the new rabbi who had not known him. Naturally I agreed. A part of me heard this as, "We need you here, but we don't really need you here." On one level I felt that I was at best a tolerated outsider rather than this community's rabbi. At the funeral I did what I believed I had been told to do: I acted as master of ceremonies and as coordinator, yet I did not venture to offer more than the most basic words of comfort.

I perpetuated this misguided humility throughout the week of *shivah*. I felt every moment like an interloper, and I shut down in the face of such emotional intensity. I attended the *minyan* at the *shivah* house in the morning and quickly shuffled out when it ended to make room for the "important" people: the close friends and family from all over the world who were camped out in Rena and Shalom's home.

One morning toward the end of the *shivah* period, as I prepared to leave their home, Rena and Shalom approached me: "We've been missing our rabbi this week." Sensing that I was being criticized, I hastily assured them that I would stay behind to speak with them, which I did. Afterward I kept feeling that my efforts had been transparently inadequate. I had to be told by people in crisis that I was needed by them. I knew that I had sorely missed the mark, and this feeling of incompleteness would stay with me for a long time. My first two years in Albany after Jon's death would be tumultuous, and my feelings of alienation from this grieving family, Rena especially, would only add to my sense of inner and outer chaos.

I Need a Rabbi

Rena

After the end of our *sh'loshim,*[4] I felt completely broken, yet the world went on as if nothing had changed. While I understood this rationally, on a primal, emotional level, I felt uncared for and abandoned. Shouldn't everyone around me share in my state of chaos and despair?

I was surprised to learn that the struggles of grief are so physical. Every breath seemed to require enormous effort, and moving through the motions of a day felt like pushing my body through molasses. I breathed, spoke, and perhaps appeared like a functioning person, but I did not feel like one. I felt as though I had been knocked down by a huge truck, one of those eighteen-wheelers that Jonathan—a lover of big trucks—had taught me about.

My wounds were too severe for anyone to heal. Yet, in those early months, many tried. People reached out to comfort me, "What can I do for you?" "How can I help you?" They sincerely wanted to ease the hurt. I appreciated the kind impulses behind these questions, but I was incapable of answering them. In the initial weeks and months after Jon's death, I had no idea what I needed. What could possibly soothe a hurt this deep?

I tried hard not to judge people's words and behavior. When they avoided the subject of Jonathan, I understood that they wished to protect themselves

---

4. The official thirty-day period of mourning.

from my pain, and that some thought they were protecting me, even though I always felt better when I was able to talk about him. I knew that as they tried to respond to my loss, many of those around me were themselves lost. Most of their words of comfort sounded meaningless; there *were* no appropriate words for this situation. Still I learned to take comfort in the simple fact that people were reaching out to me, and to accept the feelings and intentions behind their clumsily inadequate words. I held on to the beauty of the fact that people cared enough, and were brave enough, to grope their way toward my family and me through all the pain. Accepting help was something I had never done easily, but now I needed to grab every hand that was extended to me. I learned a lesson I have carried with me ever since: there is no such thing as a small kindness.

Immediately after Jon's death, some people urged me, "Be angry!" Some of them were angry on my behalf, feeling that his death was "just not fair!" I knew that I had grounds for anger, but I did not want to feel angry. In my ten years as Jonathan's mother, I had struggled to embrace what had been given me, and not to feel that I always had to fight it. Now, I needed a sense of peace and wholeness that I could find only in acceptance.

Yet there were those toward whom I felt anger. Some friends and family members were surprisingly inattentive. Most noticeably absent were various professionals: friends who are doctors and mental health professionals, some of Jonathan's doctors, and the rabbis we knew. After initial expressions of sympathy, many were strangely quiet. How odd it seemed that the "helping professionals" in our circle of acquaintances were the least helpful in comforting us! This puzzled and disappointed me. I thought, aren't these the healers, the ones who know how to respond to these tragedies? Despite my best efforts, I *was* angry at some of these people, probably because they were the people from whom I expected the most.

My most conflicted feelings were toward Dan. I had felt open to trusting him, as my rabbi, and Shalom and I had looked for his support and comfort. But in the weeks following Jon's death, he hardly spoke to us about Jonathan or about his death. When we crossed paths, we always ended up in quick exchanges about matters that jarred me with their irrelevance to my life: synagogue ritual issues, politics, and "small talk" about the community. At that time I was living in another universe, a universe in which none of those subjects mattered to me.

For me, the days moved in agonizing slow motion, whereas Dan always seemed to be rushing, in particular, rushing away from me. I was baffled. Dan seemed to be a sensitive person. I tried to be patient, as I waited for him to show concern for me, but I did not feel patient; my needs were urgent. I needed a rabbi.

On Rosh Hashanah,[5] one month after Jon's death, I sat in *shul*,[6] looking up at Dan on the *bimah*[7] and silently begging him to acknowledge us. I yearned for something from him, however irrational. Perhaps I hoped that he could uncover a secret about Jonathan's death that would make everything clear. Perhaps I had the crazy expectation that he could tell us how to end the pain. On some level I think I believed that he held special knowledge that could help me transcend the suffering. I assumed that, as a clergyperson, he would have answers, even though I could not even name my questions. But that Rosh Hashanah and Yom Kippur,[8] Dan seemed oblivious to our presence. My anger and confusion deepened. I spoke to him silently: "You are our rabbi, who just buried our child. This crowd of hopeful, boisterous people, these prayers about self-examination and repentance, all of it affronts and assaults us. The whole scenario intensifies our loneliness. Don't you see that? Why are you ignoring me?"

I did not want to cultivate my angry feelings, so in dialogues with myself, I continued to make excuses for Dan; it was the High Holydays; he was facing the complex demands of a new pulpit in an unknown community; he was under major stress. After all, my family was only one of several hundred that needed his attention. Dan and his wife were preparing for the birth of their second child, and perhaps he could not face the thought of a child dying, or perhaps there was something about my family or me. Maybe we had insulted him at the time of the funeral.

I knew that certain special dynamics complicated my responses to Dan. As the daughter and daughter-in-law of rabbis, and as someone who had at one time yearned to pursue that calling myself,[9] my history with rabbis was not a neutral one, and my relationship with my own rabbi was bound to be complicated. Part of me may have resented his being in a position of which I had been deprived. Also, the mystique of a rabbi was different for me. I know very well that rabbis are human beings. I could not be fooled or soothed when Dan presented the professional persona of Rabbi Ornstein, with formal rabbinic statements and ritual diversions. I needed the genuine person. When Dan did interact with us, he seemed to be trying to give us something complicated, something grand, befitting a rabbi. Gifts that were complicated and grand, however, went over and beyond us. We felt humbled and small, flattened by our loss.

---

5. The first of the month of Tishre observed as the Jewish New Year, beginning of the High Holydays.

6. Yiddish for "synagogue."

7. The front of the synagogue where the rabbi and cantor officiate.

8. Day of Atonement concluding the High Holydays.

9. I did pursue that calling and was ordained as a rabbi in May 2006.

On one level, I understood that I was so broken and needy that nothing and no one could satisfy me. Still, underneath all of my speculation and rationalizations lay a deep hurt and loneliness. It seemed that there was nobody who could be with me in these depths. I imagined that people avoided me, or evaded the subjects of Jonathan and of my grief, because I radiated so much intense hurt, or because I evoked something too painful to think about. When Dan avoided me, the implications for me were much greater. His apparent rejection of me suggested a number of terrifying possibilities: either God didn't care about me, or perhaps God cared but could not help. If even my own rabbi found it difficult to be in my presence and was turning away from me, did that mean there was no balm for my grief? Did it mean that I was not worthy of my rabbi's, or God's, attention and concern? If Dan couldn't face my tragedy, was facing it beyond even God's power? I could not answer these frightening questions, but I knew that I felt cut off, especially from God.

Healing

Dan

Toward the end of my first year in Albany, I began to realize that I was drowning in other people's pain. I continued to try to protect myself by being accommodating but emotionally distant, which was easier than being genuine, a mixed bag of compassion, self-interest, and real feelings. These defenses were beginning to crumble, however, and I was in great pain as a result. I had already learned in my first congregation that I did not need to be perfect. I could be myself and be liked. I could be myself and be hated. Yet this self-acceptance still felt new to me, and I was confused about how to embrace it.

At the same time, my motivations for my work as a rabbi were evolving. I no longer needed my work to bolster my self-esteem and "score points" with others. My earliest motivations for my calling no longer mattered to me, but I could not yet discern what my new motivations might be. Part of me felt dead, yet I was afraid to explore why. For the first time in my career, I began to confront the emptiness I was feeling. Nonetheless, it would take a full year more for me to begin to reclaim my own spiritual life.

A year later, on Yom Kippur evening, 1996, I told a packed house of worshippers a very personal story about how I had recently reconciled with a close friend. Taking a professional and emotional risk, I shared myself with them, not to play "true confessions," but to demonstrate that forgiveness, reconciliation, and personal growth are needed, and can be attained, by all of us. I wanted everyone to understand that this is not because people should strive to be perfect. It is precisely because we are not perfect that we are so in need of being kind with one another and ourselves. Following the story I asked everyone to spend a few minutes reconciling with or asking forgiveness of one another for wrongs done during the preceding year. It was an evening of powerful feeling and personal transformation for many people in the synagogue. I later learned that someone in the congregation who had not spoken to his brother for over twenty years decided to speak to him again as a result of my story. Clearly I had done a very good thing that evening, yet out of the corner of my eye, I could not help noticing Rena and Shalom, still grieving and angry, forcing themselves through the motions of wishing others a happy holiday just a few feet away from my speaker's stand. For two years our interactions had been nothing more than forced politeness through gritted teeth, and each time that I tried to reach out to them I badly missed the mark.

The next day, at the afternoon break in services, I saw Shalom and Rena preparing to exit the sanctuary. I knew immediately that it was the right time to approach them, although my decision to do so frightened me. Having learned from hard experience that we clergy are at times the lightning rods for others' primitive and hostile emotions, I should have been even more anxious about this impromptu meeting, but I was not. Perhaps it was the spiritual quality of the day, with its focus on forgiveness and love.

I asked Rena and Shalom to speak with me privately. I told them that I knew our communication over the past two years had been strained. I had always carried with me the disappointing sense that I had failed to reach out and be fully available to them around the time of Jon's death. There was nothing more I could say other than to ask their forgiveness and to try to start over.

I strained desperately throughout that conversation to hear from both of them that I was forgiven and that my role in helping them through the initial stages of grief had actually been positive in some way. I needed to hear simultaneously, "We think that you are a really good guy" and "We are willing to forgive you for failing to help us." Contradictory as they may seem, I needed both assurances because they reflected my ongoing struggle to accept myself as flawed, yet still worthy of love and respect. I recall little of what Rena said to me that day, only that I felt coming from her a strange combination of self-protective reserve and an almost unreal sense of peace. It seemed as if perhaps, like me, she was feeling some catharsis at hearing and saying words that had been long overdue. That afternoon marked a beginning for our relationship and for the badly needed changes taking place in me.

Rena

Just prior to Yom Kippur, 1996, we marked the two-year anniversary of Jonathan's death. Sometimes grief still felt new—the shock of Jon's absence hit me daily at unexpected moments—yet I knew that for the rest of the world a long time had passed. For most people, Jonathan's life and death were receding into the distant past. I told myself that I, too, must now turn and face forward. This anniversary, coinciding with the Jewish New Year, seemed a fitting time to turn a corner.

I had recently resumed teaching adult education, was actively engaged in writing and reading, and our family seemed intact, yet I continued to feel hollow inside. Something more than grief gnawed at me. Something else was missing, waiting to blossom. I spent a brief time in therapy, trying to open a door that would help me move forward. A wise and compassionate therapist offered me emotional support, affirmation, and insight. Therapy, however, also did not fill the empty space at the core. Only later would I understand that it was my relationship with God which needed to be healed, that it was my spiritual alienation which blocked me from feeling whole.

I sat in *shul* on Yom Kippur, feeling detached from the liturgy and drama of the day. During the long day of services, I spent several hours reading a book about death and grief by a therapist with a Buddhist orientation. The book resonated with my experience—it suggested embracing the surrender and openness that can come with intense pain and direct, honest confrontation with death. The ideas captivated me, but their Eastern framework was not mine. I needed a Jewish way to embrace and transform my pain. Yet I kept finding that we Jews, instead of learning to accept, always seemed to be fighting back against suffering. I knew that my home was still with my tradition, in Jewish prayer, texts, and ritual. Judaism was my place of solace and connection to God, yet I couldn't seem to gain access to that solace or that connection. I felt shut out. I sat in a traditional *shul,* amid a caring Jewish community, praying in the language of my ancestors, and yet I was spiritually homeless.

By this time, Dan and I had settled into a polite relationship, sometimes even working together on educational projects. At times I still sensed him trying to reach out to me, as when a few months earlier he had invited me to become his study partner. I was flattered, and the prospect of it excited me intellectually. Too many undercurrents of pain from the previous two years still festered in me, so I did not feel safe sharing my spiritual struggles with him for fear of being rejected or misunderstood. I turned down his offer of *chavrutah*[10] study and continued to keep our interactions as superficial as I could.

---

10. A traditional way of studying in pairs.

As the day wore on, I began to feel the spiritual power of Yom Kippur. Hunger and exhaustion wore down my defenses, and I felt increasingly peaceful and emotionally open. In midafternoon, services stopped for a two-hour recess. I was in the lobby when Dan asked to speak with Shalom and me. I followed Shalom into the small chapel, slightly anxious, but curious.

The previous night, before *Kol Nidrei,*[11] Dan had related to the congregation a personal story about a reconciliation he had had with a friend. I had noticed something different about him and was glad to see a more genuine side of him. Dan again seemed different throughout the morning service—there was a quietness in his tone that I had not experienced in the two years I had known him.

Now Dan sat in our small chapel, appearing very serious. First, he told us about a positive interaction he had just had with our son David. Then, in a different voice, he said that he wanted to ask our forgiveness for his behavior of two years ago: I had told him we needed a rabbi and he hadn't been one for us. His face was filled with regret. In an instant I felt layers of anger rolling off me, releasing me from their grip. Something radical was happening.

Shalom left with our two boys, and Dan and I continued to talk. I told him how shut out and rejected I had felt in my grief. I told him that I had begun to understand that, as a rabbi, he was a symbol of God's response and concern, and that he had not been that for me. He spoke about having been blocked, unable to be himself and to be present with us. After two years of painfully blocked communication, our dialogue felt like the opening of a dam, water rushing through and beginning to break down some long-standing barriers.

Dan asked how he could now "make things up" with us. Somewhat to my surprise, I heard myself ask that he study with me some Talmudic passages about suffering and acceptance that we had once learned in a community study group. We agreed to meet the following week and talked for the remainder of the recess. When it was time for services to resume, I felt as if a heavy weight had been lifted from me.

Cleansing

Dan

One day soon after Yom Kippur I sat in the office of a fellow staff member. Yom Kippur, and the first congregational evaluation of my perfor-

---

11. Initial service of Yom Kippur, known by its most prominent prayer: *Kol Nidrei.*

mance, had left me emotionally vulnerable and very tired. Not one to mince words, my colleague leveled with me about the evaluation: "Dan, people generally like you and are happy you are the rabbi here, but you never seem to slow down long enough to speak with us and to make us feel that you really care. We sense in you a certain distraction and coldness when you interact with us. You don't seem to be real. You're there, but you're not there." I was deeply insulted, but I knew that what she was saying was true. I left her office angry and confused, and needing to be alone, I drove out to the nearby Helderberg mountain range.

As I walked on one of the mountain trails, I stopped on a footbridge overlooking a valley. I felt almost glued to the spot and let out a long and anguished cry. As I stood in the silence, I imagined God saying to me, "Don't you see? I can only work through you when *you are you*," showing me what I had struggled to understand for two years, perhaps even longer. It was not that I cared or felt too little, but that I cared and felt too much. As a result, I had pushed myself away from everyone in order to feel left alone and sheltered. I was paying a high price for that, and an even higher price for having pushed God away as well. My being alone had turned into being cut off.

A few days later Rena followed up on our plan to meet again and asked me to drive with her to Jonathan's summer camp in Altamont, a small, picturesque town in the Helderbergs. Normally, I would not meet with a female congregant in an isolated place, but my heart told me that, in this case, I needed to trust my judgment, for Rena's sake as well as for my own. I also had to trust myself to remain open and receptive while Rena prepared to tell me more about my hurtful behavior. I was taking a risk, but I knew that I needed to do so.

When we got there, we walked up to a dry streambed lined with smooth stones near a bench and a log. Sitting with me in the cool autumn air, Rena interrupted the small talk in which we had been engaged. "I need to tell you how I feel about what has happened between us, but I'm not sure that I can," she said. "Rena, tell me what you need to tell me," I replied. In somewhat guarded tones, she told me again how hurt she and Shalom had been at the time of Jon's death, up until this past Yom Kippur. I had not been there for them, they had felt abandoned, and my behavior had had a profoundly negative impact on her that she had trouble letting go of.

Listening with a quiet heart, while suppressing my urge to be defensive, allowed me to take responsibility for the pain that I had caused Rena and Shalom. I could ask forgiveness of her, not out of terror that I was useless or bad, but out of full and loving acceptance of who I was. I could step beyond the strict formal boundaries between rabbi and congregant and be vulnerable. Choosing my words carefully, I told Rena what had happened to me on the mountain path a few days earlier. I began to cry as I explained to her how

my alienation from her family had been part of the larger wall that I had
built around myself in order to feel safe. Rena's silence during my weeping
felt strange. This was what *she* should have felt free to do in my presence for
the past two years, yet I had made it so difficult for her. Now the tables were
turned awkwardly. However, in its own way, this reversal of the normal
roles of rabbi and congregant was a powerful springboard for what we both
needed. Rena needed to know that my humanity and compassion were
available to her. I needed to rediscover a piece of myself that I had lost. We
both needed to transcend the resentments and misunderstandings of two
long years to begin a journey as rabbi and congregant, as friends and as
members of a spiritual community.

That day at the camp, my capacity for asking her forgiveness grew in response to her growing capacity to grant it without condescension and with
understanding. In the course of our conversations, Rena offered me insight
into the significance of what had happened between us and helped me
reframe my understanding of the past two years. "Having met Jon only in
his death, you represent this new stage in my life from which he is absent.
You symbolize his death, not his life." She did not absolve me of responsibility for my errors, yet her words captured the absurdity of the circumstances into which we had been thrust. My only relationship with her child
happened after his life was over. Upon Jonathan's death, my interactions
with his parents and with my community were intense and painful. Yet there
was no context of previous relationship, no treasure of mutual memories
that could guide me in taking these mourners through their nightmare.

In addition to providing a compassionate context for my failure, Rena's
comment revealed a deeper wisdom about relationships. What we mean to
one another at any given moment is influenced by an accumulation of symbols, fantasies, fears, hopes, and heartaches. This is especially true for relationships with clergy. Ministers of the faith are the most potent and immediate representatives of God's love and healing, as well as of our fear of God's
rejection and abandonment of us.

Coming home that day I glimpsed what was changing within me. I was
once again beginning to feel free to be the spiritual "work in progress" that I
am. It would be a few more years before I could feel the impact of these experiences in every aspect of my life. That day, they became manifest to me as
God's gifts, even if I barely understood them. They remain God's gifts today.

Rena

The morning of my appointment with Dan was a crisp fall day. The previous day I had learned that a pavilion at Jon's summer camp that was to be

dedicated in Jon's memory had just been completed. I was eager to see the pavilion, although I felt trepidation as well. Every time we remembered Jon with some kind of formal memorial, that memorial was another concrete reminder that he was really gone, that these structures were the only physical presence he would ever have on this earth.

I asked Dan to drive with me to the camp. When we arrived at the mountaintop, I stopped short. I was startled to be in this place that I associated exclusively with Jonathan, a vibrant, active, alive Jonathan, now gone for more than two years. I could almost feel him in the air, and the sensation of his presence brought him deliciously to life for a moment. Almost instantaneous with that joyous evocation, however, waves of emptiness flooded me. Without trying to explain my complex feelings, I said to Dan simply, "I have not been back here since Jonathan died." He replied, "Then I feel honored that you asked me to come here with you." I believed him, and his comment comforted me.

We followed the short wooded trails through the camp. I began to describe to Dan times I had felt unsupported by him, but my heart was not really in the conversation. He had already asked my forgiveness, and now, against the backdrop of the vast mountain vistas, my complaints seemed superficial. We shared thoughts on our painful history together, our conversation subdued and careful. I think we were both determined not to exacerbate old wounds or create new ones. While the content of our talk was serious and important, most important was the fact that, after two years, we were finally talking and listening to each other.

We sat on the porch of the main camp building, overlooking the camp's most spectacular view, a grand panorama of mountains and farmland with a crisp city skyline in the far distance. Dan told me about a powerful moment of insight he had had a few days earlier at another beautiful spot in these same mountains. It was my turn to feel honored, as Dan shared his story with me and told me about some of the internal struggles he had faced since his arrival in Albany. In the middle of his story, Dan began to cry. He sobbed quietly for a few moments, while several thoughts and feelings rushed through me. At first I thought that I should react immediately and say something comforting, but all the words that came to mind sounded silly and inadequate. I chose to remain silent, not wanting to say or do anything that might trivialize his emotions. Part of me yearned to open up and cry along with him, something I had never done, but I still could not do it. When Dan stopped I said, "You are lucky you can cry. I am not able to open up in that way."

It did not occur to me that there was anything disturbing or inappropriate about my rabbi crying in front of me. Months later Dan expressed concern to me about crying in front of me. Was it unprofessional, a sign of weakness that would undermine his authority or ability to offer leadership? Did his opening up to me inappropriately reverse our roles such that I became the caregiver and he the recipient of concern?

Perhaps I am not a typical congregant, and this was not a typical situation, but I told Dan that I had found it profoundly helpful that he had shared his vulnerability. When Jonathan died, my most intimate feelings had been laid bare to so many people, including Dan, a virtual stranger. I had felt exposed and vulnerable, all the more so with Dan because he had seemed so emotionally closed. Now it became easier for me to trust him and to share my vulnerability with him because he had trusted me in this way. I considered it a mark of strength, not a sign of weakness, that he was willing to do so.

Dan's sharing of his struggles with me, and his willingness to move back and forth between the role of comforter and the one comforted, allowed God to enter and take a place in our relationship. Healing began for us both when we acknowledged our shared humanity and our ability to reflect God's presence.

When Dan and I entered a new phase of rabbi-congregant relationship, and I began to feel compassion from him, I also began to experience God's compassion. I felt certain that it had been, in part, Dan's earlier behavior, and my anger about it, that had kept me shut off from God. I realized that I had needed Dan, in his role as rabbi, to be a facilitator, guide, and gatekeeper for me to access the Holy One. Now knowing his own struggles, I imagined how hard it must be for a gatekeeper to fulfill that role for others when he is unable to open the gate for himself.

A Scene That Could Have Been

On the evening after Jonathan's death, Dan sits with Shalom and Rena in their living room. The three of them are wrapped in an uncomfortable silence. The air around them is alive with the buzz of well-wishers, whose lively voices belie the heavy presence of death that hangs over the house.

Rena is mostly numb, as she has been since that morning of horror. While the numbness is unpleasant, it is a blessed relief from the pain that overwhelms her when the feelings come through. To even look at Shalom, and sense their shared pain, causes her defenses to collapse. Instinctively, she and Shalom know to stay quiet with each other, talking only when they need to discuss plans and logistics. Although they hardly know Dan, they are very grateful to have him there, a person to take them by the hand. For both of them, a rabbi is a moral and spiritual authority, someone in whom they can place unconditional faith and trust. He will surely show them how to do "the right thing" for Jonathan, and for themselves.

Dan's head is filled with the discordant noises of the day. He is pulled in so many directions and is already drained by the many transitions in his life. He can't imagine where he will find the resources to face this horrendous situation, let alone help others through it. He closes his eyes and prays: "I don't know what I can offer these people. I feel as if I am walking through a minefield. Please help me to be open to them and to myself."

Dan looks into the weary faces of Jonathan's parents and, after what seems like an eternity, breaks the silence. "I am as new to this as you are. I cannot imagine how this feels for you. I wish more than anything that I could undo what has happened, but I do not have that power. I will not be able to bring back your son, or to take away all of your pain. What I promise to do is to try to be with you in whatever ways are helpful to you. Please forgive me if I do anything that is hurtful to you, and please let me know when I am not being helpful. We can learn together what you need from me, and what I can do for you."

Rena hears him and she doesn't hear him. Nothing that he or anyone says can ease the agony that overtakes her at random moments—nothing, unless someone were to wake her and tell her that it had all been a dream. She wonders in silent desperation, "He's the rabbi. Can't he change all this, make it just go away?" The rational part of her knows that, of course, he cannot, and that is only another reminder that right now this is her terrible reality. Nonetheless, at the edge of her awareness, Dan's voice soothes her, reassuring her that he is present. Somehow that presence cuts into the loneliness that has begun to envelop her. It is true that he will not be able to remove the hurt, but she senses that he is willing to listen, and to speak openly with them.

Dan is not sure what more to say and is terrified that he might say the wrong thing. Should he make suggestions, offer them "advice" or rabbinic words of wisdom? He decides that there is only one appropriate subject he can raise right now. "Tell me about Jonathan," he says, at the same time wondering at the fact that any of them can be having a conversation at all.

They take out Jonathan's photo albums and share anecdotes with Dan as they flip through the pages. Their stories are typical tales of a child's life, the kind of memories that all parents have about their children. It seems important for all of them to share these moments. Dan's presence gives Rena and Shalom an opportunity to talk about Jonathan, who is all they can think about right now. Dan serves as a buffer; they can direct their thoughts and feelings toward him because sharing them with each other hurts too much right now. Dan is gaining a small sense of who their little boy was and how they see him. Tonight's conversation will help him feel more connected to Jonathan and to his parents, and more able to cope with this tragedy and its aftermath.

They close the photo albums and sit in silence for many moments. Dan feels awkward in the heavy air of despair that surrounds them. It is so tempting to find things to say, to attempt to cover the pain with words. He senses, however, that any further words would trivialize the enormity of this situation. The most honest response to this terrible moment is silence. All of them must be allowed the space to feel their feelings, however agonizing they are.

For Rena and Shalom, Dan's presence is a comfort. He is able to be fully with them in their sorrow and not turn his back on them. Although they are not conscious of it right now, he also offers them a reflection of Divine compassion and companionship. At this moment, God is remote from Rena's and Shalom's thoughts, but the fact that their rabbi sits here with them, and will continue to be by their side, lets them know that God sits here as well.

Tonight these three people are bound to one another by tragedy. Horrible events not of their own making have thrown them together. At the same time, the seeds of a healing relationship have been planted. Tomorrow, Rena and Shalom will bury their precious child along with their hopes, dreams, and fears for his future. They will have to rebuild their lives out of loss and sadness, and they will need most acutely this healing relationship with Dan.

The relationship will bring healing and growth to Dan as well. The sharing of sorrow, trust, and humanity will nourish the souls of all three of them. *His* sharing of sorrow, trust, and humanity will nourish the souls of all three of them. Dan will be challenged to walk the delicate line between struggling with his own doubts and fears and being a vehicle for God's presence with this family. The point at which the three of them have met is where God, the Healer of the brokenhearted, will be waiting.

22

T'shuvah in Sexual Violations
with Direct Implications for Other Situations:
Relational Care for Those
Who Have Sinned and Wish to "Return"

Jack H Bloom

What follows started with a phone call from Rabbi Jonathan Stein. I had barely finished complimenting him on the excellent and daring work he and the Ad Hoc Committee on Human Sexuality had done in the Symposium on Human Sexuality,[1] resulting in "Toward a Taxonomy for Reform Jews to Evaluate Sexual Behavior,"[2] when he asked if I would do a follow-up chapter on *t'shuvah*.[3] As consultant to the Ethics Committee of the Central Conference of American Rabbis (CCAR),[4] I had some experience trying to help that committee establish ways of ascertaining if a violator of CCAR norms

---

Author's Note: An earlier version of this chapter appeared as "T'shuvah for Our Time: When Sexual Violations Have Taken Place" in *CCAR Journal: A Reform Jewish Quarterly,* Fall 2005, pp. 35-67. It included some of the underlying model and presuppositions dealt with in this book in Chapter 1, "Premises of Jewish Relational Care." The original article was written for the Task Force on Jewish Sexual Values of the Central Conference of American Rabbis. It is here adapted for broader use by heterodox clergy who may not be members of the Reform movement.

1. *CCAR Journal,* Fall 2001, p. 3, quoting Selig Salkowitz from 1981.

2. In 1981, the Task Force on Jewish Sexual Values was mandated to examine "rabbinic tradition and contemporary social science concepts, to determine where they converge and how they differ on the contemporary sexual condition." *CCAR Yearbook,* Volume 92, 1982.

3. Often mistranslated as "repentance"; more accurately, "return" and/or "answer." See more anon.

4. The CCAR is the international association of Reform Rabbis. The Ethics Committe was under the chairmanship of Rabbi Sandy Ragins.

had done *t'shuvah* and could be allowed back among the employable. Flattered at being asked, I agreed to undertake the challenge. I didn't realize what I was getting myself into. I thought I had been presented with a simple question: If we accept a taxonomy of sexual behavior, similar to that put forth by Rabbi Stein, and we stand in a tradition of being *"rachmanim b'nei rachmanim,"*[5] whose mandate allows for *t'shuvah,* and violations of the taxonomy have taken place, how do we know when one has accomplished *t'shuvah?*

It was, and is, an important, tempting question. Nonetheless, it was, and remains, the wrong question. It is unanswerable. Answering unanswerable questions is a needless spinning of our wheels. There is no way one can know with surety that others and even ourselves have done *t'shuvah* and that the *t'shuvah* we may have done will hold. The "True *T'shuvah* Detector" awaits its Thomas Edison and will, when invented, require extensive field testing, which will, without a doubt, yield questionable results. *T'shuvah* is not permanent, as life is not permanent. Were *t'shuvah* a permanent fix, the tenth of Tishre[6] could be more profitably used for feasting, dancing, and assorted merriments, for those who had once done *t'shuvah.* All of us with the best intentions of doing, and sometimes convinced we have done, *t'shuvah,* repeatedly fall off the horse. That is one of the meanings of being human. That difficulty has not stopped some of the greats of our tradition from daring to answer that question.

Two different and more important questions (at least two the author thought worth tackling) are these:

1. In an era when personal autonomy, the sovereign self, and the right (even more than the ability) to make choices are not only givens but desiderata to be pursued with vigor, how can we understand *t'shuvah* in our day, especially in as fluid and in flux an arena as sexual behavior?
2. What role can we, as heterodox liberal rabbis, play in helping *t'shuvah,* imperfect as it might be, to happen?

We are charged both to remain loyal to our tradition and to explore what modern models can teach us. As rabbis, committed to the ongoing search represented by rabbinic tradition, how do we use our best understanding to-

---

5. Merciful children of merciful parents. As explained by Avraham Ibn Shoshan, *A New Dictionary* (Jerusalem, Israel: Kiryath Sepher Ltd., 1952). A popular nickname for Jews who, by their very nature, excel in feeling others' suffering. Translated from the Hebrew by the author.

6. For the uninitiated in the intricacies of the Hebrew calendar, Yom Kippur falls on the tenth of Tishre.

day to assert what *"they"* would have interpreted had *"they"* known? How can we respond, both to those in our own ranks and to those whom we serve, to help them do *t'shuvah* in the pursuit of being a holy people?[7] To help *t'shuvah* happen, we need a grounding that is both authentically Jewish and currently meaningful.

It is an audacious challenge. We are heirs to a tradition that has spent thousands of years dealing with and emphasizing *t'shuvah*. What new understanding will make a difference and what new means are usable beyond the well-worn, still indispensable tools of confession, contrition, and promises for the future? "We are not so rich that we can do without tradition. Let him that has new ears listen to it in a new way."[8]

T'shuvah must take back its original meaning as "return and/or answer." Still, the question remains: Return and/or answer to what? I will present very briefly, given its long and copious history, the traditional response to that question, and excerpts from some recent models by both orthodox and heterodox writers, suggesting where they are wanting in terms of the model I propose. This chapter is based on the model presented in Chapter 1, "Premises of Jewish Relational Care."[9] It is a useful heterodox model of human "beingness" and *t'shuvah,* both consonant with and building usefully upon our long heritage. It can be very useful in both conceptualizing *t'shuvah* in our time and helping *t'shuvah* happen in sexual, and other, contexts. In light of this model, I have in Chapter 1 suggested some rewriting of the underlying presuppositions the CCAR Ad Hoc Committee on Human Sexuality has used.[10] I will offer one model from an orthodox author that is eminently current and supports our model. I will suggest some ways of helping us to assist in the process of *t'shuvah*.

First, when we translate, we need to pay exquisite attention to the words we choose. The nuances of the words we use are vitally important. They change the meanings and overtones of our discussion. We do well not to use the words *t'shuvah* and *repentance* interchangeably, *not* to tell our people that the one is the other. They are not the same. Repentance is *not* the translation of *t'shuvah*. Repentance derives from Old French; the meanings of "repent" are as follows:

1. **reflexive:** effect (oneself) with contrition or regret for something done

---

7. Exodus 19:6, and a multitude of other places in our long and copious tradition.
8. Walter Kaufmann, "I and You: A Prologue," in Martin Buber, *I and Thou: A New Translation* (New York: Simon and Schuster, 1970).
9. See in this book Chapter 1, "Premises of Jewish Relational Care," pp. 10-14.
10. Ibid.

2. **impersonal:** to cause (one) to feel regret
3. **intransitive:** to feel contrition, compunction, sorrow, or regret for something one has done or left undone; to change one's mind with regard to past action or conduct through dissatisfaction with it or its results
4. **transitive:** to view or think of (any action, etc.) with dissatisfaction and regret; to be sorry for[11]

T'shuvah derives from the Hebrew root שוב, *S-Hu-V.*[12] Its meanings follow:

1. An answer to a question or claim
2. Turning back to one's origins
3. Cycle of time
4. Borrowed usage: return to the good way; regret, abandoning sin;[13] a return to God and to the right path[14]

The last, borrowed meaning has been the traditional understanding; תשובה[15] a return to an external persona (or even process) who has a claim on our behavior, but to whom we are accountable. The lead metaphor about the relationship is reflected in our worship:

אבינו מלכנו, חטאנו לפניך

Avinu Malkeinu Chatanu L'fanecha
Our Father, Our King, we have sinned against you.

אבינו מלכנו, החזירנו בתשובה שלמה לפניך

Avinu Malkeinu hachazireinu b't'shuvah sh'leimah l'fanecha
Our Father, Our King, help us return to you fully repentant.[16]

---

11. J. A. Simpson and E. S. C. Weiner, eds., *The Oxford English Dictionary* (Second Edition, Volume XIII) (Oxford: Clarendon Press, 1989), p. 637.

12. Overwhelmingly, Hebrew words have three-letter roots.

13. Ibn Shoshan, *A New Dictionary;* translated by the author.

14. For instance, the entry in R. J. Zwi Werblowsky and Geoffrey Wigoder, eds., *The Encyclopedia of the Jewish Religion* (New York: Holt, Rinehart and Winston, Inc., 1965).

15. From this point on the transliterated Hebrew *(t'shuvah)* will be used instead of repentance.

16. Rabbi Jules Harlow, ed., *A Prayer Book for the Days of Awe* (New York: The Rabbinical Assembly, 1972); Chaim Stern, ed., *Gates of Repentance* (New York: Central Conference of American Rabbis, 1996).

One appears before a ruler, the ultimate father, God, royalty to whom we owe obeisance. He is a celestial monarch whose commands we have violated, or, alternatively, we have sinned against one of His creatures. He is enthroned and passing judgment (especially on Yom Kippur) and is capable of both judgment and mercy, though we are reassured that He has a strong streak of forgiveness in His nature. We are obliged/advised to implore and engage this quality in Him. The rules of this crucial game involve recognition of one's transgressions, confession, imploring God's forgiveness, and receiving pardon in return for promises (sincerely meant) not to repeat the offense.

Alternatively, in a traditional high point of the High Holyday liturgy, there exists a seemingly kinder, more evocative, more benign metaphor—though it leaves humankind in the position of sheep—of a (divine) shepherd counting and determining the destiny and fate, sometimes deserved but often quite capricious, of each member of His flock. The metaphor of God accepting and dispensing *t'shuvah* does not resonate for most of us as it did with our ancestors. It has an antiquarian sound, which we might mine for meaning as we would Chaucer or Shakespeare, but it is not contemporary. Even that of the divine shepherd counting (a metaphor within a metaphor) and determining the fate of His flock rings somewhat hollow for us who are puzzled by a God whose cognition allows cancer in the world, the good to suffer, and the evil to triumph. We are no longer capable of talking about reward and punishment in the traditional manner. Only the fundamentalists among us are sure that specific acts and innocent deaths are a result of violations of the 613 commandments. After Auschwitz especially, one cannot believe, even if one believed it before, that there is a simple correlation between living the religious/ethically good life and being rewarded in this world. Evil in the world may result from our doing terrible things—it is not the result of God on His throne dispensing just desserts to the "goodies" and the "baddies."

We are reassured in somewhat equivocal terms:

ותשובה ותפלה וצדקה מעבירין את רע הגזרה

Ut'shuvah, ut'fillah, u-tzedekah ma'avirin et roa hagezerah
But penitence, prayer and good deeds can annul the severity of the decree.[17]

---

17. See Harlow, *Prayer Book for Days of Awe.*

Alternately:

> *But Repentance, prayer and Charity temper judgment's severe decree.*[18]

The Traditional Understanding

T'shuvah is perhaps best described by the words of two scholars whose names I never heard in rabbinical school:[19] Kaufman Kohler and Max Scholoessinger, who wrote the article "Repentance" in the original *Jewish Encyclopedia:*[20]

> The full meaning of repentance, according to Jewish doctrine is clearly indicated in the term "teshubah" [*sic*] (lit. "return"; from the verb). This implies: (1) All transgression and sin are the natural and inevitable consequence of man's straying from God and His laws. . . . (2) It is man's destiny, and therefore his duty, to be with God as God is with him. (3) It is within the power of every man to redeem himself from sin by resolutely breaking away from it and turning to God, whose loving-kindness is ever extended to the returning sinner. . . . the manifestation of repentance[21] consists in: (1) Confession of one's sin before God (Lev.V;5; Num.5;7), the essential part of which, according to rabbinical interpretation (Yoma 87b; Maimonides), is the solemn promise and firm resolve not to commit the same sin again. . . .

The modern Reform position remains essentially the same. Writing in *Reform Judaism,*[22] author Grant Perry describes his "hero" as doing *t'shuvah* (literally "returning"), which the author describes as "a process that includes confession, seeking forgiveness, change of behavior, and ultimately a change in character"—an outcome devoutly to be wished for.

---

18. See Stern, *Gates of Repentance,* though Stern's translation of *ma'avirin* is inaccurate. See Ibn Shoshan, *A New Dictionary.*

19. The reader should be advised that I attended Jewish Theological Seminary in New York. Kaufman Kohler, PhD, was Rabbi Emeritus of Temple Beth El in New York City and President of Hebrew Union College (HUC) in Cincinnati, Ohio, and Max Scholoessinger, PhD, was Librarian and Lecturer on Biblical Exegesis of HUC in Cincinnati.

20. *The Jewish Encyclopedia* (Volume 10) (New York: Funk and Wagnalls Co., 1905), p. 376 ff.

21. They immediately miss the nuance of what they have just written.

22. Grant Perry, "The 'Good Jew' Who Went to Jail," *Reform Judaism,* 32(2) (Winter 2002), p. 31.

We are, most of us at least, no longer able to think of *t'shuvah* in terms of obedience to a sovereign, even when we mean it metaphorically. The traditional notion of *t'shuvah* is of limited usefulness to us. Living in such a world, what is the place of *t'shuvah*? What does it mean? How is it useful to us as heterodox Jews?

The second *Avinu Malkeinu* beseeching full and complete *t'shuvah* gives us *fits*. Deeply problematical, how to be able to identify, recognize, and acknowledge that full/consummated *t'shuvah* has taken place is a question that preoccupied our forbears, who had little trouble with the monarchical *Avinu Malkeinu*. It is clearly not the promise and firm resolve alone, not even the sense, of being forgiven. Fearlessly, RaMbaM, who always went where others feared to tread, offers "an example of fully consummated *t'shuvah*." RaMbaM asserts that *t'shuvah* is possible because humankind is endowed with free will:

> Free Will is bestowed on all. If one desires to turn toward the good and be righteous, one is at liberty to do so. If one wishes to turn toward evil and be wicked, one is at liberty to do so. Thus it is written in the Torah, "Here, the human has become like one of us, in knowing good and evil.[23] ... humankind by the exercise of their own intelligence and reason, (Maimonides' understanding of the Tzelem)[24] knows good and evil, and none can prevent them from doing either good or evil.[25]

RaMbaM[26] continues:

> Every human being may become righteous like Moses ... or wicked like Jeroboam;[27] wise or foolish, merciful or cruel, niggardly or generous, and so with all other qualities. There is none to coerce nor de-

---

23. Genesis 3:22. Translation of Torah text by Everett Fox, *The Five Books of Moses: A New Translation with Introductions, Commentary, and Notes* (New York: Schocken Books, 1995), p. 25.

24. Compare Maimonides, *Guide of the Perplexed,* trans. M. Friedlander (New York: Hebrew Publishing Co., 1881), Chapter 1. "In man the 'form' (צלם) is that constituent which gives him human perception: and on account of this intellectual perception the term צלם is employed."

25. Moses ben Maimon, Mishneh Torah Hilchot Teshuvah 5:1. The translation is the author's.

26. Maimonides, in Hebrew **RaMbaM** (Rabbi Moshe ben Maimon), 1135-1204. Arguably the greatest Jewish commentator and philosopher, he was also physician to the court of Sultan Saladin of Egypt.

27. In the view of the rabbis, *the* paradigmatic evil King.

cree how one is to be, nor anything to draw one to either of the two ways. Each person, of one's own volition turns to the way which s/he desires.[28]

We have always been the prisoners and the beneficiaries of our era's ways of seeing and experiencing the world. It cannot be otherwise. We moderns no longer think uncomplicatedly of having or not having free will. We recognize that we are both free and not free.[29]

What *t'shuvah* will mean to us, given the changes in our experience, will depend on our particular view of the world, on what we accept as religious "facts." We need to think of *t'shuvah* in a new way, yet, being covenanted inheritors of our tradition, it has to be in a way that has deep roots in our past. There are for us no deeper roots than the biblical story of human creation.

What the biblical author presents as the "facts" of our creation,[30] in the two creation stories which daringly assert that humankind, created [*Tzelem* ⇔*N'shamah*],[31] is modeled after and molded by Divinity, and filled with the Divine Breath, is the foundation of our religious beliefs. All of Jewish tradition is an exposition, expansion, and a playing out of those "facts." Accepting our having been created [*Tzelem*⇔*N'shamah*] leads to a sea change in our thinking about the process and meaning of *t'shuvah*. What can we say of *t'shuvah* in our time that takes into account how these religious "facts" affect our understanding?

We dare assert that *t'shuvah* is responding to and answering the call of the [*Tzelem*⇔*N'shamah*]. *T'shuvah* is taking the time and making the effort to turn back to our origins and reclaim and repair our [*Tzelem*⇔*N'shamah*] relationship, which the vagaries of life have often damaged and wounded, yet which always awaits our return. *T'shuvah* is turning to witness and experience our [*Tzelem*⇔*N'shamah*] *"selves"* and what we have until now referred to as our Self in a new way. Having done that, we then inexorably experience others, the world, and God in a new way.

---

28. Moses ben Maimon, Mishneh Torah Hilchot Teshuvah 5:2.

29. The insanity defense is probably the outstanding example, but so is the nature versus nurture argument.

30. For a fuller explication of our creation myth and [*Tzelem*⇔*N'shamah*], see Chapter 1, "Premises of Jewish Relational Care," pp. 10-14.

31. [Breath-Taking⇔Model of Divinity]. See *ABC's of Jewish Relational Care* in this book; for further explication, see Jack H Bloom, *The Rabbi As Symbolic Exemplar: By the Power Vested in Me* (Binghamton, NY: The Haworth Press, 2002), especially Chapters 6 and 8.

What makes *t'shuvah* difficult is our having been raised and carefully taught to experience the world in an [Either/Or] manner. [Either/Or] thinking has dominated our internal and external maps for a long time. Monotheism can be taken to imply an essential oneness in the world, and in us. Our thinking has been dominated by the pursuit of that unity, and the ultimate meaning seemingly implicit in it. Monotheism, and the quest for ***ultimate*** meaning, for all its truth and benefits, has unfortunately produced a dangerous by-product: [Either/Or] thinking. [Either/Or] thinking pervades much of what we think and do. Things, ideas, etc., are either one way or another. It is in the dichotomies of sacred/profane, good/evil, clean/unclean, rational/irrational, and seemingly endless other splits. [Either/Or] thinking is at its core a fundamentalist position. There is ***one*** way.

The quest for oneness has had a profound effect. The pursuit of what our singular identity is, and precisely who we are, has been a theme weaving its way through our tradition. It finds its expression even in the watchword of our faith. The presupposition that underlies this thinking is that we are ***one*** and need to integrate the disparate aspects of ourselves to bring us to ***oneness.***

T'shuvah cannot afford [Either/Or] thinking that makes a desideratum of conquering, transforming, or getting rid of the other parts of us. We need to think differently. We have to learn to think in a way that affirms our multi-faceted *"selves"* and know that they can coexist and enrich our total being.[32]

[Both/And] thinking makes *t'shuvah* a more viable possibility.

We have increasingly been realizing that there is overwhelming evidence "that people apprehend reality in at least two fundamentally different ways: one, variously labeled intuitive, automatic, natural, non-verbal, narrative and experiential [the *N'shamah*[33]], and the other analytical, deliberative, verbal, and rational [the *Tzelem*[34]].[35]

The New York Times[36] reported on the discovery of another brain, located in the gut, that produces a variety of experiences independent of the brain in the head. All of this implies a new way of thinking about our *"selves"* (and others), a way that involves [Both/And] thinking. We are not

---

32. Adapted from Bloom, *The Rabbi As Symbolic Exemplar*, p. 179 ff. See also Chapter 1, "Premises of Jewish Relational Care," in this book.
33. Our breathing somatic self, from the Hebrew root *N-Sh-M*, breath.
34. Our mindful cognitive self.
35. S. Epstein, "Integration of the Cognitive and the Psychodynamic Unconscious," *American Psychologist,* August 1994.
36. Sandra Blakeslee, "Complex and Hidden Brain in the Gut Makes Cramps, Butterflies and Valium," *The New York Times,* January 23, 1996.

solely one or the other aspect of ourselves. We are at all times [Both/And]. *No* part, aspect, or characteristic stands alone. Each can serve as context for the other. Our challenge, and the purpose of *t'shuvah,* is how to have our various *"selves"* be in a [Both/And], loving, respectful relationship with each other. A relationship in which both are blessed and neither needs to be "converted" or eliminated in a futile quest for oneness. When our [*Tzelem* ⇔*N'shamah*] relationship is [Both/And], head and heart, rational and emotional, and so forth, and experienced as "just there," that is when we are just going about our regular business with little or no awareness of life being a problem. This working covenant enables the covenant life to be lived. When life is a problem, when sexual violations or abuse happen, and others are treated with disrespect, that is prima facie evidence that the [*Tzelem*⇔ *N'shamah*] relationship has been disrupted. Whatever happens takes place in the context of relationship, and not because of any individual characteristic in our *"selves"* and in the others with whom we deal. In [Both/And] thinking, these at least two *"selves"* are in relationship. [Both/ And] thinking allows for the existence of multiple, constantly changing truths. We need to learn how to be in touch with, accept, and *love* our other *"selves."*

Unfortunately, virtually all of our texts are read and understood through the lens of an aperceptive mass which assumes that, though modeled after and molded by Divinity—a phrasing recognizing the [Both/And] nature of our creation—we are singular beings with a singular will, tractable desires, a oneness, a singular self who turns away, sins against, and violates the decrees of a divine author, who is also perceived as a singular Self, despite much evidence to the contrary. Such references are often simply ignored or treated as whimsical fantasies.

Ari Mark Curtin points out that this odd mix of singular and plural comes to teach something very important (I am taking some liberties with Curtin's translation of the Hebrew; they are italicized):

> By using these first-person plurals, God is revealing something special about God's nature and what it means for humanity to be *modeled after and molded by Divinity.* The . . . divine plural self-references . . . acknowledge[s] . . . paradoxical "plural" images/likenesses of the God who is, nevertheless, overwhelmingly One. Just as humanity's "God-image" is somehow singular while plural, so is God. God and humankind are to be seen as fundamentally unified while also multiple. God and humankind's nature are each poised between these pluralities: simultaneously singular and plural. Human form *modeled after and molded by Divinity* is plural. Human knowledge *modeled after and molded by Divinity* is plural. Fittingly, the human ability to

conceptualize and communicate is also plural, *because humankind is modeled after and molded by Divinity.*[37]

That God is both singular and paradoxically plural is referred to many times in Jewish tradition[38]: for example, God said to Moses:

> You want to know my name? I am known by what I do. I am called many things. When I judge humanity, I am *Elohim*. When I war on evildoers, I am *Tzevaot*. When I suspend judgment, I am *El Shaddai*. When I am merciful to My world I am YHWH. (My name is) EHYEH ASHER EHYEH. I will be there howsoever I will be there. I am known by what I do.[39]

Or noting God's prayer:

> May it be My will that my compassion overcome my anger and may my mercy prevail over my attributes [of justice and judgment]. May I deal with my children in accordance with My attribute of compassion. May I act towards them beyond the letter of the law.[40]

That God is a [Both/And] personality is amply present in rabbinic tradition: the twelve-hour divine day is said to include a variety of activities; God spends three hours studying Torah, three hours dispensing justice, three hours providing for the needs of the world's creatures and three hours playing with Leviathan.[41] It would have been hard for Rambam to assert that one could be [Both/And] for he was limited by an [Either/Or] position. One either turns to the good or to the bad.

Relationship, a [Both/And] position, has a great claim to being a Jewish religious value and is worth pursuing. Human beings, though enveloped in one skin and, until recently, thought of as possessed of a single brain,[42] are

---

37. See Ari Mark Curtin, "When God's References Are Plural: A Look at Gen. 1:26, 3:22, 11:7 in an Overarching Context," *CCAR Journal: A Reform Jewish Quarterly,* Fall 1996. In a personal communication, the author indicated that the full title was supposed to have been "When God's Self-References Are Plural," but the "Self" got lost on the way to the printer.

38. See Jack Miles, *God: A Biography* (New York: Alfred A. Knopf, Inc., 1995).

39. Exodus Rabbah. 3:6.

40. Babylonian Talmud, B'rachot 7a.

41. Babylonian Talmud, Avodah Zarah 3b.

42. Blakeslee, "Complex and Hidden Brain in Gut."

multiple, from the atom on up. We have many inner *"selves"* that we instinctively understand to operate "independently" of one another. We are
not a Self; we are a relationship between *"selves."* Relationship is the basic
psychological and religious unit. Self is a context, not a position.[43] The first
question, therefore, is not only about the relationship between man and
woman, man and man, woman and woman, or each of those with God. The
first question is the relationship between our multiple inner *"selves."*

To elucidate that thinking this way makes a difference, we can look at
some other recent models of *t'shuvah*. Excerpts from those models are presented here. Their limitations in terms of the model presented in this chapter
will be noted immediately following each excerpt.

Adin Steinsaltz,[44] one of the greats of our time, writes:

> In fact, two essentials are found in every kind of t'shuvah; the renunci-
> ation of a regretted past and the adoption of a better path to be fol-
> lowed henceforth. Put concretely t'shuvah is simply a turning, be it a
> complete, abrupt change of direction or a series of smaller turns. . . .[45]

What is needed is the very opposite of renunciation. *T'shuvah* is not a turning away from a regretted past. *T'shuvah* requires a respectful relationship
with that past even as we move to a "new" identity.

Steinsaltz continues: "The desire to do t'shuvah always springs from
some sense of unease or disquiet."[46] True! Steinsaltz is on target. If life is
not experienced as a problem, *t'shuvah* is unlikely. The unease or disquiet
stems from a disruption in the ongoing relationship within the [*Tzelem*⇔
N'shamah]. The unease or disquiet is experienced on a somatic level first.
The *Tzelem* then labels what is happening as being a problem. One often
tries to ignore or rationalize or otherwise subdue it, but, ultimately, to resolve the problem, one must return to an [I–You][47] relationship with it.

---

43. Bloom, *The Rabbi As Symbolic Exemplar*, p. 162.
44. Adin Steinsaltz, *Teshuvah: A Guide for the Newly Observant Jew* (New York:
The Free Press, 1987).
45. Ibid., p. 4.
46. Ibid., p. 5.
47. After Walter Kaufmann, who in "I and You: A Prologue," in Buber's *I and Thou,*
spends sixty pages demonstrating conclusively that I–You is better English usage than
I–Thou, and in consultation with my wife, Ingrid, a native speaker and teacher of German, who affirms that *you* is a better expression of what Buber meant by the German intimate *Du*. The publisher, concerned about market share, no doubt retained the more
familiar *I and Thou* title as better for sales.

The great obstacle in the way of t'shuvah, an obstacle confronting all of us, wicked and righteous alike, is self-satisfaction, the smug conviction that "I'm okay, you're okay," that whatever flaws one may have are the inevitable lot of human beings. Such spiritual and moral complacency has no necessary relation to one's objective condition.[48]

"I'm okay, you're okay" may be a nonuseful, simplistic, inelegant way of expressing a great truth. What else can we ultimately say, if we accept as religious "fact" that all humankind is created modeled after and molded by Divinity, with the breath of God infused into us? It is saying, to paraphrase the words of Martin S. Cohen, "that no quality assigned to God is by definition beyond (our) grasp."[49] We may turn away from our [*Tzelem* ⇔ *N'shamah*], or life's inevitable wounds may do that to us, yet we are ultimately okay. Created [*Tzelem* ⇔ *N'shamah*] behooves us to honor all parts of us, including those which are different, obstreperous, and difficult. Entering into a respectful, even loving relationship with them is, I would suggest, the very opposite of "spiritual and moral complacency." Turning away from them, not recognizing both their/our woundedness and specialness, has within it the seeds of the spiritual and moral arrogance that Stensaltz rightly fears.

Steinsaltz describes *t'shuvah* as a self-creation, a rebirth experience:

Another common aspect of t'shuvah concerns one of its most essential, and paradoxical, components. On the one hand, t'shuvah entails a break with the past, fixing a cut-off point that divides one's life into a "before" and an "after." Indeed, the ability to atone for and rectify one's mistakes rests on the assumption that such a break is possible, that t'shuvah results in the creation of a completely new being. The past is severed from the present; one's former self becomes a stranger or ceases to exist. Or, as the Sages put it, the sinner one dies and passes from this world; the penitent self is a new creature. T'shuvah is thus a kind of spiritual death and rebirth.[50]

Joseph Soloveitchik, one of the true greats of modern Orthodoxy, in his classic *Halakhic Man* weighs in with self-creation:

---

48. Steinsaltz, *Teshuvah,* p. 5.

49. Martin Samuel Cohen, "Forgiveness and Subtlety," *Conservative Judaism* 56(4) (Summer 2004), p. 49.

50. Steinsaltz, *Teshuvah,* p. 13.

Repentance,[51] according to the halachic view,[52] is an act of creation—self-creation. The severing of one's psychic identity with one's previous "I" and the creation of a new "I" possessor of a new consciousness, a new heart and spirit, different desires, longings, goals—this is the meaning of that repentance compounded of regret over the past and resolve for the future.[53]

Though we would wish it so, we are never, nor can we ever be, completely new beings. Our DNA, in addition to the lives led by those who bore us, denies us that. Humankind has always pursued the chimera of a new birth, believing that it is a new start from a totally new beginning. We talk hopefully about the death or obliteration of an old part and creation of a totally new being. This is a remnant of [Either/Or], fundamentalist thinking that violates the ongoing constant relationship of our [Tzelem⇔N'shamah]. Whatever is created is a continuum, not a "that was then, this is now" break.

The challenge of t'shuvah is in how we move forward, including both past and present, good and bad, in a new relationship. When we talk of a new creation or a new birth, what we are at best talking about is a new identity, which is very different from a new being. When we talk about a new identity, we are talking about a new relationship of our multiple "selves." Anyone who has observed a marriage knows that 1 + 1 = 3. When each partner makes room for the other in the fullness of his or her own being and the other's, when the relationship is working, with neither dominant, a new identity, a "we," is created. Likewise, within our own being, a new "I" identity, an inclusive one, follows a reorienting of the [Tzelem⇔N'shamah] in us when we create a loving [I–You] relationship between our "selves."

T'shuvah is not about obedience or obeisance or even rebirth. T'shuvah is not about being rid of our past. Our past is in and of us. T'shuvah is the answer we give to the claim our being created [Tzelem⇔N'shamah] makes on us, and our return to the bedrock of our faith and tradition. Nothing else, not the relationship to other members of the species nor to God, can take place without first turning back and attending to our "selves" and our "selves"' relationship to one another within the larger context of our "being." T'shuvah is reorienting to the interactive [Tzelem⇔N'shamah] that is our essence. Everything thereafter is an attempt to sustain that balance. When that

---

51. *Repentance* is the translator's word. In the original Hebrew, Soloveitchik of course, used תשובה.
52. Halachah, for traditional Jews, is the proper path of religious observance.
53. Rabbi Joseph B. Soloveitchik, *Halakhic Man*, trans. Lawrence Kaplan (Philadelphia, PA: The Jewish Publication Society, 5743/1983), p. 110.

relationship is working, then we can have a relationship with others and ultimately with the Divine "being" beyond us. Our internal compass needs to be in working order. We start with our *"selves."* We need to turn inward before turning outward. Even turns outward are done from the inside.

A modern heterodox colleague, Rabbi Elliot Dorff, in his monumental work *This Is My Beloved, This Is My Friend: Sex and the Family,* has produced a wonderful piece of work that bears reading by every Jew. Dorff begins by affirming that Jewish tradition sees

> the human being as an integrated whole created by God. . . . For the Jewish tradition, God created each one of us as an integrated whole, with no part of us capable of living apart from any other part of us. . . . This integrated view of the human being has an immediate implication for our sexual activities—namely, that on a level as conscious and deliberate as possible, our sexual acts ought to reflect our own values as individuals and as Jews.[54]

It will be clear to the reader who has come this far where I differ from my student and my teacher, but most of all my beloved friend. Mine is not a trivial quibble. It is intrinsic to the way we as rabbis are able to work to assist *t'shuvah.* In contradistinction to what Dorff writes, we are not integrated wholes. It is not achievable, nor may it be worth aspiring to. Life would be incredibly simpler if we were that way, but life itself, in all of its vagaries, has intervened. We are the sum of "independent" parts/*"selves,"* many wounded, all in relationship. That is certainly the human experience, and it is in our experience that we live. Each human being is a relationship. between *"selves."* That experience, especially when it is a problem, is quite different from wholeness or integration.

Martin Buber's [I–You] relationship has something to offer on the subject, as well. Even Buber's "I" is a relationship, an ongoing dialogue between our own "It" and our own "I." In seeking to repair our own [*Tzelem* ⇔ *N'shamah*] relationship, it is crucial to maintain an [I–You], not an [I–It] relationship. We too easily turn our relationship to our wounded parts into an [I–It] relationship, as when we give it a negative name: anxiety, greed, lust, lasciviousness, low self-esteem, depression, anger, boredom, fear, and so on. We turn it into an IT and make it something to be rid of, rather than a partner in an [I–You] relationship:

---

54. Elliot Dorff, *This Is My Beloved, This Is My Friend: Sex and the Family* (New York: Rabbinical Assembly, 1996).

Even as a melody is not composed of tones, nor a verse of words, nor a statue of lines—one must pull and tear to turn a unity into a multiplicity—so it is with the human being to whom I say You. I can abstract from him the color of his hair or the color of his speech or the color of his graciousness; I have to do this again and again; but immediately he is no longer You.[55]

Relation is reciprocity. My You acts on me as I act on it. Our students teach us, our works form us. The "wicked" become a revelation when they are touched by the sacred basic word . . . we live in the currents of universal reciprocity.[56]

When we are in loving relationship with our own *"selves,"* those difficult *"selves"* which we have been trained to turn into "Its," something wonderful can happen. [I–You] relationships with others become possible.

In each person there is a priceless treasure that is in no other. Therefore, one shall honor each person for the hidden value that only this person and no one else has.[57]

The work of Abraham Isaac Kook[58] is most useful for this heterodox model of *t'shuvah*. Kook presents a religious framework that allows for multiple *"selves"* and explicitly affirms having a loving relationship toward them.

Jacob B. Agus's preface to Ben Zion Bokser's book on Rav Kook notes Rav Kook's determination to search out "the *nitzotzot k'dushah*"[59] in every ideology, since "all 'lights of holiness' derive from God and lead back to Him."[60]

As rabbis, our task is to redeem "the sparks of holiness" that are scattered throughout the world and, to coin a neologism, *relationshipize* them, or enter into relationship with them. Ben Zion Bokser in his introduction of-

---

55. Kaufmann, "I and You: A Prologue," p. 59.

56. Ibid., p. 67.

57. Martin Buber, *Hassidism and Modern Man,* trans. Maurice Friedman (New York: Harper and Row, 1958), p. 115.

58. Excerpts from *Abraham Isaac Kook: The Lights of Penitence, The Moral Principles, Lights of Holiness, Essays, Letters, and Poems,* The Classics of Western Spirituality, translation and introduction by Ben Zion Bokser. Copyright © 1978 by Ben Zion Bokser, Paulist Press, Inc., New York/Mahwah, NJ. Used with permission of Paulist Press. www.paulistpress.com.

59. Holy sparks.

60. Quoted in Agus's preface to *Kook: The Lights of Penitence,* p. xiii.

fers that, in Rabbi Kook's world of thought, the love of God carried with it a love for all God's creatures, an openness to all ideas, and a continued passion to perfect life through reconciliation, harmony, and peace. In Rabbi Kook's words:

> Whoever contemplates divine ideas in their purity cannot hate or be disdainful of any creature or any talent in the world, for through each does the Creator reveal Himself. . . .[61]

> But man's response to his fellowman must be more than the negative response of tolerance; it must reach the higher category of love. . . . The higher holiness abounds with love, kindness and tolerance. . . . Hatred, sternness and severity are the result of forgetting God and the suppression of the light of holiness. The more the quest for God grows in a person's heart, the more does the love for all people grow in him, and he loves even wicked men and heretics.[62]

Rav Kook might well have also added "even those difficult recalcitrant parts in oneself."

Bokser continues:

> Another attribute of life that aids man's quest for enlightenment is the phenomenon of t'shuvah which, for Rabbi Kook, has much deeper significance than the conventional notion of remorse and atonement for specific wrongdoings, in response to traditional admonitions.[63]

> In truth, t'shuvah is a universal and an essentially positive phenomenon, acting on some levels as a natural process, and expressing a revolt against deficiency and the quest for perfection. We are not directed by the automatic workings of our nature to embrace divine ideals, but an affinity, a predisposition for those ideals, is part of us. . . .[64]

> T'shuvah derives from the yearning of all existence to be better, purer, firmer, nobler than it is.[65]

---

61. From Bokser's introduction to *Kook: The Lights of Penitence,* quoting Orot Hakodesh, Volume I, p. 327.

62. Ibid., p. 8, quoting Orot Hakodesh, Volume I, p. 317.

63. Ibid. Orot Hat'shuvah, Yeshivat B'nei Akiba "Or Etzion," Ikve Hatzon, "Avodat Elohim," in *Eder Hayakar* (Jerusalem, Israel: Merkaz Shapiro, 1966), p. 145.

64. Ikve Hatzon, "Avodat Elohim," in *Eder Hayakar,* p. 145.

65. Orot Hat'shuvah, Yeshivat B'nei Akiba "Or Etzion," in *Eder Hayakar.*

Thus we are able to turn away from the [*Tzelem⇔N'shamah*] in which we are created and bring much evil to the world. Also note, Kook affirms that *t'shuvah* is not about regret and rejection and turning away; it is about acceptance and love. In his own words:

> I love everybody. It is impossible for me not to love all people. . . . I desire to see them grow toward beauty, toward perfection . . . my inner desire reaches out with a mighty love toward all.[66]

In his classic essay "Concerning the Conflict of Opinions and Beliefs," Rav Kook asserts much that we have proposed here:

> The concept of higher comprehensiveness, however, through its breadth and certainty, offers us an ideal system in stressing the principle of singularity. . . . Because it is universal, because everything is included in it, it cannot by nature exclude anything from its domain, it finds a place for everything. In doing this it only increases our perception of the light in all life-styles and in all expressions of the spirit. The basic thrust of its kind of tolerance is to find a place for every form of illumination, of life and of spiritual expression. . . . This concept of tolerance is aware that there is a spark of divine light in all things . . . even in the crudest husks that cover and blunt man's higher self is hidden that spark of the good, the light of God, the supreme light that we cannot define.[67]

> There remains within, in full force, the inner impulse that is pushing the good sparks to become manifest, and the good sparks, which are flashes of the light of the good emanating from the light of the God of truth, begin to be seen through the openings in the zone of darkness. . . . Therefore, instead of rejecting every pattern of ideas from which the tiny elements of good have begun to sparkle and which in themselves have trapped souls to lead them to the depths of the abyss—the place where reigns the darkness that deadens the soul in its prime of vigor . . . it is for us to enhance the original light. . . . It is for us to clarify how every spark of the good that is manifest in the world stems from its source and is linked with it in a natural bond.[68]

---

66. From Bokser's introduction to *Kook: The Lights of Penitence,* p. 29, quoting Aple Tohar, p. 22.

67. Ibid., p. 273 ff.

68. Ibid.

About rebirth Rav Kook says:

> The principle of "renewal," *b'yisod hachidush,*[69] in the order of creation . . . refers to the core element of the principle . . . to the very fact that the phenomenon of "renewal" (החידוש) exists as it does in its operative character. We know intuitively that true "renewal" derives from the substantive content of everything preceding it, that it emerges from its energizing essence. The fruit derives from the whole nature of the tree, from the depths of its trunk and roots, from the source whence it absorbs its juices, to its outer bark and the spread of its branches and foliage.[70]

Rav Kook offers an exemplary expression of [Both/And] thinking:

> T'shuvah . . . bestows a great benefit in purifying souls, in refining the spirit and purging behavior from its ugliness. But together with this it necessarily bears within itself a certain weakness that even the most heroic spirits cannot escape. When one shrinks the will, when one restrains the life force through inner withdrawal and the inclination to avoid any kind of sin, there is also a shrinking of the will for the good. The vitality of the virtuous life is also weakened . . . the person suffers from the cleansing of his moral state the kind of weakness experienced by the patient who was cured from his illness through a strong current of electric shock. It may have eliminated the virus of his illness, but it also weakened his healthy vitality. The penitential season is therefore followed by days of holy joy and gladness[71] for the self to restore the will for the good and the innocent vitality of life. Then will t'shuvah be complete.[72]

Sex

Not too much needs to be said, and not too much can be said, about sex and its elemental driving power. Sex is a most powerful somatic urge. Sex

---

69. *Novelty* was the word used by Bokser. Novelty would be חדש. חידוש suggests "renewal."

70. *Kook: The Lights of Penitence,* letter to David Ha-Kohen, p. 361.

71. *Sukkoth* (the feast of tabernacles; the Jewish harvest festival) and *Simchat Torah* (the annual festival rejoicing in the completion of the reading of the Torah) come just five days after the end of the ten days of *t'shuvah.*

72. *Kook: The Lights of Penitence,* p. 73.

all too often drags the cognitive around and takes unacceptable risks, leaving havoc in its wake. Sex drives us, affects our thinking; gets the cognitive focused, even against its best interests; intrudes in our visualizing, our breathing, the very flow of blood in our body; shows up in our sleep; and violates oaths the cognitive in good faith has taken. It is engendered in the breathing, pulsating, somatic part of us in a dynamic, exceptionally vulnerable tension and relationship with the *Tzelem,* whose task is to affirm, rein, channel, and bless that drive so that it may find its proper covenantal place.

Our tradition first recognizes the sacred blessedness in humankind, not externally, but in our ability to be fertile, implying sexual.[73] Sex as sex only enters the scene in Genesis 4,[74] after the creation of humankind from the dust with the breath of God breathed into them. Sex thus appears after self-consciousness and shame have arrived on the scene. Shame's abortive attempt with a fig leaf loincloth, covering our somatic nakedness (sexual organs), is perhaps the cognitive's first attempt to do something, almost anything, to ride herd on this driving urge. After the expulsion from Eden, only in the human is sex a problem. A stray dog might wonder, "What's the fuss all about?"

David Biale[75] recounts in great detail the energy and the monumental efforts of our very cognitive tradition to limit sex, negate its power, channel it, contain it formally, and shackle its excesses by establishing strictures and structures and injunctions of all kinds. Biale recounts long arguments about men's duties, the struggle with desire and procreation, women's rights in sex, and solutions ranging from celibacy to thinking appropriate thoughts during the act, to allowing it at only certain times of the month. He recounts changing mores: certain behaviors biblically and talmudically were considered violations of sexual norms, while others were permitted.[76]

In sexual mores as well, we are prisoners of our age, dragged along with the times. We are in a new sexual world. Some may wish to go back, but that does not seem to be where we are headed. Fifty or seventy-five years ago, people could present for psychiatric treatment if they preferred oral sex. Such a preference was treated as an aberration to be cured by massive doses of psychotherapy. Today, if one says "Yuck, I can't stand doing that," psychotherapy will be employed in the opposite direction. After all, those up-to-date say, "There are so many ways to enjoy one's body. And if it's con-

---

73. Genesis 1:28.
74. Genesis 4:1. "The Human knew Havva his wife, she became pregnant. . . ."
75. David Biale, *Eros and the Jews: From Biblical Israel to Contemporary America* (New York: Basic Books, 1992).
76. Ibid., p. 50 ff.

sensual, why not?" In the nineteenth century, young men were warned that masturbation could blind them. Now women, whom few thought needed such warnings, are provided with books that teach them how to do "it" elegantly.[77]

When I entered the rabbinate, *b'tulta*[78] in a *ketubah*[79] had a specific meaning. Very few officiants today seriously assume that the thirty-something bride is blushing under the *chuppah*[80] because she is about to lose her virginity. Were she so, she would be considered problematic. Many of our orthodox young men know what the evening is going to include when they are lovingly reminded to bring their *t'fillin*.[81]

Notwithstanding all this, sex with others as mere sex objects is an abandonment of our covenant commitment to be a holy people. It is surrender to the somatic part of us and abandonment of the [*Tzelem⇔N'shamah*] relationship. We see all too often how people are dragged around by their feelings, leading to promiscuity and other violations of the "sexual taxonomy."[82] It happens when the somatic is abandoned by the cognitive.

Sex at its truest can be the very exemplar of relationship, the very treasure house of [I–You] relations. "Human sexuality, as a powerful force in our lives, has the potential for physical closeness and pleasure, emotional intimacy and communication."[83] Sex, when covenantal, is a prime example of [Both/And] thinking. Sex relies on the presence, real or imagined, of an "other," even if it is a fantasized other, as in masturbation. As any sex therapist knows, sex requires a self whose *"selves"* are in relationship, before sex can take place with another self whose *"selves"* are likewise. And, as in most relationships, sex is vulnerable and touches wounded places easily with many resultant difficulties. Sex on a holy level is in the relationship, and is vulnerable, to the [*Tzelem⇔N'shamah*] being out of balance. Sex is holy when it is about a Buberian [I–You] relationship. [I–It] sex is little different from animal fornication.

Marital sexual infidelity is an example that sex is first and foremost about our [*Tzelem⇔N'shamah*] relationship, and how this impacts a new way of

---

77. Lonnie Garfield Barbach, *For Yourself: The Fulfillment of Female Sexuality* (New York: Doubleday and Co., 1975).

78. Virgin.

79. Marriage document outlining the rights and obligations of the couple to each other.

80. Marriage canopy symbolic of the Jewish home to be established by the couple.

81. Phylacteries worn by many Jewish men for morning worship.

82. "Reform Jewish Sexual Values," *CCAR Journal,* Fall 2001.

83. Ibid., p. 12.

thinking about *t'shuvah*. As Rabbi Daniel Schiff observes, "classic" adultery is

> the form of adultery most widely embarked upon and also the one usually thought of when the term "adultery" is mentioned. In most instances of classic adultery, the adulterous relationship is conducted in secret from the partner. If the secret were to be known by the spouse (and it is often discovered as the affair progresses), it would be perceived as a hurtful violation of the marriage covenant, both because of the infidelity itself and because of the lies and deceit that usually accompany it.[84]

If marriage calls for conjugal loyalty and personal intimacy (i.e., informing the partner at all times of any information that is crucial to the relationship), the intimacy has already been breached by the preparatory thoughts that precede the act of adultery being untold to the partner. The breach in intimacy is an obvious violation of the pledge of intimacy, but it is, first and foremost, a break in the relationship/love intimacy of our own [*Tzelem⇔N'shamah*]. Whatever the wounded place that interferes with the [*Tzelem⇔N'shamah*], that relationship must be repaired first. To do that requires an act of personal *t'shuvah*. When that is done, *t'shuvah* in the marriage has a chance.

Why Us?

Much of the work of *t'shuvah* has been subcontracted in our society to "therapists." They are in a sense our "hit men" with whom we contract to rub out parts of us that cause trouble. As rabbis, our seminaries have often taught us about morality/immorality, *chet/kaparah*,[85] good/bad, and suggested that when there are violations, and the violators have given hints of wanting to change, these are better dealt with by the new priesthood, the legions of the psychotherapeutic community. And we have been instructed that our job is to make good referrals. I posit that the opposite is true; when *t'shuvah* is required, rabbis, and other Jewish clergy, because of symbolic exemplarhood, because they believe that all are created [*Tzelem⇔N'shamah*], because of their leadership in shaping the covenantal community, have, if trained, much greater efficacy. In helping *t'shuvah* happen, rabbis have a unique place as the guardians in the covenantal community of multiple relationship systems—those being *beyn adam l'atzmo, beyn adam*

---

84. Ibid., p. 17.
85. Sin/forgiveness.

l'chaveiro, uveyn adam lamakom.[86] The rabbi is also the *eid ne'eman*[87] to the [*Tzelem⇔N'shamah*], is *shomayr hab'rit,*[88] and hopefully is *doveir emet bil'vavo.*[89] All of these increase the rabbi's potential influence and power in helping *t'shuvah* happen.

Because *t'shuvah* is ultimately turning back to our [*Tzelem⇔N'shamah*], which is so easy to stray from, as rabbis, our charge is always to be aware of the holy sparks and be imbued with a love for them. Those hidden sparks may open the door to *t'shuvah.* We are the opposite of "hit men." Our task is not to get rid of unwanted parts; it is to help create loving respectful relationships with "them." We are uniquely suited to that task. **That's why us.**

What Do We Do? How Do We Do It?

We have some of the old tools that have stood the test of time. We have our pulpits and our teaching. We need to continue and improve using these to teach norms, to help establish a caring community that can support these norms and can welcome back those who are struggling with *t'shuvah.* We are uniquely in a position to teach about the *nitzotzot* and to teach this model in a non-Pollyannaish fashion, for it is a tough world out there. Confession is a tried-and-true ally. Telling what had been an embarrassing secret is often the first step toward bringing it into human "being." We have a calendar that sets aside time for all to focus on *t'shuvah,* with emphasis on those ten days of *t'shuvah* at the turn of our year. We are, or need to be, masters of ritual, which will provide context and symbols for welcoming the one doing *t'shuvah* back into the covenant community. We are also symbolic exemplars for those who are struggling with their own [*Tzelem⇔N'shamah*] relationship. We need to feel safe being transparent about this. And we hope a new liberal sexual taxonomy, either that of the CCAR or another, will support the work we do in cases of sexual violations, by providing a normative framework appropriate for new realities, yet covenantal in nature.

We are not judges, acting on behalf of the Divine. We are involved guides, working to make multiple contacts. So some tools are no longer available to us. *Karet,*[90] cutting an individual off from the covenant community, the biblical solution to problems of sexual deviation, doesn't cut much mustard nowadays. Sexual deviations may lead to a cutoff, but that is

---

86. Between humans and their *"selves,"* humans and their fellows, humans and the Divine.
87. Trustworthy witness.
88. Guardian of the covenant.
89. Recognizes and is in loving relationship with one's own impulses.
90. Biale, *Eros and the Jews,* pp. 28–29.

an outcome of our actions, not a divine punishment. We are no longer a corporate, isolated community where each is fully dependent on the other, so *cherem*[91] is not an option.[92]

Community is vital. Personal autonomy is not enough. Violations are often facilitated by the absence of a supportive loving community, which undercuts proper behavior and denies our responsibility to others for our behavior. *T'shuvah* cannot be separated from the covenant community and its norms of respect for oneself, and for others. The covenant community makes a claim on us, and *t'shuvah* makes a claim on the covenant community. Many life experiences, *t'shuvah* among them, may be impossible without community. It is not accidental that birth, marriage, and mourning require community. It is tragic that, in our day, divorce has little community structure to help that transition. *T'shuvah* requires community.

Though community is indispensable, still we start with our *"selves."* There is no other way. We are all Jonahs, about whom we read in the quintessential Yom Kippur afternoon *t'shuvah* portion. Jonah learns caring for others by starting with caring only for himself,[93] then caring for the plant, then being lectured about caring for Nineveh, and implicitly making room for *t'shuvah* for all of God's creatures. We, too, start with our *"selves."* We can start nowhere else. As heterodox Jews we have nowhere else to start but with our self—not only our self, but our multiple *"selves,"* our own [*Tzelem ⇔N'shamah*], our own internal community, as it were.

Assisting *t'shuvah* in others requires multiple skills. It requires that we be centered and in touch with our own [*Tzelem⇔N'shamah*]. Being centered is not just California psychobabble. Centering is a skill that is learnable. Saralee Kane writes:

> Centering allows one to shift primary or "first" attention away from other people, away from one's racing thoughts, away from past im-

---

91. Excommunication by community officialdom, allowing no contact with the offender.

92. As pointed out by Ismar Schorsch, in a speech at Fairfield University on February 12, 2003. Yet, *The Jerusalem Report,* December 2, 2002, reports, in an article titled "Tribal Tribulations: High-Profile Peruvian Jews are Caught Up in a Slew of High-Profile Cases":

They have betrayed the trust that members of the community had put in them . . . the *psak din* [ruling of the rabbinic tribunal] . . . effectively excommunicating the Jewish directors . . . they cannot be called up to the Torah . . . be counted in a minyan or participate in parental activities at the Jewish School. One director . . . recalls attending a . . . funeral at which the gravedigger was chided for allowing him to throw earth on the coffin.

93. Jonah 4:5-11.

ages, and let it settle in the present moment on the breathing, focused/relaxed somatic (Neshamah) self. . . . Mindfulness (Tzelem) is a related practice of just observing and being aware of what is happening in each moment, without any need to try to change it. It is a process of deep awareness and acceptance . . . both internal and external.[94]

Muriel Singer describes her experience of being centered:

There is enough space within and without for all my selves to be included and welcomed. One part of me does not cancel out another part nor does the co-existence of several divergent parts mean that one or the other is inauthentic. They all have a home . . . even if it does not last.[95]

Being centered is experienced as a calm alertness of body and mind. It is simultaneously being in touch with your own experience and that of the other human being you are with. It is the state in which you have the ability to be both with your *Tzelem* and your *N'shamah,* as you attend and listen to the [*Tzelem*⇔*N'shamah*] experience of the other (by the way, a great asset in a marriage). Being centered means paying attention to what your cognitive being is producing inside yourself and how that is connected to the relationship you are having with the other.

In situations where the [*Tzelem*⇔*N'shamah*] resources are honored and used appropriately, relational differences can operate in a [Both/And] setting with a tone of conversational connectedness: the sort of [I–You] relationship described by Martin Buber. In this kind of intimacy, the experience of a "me," a "you," and the relational self of "us" is felt when both the "I" and "You" are respected and treasured. That "us" means that the *t'shuvah* candidate and the rabbi are part of one relational system, modeled after and molded by Divinity, and hopefully ready to return to, and simultaneously move forward from, that point of creation.

You will inevitably be knocked off center. Your mind may wander; you may feel bored, get a headache, start thinking about whether the plumber has shown up at your house to fix the leaky faucet, or whatever. We get knocked off center easily. Know that to have a problem you have to have let

---

94. Saralee Kane, "Self-Relations Psychotherapy with Couples," in *Walking in Two Worlds: The Relational Self in Theory, Practice and Community,* eds. Stephen Gilligan and Dvorah Simon (Phoenix, AZ: Tucker and Theisen, 2004), p. 103.

95. Muriel Singer, "A Personal Narrative of Self-Relations Therapy," in *Walking in Two Worlds,* pp. 27-28.

go of your center.[96] When knocked off center, it is crucial to have ways of getting centered again. The first place to turn is to your own breathing. It will always have been affected. Centering is a learned skill. Learning how to do it expertly is beyond the province of this chapter.

Still there is much that each of us already knows about being centered, and ways we can get there. We know that these, what might be called [*Tzelem*⇔*N'shamah*] states, are often marked by an absence of internal dialogue, accompanied by a comfortable breathing pattern; they are those special times when we are so absorbed that time and boundaries are not issues. A rabbi may access these quintessentially [*Tzelem*⇔*N'shamah*] resources in study, prayer, doing a *mitzvah*,[97] walking in the woods, painting, writing, talking with a friend, playing or listening to music, or a myriad of other experiences. Bringing the experiential state a rabbi has while doing these into ongoing relationship with oneself, with others, and with the tradition itself is a crucial undertaking. Shuttling back and forth between what is going on and those resources is a skill to be carefully honed.

Assisting *t'shuvah* requires expertise in searching for the *nitzotzot* implicit in and lurking behind "bad" behavior. The *nitzotzot* struggling to have human existence are often experienced as the "not me." The "not me" that is in some way responsible for the violation of the sexual taxonomy is often where the *nitzotzot k'dushah*, the holy sparks, are in hiding or veiled.

A useful question in the search for the *nitzotzot* that need uncovering, and then naming and blessing them in the process of *t'shuvah*, is **"If only I didn't do or experience (or could get rid of) X, then this really wouldn't be a problem." X marks the spot where the *nitzotzot* may be found.**[98]

For example:

"If only I didn't feel so *lonely,* I wouldn't have had the affair."
"If only I didn't feel so *sexual,* I would have controlled myself."
"If only I wasn't so *aroused,* I wouldn't have done it."
"If only I felt *appreciated,* I wouldn't have strayed."
"If only my husband was *kinder,* I wouldn't have been vulnerable."
"If only my wife was more *sexy,* I would be loyal."
"If only she wasn't so *seductive,* I could have resisted."
"If only I didn't feel *inadequate,* I wouldn't have done it."
"If only I wasn't afraid of *commitment,* I would have married."

---

96. Stephen Gilligan, PhD, from personal correspondence with the author.
97. In Hebrew, fulfilling God's command; in Yiddish, a good deed.
98. Adapted from Stephen Gilligan, *The Courage to Love* (New York: W.W. Norton and Company, 1997).

Realizing what it is in others, which is often unexpressed, witnessing the struggle and essence that begs inarticulately for naming and blessing, and blessing both struggle and essence with words of one's own, words not received and not encoded in the text, are rabbinic skills of the first magnitude. To bless those wounded, hidden parts is a great art and skill to be carefully learned.

Witnessing the holy sparks in every act, good and bad, is of supreme import. Awareness and uncovering of the *nitzotzot* involves shifting our focus away from what is being presented by the other. It requires looking for who else is in the room. By opening one's view and searching behind and seeing beyond, one is always looking for the *nitzotzot*, while making room for, and not denigrating, what is being presented.

Our colleague and teacher Lawrence Kushner, in his inimitable style, no doubt influenced by Rav Kook, gives examples of how to look for *nitzotzot k'dushah:*

> We go down into ourselves with a flashlight, looking for the evil we have intended or done—not to excise it as in some alien growth, but rather to discover the holy spark within it. We begin not by rejecting the evil, but by acknowledging it as something we meant to do. This is the only way we can truly raise and redeem it.

> We lose our temper because we want things to be better right away. We gaze with lustful eyes because we have forgotten how to love the ones we want to love. We hoard material possessions because we imagine they will help us live more fully. We turn a deaf ear, for we fear the pain of listening would kill us. We waste time, because we are not sure how to enter a living relationship. We even tolerate a society that murders, because we are convinced it is the best way to save more life. At the bottom of such behavior is something that was once holy. And during times of holiness, communion and light our personal and collective perversions creep out of the cellar, begin to be healed, freed, and redeemed.

> This does not mean we are now proud of who we were or what we did, but it does mean that we have taken what we did back into ourselves, acknowledged it as part of ourselves. We have found its original motive, realized how it became disfigured, perhaps beyond recognition, made real apologies, done our best to repair the injury, but we no longer try to reject who we have been and therefore who we are.

We do not simply repudiate the evil we have done and sincerely mean never to do it again; that is easy (we do it all the time). We receive whatever evils we have intended and done back into ourselves as our own deliberate creations. We cherish them as long-banished children finally taken home again, and thereby transform them and ourselves.[99]

Our mandate was, and is, "Be a blessing"[100]—that having been blessed, we are obliged to bless others. We can honor that covenantal obligation by helping ourselves and others do *t'shuvah* in keeping with both our tradition and our generation's understanding of human "beingness."

---

99. Excerpt is from *God Was in This Place and I, I Did Not Know: Finding Self, Spirituality and Ultimate Meaning.* © 1994 Lawrence Kushner (Woodstock, VT: Jewish Lights Publishing). Permission granted by Jewish Lights Publishing, P.O. Box 237, Woodstock, VT 05091; www.jewishlights.com.
100. Genesis 12:2. Translation from Fox, *The Five Books of Moses,* p. 55.

23

Jewish Relational Thinking and a Difficult Text: Amalek and Us

Jack H Bloom

זכור את אשר עשה לך עמלק בדרך בצאתכם ממצרים:
אשר קרך בדרך
ויזנב בך כל הנחשלים אחריך ואתה עיף ויגע
ולא ירא אלהים¹

Remember what Amalek did to you as you left Egypt. . . . Therefore, when the Lord your God grants you safety from all your enemies around you, in the land that the Lord your God is giving you as a hereditary portion, you shall blot the memory of Amalek from under heaven. Do not forget![2]

This implacable text is drilled into us from childhood: *Zachor, Zachor, Zachor*—Remember, Remember, Remember what Amalek did to you. It has been reinforced by the Jewish Experience from Haman to Hitler, all reputed to be descendants of Amalek. The promise from Exodus that God "will utterly blot out the memory of Amalek from under heaven"[3] and the reassurance that "The Lord will be at war with Amalek throughout the generations" resonate in us. This text has always been translated and read a specific way. (I offer it in the Hebrew original because an Italian proverb has it correctly: *Traduttore traditore,* or "The translator is a traitor"; to which I add, the only question is degree.) To look at this angry traditional text relationally we need to minimize the distortion and examine the original.

Author's Note: An earlier version of this chapter appeared as "Amalek and Us" in *CCAR Journal: A Reform Jewish Quarterly,* Spring 2001, pp. 51-55.
1. Hebrew text of Deuteronomy 25:17-18.
2. Deuteronomy 25:19 (Philadelphia, PA: Jewish Publication Society, 1962/1985).
3. Exodus 17:14-16.

My own translation follows the literal sequence of the Hebrew, adding or subtracting nothing:

> Remember what Amalek did to you on your journey, after you left Egypt—how he surprised you on the way, cut down all the stragglers in your rear, and you, famished and weary, do not fear God.

The traditional Jewish Understanding and the translating that followed and supported this understanding is that it was Amalek who did not fear God. The translations, examples of which follow, do this in a number of ways.

The New Jewish Publication Society translation of 1985, while claiming fidelity to the traditional Hebrew text, nevertheless *rearranges* the sentence order, inserts the words *undeterred by fear of God,* then adds a *he,* so as to unmistakably point the finger at Amalek. It makes a fine English sentence but distorts the meaning (in the following quotes all emphases are mine):

> Remember what Amalek did to you on your journey, after you left Egypt; how, *undeterred by fear of God, he* surprised you on the march, when you, famished and weary, and cut down all the stragglers in your rear.[4]

Traduttore traditore.

Others do it more simply with the judicious addition of *he* or *they,* neither of which is in the Hebrew text:

> Remember what Amalek did unto thee by the way as ye came forth out of Egypt; how he met thee by the way, and smote the hindmost of thee, all that enfeebled in thy rear, when thou wast faint and weary; and *he* feared not God.[5]

> Bear-in-mind what Amalek did to you on the way, at your going-out from Egypt, how he encountered you on the way and attacked-your-tail—all the beaten-down-ones at your rear—while you weary and faint, and (thus) *he* did not stand-in-awe of God.[6]

---

4. *TANAKH: A New Translation of The Holy Scriptures According to the Traditional Hebrew Text* (Philadelphia, PA, and Jerusalem, Israel: Jewish Publication Society, 1985).

5. *The Holy Scripture* (Philadelphia, PA: Jewish Publication Society, 1917).

6. Genesis 25 ff. Translation of Torah text by Everett Fox, *The Five Books of Moses: A New Translation with Introductions, Commentary, and Notes* (New York: Schocken Books, 1995), p. 967.

The Christian translations join the parade:

> Remember what Amalek did to you on the way as you came out of Egypt, how he attacked you on the way, when you were faint and weary, and cut off at your rear all who lagged behind you; and *he* did not fear God.[7]

> Remember what Amalek did to you on your journey out of Egypt, how he attacked you on the way, when you were faint and weary, and struck down all who lagged behind you; *he* did not fear God.[8]

> Remember what the Amalekites did to you on your way out of Egypt, how they met you on the road when you were faint and weary and cut off your rear, which was lagging behind exhausted; *they* showed no fear of God.[9]

Our tradition and its foundational texts, even their calls for total monotheism, are full of direct or implied [Either/Or] statements. Do whatever it is a specific way or bad things will happen to you. When understood by humans desiring to be loyal to Divinity, these texts easily lead to, and provide support for, a fundamentalist point of view: "Either my way or the highway." As I have written elsewhere:

> A monotheistic worldview complicates our accepting multiple "truths" by implicitly postulating that there is only *one* ultimate truth. So we hold to our own (often inculcated) perceptions and reject others' "realities," assuming that they are wrong or, at best, woefully inaccurate.[10]

Or in another place:

> The move from polytheism to monotheism has not been without its costs and dangers. The belief that there is only One True God has sometimes led to the blessed affirmation that all humankind is equal.

---

7. *The Holy Bible* (Revised Standard Version) (New York: Thomas Nelson and Sons, 1952).

8. *The Holy Bible* (New Revised Standard Version) (New York: American Bible Society, 1989).

9. *The New English Bible* (New York: Cambridge University Press, 1971).

10. Jack H Bloom, *The Rabbi As Symbolic Exemplar: By the Power Vested in Me* (Binghamton, NY: The Haworth Press, 2002), p. 98.

It has with less benign consequences also led to rejecting that there is more than one way to know the one God, especially if that way is different from what we are told that God has commanded. Monotheism can be taken to imply an essential oneness in us and the world. . . . It is a dangerous yet understandable inference drawn from monotheism that as there is only one God, there is only one way to the divine. . . . *You either* acknowledge that "truth" *or you* are in some way benighted, and must be set right. Monotheism, and the quest for *ultimate* meaning, for all its truth and benefits, unfortunately has produced a dangerous by-product: [Either/Or] thinking. [Either/Or] thinking is found throughout our own and other traditions. Things, ideas, etc. are either one way or another. . . . [Either/Or] thinking is at its core a fundamentalist position. There is *one* way. Both intrapersonally and with others, an attribute, idea, person or whatever that is not that *one* way needs either to be converted to the "true" thinking or gotten rid of. We are obliged to bring both ourselves and others into line both for the wayward's benefit. [Either/Or] thinking allows no other way.[11]

To think about this text in a relational [Both/And] setting is no easy thing. It is as far from "You shall love your neighbor as yourself" as you can get. It is a text well described by Judith Plaskow as "hard and perplexing in many ways, an embarrassment to many. No mitigating circumstances are possible, no way to end the enmity short of blotting out the memory of Amalek."[12]

Why get *so* worked up? Why a call for eternal battle, for a war of extermination? War with Amalek was, after all, only one of a whole series of battles as the Israelites made their way to Canaan. In Numbers (14:45) is yet another battle—a defeat—yet no cry of eternal revenge. What is all the fuss and fury about? There are endless battles with seemingly countless enemies. Only one becomes a paradigm. Only one evokes the motto "God is at war with Amalek in every generation." Only one carries the terrifying injunction to "blot out the memory of Amalek from under heaven." A hard text for a people subjected to wars of extermination, and for those of us who would not want to do unto others.

We return to the Hebrew text. In Deuteronomy (25:18), we take note of a sequence that raises a question. The sequence in which *"do not fear God"* appears, seems different from that indicated by the Jewish Publication Soci-

---

11. Ibid., pp. 179-180.
12. Judith Plaskow, "Dealing with the Hard Stuff," *Tikkun,* September/October 1994.

ety of America's translation of 1962/1985, which, in keeping with Jewish tradition and most translations, understands *"do not fear God"* as referring to the Amalekites, who because they *"do not fear God"* could perpetrate their unforgivable act. The Hebrew sequence has *"do not fear God"* follow immediately after "and you, famished and weary," "do not fear God."

זכור את אשר עשה לך עמלק בדרך בצאתכם ממצרים:
אשר קרך בדרך
ויזנב בך כל הנחשלים אחריך ואתה עיף ויגע
ולא ירא אלהים

ולא ירא אלהים = **"do not fear God"**

Located at the very end of the verse, to whom, then, does *"do not fear God"* apply? In its Hebrew location, *"do not fear God"* seems to apply to the Israelites. They are "famished and weary," and they (the Israelites) *"do not fear God."* Read one way the Amalekites *"do not fear God"*; read by its place in the sentence, the Israelites.

What does *fearing God* mean? This expression appears at the beginning of Exodus.[13] The midwives, Shifrah and Puah, ordered by Pharaoh to kill all newborn Israelite boys, do *not* do so because they *fear God*. The midwives understand that the babies, though weak and helpless, are human, modeled after and molded by Divinity, and therefore are not to be killed. Their *fear of God* governs their actions. They disobey Pharaoh and risk life and position by lying to Pharaoh in their account of how it was that the baby boys survived. So the text is clear: *fear of God* motivates compassion toward the helpless.

Back to Amalek. Amalek infuriatingly attacks and kills those who cannot keep up. Killing the weak and stragglers is of no military or strategic importance. It is a waste of energy and resources. To defeat the Israelite enemy by killing in battle is one thing, but the women and children, the "famished and weary," those who cannot hurt you and are no threat—what is the point of killing them? You kill them because they happen to be Israelites, the enemy, because they're different, because they're not you. To kill them, you have to depersonalize them. Amalek attacks and kills the "other" simply because they are the "other," a depersonalized other.

If *"do not fear God"* applies to the Israelites, it applies to all of them, not only to the stragglers, but equally to those in command. "Equal over" against "equal." Perhaps at an Israelite army staff meeting, when an officer noted that there were those who trailed behind the camp, unable to maintain

---

13. Exodus 1:17.

the stringent pace, no junior officer or commanding general stood up to say, "We have stragglers out there; we have women and children, the famished and the weary, young and old, who can't keep up—we have to protect them somehow."

No troops were deployed, no armed escort dispatched, no protection provided. The stragglers were not protected for the selfsame reason the Amalekites attacked them. The Israelite high command had depersonalized their own people. They were the refuse, the impoverished, those no longer of any use in the long trek to Canaan. They were no longer of value. They did not matter. They had *become other. They were depersonalized,* left to perish in the desert, to be exterminated by Amalek. The Israelite leadership itself did *not fear God.*

Because Israelites and Amalekites *both "do not fear God,"* they, unlike the midwives of old, did not recognize the Divinity in and of each person. Both were guilty of depersonalizing the other. Both were responsible for the awful outcome. So one can read the verse as applying to both Israel and Amalek. Neither *feared God. Fearing God* means recognizing the ultimate personhood, the ultimate value, of each human being, taking none for granted, depersonalizing no one.

God's war with Amalek is an eternal war against depersonalizing people, against the kind of thinking that allowed both Amalek and Israel to collude in what happened in the desert so long ago, and so many times in so many places, to our own day.

In my early courtship of the woman who is now my *yekkeh rebbitzen,*[14] I had to deal with her German-ness. I was stunned to hear that when she heard the words *six million,* she also thought of the six million German men who had died in the war. "No comparison," I said. She agreed. Yet it started me thinking about those on the other side who had died. One night after viewing a documentary titled *The Siege of Leningrad,* I called her, sharing with her that I had seen it. Her first comment was, "It's terrible how many Germans died there." I exploded! "Who began the war?! Who attacked whom?! Who was shelling whom?! Who was encircling and starving Leningrad anyway?!" She interjected in the midst of my outburst, "You think those students, those farmers, those clerks, those men like my uncle . . . you think they *wanted* to die there?" I was caught up short. I realized that I was doing what had been done to my people. I had depersonalized them all. They were Germans, and their deaths did not count because my people had suffered so!

We are each of us expert at depersonalizing others. We do it with our spouses, our friends, the other sex, our neighbors, ethnic groups, religions,

---

14. *Yekkeh* is Israeli colloquial for German Jews, perhaps because they insisted on wearing their jackets on hot Middle Eastern days. *Rebbitzen* is a rabbi's wife.

and races—with whomever we perceive as "other." Each of us, in any and every relationship, is living and dealing with an alien reality. Depersonalizing is a simple way of dealing with "alien-ness." It is simpler to *not fear God* and to depersonalize the other. No problem!

Fearing God is much tougher. Recognizing the divine uniqueness in every other, not depersonalizing them, is difficult for another reason. It runs headlong into what we humans have to do to get by in the world. We *have to generalize.* If every time we met a new person we started de novo, wondering, "Is this creature human or an orangutan?" and not knowing whether to shake hands, how to say hello, whether to smile or run for cover, we would be stuck. We learn by *generalizing.* Whether in Chicago, Illinois, or Fairfield, Connecticut, a red light means stop. We drive on the right (in the United States, at least) and generalize that others have learned the same. Otherwise it would be even more insane to drive down the road than it already is. Much of our learning and behavior comes from our ability to generalize from one situation to another, from one person to another. Otherwise we could predict nothing. We would be starting from square one all the time. And *generalizing* is the direct opposite of recognizing each human being as a specific and different person, each modeled after and molded by Divinity, each unique and ultimately valuable—a hard thing to do. Depersonalizing is a lot easier. It's in our bones. To *not fear God* is both natural and effortless.

So the text, indeed a "hard" text, remains intense and resolute. Only its focus changes. God is at war with the Amalek present *in us* and *in others* in all generations. God has sworn us to an oath to wipe out Amalek, to do the patently impossible, yet to undertake the mission. We are covenanted to overcome the tendency to depersonalize others, which has wreaked so much havoc in human history. Our task is to be counted among those who *fear God.* Our mission is to see the personhood in ourselves and in all others. Our battle is to recognize and relate to the Amalek in ourselves and others and, with fear of God, neutralize the Amalek that depersonalizes and destroys, both others and ourselves, lest it destroy the world.

– 24 –

Jewish Relational Care with the Healthy Aging

Richard F. Address

You are to love God with all of your heart, all of your soul, and all of your might."[1]

Jewish relational care with the aging presents new and exciting challenges. The emerging twenty-first century is witness to demographic and social changes that have transformed the face of aging within our community. Old stereotypes are vanishing and multigenerational cohorts are evolving as "new" Jewish older adults. Given the nature of the changes, we as clergy are often part of this emerging "longevity revolution," caring for congregants at the same time as we care for ourselves and our own families. The foundation for approaching this revolutionary new time is rooted in what may be called a "theology of relationships." Simply put, this is a belief that the most powerful element we can bring to working with the aging is the presence of relationships based on sacred texts that, when translated into our own rabbinate, speak to the basic needs of our people and ourselves as we age: that of seeking meaning and purpose in life.

---

1. Deuteronomy 6:5. Translation is the author's.

One of the basic issues relating to this discussion is that it is difficult to actually define what "old" is. Walter Jacob, in an article summarizing the issue of how texts define "old," points out that there is no precise definition within the texts; there are no special tractates devoted to the elderly, no calls for a special social class. Rather, as Jacob points out, it is always the person rather than the age that matters.[2] This reality is often lost in the way we have come to see older adults within our contemporary society. Relational caregiving with the elderly too often is stereotyped as working with individuals at the end of life, individuals who are dealing with illness and suffering. In this traditional approach to the subject of caring for the aging within our community, the rabbi and clergy are often called upon to provide avenues for comfort that deal with the feelings of loss and estrangement that illness and suffering can cause. Within this arena rests the call, on the part of our people, for some sense of meaning that may be derived from these experiences, and it is in this forum that we often receive our first tests as clergy. This role remains one of our most powerful and important. The power of the relationships that we create within these moments can impact individuals, families, and our own sense of self in ways that can be measured only through the experience itself. All clergy have had the experience of being only present at these moments and knowing that their presence helped ease a passage from illness back to health or, perhaps, into another world. Families never forget that relationship, and rarely do we.

With increasing frequency we are seeing the expansion of the needs of older adults and their families for clergy involvement in an ever-widening definition of caregiving. The reason for this is the radical restructuring of the Jewish community that is taking place before our eyes. The so-called longevity revolution is changing the face of our community and presenting us with new challenges and opportunities. Jews sixty-five years of age and over are now close to 20 percent of our community, with the fastest growing segment being those over seventy-five. They represent the longest-living, healthiest, most secure, and spiritually challenging generation of older adults that has ever lived. Joining them within a decade will be the first wave of the baby boom generation, bringing their cultural and social baggage of the "sixties," "seventies," and "eighties" into the field of aging. Increased concerns regarding entitlements, resource allocation, and the impact of multigenerational caregiving will be present in ever-expanding ways for the next few decades. Our role in this revolution will be critical. As longevity increases, so will demands from our people for guidance from our

---

2. Walter Jacob, "Beyond Methuselah—Who Is Old?" *Aging and the Aged in Jewish Law* (Pittsburgh, PA: Freehof Institute of Progressive Halakhah, 1998).

tradition regarding the meaning of this new longevity. Personal security, increased education, mobility, affluence, and health, many of the key characteristics of the new aging, will still be rooted in the individual's basic search for ways to seek meaning in light of mortality. We are already seeing redefinition of the concept of retirement, a concept that may soon be obsolete.[3] Increasing numbers of our community, including ourselves, will be faced with a reality of several decades of—God willing—healthy life after children leave home and the demands of career and work formally end. A challenge for the Jewish relational caregiver will be how to deal with the traditional questions of life's meaning and purpose from the perspective of this revolution in years, a revolution made possible by the blessings of medical technology, economic gains, and personal security. Part of our challenge in working with the new older adult population will be to create and sustain a sense of community, meaning, and relational presence within a society that is fragmented, private, rootless, and secular. We are being blessed with years in a society that still has yet to value them. Within this reality resides the opportunity to redefine how we see ourselves in relation to God and, thus, the people with whom we interact. In redefining such relationships, we can, if we are so open, invite our own souls to reflect upon and re-vision our own relationship patterns.

How we create relationships with others will rest on how we stand in relationship to God. That fundamental relationship is the foundation from which emerges our own search for meaning. What the longevity revolution will be teaching us is that our ability to develop sacred relationships with this multigenerational cohort will reflect our own ability to evolve our own relationship with God.

One of the issues that confronts contemporary Jewish synagogue life is the growing decline in older-adult membership. One of the reasons cited for this affiliation gap is the "pediatric" nature of much of synagogue life. That is also reflected in theologies that still present a parent-child attitude in discussing our relationship with God. What many of our older adults are now telling us is that their life experience and intellectual and spiritual maturity demand a different approach. They require a theology that understands the contingencies and realities of life experience, an experience that encompasses new life stages and challenges for individuals who may be living well into their ninth decade.

David Ariel examines this challenge, noting, "All the images that we have of God are based on our ideas of relationships. Too many of the images of the past are based on parental images of God that emphasize our depend-

---

3. See Chapter 25, "Jewish Relational Care and Retired Clergy," in this book.

ence, inadequacy, and need for protection."[4] Ariel notes also the need for developing a new way of looking at our fundamental relationship with God, a view that reflects the changes in our own society. He suggests that the parent-child model may not be as compelling as it once was:

> We can use a new imagery of God based on a mature understanding of relationships. We can replace the parent-child model for our relationship with God with a new model of father to adult and mother to adult. We can find new images from within the tradition that reflect these more appealing notions of our relationships with God.[5]

This charge challenges us as caregivers to seek continually our own re-visioning and redefinition of our own relationships with God. In our interacting with older adults, we can audaciously dare to be open to allowing our relationship with God to be constantly evolving, and theirs as well. The "maturing" of our own relationship can be of immense value as we are called upon to take care of and guide our people. We are reminded of the value of this openness to new relationships with God in God's charge to Moses in Exodus 3:14. There, God responds to the request from Moses for God's name with words that reflect the idea that our relationship with God continually evolves, based on our own life stages and life experiences. As our lives and relationships are never static, so too our relationship with God continues to evolve as we grow and age.

The idea that our relationship with God should never be fixed is equally crucial when we examine our relationships with others and, by extension, our own *"selves."* Change is a positive and important value within Judaism. It is an essential element in healthy relationships. One of the beautiful aspects of working with older adults is that they often model, through their own life experiences, the value of change and the ability to be open to dealing with what is often unexpected. This tension of holding on and letting go can inform us as we seek to be in a caring relationship with them. If our involvement and caring is a door that leads to a pathway of meaning, then sacred relationships are a key to unlock that door. In this sense, relationships become more important than belief in the achievement of meaning and purpose in life. Change is part of the development of those relationships, and, thus, relational caregiving involves an embrace of change and an acceptance of the possible. Daniel Gordis, reflecting on the dynamism inherent in the development of relationships that reflect God, wrote:

---

4. David Ariel, *Spiritual Judaism* (New York: Hyperion, 1998), p. 3.
5. Ibid.

Relationships implies gradual growth and learning with fits and starts, with periods of tremendous progress as well as deeply frustrating and painful times. . . . It is not certainty that Jews seek; Jewish life is about searching for God's sheltering presence.[6]

Caring for older adults reminds us that few things remain certain and that one's meaning is derived from being open to the search.

In seeking to create this theology of relationships, we return to the basic concept of Genesis 1:27 and Genesis 2:5 that we are modeled after and molded by Divinity and created [*Tzelem*⟺*N'shamah*],[7] with mind and body in relationship. The Hebrew word *Tzelem*[8] represents one aspect of this theology, and key values can be gleaned from looking at the three letters that form the word. The creation of sacred relationships, based upon our fundamental relationship with God, and the ability to model that relationship with people can be enhanced by values contained in the letters *tzadi, lamed,* and *mem.* Contained within the word for our divine reflection of God are the important values of justice, dignity, self-worth, balance, love, and deed. Contained within the word *N'shamah*[9] are values associated with the letters *nun, shin, mem,* and *hei.* *N'shamah* helps define the fundamental relationship we have with God, as expressed by *Tzelem.* Values such as faithfulness and a search for a sense of completeness or wholeness seek to help manage the creative tension in the [*Tzelem*⟺*N'shamah*] model. These values meet in sacred deed and, in doing so, invite the mystery of God into the way we deal with our competing *"selves"* and with others. These values can be applied to our work with older adults, for they reflect the realities of lives being lived, of the need to deal with the randomness of existence and, above all, the search to find meaning in our own *"selves"* and our own existence.

The *tzadi* in *Tzelem* reflects the concept of *tzedek.*[10] Being modeled after and molded by Divinity reminds us that, no matter what our status or position, we have a spark of God in each of us. Thus, by the very fact that we have been created, each of us possesses dignity, worth, and value. This, all of us affirm. Yet, as we age, we are often confronted by realities that test

---

6. Daniel Gordis, *God Was Not in the Fire* (New York: Scribner, 1995), p. 55.

7. [Breath-Taking⟺Model of Divinity]. See *ABC's of Jewish Relational Care* in this book; for further explication, see Jack H Bloom, *The Rabbi As Symbolic Exemplar: By the Power Vested in Me* (Binghamton, NY: The Haworth Press, 2002), especially Chapters 6 and 8.

8. Our mindful cognitive self.

9. Our breathing somatic self, from the Hebrew root *N-Sh-M*, breath.

10. Justice, equality, and worth.

these basic Jewish axioms. Indeed, we often forget to remind our people as they grow that these are basic Jewish values. The challenges of longevity and caregiving often test an individual's feelings of worth, dignity, and value. They are opportunities to seek that evolving, maturing relationship with God. The older we get, the greater the need to seek a balance within the stresses and contradictions of life. Perhaps this sense of harmony or balance is implied with the mystical concept of *d'veikut,*[11] which implies, within our various *"selves,"* a need to seek a sense of spiritual harmony within the stresses and strains of reality.

This search for a sense of balance and spiritual harmony within our competing *"selves"* and in our relationships with others can also be gleaned from the letter *nun,* the first letter of *N'shamah*. This *nun* represents the value of *ne-eman,*[12] of faith in one's self to search for the appropriate ways to model the fundamental relationship we have with God. Tradition is instructive in giving us insight into the competing ways that faithfulness can define how we engage in relationships. There are several comments in the tradition as to the two ways to write the letter *nun;* the letter that appears in the beginning or middle of a word, and the letter that appears at the end of a word, the final *nun*. One letter is bent, the other is erect. The MaHaRal[13] taught that the bent *nun* represents a sense of humility, bent in respect, whereas the final letter, written as if erect, reflects a more unwavering, dedicated approach to life and faith. Can we say that one is more inner directed, the other outer directed, as if representing competing aspects within the same person? These are two representations of the challenge that we face in how we approach every relationship. In seeking to define each encounter in terms of dignity and value and worth, we often struggle in our approach. There is no one fixed way of dealing with people, especially people who have lived and experienced decades of life. How do we balance our competing internal *"selves"* so as to treat each relationship with justice and equity?

In working with the members of the "longevity generations," the ideas of justice, self-worth, equity, and faithfulness will focus on the growing need for meaning. Here again the texts are insightful. As we and our people live longer and experience more, the reality of our own mortality becomes more crystallized. How many of us have people coming to our offices to ask for help in dealing with a feeling that something is not right. They have achieved financial security, personal success, and yet they bring a spiritual hunger that has been called a crisis of meaning. Here again is an opportunity

---

11. A desire to be in relationship with the sacred.
12. Faithfulness.
13. Rabbi Judah Leow, MaHaRal of Prague (1525-1609).

to create relationships that are based on life experience and a mature view of how God and tradition can guide and embrace the search for meaning. Genesis 3, perhaps the greatest chapter ever written, constantly reminds us that, in the end, life comes down to basic questions of *why:* Why was I born? Why must I die? Why am I here? With the longevity revolution upon us, answers to these questions cannot be framed in parent-child language. Life has presented us with contradictions, challenges, randomness, and choices that demand we engage our people in relation to their experiences and the contexts from which they come. The relationships we create as we work with our older adults will be ones that speak to a basic mood of Judaism, a mood that has stretched from Genesis to Heschel;[14] we are beings in search of meaning; we need to be needed. As we age and diminishing health reminds us that the reality of death encroaches, these feelings form a basic component of what it means to be in relationship with God and others.

The *lamed* of the word *Tzelem* speaks to an aspect of relationships that is in increasingly short supply. The *lamed* can represent the Hebrew word *lev,*[15] the epicenter of our breathing, pulsating *N'shamah,* and carries with it the need for us to infuse our work and relationships with a sense of love. This does not necessarily mean romantic love, although the realities of new life stages within the longevity revolution have destroyed stereotypes regarding sexuality and aging. Rather, it is suggested that we revisit the role of love, intimacy, and companionship within our relationships with older adults. If it is not good that we be alone,[16] then part of what we need to look at may be new definitions of community, new celebrations of intimacy and cohabitation, and a redefinition of love. This idea of love springs again from the fundamental relationship we have with God. The impact and power of this concept is even part of our daily worship experience, for we are constantly reminded in the *Sh'ma*[17] and *v'ahavta:*[18] "You are to love God with all of your heart, all of your soul and all of your might." Over a decade ago, one of the foremost scholars on aging issues, J. J. Seeber, looked at the Deuteronomy text and saw its importance to how we relate to issues of aging and caring:

> The command is to love God consistently with all dimensions of ourselves. . . . The multidimensionality with which persons are seen is

---

14. Abraham Joshua Heschel (1907-1972), prominent Jewish theologian of the twentieth century, author of *The Sabbath* (1951), *Man Is Not Alone* (1952), *Man's Quest for God* (1954), and *God in Search of Man* (1956).

15. Heart.

16. Genesis 2:18.

17. "Hear O Israel the Lord is One, The Lord alone"—watchword of Jewish belief.

18. The text that follows the *Sh'ma* and thought of as part of it.

important today in a society that stereotypes the elderly as only de-
clining bodies. . . . Human life is a complex mixture of heart and soul,
mind and strength, and aging is a complex process of change.[19]

Looking at the words of the *v'ahavta,* we see that Judaism teaches a holistic approach to the creation of our relationships. This is something that in
our Western world we often forget. In seeking to be in relationship with others, we are called upon to invest all of our *"selves":* mind and heart, body
and soul, all of which need to interact with one another. Likewise, in our relationship with God, and thus with our own soul, we are reminded that everything is interrelated. There can be no divorce of heart from soul, of mind
from body. Sacred relationships require the total commitment of all our
"selves," those we accept and those we are tempted to reject. In dealing
with the challenges of aging, this is important. Rarely do we deal with just
an individual. In truth, every relationship is in relation to others. Every person is a universe unto himself or herself. Those with whom we choose to interact are part of other similar worlds. In creating sacred relationships with
our people and in enabling those relationships to be created by our communities, we need to be reminded of the interconnectedness of life. Thus, we
see the "systems" approach to establishing these relationships. Our role as
clergy again impacts, not only older adults and their relationships to their
own multiple *"selves,"* but also the universe of relationships that encompasses them. The message of *lev* is to see the power of love in the creation of
those relationships—love in the sense of respect, and love in the sense of
welcoming God's love into the relationship. Caring for the growing numbers of people who represent the longevity generations will call upon us
to speak of the power of love within the relationships that we establish. Being created [*Tzelem*⇔*N'shamah*] or [Breath-Taking⇔Model of Divinity]
means that we do not split our minds from our hearts and our souls from our
bodies. Inviting the concept of love into our dialogues means that we reinforce a basic aspect of our working with all people, especially the aging; we
seek meaning in our existence, we seek to be needed, and the mutuality of a
mature concept of love speaks to a covenant of need, a covenant between
God and humankind that is exemplified by the ideal of [*Tzelem*⇔
N'shamah] and is demonstrated by the value of religion. In looking at a theology of relationships as it can influence a sense of relational caregiving, it
is noteworthy to look at the root meanings of religion and relation. Dictio-
naries note that the root of religion has the sense of binding, or bringing to-

---

19. J. J. Seeber, PhD, "Beginnings of a Theology for Aging," *Generations,* XIV(4)
(Fall 1990), p. 48.

gether, while relation carries with it the sense of connection. To be truly religious, then, we go about the work of bringing people together and creating sacred connections. Love is key to making those connections sacred.

Often, in trying to bring people who are in conflict together, we seek a sense of completeness or wholeness. The *shin* from *N'shamah* reflects this ideal of *sh'leimut*.[20] To this end, we need to be reminded that the value of love as represented by the *lamed (lev)* cannot always lead to *sh'leimut*. Again we face the reality of life and people and the creative tensions that reside within each of us and within each of the relationships we encounter. Often our older adult congregants will tell us that their ability to accept certain realities in their lives has allowed them to make "peace" with their circumstances and has helped define the purpose of their lives. One of the lessons we may be able to take from the concepts of *lev* and *sh'leimut* may be that, in seeking honor, respect, love, and wholeness, we can come to honor and see the wisdom in compromise, the acceptance of what "is," and gain the ability to let go of what cannot be changed. A lesson of the longevity revolution will be the affirmation of the need to celebrate the fact that we can never achieve *sh'leimut*, that our lives are continually open to new ideas and possibilities, and that in seeking a balance among the realities of life's experience we may actually achieve meaning and purpose.

Through service to others, the *mitzvah*,[21] we actualize the concept of [*Tzelem*⇔*N'shamah*] in the world. The creative duality of [*Tzelem*⇔ *N'shamah*] meets in the *mem*, the doing of *mitzvoth:* deeds that give definition and substance to being in relationship with God. In working with the aging population, the concept of *mitzvah* may be the most valuable lesson we can teach. It is in the performance of the *mitzvah* that we elevate the ideal of meaning in life. In creating sacred relationships, we model the belief that the *mitzvah* helps focus the individual to a place beyond the self. Being in a relationship with someone else allows us to teach and live the concept that we derive meaning from a place outside of Self. It teaches that individuals, no matter how old in years they may be, always have the capacity for growth. Involvement with people, as study after study shows, benefits the doer of the deed far more than the recipient. This speaks to the traditional belief that, to be truly human, we need to relate to something beyond our own self. As our work with older adults evolves, we often become aware how present this search for meaning outside of self becomes. As we move toward the end of life, we are reminded of the poetry and symbolism of Ec-

---

20. An unimpaired condition; soundness; the quality or state of being complete or undivided.

21. In Hebrew, fulfilling God's command; in Yiddish, a good deed. The plural form is *mitzvoth*.

clesiastes 1, which tells us that we are all part of a greater something that is beyond our self. This age of "generativity," even though it now may encompass decades instead of years, is allowing us as clergy to impact significantly the value and quality of increasing numbers of people. The search for the transcendent is a search that is all too often missing from our community and our society in general. Working with and caring for the elders of our people will continue to provide us with a unique opportunity to gather the spiritual capital of several generations and to teach that being created [*Tzelem*⇔*N'shamah*] is about giving of oneself in relationship to *"self"* and others. In this way we seek to model the fundamental relationship that exists between human beings and God, a relationship that is never fixed and is always evolving.

Thus, values embedded in the *tzadi* and *lamed* of *Tzelem* and the *nun* and *shin* of *N'shamah* meet in the *mem* of *mitzvah,* which allows us to transcend our culture's primary focus on seeing meaning only in the moment. Viktor Frankl emphasized this when he wrote:

> From all of which we see once again that life can never be an end in itself, and that its reproduction can never be its meaning; rather, it acquires meaning from other, non-biological frames of reference, from sources that necessarily lie beyond itself. To be bestowed with meaning, life must transcend itself, but it must do so not in "length"—in the sense of living on in one's children—but in "height"—in the sense of spiritually growing beyond oneself—or in "breadth"—in the sense of social engagement.[22]

The *mitzvah* places us in relationship with others and thus provides us the means through which the height and breadth of life can help define the covenant of meaning, a covenant that speaks to our involvement with people and our community, defined by values of dignity, worth, and love. For the longevity generations, who will come to us with increasing requests for us to facilitate or guide their own journeys to meaning, relationships defined by *mitzvoth* will be necessary, if they, and we, are to seek meaning beyond the moment.

What embraces the [*Tzelem*⇔*N'shamah*] concept is symbolized by the letter *hei,* a traditional shorthand symbol for God. What defines our ability to create caring and supportive relationships with older adults? What should be the foundation for how our own communities welcome, work

---

22. Viktor Frankl, "Facing the Transitoriness of Human Existence," *Generations,* XIV(4) (Fall 1990), p. 8.

with, and value the members of these longevity generations? We return to the fundamental relationship that infuses all we do as Jews. The creative covenant with God that we are given by the fact of our own creation is the foundation for what we do and how we care. It is, as Leviticus 19 reminds us, the refrain for our actions and our lives: *Ani Adonai*.[23]

The [*Tzelem⇔N'shamah*] model of creating relationships can serve as a value-based guide to creating sacred relationships with those with whom we work. It is a continually evolving theory, a dialectic that flows between the fundamental relationship we have with God and the lifelong encounter that our soul has with God as to who we are and how we will be. It is also the translation of that struggle as to how we model and create relationships with others, relationships that we hope will model the fundamental creation-based relationship with God. Thus, we are in constant dialogue between self and *"self," "selves"* and others, and God. This fluidity speaks to one of the challenges of the longevity revolution. A characteristic of this revolution is the ongoing search for meaning. Longevity has provided opportunities for older adults to explore new avenues of meaning. Their life experiences now demand that we, as clergy, speak to them in ways that can bring the power of our tradition to their experiences, and thus have that tradition serve as a foundation upon which they can construct lives of meaning. The explosion of religious options and new expressions of community that we are now seeing validate the fact that people have a need for meaning, a need to be needed. From our beginnings, human beings have sought out one another for community; they have engaged in the creation of relationships. Healthy, sacred aging implies moving from a focus on only oneself to an embrace of the notion that we are part of something greater, something transcendent. This is the sense of mystery that resides within each of us, and it is in the search for our understanding of this mystery that we can find meaning.

In the next few decades the Jewish community will experience a revolution in aging. No single definition will be adequate to describe the inhabitants of this exciting new world. We, as clergy, will be called upon to work with this community in new ways. Increasingly we will be asked to bring the richness of our tradition to the ever-expanding life experiences and new life stages that are already emerging. People living into their ninth and tenth decades will look to us for adult, mature guidance. They will seek relationships and community to provide comfort and support and to gain meaning in the mystery that is life. We, as clergy, and the communities in which we serve, can be the bridge that brings people together, and the relationships we create can serve as examples that connect our people with the sacred, by

---

23. Hebrew for "I am the sovereign God."

modeling relationships that honor, celebrate, and reflect the values inherent in the [*Tzelem⇔N'shamah*] model: dignity, worth, uniqueness and love, faithfulness and wholeness, values that meet in sacred deeds and are reflective of our search for the transcendent mystery that is God.

Jewish Relational Care and Retired Clergy

Jack H Bloom

"Are you senior citizens?" they ask at the ticket booth. We answer, "Yes," ambivalently at best. That response gets Ingrid and myself more reasonable tickets for the movies and cheaper seats on the commuter train, and it sometimes evokes a challenge—Does Ingrid really pass as a senior? Welcome to the "golden years," or is their glitter simply American promo and hype? Is it a lie—BS—or is it based on something? Each of us knows that old age is not for sissies, and as George Vaillant has put it, in his seminal book *Aging Well,*[1] we know that old age is rarely getting exactly what you want.[2] Is there some/any truth in the term *golden years*?

Years back, a perturbed woman came to see me in my office. Her husband had just retired from being a security guard at the local City Trust Company bank in Bridgeport, Connecticut. For forty-five years, he'd left the house at 8:30 a.m., arrived at work at 8:50, did his job until 5:00 p.m., and then returned home. She told me in her first session that she was eager for him to retire finally after forty-five years. One morning, three weeks after he had retired, he went out to get the paper and some cigarettes, and the next thing she knew he was gone. Disappeared. Not a word! Four months later she found out that he was in Seattle, Washington, which is about as far as you can get from the City Trust Company in Bridgeport.

The Chancy Path Ahead

So old age is not always getting what you want—or think you want—for the retiree, or the retiree's partner. No matter how we gussy it up, it's a downward slope, the days moving by ever more quickly to the end of the run. It is a slippery slope that needs to be negotiated with as much flexibility

---

1. George E. Vaillant, *Aging Well* (New York: Warner Books, originally published by Little, Brown and Co., 2002).
2. Ibid., p. 186.

and grace as you can muster. The obstacles and impediments show up, suddenly surprise you, knock you off course, and can even kill you. However, it *can* be a good time, and oddly, for some people, it turns out to be the best time. For some it's Jerusalem at sunset, when the walls are most golden and radiant, marking the end of the day.

Edgar Bronfman,[3] in his book *The Third Act,*[4] asked Philip Johnson (the ninety-plus-year-old who collaborated with Ludwig Mies van der Rohe in the design and construction of the "Building of the Millennium"—none other than the Seagram Building) what piqued his interest most at this point in his celebrated career. Which of his famous projects held him most in its thrall? Johnson leaned across the table without hesitation and said:

> What interests me most is the next project I'm doing. And the next one after that. All my attention is focused on the horizon, though I don't know what's on that horizon. But I'll find out. If you don't keep learning, you're finished. The only reality in the world is change. As Heraclitus said, "Change is the only absolute in life." Luckily, I love change.[5]

Talk about change: Who could have imagined the path each of us has come? As mature adults we know that we have traversed an ever-changing terrain: peaks of achievement and valleys of despair; too many bumps and too few meadows; times when the road was clear and times when pebbles made us fall flat on our faces. We know well that life is a [Both/And] proposition. A favorite aphorism of mine, attributed to Winston Churchill, is this: "If you think you know your path, it's not yours."

Vaillant suggests that the vital question retirees in the golden years must answer is, "What is the most important thing that makes you want to get out of bed in the morning, eager for a new day—excluding your bladder?"[6]

In choosing whatever it's going to be that gets us out of bed day by day, we have to recognize that our future is, to some extent, predicted by our past, our genetic heritage, parental influences, childhood, education, and, of course, health. Yet chance has a very crucial place; sometimes what happens is totally unexpected.

---

3. I bought his book because I owed him: he was reading my book, *The Rabbi As Symbolic Exemplar: By the Power Vested in Me* (Binghamton, NY: The Haworth Press, 2002), shuttling between one of his many homes.

4. E. M. Bronfman and C. Whitney, *The Third Act: Reinventing Yourself After Retirement* (New York: G.P. Putnam and Sons, 2002).

5. Ibid., p. 136.

6. Ibid., p. 5.

In 1959 I was the obvious candidate to be the assistant rabbi at the Society for the Advancement of Judaism (SAJ), the mother synagogue of the Reconstructionist movement in New York City. The SAJ had been founded by Mordecai M. Kaplan, who took no salary for many years. By 1959 Jack Cohen was the rabbi of a thriving congregation, and they wanted an assistant rabbi in charge of youth work. At that time I was probably the last unreconstructed Reconstructionist at the Jewish Theological Seminary; ideologically I was the right candidate. Being someone who had been in charge of the teenagers at Camp Ramah in Wisconsin, and having done a reasonably successful job of it, I was the right candidate in that way, as well. The other candidate was very different. As far as we knew, he was anti-Reconstructionist and had little experience with children. The choice seemed obvious—the key word being *seemed.*

On July 1, 1959 (a date that features large in the annals of my life), I, as a newly ordained rabbi, was assisting at my very first wedding—that of Joel and Ann Zaiman[7]—at Beth El Synagogue Center in New Rochelle, New York, where Rabbi David Golovensky held sway. As the reception line formed, I looked for a public phone and confidently called up Jack Cohen at the SAJ. The board meeting to ratify my selection as assistant rabbi had taken place that night. Jack picked up the phone, and I said, "Well, Jack, how did it go?" He said, "Jack, they picked the other guy." *"What?"* I had already rented a brand-new apartment in New York. I had a datebook full of names and phone numbers of prospective *rebbitzens.* I had my shrink appointments set up for three times a week in New York. I had everything all set. I said, "They did *what?"* He said, "They picked the other guy." I said, "Jack, how could that happen?" He then said something to me that has reverberated in my mind down through the years,[8] *"Jack, that's how boards are!"*

Rosh Hashanah was just a couple of months away, and I was going to St. Louis, Missouri, a day or two later, to court the woman who is now my ex, whom I had known for about a week. I came back in the middle of July. I didn't have a job. Finally a job appeared on the Rabbinical Assembly list[9]—in Bridgeport, Connecticut, fifty miles from Times Square.[10] They wanted

---

7. They were, and are, exemplars of a rabbi and a gracious talented wife.

8. A couple of years ago, I had the privilege of sitting next to Jack, at Cong Mevakshei Derech in Jerusalem, and I told him this story and what he told me on July 3, 1959. "Well I *was* right!" he responded.

9. The Association of Conservative Rabbis. I am now both a Conservative and a Reform rabbi.

10. An arcane fact that only few know was that Wolfe Kelman *z'l,* Director of Placement for the Rabbinical Assembly, had a map on his wall noting how far everything in the world was from Times Square.

an assistant rabbi to Harry Nelson, one of the greats of our time, and, as it worked out, I ended up going to Bridgeport to be in charge of a suburban congregation in next-door Fairfield, Connecticut. I spent ten years there as a congregational rabbi, and I've been in Fairfield ever since. I arrived there by mistake. Happenstance changed my life.

From one chance occurrence to another—in 1969 I decided to take my family to Israel. I was leaving congregational life and doing a second psychology internship at Hadassah Medical Center. My office was distinguished, not because it was four feet by six feet, but because it was ten feet from the world-famous Chagall windows, right across a small divide. My daughter Rebecca was one of three kids who constituted the Anglo-Saxon *landsmanschaft*[11] in a *gan*[12] on 11 Ibn Ezra Street in Rechavia, Jerusalem. The *landsmanschaft* consisted of Ray and Roz Arzt's daughter Ilana (they were our friends and neighbors in Fairfield and lived at 9 Ibn Ezra), Rebecca, and a little boy, Jackie, about whose existence I had no inkling. The three English speakers skipped class one day and went exploring Rechavia. The teachers, distraught about these three three-year-olds wandering around Jerusalem, found them within an hour. The father of Jack Glaser was Rabbi Joseph Glaser *z'l,*[13] who was spending a year in Israel prior to taking over as executive vice president of the Central Conference of American Rabbis (CCAR). He invited me to his apartment and, over a cup of instant coffee, asked, "What are you studying?"

"I'm studying clinical psychology."

"Why are you studying clinical psych?"

"This is going to sound weird, Joe, but I want to help rabbis *not* to do what I did."

"What do you mean not to do what you did?"

"Well," I said, "I essentially left the pulpit."

He looked at me quizzically and said, "You want to help rabbis not do what you did."

"That's right." That was it, nothing more.

Years later, back in the States, out of the blue, Joe called up and said, "What do you know about midlife crisis?"

"Joe, whatever you want me to do, I'll do."

That's how I became the Director of Professional Career Review of the CCAR—totally by accident. No one would have dared predict that we would meet, and that my life would change as a result.

---

11. A group organized in their new home on the basis of country of origin—in this case, all were from the United States.

12. Nursery school.

13. An abbreviation for the Hebrew *zichrono l'vrachah:* "May his or her memory be a blessing."

As it was in the past, so it is with retirement. Many of the things that are going to happen to us, no matter how thorough our planning, will happen by chance; others inevitably accompany aging. This is even more true for our future than our past. The challenge, then, is, What do we do with them? Our problem is not about retiring to doing nothing, but about what we are going to do with these, perhaps, bonus years. How will we respond? Rob Rossel, a therapist colleague about to retire, has noted that "the word end . . . can mean both a terminus (end of the line) and a purpose (an outcome worked toward). . . . I have learned so much in going through this passage and find myself wondering what I will find in my new 'ends.'"[14] His question resonates for us all. What will our new "ends" be?

Developmental Tasks of Later Maturity

If one thinks back thirty, forty, or fifty years ago, these retirement years that modern seniors are currently engaged in were considered an endpoint, not a new beginning. Those who know the name Robert Havighurst know also that he wrote *Developmental Tasks and Education*. Havighurst eventually wrote about developmental tasks for people in the golden-years age bracket, and, of course, these tasks are all about dealing with how things go downhill. He outlines a truly sorry, disheartening set of later-maturity developmental tasks:

1. Adjusting to decreasing physical strength and health
2. Adjustment to retirement and reduced income
3. Adjusting to death of a spouse
4. Establishing an explicit affiliation with one's age group
5. Adopting and adapting social roles in a flexible way
6. Establishing satisfactory physical living arrangements[15]

There may be a lot of truth to this list, but not much impetus to get one out of bed each morning.

As late as 1978 Daniel Levinson, then in his fifties, in his very popular book *The Seasons of a Man's Life,* wrote gloomily that men approaching sixty may

---

14. Slightly adapted from *SR-L Digest,* October 8, 2004–October 12, 2004 (#2004-195).

15. R. J. Havighurst, *Developmental Tasks and Education* (Third Edition) (New York: Longman, 1971).

feel that all forms of youth . . . are about to disappear . . . [A] man fears that the youth within him is dying and that only the old man—an empty dry structure devoid of energy, interest or inner resources—will survive for a brief and foolish old age.[16]

That's what they call "golden years"?!

Vaillant suggests that "to see age as continued human development involves a revolutionary paradigm shift,"[17] and that's exactly what he sets about doing. He starts with some facts from *The Study of Adult Development,* which he describes as a rarity in medicine, for it quite deliberately set out to study the lives of the well, not the ill. In so doing, it has integrated three cohorts of elderly men and women, all of whom have been studied continuously for six to eight decades:

> **First,** there is a sample of 268 socially advantaged Harvard graduates born about 1920—the longest prospective study[18] of physical and mental health in the world.
> **Second,** there is a sample of 456 socially disadvantaged inner city men born about 1930—the longest prospective study of "blue collar" adult development in the world.
> **Third,** there is a sample of 90 middle-class, intellectually gifted women born about 1910—the longest prospective study of women's development in the world.[19]

In the general population, only one-third of adults alive at sixty will live past eighty, but in the three previous cohorts, 70 percent of college-educated members alive at sixty will be alive at eighty—twice as many as expected. In other words, many study members are now enjoying the exceptional longevity and prolonged retirement that will become the rule for American children who were born in the year 2000.[20]

Among the many significant findings to emerge from Vaillant's study of adult development thus far are the following:[21]

---

16. D. J. Levinson, *The Seasons of a Man's Life* (New York: Knopf, 1978), p. 34.

17. Ibid., p. 37.

18. To call a study prospective means that it studies events as they occur, and not in retrospect.

19. Levinson, *Seasons of a Man's Life,* p. 16.

20. Ibid., p. 12.

21. Ibid., p. 13.

- "It is not the bad things that happen to us that doom us; it is the good people who happen to us at any age that facilitate enjoyable old age."
- "Healing relationships are facilitated by a capacity for gratitude, for forgiveness, and for taking people inside. Allowing them into your life. (By this metaphor I mean becoming eternally enriched by loving a particular person.)"
- "A good marriage at age 50 predicted positive aging at 80. Surprisingly, low cholesterol levels at age 50 did not."
- "Learning to play and create after retirement and learning to gain younger friends as we lose older ones add more to life's enjoyment than retirement income."
- "Objective good physical health was less important to successful aging than subjective good health. It is all right to be ill as long as you do not feel sick."
- "In a world that seems ruled by genetic predestination, we need hope that we still can change. The lives of the Study members offer us guides."

An Early Guide for Me: Mr. Krane's Dad

Mr. Charles Krane, my beloved cello teacher, totally failed to teach me cello. My two older brothers were musicians, excellent musicians. My eleven-years-older brother played the piano. My middle brother, Sol, played the violin. It was determined by father and brothers that Jackie would play the cello. *I was terrible.* Mr. Krane soon figured out that it was better to take me to the Brooklyn Dodgers' games at Ebbets Field, and that reading the comics during our Sunday morning lessons and filling the conversation with other tidbits diminished the hour lesson to about half an hour. One Sunday morning he told me a story that I have never forgotten. He told me about Pittsburgh, Pennsylvania, where he had grown up, and where a white shirt donned in the morning would turn black by midday. He told me also of his father, who had done hard, tough, physical work in the steel mills, hauling and shlepping large ingots of steel all day. When his father had retired at age sixty-five, the doctor performing his exit physical had said to him, "Mr. Krane, if you don't find something that's going to keep you active, you're going to be dead in six to nine months." That quickly. He told me that his father had heeded this advice, moved to Florida, learned ballroom dancing, and, with that new skill, charmed all of the women there, and so ballroom danced his way through his seventies, and then through his eighties, and died in his early nineties, still ballroom dancing. So Mr. Krane failed at teaching me cello, but he sure did teach me something about learning to play after retirement.

The Stages of Adult Development

Vaillant credits Erik Erikson with being the first social scientist to clearly conceptualize adult development as progress, not decline. Erikson believed that, through a sequence of stages, adults participate in life within a widening social radius. Life after age fifty need not be a staircase leading downward, but a path leading outward. Erikson's original four stages were "Identity vs. Identity Diffusion," "Intimacy vs. Isolation," "Generativity vs. Stagnation," and "Integrity vs. Despair."[22] Erikson later emended the last stage to "Renunciation and *Wisdom*."[23]

Vaillant's study of adult development at Harvard has allowed him to investigate Erikson's theory empirically. Similar to time-lapse photography of blooming flowers, the different stages of Vaillant's study of adult development permitted him to remain the same while "watching" study members evolve from adolescents into great-grandfathers and great-grandmothers. Similar to Erikson, Vaillant concluded that one way to conceptualize the sequential nature of adult social development may lie in appreciating that it reflects each adult's widening social radius over time. Imagine a stone dropped into a pond: it produces ever-expanding ripples, each older ripple encompassing, but not obliterating, the circle emanating from the next ripple. Adult development is rather like that.

Vaillant's revision of Erikson's model notes that, for charting adult development, a term such as Robert Havighurst's *developmental tasks* is more scientifically correct than Erikson's *stage*. Adult developmental tasks are, more often than not, sequential. To Vaillant, the penultimate life task is to become a "Keeper of the Meaning":

> This task involves passing on the traditions of the past to the next generation. . . . [B]ecoming a Keeper of the Meaning allows one to link the past to the future. Finally, there is Integrity, the task of achieving some sense of peace and unity with respect both to one's own life and to the whole world.[24]

The virtue inherent in the task of Keeper of the Meaning is justice, for justice involves a more nonpartisan and less personal approach to oth-

---

22. E. H. Erikson, *Childhood and Society* (New York: W.W. Norton and Co., 1961), quoted in Vaillant, *Aging Well*, p. 43.

23. Erikson, *Childhood and Society,* footnote on p. 273, in the "Afterthoughts" section: "The italicized words are called *basic* virtues because without them, and their reemergence from generation to generation, all other and more changeable systems of human values lose their spirit and their relevance."

24. Vaillant, *Aging Well*, pp. 43-45.

ers. Society needs dispassionate judges as much as it needs passionate trial lawyers. If the task of young adults is to create biological heirs, the task of old age is to create social heirs.[25]

The task according to John Kotre is "to invest one's substance in forms of life and work that will outlive the self."[26] According to Ashley Montague, the idea is to be young as late as possible.[27] I would add to this: be young as late as possible but with the advantages that age can give.

Reconceptualizing the Value of Aging

Age can confer advantages and special resources needed in one's life. Among others are these:

- New and and more useful frames
- A refurbished and renewed past
- Freedom to be who we are
- Wisdom and all its manifestations

New and More Useful Frames

The frame[28] through which we see our older years can determine what we see, what is clear, what is fuzzy, what we include, what we ignore, and how we experience and value the world in which we live. We can enter these years wondering how terrible they are going to be, or we can approach them eagerly wondering how to make them rewarding and, yes, even fun. Learning and satisfaction are in store for us.

The frames for people our age are starting to change, becoming much more hopeful. As Vaillant has noted, good physical health is less important to successful aging than subjective good health: "It is all right to be ill as long as you do not feel sick." That's not easy but very important. When facing a medical procedure typical of the golden years, one can, of course, be frightened of the possible outcome, or one can choose to frame it in a positive light: "Others have gotten through this; if they could, I can." The frames we have and the perspectives they provide are what's important.

---

25. Ibid., p. 144.

26. Ibid., p. 115, footnote p. 352. J. Kotre, *Outliving the Self* (Baltimore, MD: Johns Hopkins University Press, 1984), p. 10.

27. Bronfman and Whitney, *The Third Act,* p. 135.

28. For explication of frames and their use, see in this book Chapter 2, "Language As a Relational Tool: Using Your Mouth with Your Head?"

Zalman Schachter's reframing, indicated by the very title of his book, *From Age-ing to Sage-ing*, suggests the need to adjust our frames. He offers:

> The years beyond sixty, the years of our second maturity, may be evolution's greatest gift to Humanity. . . . No longer needing to compete and to be acceptable, likeable, and all those other things considered respectable in society, people are finally uncaged in their elder years, free to release energies and capacities that the culture restrained in them when they were younger. The energies that people release after age sixty-five are not really new at all, but exist in a state of latency within the mind-body system. When we don't have to devote a large percentage of our time in fulfilling social obligations and meeting other people's expectations, we can unleash these energies and harness them for self-awareness, spiritual development, and creativity.[29]

Betty Friedan, writing in her seventies, offers a useful new frame: "We have barely even considered the possibilities in age for new kinds of loving intimacy, purposeful work and activity, learning and knowing, community and care."[30]

A Refurbished and Renewed Past

We need to reprocess our past, to change and rewrite it, and it's something we do anyway, quite unconsciously. It is okay to do this more overtly, as long as the change is positive and nourishes our present and our future. Victoria Fitch notes:

> Gerontologists tell us that one of the major tasks of old age is to reflect on the wealth of our past experience—our personal achievements as well as our unresolved conflicts—in an attempt to understand what life has meant. [Fitch] describes this process of introspection as "a kind of inner cooking or brewing. . . . The flame is the knowledge of mortality, the ingredients are a lifetime of perceptions, experiences, and relationships as yet unprocessed, and the vessel is the human heart."[31]

---

29. Zalman Schachter-Shalomi and Ronald S. Miller, *From Age-ing to Sage-ing: A Profound New Vision of Growing Older* (New York: Warner Books, 1995), p. 34 ff.

30. B. Friedan, *The Fountain of Age* (New York: Simon and Schuster, 1993), p. 87.

31. Victoria Fitch, "The Psychological Tasks of Old Age," *Naropa Institute Journal of Psychology* 3(1985): 90-106, quoted in Schachter-Shalomi and Miller, *From Age-ing to Sage-ing.*

Freedom to Be Who We Are

A certain freedom comes with age. We often envy the freedom our older citizens feel about saying and doing exactly what they want—no holds barred. Edgar Bronfman describes how Mike Wallace laughed when saying, "One of the great things about getting this old is the absolute freedom to say what you want. What the hell? What are they going to do? Fire me? Kill me? I'm fearless." Mike's colleague Walter Cronkite concurred: "I am in a position now to speak my mind. And that is what I propose to do."[32]

A longtime rabbi friend shared with me his experience of being called back to serve the same congregation he had served for many years before his retirement. He described it as a totally different experience from his first go-round: He is free now to be the rabbi he wants to be, rather than the rabbi others want him to be. They treated him one way ten years ago, and now it's a whole different story. An integral theme of that different story is his different sense of himself, providing him with the freedom to say precisely what he wants to say, in the way he wants to say it.[33]

Wisdom and All Its Manifestations

Another advantage to staying young until we're very old is wisdom, in all its manifestations. Golden-agers know a lot about what counts and what doesn't, and what battles are worth fighting, ranging from who will put the dishes in the dishwasher to getting spouses to change habits that they may still consider to be vitally important.

A great danger in the senior years is the tendency to become very crotchety and rigid. Sometimes I get a little frightened when recognizing that tendency in myself. For instance, sometimes I come home after the cleaning lady has made her appearance to find that she's moved the things I keep in one place to someplace else. It's not only because I have to guess where the thing is, but there's something in me that says rather petulantly, "That's the place for my nail clippers; don't move them around," but I have to respond lovingly to that other *"self"* that is alive and well within me: "Thanks for your help in keeping me organized, but just because we've done something a certain way doesn't mean that it's the only way. If I attend only to you I'll start to sound like a crotchety old geezer. I'll pay attention to your keeping me organized in a familiar way, but don't make such a fuss. You and I can deal with the clippers being in another place." We need to be careful about

---

32. Bronfman and Whitney, *The Third Act,* p. 136.
33. Rabbi Donald Crain, personal communication with the author.

getting rigid. Old folks can easily slip into being fundamentalists, forgetting that it's a [Both/And] world, which their life experience has taught them, resorting instead to, "It's my way or the highway." Rigidity, self-imposed, is a great risk and endangers the very wisdom that is so available to us.

Erikson offers reassurance: "Those in late mid-life describe both themselves and their aged contemporaries as more tolerant, more patient, more open-minded, more understanding, more compassionate and less critical than they were in their younger years." He quotes the septuagenarians whom he studied: "Patience is one thing you know better when you're old than when you're young"; "Now I can see both sides"; "Nothing shakes me any more." That whole business of having wisdom is very, very important.[34]

Paul Baltes, of the Max Planck Institute in Berlin, Germany, and perhaps the leading scholar in the world of wisdom development, has wisely pointed out, "Everybody's definition of wisdom will be different in the words, but the melody I suspect, will be the same."[35]

Pursuing Your Passion—The Symbolic Exemplar Option

If we were Havighurst today, knowing all the changes that have happened since 1971, we would ask, What are the developmental tasks that are required of us, that we need to undertake (given the added assets of useful frames, a refurbished history, freedom, and wisdom) to answer this crucial question: *What is the most important thing that makes you eager to get out of bed in the morning so you can do it that day? Or, to put it another way, What is the passion you will pursue?*

A characteristic of PASSION is total involvement in an activity, to the point that it absorbs you completely. To test whether a passion absorbs you completely, consider this scenario: I come up to you *while* you are absorbed in your passion and ask: *"Where at this moment do you end and the world begins?"*[36] You are abruptly interrupted. Taken aback, you do a quick double take. This is an almost impossible question. You have to reorient yourself to respond. We have all had that experience of being absorbed in doing something and then suddenly disrupted. I get that at times when I'm writing. Others experience it when deep in a gripping book or doing research, or while exercising or absorbed in prayer. Others experience it when the phone rings while they're deep in conversation with their spouses. The list is end-

---

34. Erickson, *Childhood and Society.*
35. Vaillant, *Aging Well,* p. 251.
36. Stephen Gilligan, PhD, from personal communication with the author.

less. When you're absorbed in your passion, the boundary between you and the world is blurred.

So these questions remain: What is your special passion? What fits who you are and how you've been trained? What will get you out of bed each morning eager to seize the day? For those for whom the covenant of our people has been our historic calling and vocation, it is an updating and re-working of Vaillant's "Keeper of the Meaning," making it appropriate to who we are. Our father Avraham, in whose footsteps we walk, was com-manded: "Be a [source of] blessing."[37] As symbolic exemplars[38] of both the God who intended that and of the Jewish People who took on that task, for us, the ultimate passion is that we be a blessing in the world, by our presence and by our activity. Being a blessing lies in implementing the charge of realizing fully the [*Tzelem*⇔*N'shamah*][39] in which each of us is created and with which each of us is blessed. It is in searching for and blessing the [*Tzelem*⇔*N'shamah*] in others around us, and in those who follow us, that our lives take on meaning. Doing that means blessing the [*Tzelem*⇔ *N'shamah*] and its signs, no matter how obscured, in ourselves and others.

As symbolic exemplars we've been important in other people's lives— sometimes too important, it seems. We have struggled to be loved and needed, and all too often we have made our self-worth hostage to, and de-pendent on, doing for and pleasing others. Hopefully, now possessed of the wisdom that comes with years, no longer professionally dependent on com-munity or congregation, we are free to take on a task that can absorb us, and for which we are uniquely suited.

We know we are both symbolic exemplars and regular human folks. We intimately know both sides of that equation and that relationship with which we have struggled. We know both the power of being a symbolic exemplar and how difficult the experience can be. We've learned from our "indispens-ability" and our "dispensability" that to do the job we need to see life as a [Both/And] proposition. [Either/Or] thinking is a ticket to nowhere.

We are symbolic exemplars because we have been ordained, and thus our "being in the world" is distinct and blessed. Whether professionally em-ployed or not, as symbolic exemplars, we have no retirement age. Blessing others is the path we have chosen and with which we have been endowed.

---

37. Genesis 12:2. Here "[source of]" is the author's addition.
38. See especially Chapters 6 and 8 in Bloom, *The Rabbi As Symbolic Exemplar.*
39. [Breath-Taking⇔Model of Divinity]. See *ABC's of Jewish Relational Care* in this book; for further explication, see Bloom, *The Rabbi As Symbolic Exemplar,* espe-cially Chapters 6 and 8.

We have made it our destiny, our passion, and our very special *mitzvah*.[40] Being a blessing by blessing others is a passion behind which lies no ulterior motive, except for spreading God's blessing, and this is what we are all about. It is a passion whose motive and outcome is letting others know and hopefully experience that they are created [*Tzelem⇔N'shamah*]. Blessing others is the passion that can absorb us. Following Vaillant, we are "Keepers of the Meaning." Beyond Vaillant, the special meaning we carry is that life is blessed and that we are to bless it in every way possible. The symbolic exemplar's special work is about witnessing, naming, and blessing[41] the signs of the [*Tzelem⇔N'shamah*]—exponentially multiplying the *mei'ah b'rachot*[42] of each day. With our life experience, we can have a better and fuller perception and view of things, enabling us to witness, in the words of Rav Kook, the ניצוצות קדושה—*nizotzot k'dushah*.[43]

To do a passion well requires skill. A major skill is being, and staying, centered. That in itself is a task. What does it mean to be centered? Centered has a very special, experiential meaning. A mark of being centered is being in the moment and not in the moment, at the same time. Being with yourself, paying attention at one and the same time to your own being, your own breathing, and simultaneously paying attention to the breathing and the sounds, the appearance and all the varied emanations, coming from the other person. Being centered means not having to change the other and, at the same time, knowing that what you do will inevitably have an effect. We all know when we are off center. We know we are off center if, when we are with somebody, we lose focus and our attention wanders to something seemingly irrelevant. To return, the first thing to check is how our breathing is going. Because we're freed from certain burdens—such as "How will this encounter play back at the board meeting?" or "Is this what I should be saying or thinking?"—our ability to be centered, to make room for the others' personhood, who they are as we hear them and as we attend to them, is enhanced exponentially. Even so, much can, and will, knock us off track, and,

---

40. In Hebrew, fulfilling God's command; in Yiddish, a good deed.

41. See Bloom, Chapter 10, "Witnessing, Naming, and Blessing," in *The Rabbi As Symbolic Exemplar.*

42. The 100 blessings every Jew is to recite daily.

43. The holy sparks present in all that has been created. See Jacob B. Agus's preface to *Abraham Isaac Kook: The Lights of Penitence, The Moral Principles, Lights of Holiness, Essays, Letters, and Poems* (The Classics of Western Spirituality, translation and introduction by Ben Zion Bokser. Copyright © 1978 by Ben Zion Bokser, Paulist Press, Inc., New York/Mahwah, NJ. Used with permission of Paulist Press. www.paulistpress .com), which notes Rav Kook's determination to search out "the *nitzotzot k'dushah*," the "holy sparks" in every ideology, since "all lights derive from God and lead back to Him."

paradoxically, we have much to keep us on track. Age is an aid in the ability to be centered—because of history, because of all of our life experience. We've seen it all and done most of it; nearly all of our battles are behind us; we're no longer accountable for our failures. We have a different perspective on life and its vicissitudes. Wisdom helps us to be centered in who we are and assists us in recognizing simultaneously the [*Tzelem*⇔*N'shamah*] in our *"selves"* and in others' *"selves."* The relation between them and in doing our passion allows us to bless the *nitzotzot* wherever they may be found.

In a sermon delivered to his fellow summer residents on his beloved Block Island, Judge Oliver Holmes said that

> an old Quaker expression has it that when attending Meeting for Worship, one should try to "center down." We are to sit quietly and listen and reflect, in the hope that what is important to life will emerge. Block Island helps me center down.[44]

Wisdom is a great attribute for staying centered.

Vaillant quotes his wise young son-in-law: "what all definitions of wisdom have in common is the capacity and the willingness to step back from the immediacy of the moment—whether it is an affect, a judgment, or a conflict—in order to attain perspective."[45]

V'heyeh b'rachah[46] requires blessing others. Relational caregiving is not limited to the indigent, ill, and infirm. All need blessing. Blessing is the task that can get us up in the morning. This is the task that can give meaning to our days and be the fulfillment of our lives. This is a task that we are never too old to do. That having been blessed by God, we can impart that blessing to others.

Neil Gillman and Myself

Neil Gillman and myself (we were children then—about sixty, both of us) were at a Rabbinic Training Institute,[47] working to help rabbis be more of who they are. We were working side by side for the first time in years. We said (I don't know anymore who said what because Neil and I are old friends), "Isn't it great to be sixty? We're still relatively healthy. We've

---

44. Vaillant, *Aging Well*, p. 258.
45. Ibid., p. 256.
46. To be a blessing.
47. Where I taught for fifteen years, sponsored by the Jewish Theological Seminary of America.

fought all the battles. The political machinations are ultimately not going to bother us very much." We pondered the advantages of age and wondered, "Can we teach this stuff to these thirty-five-year-olds? They're children." We both decided, "Well, I don't know if they can learn it—maybe they have to go through the years to learn it—but we have an obligation to do it anyway. That's why we're here."

We're still HERE! We can have no better motto. Each of us can respond, *"Hineni."*[48] Each of us is more than enough. Each of us, and all of us, is blessed. Know and be assured that our blessedness is not in the doing; it is in the *being*—through no choice of our own. So, when the going gets tough, and assuredly it will, we can do no better than to respond: *"Hineni"*—*"I'm still here."*

Though a bit shabby and worn, I'm gentler than I used to be. God has blessed me with some good years. I'm hopefully wiser than I was, and I am free to be a blessing, and to bless others so that they may realize the [*Tzelem⇔N'shamah*] in which they have been created. *Hineni*—Do with me what you want. Each of us is more than enough.

What is the blessing for these years? I dare not end without a blessing:

When a child became of age, our forbears would say:

ברוך שפטרני מענשו של זה

I am blessed to have been freed from the punishments of this one.
It seemed superflous to say:

ברוך שנתן לי נחת של זה

I am blessed with *naches*[49] from this one.
We each of us pray:

ברוך שיפטרני מענשו של זה

May I be blessed by being freed from the punishments of advanced years, and

ברוך שיתן לי נחת משנים אלה

May I be blessed with *naches* from these advanced years, no longer seems superfluous.

---

48. "Here I am."

49. *Naches* is deriving pleasure from others, mostly loved ones. The feeling a grandparent has when a grandchild does some wondrous act is *naches*. It is also okay to have *naches* from grandparents.

And if that *yod*[50] that we added, one for each blessing came from the

שם המפורש

The Holy Name of God itself we would be left with **הוה (יקהמ᷒י)**—being Present—not past, not future, but truly present.

And for our wisdom, our blessing, our freedom, our presence, for being part of Eternal Israel, created like all humankind [*Tzelem*⇔ *N'shamah*], we give thanks:

ברוך אתה יי אלהנו מלך העולם שנתן מחכמתו לבשר ודם וברכה ליראיו

Blessed be God who has given wisdom to humankind and blessing to the reverent.

And for those we encounter over the years bearing witness to who we are, who name

The **נצוצות קדושה** in us, may they bless us when they see us:

ברוך אתה יי אלהנו מלך העולם הטוב והמטיב

Blessed be God who, being good, shares that goodness with all.

---

50. The tenth letter of the Hebrew alphabet. When two are used together they serve as an acronym for the name of God, which is YHWH. When the *Y* is removed we are left with HWH **הרה** *(hoveh),* Hebrew for present tense.

JEWISH RELATIONAL CARE WITH THE TRAUMATIZED

– 26 –

There and Back Again— Journey into the "Death Zone": Jewish Relational Care and Disabilities

Judith Z. Abrams

Who I Am and Who I Was

I am a Reform rabbi, ordained by the Hebrew Union College Jewish Institute of Religion (Cincinnati, Ohio) in 1985. I also earned a PhD in Jewish Studies from the Baltimore Hebrew University in 1993. My area of expertise is rabbinic literature, and my dissertation was eventually published in 1995 by Gallaudet University Press as *Disabilities in Judaism from the Tanakh Through the Bavli.* I had chosen the topic of disabilities because of a beloved aunt, a professional musician who gradually lost all her hearing. She handled it so magnificently that she became a great inspiration to me. All I can say is, "Beware the energy you beckon toward yourself." Having written a book about disabilities would not qualify me to address the relational aspects that arise between a sick and/or disabled person and a rabbi. My bona fides come from my own personal suffering.

Until I became ill, I considered myself to be physically strong. I flew about the country at ease, carried heavy loads (especially our three children as babies) and jogged on a regular basis. I could sit at the computer, working, for hours at a time. I had arranged my life so that I was our three children's primary caretaker for the first eighteen months of their lives. I did not, however, give up my professional life. I knew when they'd take their major nap of the day and would set everything in readiness for that moment. The computer would be on and the coffee set to brew. As soon as they went to sleep, I would sit down at the computer and write until they awoke. I also served small congregations part-time during this period of my life.

Things Changed

Then, to put it mildly, things changed. Imagine, if you can, what it is like to sit at a park, watching your toddler and preschool-age children play and suddenly feel hot flashes. The other mothers looked at me as if I were crazy. It wasn't only that though. At thirty-eight and a half, besides going through menopause, my hair turned gray, my memory left me, my energy disappeared, and I became depressed as my thyroid began to fail. Then worse things started to happen. A sarcoma on my chest began to grow larger and larger. My hands were often numb and pain arced down my arms. The worst of it, though, was that I felt as if two inches of raw nerve endings, right under my collarbone on both sides, were being stepped on by stiletto heels. I thought surely there must be some overarching diagnosis that would explain this wretched mess of symptoms, thereby hastening a cure. There may have been, but no physician I saw could identify it.

I started taking thyroid medication and estrogen, which helped with the energy and depression problems. I had a five-hour operation to remove the sarcoma. I had carpal tunnel release surgeries on both hands. When I showed precancerous signs in my uterus, I had that removed too. Still, the worst pain continued. Finally, it was determined that I had thoracic outlet syndrome on both sides. Thoracic outlet syndrome is brought on by incorrectly lifting or carrying too much weight. The nerves coming out of the spinal column are entrapped in the shoulders' scalene muscles and squeezed by them, thereby causing great pain. The only true "test" for this is for you to hold an arm up to see if your pulse decreases. I had the operations to remove the first rib and three neck muscles on each side of my body. I jokingly asked the surgeon if I could get a wife in return for each rib. (I didn't get even one, alas.) However, it had taken so long to make the diagnosis that the nerves were damaged. It has taken them years to heal gradually, and they still have not done so completely, nor do I expect them to do so.

In the course of being ill I came to understand that physicians, by and large, depend on tests to identify what is wrong with the patient. It is axiomatic among physicians that if a patient describes one thing and a test indicates something different, the physician should believe the test. So patients, especially patients with problems that are difficult to diagnose, or patients who have more than one thing going wrong with them at the same time, have to undergo many tests. For example, I have been injected with radiation of such strength that I was told not to hold my children in my lap for a few days. I have had EMGs,[1] whereby the nerves in your arms are given ever more powerful electric shocks that, as you might imagine, can be quite painful. I have had MRIs and CT scans. I have been under a fluoroscope while an anesthetic agent was injected directly into a specific nerve. I have had a myelogram. This one, in particular, reminded me of the rack. I lay down on a table, face down, in my hospital "patient uniform" (I won't dignify it by calling it a gown). Nothing about the procedure was explained to me ahead of time. A stranger came into the room and punctured my spinal column. At this point in the proceedings, I noted that I seemed to feel some liquid dripping on my back. The gowned stranger said, "Yes, that's spinal fluid." Next, he injected dye into my spinal column, attendants put my feet into restraints, and the entire table was tilted down to a forty-five-degree angle while the physician ordered me to yank my head back as far as I could to keep the dye from getting into my brain. I have had an arteriogram. For that test, you are wheeled into an exceptionally cold room with another (in my case, older, male) patient. A paper towel is summarily placed on your pubic area and taped down, and then you are shaved without a word of warning or explanation. Then another complete stranger comes into the room and proceeds to inject dye into your femoral artery. And let's not even begin to delve into the tests for the digestive tract.

All of the tests I just mentioned are called "procedures." In days gone by, you would have been checked into a hospital for these tests. Now, cost cutting mandates that you go home after the tests. Truthfully, who would want to stay in a hospital? Staffing shortages often put doctors, nurses, and other health professionals under great pressure, and, predictably, they begin to see patients and their needs as "the enemy." For a generation that grew up watching *Marcus Welby, MD,* the reality and brutality of medical care today is going to be a very rude awakening. (That being said, competent, even saintly, physicians and other health care providers do exist, and I have been blessed to be cared for by several of them. I am deeply grateful for their expertise and compassion.)

---

1. For fuller explanations of medical procedures, see Web sites such as www.mayoclinic.com or www.webmd.com.

Most physicians have about five minutes to spend with you. (You may wait fifteen minutes or five hours to see your physician, depending on how late he or she is running. Your time has no value in this system.) If your situation is difficult to diagnose, or needs thinking through, it is quite possible that you will be palmed off on another physician by referral or told that it's all in your head. Well-meaning friends may complicate things still further. They will urge you to try acupuncture, vitamins, magnets, diets, tuning forks (I kid you not), massages, and other alternative therapies that cost a fortune and involve dragging yourself out to yet another appointment—the very last thing you want to do.

The Death Zone

During my illness I grew fascinated with literature about Mount Everest. The first book I read was the most popular account describing the disastrous climbing season of 1996: Jon Krakauer's book, *Into Thin Air*.[2] Then I read several different books about that same climbing season by other people who had teams on the mountain that spring. It was very much like studying Talmud: everyone had his or her own truth to share, even though they all appeared to contradict one another on some points.

Climbing Mount Everest means enduring unending hardship, a gradual deterioration of the body because of lack of oxygen, and, finally, when you are at above 25,000 feet, you enter into the "death zone." There is simply not enough oxygen above 25,000 feet to sustain life. If you were taken from sea level to the top of Mount Everest (approximately 29,000 feet), you would be unconscious in thirty seconds and die within a few minutes from lack of oxygen. Add to that the snow, the cold, the nausea, the coughing so severe that separated ribs are common, and you begin to realize just how much suffering it takes to reach the summit.

I believe the reason I became so fascinated by these accounts of climbing the world's tallest mountain is that they resembled my life during the worst period of my illness. I was in my own death zone. I was barely a person. I was a thing to be tested or cut. My person, my profession, and my individuality were unimportant. Take, for example, the preoperative "holding pen" in which I was frequently kept. Approximately twelve beds fill a rather small room and no relatives are allowed. (In this I was fortunate: my husband is a physician and so was allowed to keep me company there.) No curtains hang between the beds to offer some semblance of privacy. Anyone

---

2. John Krakauer, *Into Thin Air: A Personal Account of the Mt. Everest Disaster* (New York: Anchor Books, 1998).

walking by could take your chart from the end of your bed and start flipping through it. No certainty existed there either. Emergencies would arrive and take the operating room I was slated for, so that I then had to wait for a new operating room, and a new anesthesiologist, resulting in more hours of waiting without anything to eat or drink.

The very worst part of my being ill was the unending, unendurable pain—pain that turned me into a howling animal; pain that caused my time frame to shift. My definition of "the future" became "getting through the next second." I learned that if you're in enough pain you'll do anything, say anything, and betray anything to make it stop. Incidentally, this made me realize that "intelligence" pried out of a person through torture is likely to be of little practical use. The tortured person soon understands what the torturer wants to hear and will say it to stop the pain. It was pain as bad as the hardest stages of labor in childbirth. But when a woman is in labor, she is given Demerol, she knows the ordeal will end somehow, and she can see her baby when it is over. People make allowances for pain in that type of situation. But when you are in this sort of pain every single day, nobody wants to hear about it or make allowances for it. Indeed, a middle-aged woman in great pain, with a difficult-to-diagnose disease, is often assumed to be making it up.

God, Pain, Punishment, and Death

I believed, and still believe, that the pain I suffer is punishment for sins I have committed. I find it more comforting to believe that the suffering is a punishment than that there's no reason for it at all. Indeed, being able to make meaning out of pain is what makes it bearable. At one point I wondered if my sin was forgetting Jerusalem, since it says in Psalm 137:5, "May my right hand forget its cunning if I forget thee, Jerusalem." I also find comfort in the idea, expressed in T. Yom Kippur 4 [5]:8, that suffering in this life helps one achieve atonement and peace in the next.

During my worst days, the idea of suicide became quite attractive. I came to realize that death is one of God's greatest gifts to us. God could have created a system in which we would all become progressively more disabled and that the pain would never end in death. At least we know that the pain will end. Often, only two things kept me from suicide. The first was my children, knowing that I would severely devastate their lives if I did this horrible deed. The second was that I believe in reincarnation. Therefore, I am determined to do everything I have to do in this incarnation so that I will never, ever have to return to a body again.

What I Lost

I lost a great deal through these trials. I lost the confidence that my body could carry me and respond appropriately to stress. In particular, I lost the ability to travel easily and this had a direct impact on my ability to make a living. Thankfully, distance-learning technology has allowed me to continue to teach those who are far from my home in Houston, Texas. I am unable to write for as long as I'd like or do as many activities as I'd like. I do not adjust to limits easily, but I've had to learn to do so. Finally, I am caught in an uncomfortable role. I am not utterly well, but I am not completely ill. I am not in extreme pain most of the time, but if I don't listen to my body and rest, I know I will be. I do not have a day without pain. So I do not fit comfortably into the role of "disabled," "ill," or "healthy."

What I Gained

What, then, from this hideous montage of experiences, could I possibly have gained? Surprisingly, a great deal. I can now talk with anyone about anything relating to illness and/or disability without becoming anxious or bored. Indeed, I'm able to listen to the range of tests and medications people are taking and truly identify with them as, at one point or another, I was on a good number of these same meds and endured most of these tests myself.

I am also able to share my "oral torah" about the medical care system with them. We are so conditioned by television and movies to expect doctors to care personally about patients that most of us don't realize that this is pure fantasy. We assume that if we fall ill and go to the hospital that the hospital staff will look after us. Reality is quite different. Nurses and physicians are overworked. You, or a loved one, must become advocates for your care. For example, it is not uncommon for a person to have nausea after being under general anesthesia for a long time. So you can wake up from a huge operation to find yourself vomiting, which increases postoperative pain and discomfort. However, if you tell the anesthesiologist (a stranger upon whom your life depends) about your concerns regarding this issue, he or she can administer a medication that erases the problem. But you have to ask for it. You must become your own advocate in terms of your medical care.

Having been through these experiences makes it much easier for me, as a rabbi, to be empathetic to those who are very ill, or who have disabilities but who are leading as normal lives as they can. I can be empathetic and unafraid to be in the "death zone" with people. No matter how depressed, agitated, or angry they are, I can truly be with them. I have not walked through the portal from this life to the next, but I've come mighty close, and I am not afraid to be in this realm.

I don't know if a rabbi who has not been through this particular region of hell can really understand it. My own advice to rabbis would be, "If you cannot be truly present with the sufferer, then don't show up at all." Few things are more annoying than a rabbi entering your hospital room (which almost never happens thanks to the new privacy laws) or making a telephone call when you know that the rabbi is just crossing you off the list of calls to be made that day. Mostly, what kept me going were friends who helped by bringing meals to the house after multiple surgeries and lending their emotional, intellectual, and spiritual support through the agony and depression.

Some Examples of Relating to Those in Agony: Did I Do the Right Thing?

For some reason I still do not understand, I was asked to visit a woman in a distant hospital whom I had never met. She had cancer but wasn't thought to be actively dying. When I arrived in her room I immediately recognized the signs of intense pain: a rigidity of the body, a biting off of every word, a flinch at every touch. I asked her if she wanted to say the *Sh'ma*.[3] She began crying and shook her head. I knew what she meant. She was in so much pain she couldn't hear anything at the moment. I went out into the hall and asked her nurse to give her some more pain relief medication. The patient, you see, had been moved to a new unit, but the orders for pain meds in her chart had not been moved, so she was going through withdrawal and enormous pain at the same time. I urged the nurse vigorously to get a doctor to give the order. I went back to the woman. Gently taking her hand in my hand and stroking her arm, I softly hummed the *Mi Shebeirach*[4] tune used in her synagogue. This made her cry but also relaxed her to some extent. When she was calmer, I went outside, pinned that nurse to the sticking point, and convinced her to bring a shot of something and to have the physician write the orders later. To her great credit, the nurse did just that. When I saw that the patient could finally relax, and her family came, I departed. She died that evening. I feel guilty about this incident somehow. Did I hasten her death? Or did I bring her comfort?

---

3. "Hear O Israel the Lord is One, The Lord alone"—watchword of Jewish belief.
4. A specialized prayer in the synagogue liturgy often, but not exclusively, used for healing: "May the God of our Ancestors bless (and heal) So-and-So, the child of So-and-So."

The Wrong Thing

More typical of patient care is the following incident. This scenario took place first thing in the morning at a hospital's Nuclear Medicine Suite into which I'd gone to have a test. An elderly man wheeled his wife into the waiting area. She was clearly in a great deal of agony. She shook with the strain of not screaming (a state you recognize once you've been in it). The man urgently asked the secretary, who was powering up the computer and messing around with some wires, if she couldn't get his wife somewhere to lie down. The secretary just said, "You'll have to wait till we get started." She had no idea that fifteen minutes would seem an eternity to this woman.

The Best Thing

A quite different story took place in a different hospital. At this hospital (as at many others) you are given a number on a piece of plastic similar to a credit card. Just as you are the sum total of your lab results, so you are also just the patient number on your card. I was going to have a CT scan and so joined a good-sized line at the check-in desk. When I reached the desk, I presented my card to the secretary. She then asked me an unexpected question: "Is there anyone accompanying you today?" At that point, I had had so many tests that it hadn't occurred to me that having someone along might have made the day easier. I simply began to cry. The secretary stood up, came out from behind her desk, and, hugging me to her very ample bosom, asked me, "Did you wake up today?" I nodded. She asked, "Did you know who you were?" Again, I nodded. She said, "Then you are blessed." Those words and her deed have stayed with me ever since.

27

When the Rabbi Needs Care

Andrew R. Sklarz

Could this really be happening? Why would God do this to me, to my beloved wife and partner, and to my little loves—our zestful, darling, little daughter and our bright-eyed, ever-smiling baby boy? Why should my mother be forced to witness the lingering and gut-wrenching road to death of the child she had waited so many years to have, and whom she nurtured, supported, and championed, while at the same time watching my father enter the downward spiral in the final chapter of his life? Did I, the rabbi, the social worker, the hospital chaplain, and hospice volunteer, the one who had truly believed that humankind was molded after and modeled by Divinity, and who sought to exemplify being created [*Tzelem*⇔*N'shamah*],[1] deserve such a fate? Was the chromosome that had gone berserk in my otherwise healthy body, causing the deadly cancer, a fluke of nature, or was God meting out a just punishment for some transgression I was too arrogant to know I had committed?

Oh, how these questions wracked within my tortured head, as I tossed and turned throughout the sleepless nights in the weeks following my diagnosis of leukemia. Indeed, it seemed as though a blood-soaked "scarlet L" had been placed upon my neck, branding me for death under the watchful and sadistic eye of a masked executioner, an expert who would squeeze all vestiges of dignity from me, while plaguing me with untold physical pain and emotional anguish. Shifting my thoughts to another gruesome flashback, I heard again and again the voice of the oncologist, who had announced to me, only hours before I was to lead the evening service that would herald the Jewish New Year before hundreds within my congregation, that my only brother, fourteen years my senior, whom I had been led to

---

1. [Breath-Taking⇔Model of Divinity]. See *ABC's of Jewish Relational Care* in this book; for further explication, see Jack H Bloom, *The Rabbi As Symbolic Exemplar: By the Power Vested in Me* (Binghamton, NY: The Haworth Press, 2002), especially Chapters 6 and 8.

believe contained the needed bottle of medicine within his body for me, namely, his bone marrow, was not a suitable match. Furthermore, the doctor's words—"A bone marrow transplant is an extraordinarily dangerous procedure"—echoed relentlessly, violently, and without pause in my head.

I recalled my days as a chaplain, comforting cancer and leukemia patients who had suffered and died subsequent to bone marrow transplant, albeit in the late 1980s, which I am told, is light-years in the past in the field of transplantation. As the tape in my head replayed these scenes, interspersed with others that were equally as frightening, the words that characterize the theme of the Jewish High Holydays—"Who will live and who will die?"— were most pronounced.

How suddenly and dramatically life had changed. Only weeks before at my annual physical, an abnormality in my blood test led to further testing, which resulted in the grim diagnosis. "Wasn't this merely a lab error?" I mused. No symptoms had manifested to suggest that I had been stricken with a life-threatening, and potentially terminal, illness. I struggled with the then limited, but horrific, available medical options, while attempting to find a physician willing to place me on a protocol with an experimental drug, at that time approved only for those in the last stage of the illness, for whom all other courses had failed. However, I needed to continue my daily existence with my roles as rabbi, husband, and father. On the surface, I attempted to simulate the activities of the person I had worked so hard to become; on the inside, I felt but a shell of my former self.

Perhaps this was all retribution, I thought. While I was drawn to the rabbinate by the prophetic ideals for social justice and righteousness inherent in our great tradition, the question of God's existence was a theme that haunted me throughout my youth, my rabbinic school days, and my early years as a rabbi.

The concept of spirituality and the quest for an [I–You] relationship,[2] as described by Martin Buber, were not a part of my consciousness; they lay dormant and repressed deep down inside. Although I had sat by many a bed as a pastoral counselor, holding hands and doing my utmost to bring comfort to those who were in pain and experiencing untold fear, especially while serving as a pastoral counselor at Memorial Sloan-Kettering Cancer Center in New York City, and later on at a New York hospice, I so often felt myself to be a fraud when I agreed to recite the *Mi Shebeirach*.[3] Perhaps, as

---

2. After Walter Kaufmann, in "I and You: A Prologue," in Martin Buber, *I and Thou: A New Translation* (New York: Simon and Schuster, 1970); see also in this book "A Guide for the Reader," p. 2, n. 3.

3. The prayer for healing.

inconceivable as it seemed, the God whose existence I had so long held in question was punishing me for donning the rabbi's cloak over the body of an agnostic or, worse yet, an unbeliever.

With a paucity of answers from the medical profession, I desperately sought for something to hold on to, and believe in, within the spiritual realm. Although my professional life had always been devoted to providing comfort for others, I had truly never sought spiritual care from other rabbis. Nevertheless, desperate people do desperate things. Not knowing where else to turn, I called upon another rabbi—a friend, professor, and mentor, some twenty years my senior, who some seven years earlier had been given a diagnosis of a rare cancer, and a rather grim prognosis. His well-meaning words were not encouraging, though in retrospect were rather prophetic, when he opened our conversion by stating, "The Andy you were is dead," repeating them when I protested his statement.

My beloved and esteemed rabbi's words cut through me like a knife, bru- tally hacking away at the few remnants of myself that I still recognized. Within this deserted island—for I, whose body seemed to be working against my mind, couldn't help but feel as though I were completely alone; no one else, even those closest and dearest to me, could possibly understand my pain—I began my quest to find God. Indeed it was now my turn to begin a truly spiritual journey—a journey only I could take, alone. Although oth- ers could cheer me on, so to speak, and help me pack my bags, no other could travel on the road as I sought to encounter the Divine.

As a young rabbinic student, I sought an internship as a clinical pastoral counselor at Memorial Sloan-Kettering Cancer Center in New York City. Always drawn to supporting others during their times of need, this was a most meaningful experience for me. Although I believe I extended kindness and care to my patients, the reality was that, in those days, cancer was a di- agnosis given to others, certainly not one I ever expected to receive. My then supervisor, Pesach Kraus, a rabbi many years my senior, would walk into a room of the newly diagnosed individual and proclaim, "You have been given a terrible gift." Although I had great respect for Rabbi Kraus, I was troubled by this statement, and I later put it in a similar category as the words of my beloved rabbi and friend who had proclaimed, "The Andy you were is dead." The truth was, as much as I resisted my beloved rabbi's state- ment, there was no escaping the reality that he was absolutely on target. When you receive a diagnosis of cancer, or of another life-threatening dis- ease, you are irrevocably changed; your innocence is lost; all naive delu- sions of your immortality are forever gone.

The option, however, is what one does upon acceptance and acknowl- edgment of such a truth. In time I came to understand what Rabbi Kraus meant by a "terrible gift," and that the adjective *terrible* could be understood as *awesome*. No doubt, a diagnosis of a potentially fatal disease is life altering, but life altering does not necessarily mean irrevocably awful. In fact, it can mean quite the contrary. While receiving such a diagnosis is initially quite frightening, it can be transformed into a gift, a blessing, if one is willing to put in the necessary work.

Each human being travels through life with his or her own baggage, and I have always said that some carry only a backpack, while others travel with footlockers; all of course can be modified throughout one's travels. During my time as a chaplain at Memorial Sloan-Kettering, it occurred to me that when an individual is given the diagnosis of cancer, he or she suddenly receives an additional set of luggage. The baggage the individual has carried until that point will surely have an impact upon the way he or she handles the new luggage, or the diagnosis. However, the way an individual ultimately chooses to deal with the diagnosis will have a profound impact on his or her lifetime baggage, either lightening it or making it so weighty that the individual cannot function.

We all know people who express nothing but bitterness over an illness or a condition, while others handle it as though it is merely an impediment but refuse to let it interfere with what they really wish to do. While obstacles may interfere, the extent of this boils down to choice. It may be difficult to embrace Rabbi Kraus' statement that the receiving of cancer is a terrible gift, but we do have the power to make it into a gift, to lighten our baggage and make our lives more whole—regardless of what the ultimate physical outcome might be. Depending on how we choose to conduct ourselves, we can bring so much healing to our [*Tzelem*⇔*N'shamah*] and our relationships. Without question, as a result of my diagnosis, I began to develop the type of relationship with God for which I believe I have unconsciously yearned, if not hungered, my entire life.

From a background in which rational thought reigned, with the manifestation of my diagnosis, I came to accept how much I needed a spiritual relationship. Perhaps, in retrospect, it was unconsciously what led me to the rabbinate. Not feeling satisfied with the answer of the rabbi I initially called, and not secure enough to turn to other rabbis within my movement, I looked for a safe place in a world diametrically different from anything resembling my approach to Judaism.

I first turned to my wife's Great-Aunt Marcia, known affectionately as Mishie. Mishie's Orthodox Judaism had been a guiding force throughout her then eighty-six years. Wise, loving, respectful, and deeply spiritual, she has seen her faith carry her through every storm. Days after my diagnosis, I sat alone with Mishie for hours where she is best known for holding court—her kitchen table. While sipping tea and eating her home-baked cookies, I approached her as if I were with a priest at confession, unabashedly airing my spiritual questions, emotionally pouring out my heart and innermost thoughts, desperately hoping to deepen my relationship with God. How strong Mishie was, as she spoke of events in her life; yet at that juncture it was early for much, at least consciously, to penetrate.

I next called the famous Orthodox author and speaker Rebbitzen[4] Esther Jungreis, whose wisdom and compassion is palpable; her words to me were, "We will pray to God for a miracle." Her fervent prayers were indeed heartfelt, but similar to my encounter with Great-Aunt Mishie, I was not yet ready to let them enter. Finally, I called upon Rabbi Aryeh Weinstein, an Orthodox rabbi of the Lubavitch sect, with whom I had studied and for whom I had great respect. The kindness extended by him and his wife, Rosie, abounded, as did his suggestions that I incorporate more traditional rituals into my life; yet I was just not ready truly to consider them. Finally, however, I did take the suggestion of the rabbi whom I had first called, who had told me that the person I had been "was dead." His advice to find a good therapist was one that I took to heart. Rather than seeking the therapy that I had known best, which I had trained in and practiced with my own patients, I looked this time for a therapist who was a cancer survivor, and, interestingly enough, I was blessed to find one who also possessed an abiding respect for the spiritual. The truth, however, as I came to understand it, was that it is not enough to look to other people, no matter how profound their faith, for answers; the spiritual journey that I needed to take was mine and mine alone.

Along with the solitary spiritual journey, rabbis grappling with their own fate are simultaneously required to hear and often endure the thoughts of their congregants and other acquaintances. As with anyone who receives such a diagnosis, the reactions and responses of others are varied, and so reflect the state of their own egos and needs. Some quite understandably are at a loss as to what to say or do and thus, unfortunately, choose to retreat. This is indeed terribly hurtful if you already feel afflicted and alone. Others may barrage you with phone calls, asking detailed questions, demanding information, and offering anecdotal information or "horror stories," ostensibly "to help," but which do anything but lift the spirit. Oh, how I remember, early on in the first days and weeks following my diagnosis, how well-meaning individuals would demand that I read accounts of those with similar illnesses, not from scholarly periodicals but, rather, from magazines they had read while having their hair or nails done, or while waiting in the supermarket checkout line—tabloids replete with anecdotal accounts of those

---

4. *Rebbitzen* usually refers to a rabbi's wife. However, here it is used to refer to Esther Jungreis, who, being Orthodox, cannot carry the title "rabbi."

who had been diagnosed with leukemia. Some people were actually convinced that I would receive more cutting-edge medical data from a magazine than from the recommendations of top physicians; ironically, in some cases, they may have been correct.

Even worse are those who feel licensed to invade your personal space or family circle to express pity or advice, as though you were already dead, dying, or planning to die. Shortly after my diagnosis, when working with an upcoming *bat mitzvah*[5] family, the mother of the young woman commented, "Oh, rabbi, I wouldn't wish upon my worst enemy what you have. My cousin had the same thing and died." Unfortunately, this is not an anomalous type of behavior or comment. So often, I will lead a full service or officiate a life cycle event with the same gusto people have always associated with me, and still, immediately following, someone I don't even know will appear before me, a pathetic look on the face, take my hand, and, in an attempt to show me that he or she truly empathizes with my plight, comment, "Oh, rabbi, I understand what you're going through. My so-and-so had exactly what you had and died." This is particularly horrendous when you are attempting to shield your children, let alone when you have chosen to go on with life in a positive direction. Nevertheless, many consider it their right and prerogative to say whatever they wish to the rabbi, who is obliged to stand there and smile or say, "Thank you for expressing your thoughts." If only I had a penny for each time I have tried to redirect the conversation so that my children, let alone their mother and I, would not have to endure this. If only such persons considered the emotions and, in some instances, tears we were left with long after they walked away.

Rabbis are always expected to listen, swallow, and absorb whatever is hurled at them, as though their feelings are coated with Teflon. Regardless of the pain or turmoil that rabbis may be experiencing, they just can't walk away or reply, "Please stop—your words are hurtful to me." Some ten months after my diagnosis, I was asked to officiate at a wedding ceremony in New York City for a cousin of my wife's. I was delighted to be presiding over the marriage of a woman whom I had known since her childhood and to whom I felt close. The formal Saturday night affair was to be held in one of Manhattan's premier hotels, and we were looking forward to enjoying the lavish evening to the fullest, and to seeing family and friends, as our children stayed in our room with the sitter. However, the reality is that there is not a day, perhaps not even an hour, during which I am not consciously

---

5. At age thirteen, a young person is obligated for the fulfillment of God's commands. The occasion is marked by being called to the reading of the Torah, and participating as an "adult" in the service.

aware that my identity has changed: I am no longer only a Jew, a father, a husband, and a rabbi; I am also a person who is surviving leukemia. Nevertheless, I wanted to leave my diagnosis at home and take full advantage of our weekend in New York.

Immediately after the ceremony, as I milled around the room in my tuxedo, I was pleased to meet and greet, hug and kiss, and receive feedback on the very personal ceremony I had prepared. After cocktails, while enjoying ourselves among those for whom we truly care, an older woman, a relative of a relative, whose children are approximately my age, sprinted over to me and said, "I just heard about you. . . . My brother . . ."—who was old enough to be my father, perhaps grandfather—"recently died of cancer." I needed and wished to hear this story like I needed a hole in the head, but rather than casting her away from the table, in a proper and sympathetic rabbinic tone, I responded, "I'm so sorry." However, she was relentless, adding insult to injury: "You have to be grateful for the time you have." With that comment, my face dropped, and I excused myself from the table, quickly fleeing the party Susan and I had so anticipated, and ran out to the street. I'm neither a smoker nor a drinker, but I sure could have used a cigarette and a glass of Scotch—maybe even a double—though the taste of such makes me gag.

Most often, after such "necessary" comments, I cannot leave the room, for generally I must continue with my rabbinic work. This time, I took a few minutes to comfort myself and regain my composure before returning to the "scene of the crime." Needless to say, such behavior sure puts a damper on things. It is bad enough to know I have the "scarlet L," but why do others, often otherwise intelligent, compassionate people, feel the need to remind me of its menacing presence?

I call these types of comments the "bowling-ball approach" to sympathy. It is as if someone has dropped a large bowling ball into your arms and then turned away, leaving you along to struggle with its weight. Many of us with major diagnoses are dealing with our own bowling balls, but, too often, well-meaning individuals feel the need to thrust yet another one in our arms, not stopping to consider whether it's more thant we can bear.

Of course, others may treat rabbis as dispensable or disposable—there for only their own needs. After spending a terrifying day in a cancer clinic, my temple president informed me, with great embarrassment, about an irate congregant who had complained that I had not returned a call she had left on my home voice earlier mail that day. It was of no interest to her that I had spent a full day being evaluated by a team of oncologists and had undergone a bone marrow biopsy. Still another congregant, who several years prior had insisted that I not take my normal scheduled summer vacation so that I could be available to officiate at her daughter's wedding, hired another clergy member immediately upon hearing of my diagnosis, for fear that I would not be alive to do the service. Obviously, the insensitivity of her actions completely eluded her. Still another congregant, whom I telephoned after not having seen her for a while, responded, "Oh, rabbi, I'm glad to know you're still alive."

However, there are indeed many whose compassion resonates far beyond the clueless behavior of those previously mentioned. Such loving individuals stayed with our children, sent meals to our home, and offered help with transportation. Some have even been in the position to extend medical expertise and suggest viable options that we had not explored. This is when you begin to feel that God has sent angels into the world.

I have never refused caring congregants, if it appears that their desire to be a part of my life is genuine. However, as rabbis, we must always be especially cautious when it comes to sharing the personal pages of our lives. Our dear friend Suzanne, a congregant and a maternal force who has been there for my family both emotionally and physically over the years, came to celebrate Chanukah[6] with us shortly after I was diagnosed. As my children, then six years and eighteen months unwrapped their gifts, I suddenly felt overcome with emotion and my eyes welled up with tears; I fearfully wondered if this would be the last time I would witness such delight in them. To conceal my tears, I ducked into another room. Lovingly, Suzanne followed after me, but once alone she said most emphatically, "Don't go into that corner—for I will not go there with you." With tough love, my dear friend was reminding me that my focus needed to be on being and staying alive. Another close friend, Gail, had been diagnosed with breast cancer shortly after the birth of her third child, several years before my diagnosis. She, too, reminded me constantly of the power of positive thinking, working to boost my spirits whenever we spoke.

Vivan, another special friend and a cancer survivor, who ultimately passed from the disease several years later, and whose son's life had been claimed by cancer the year before, also fully extended herself to me in a wide variety of ways upon learning of my diagnosis. Some years earlier, her other son's partner, David, who later died of AIDS-related complications from an infection he had received years prior to their relationship, had put together a series of positive affirmations. Among the number of books and truly helpful medical advice she offered me, not to mention the continual

---

6. Eight-day festival commemorating the rededication of the Temple in Jerusalem by Judah Maccabee and his followers (165 BCE).

emotional support, were these typed-up and framed statements. David's words transmitted through Vivian:

- Be positive.
- Know you're going to win.
- Treasure the moment.
- Think of yourself.
- Think of others.
- Be honest.
- Be educated.
- Know your options.
- Don't harbor hate.
- Keep a sense of humor.
- Don't sweat the small stuff.
- Talk it out.
- Be alive.
- Stay alive.

A powerful gift, these statements sit on my desk and serve as a mantra for me. Another profoundly wonderful gift that Vivian and others who have come into my life have taught me is that no two human beings are identical, and, therefore, the course of any given illness is different for each individual. As I have come to learn, for a myriad of reasons, way beyond those that Western medicine can offer, one individual may succumb to a given illness when another may not only survive but thrive.

Often, however, even the best of intentions are just not well thought out. Early on after my diagnosis, some extremely kind people persuaded me to speak to others with a similar diagnosis, whom they were certain would be of help to me. One such person had been diagnosed with chronic myeloid leukemia (CML) some ten years earlier and had undergone a bone marrow transplant. Complications, however, led to a stroke, and as a result, he is unable to work full-time and cannot drive a car. When I expressed this to my friend, her comment was, "But, Andy, he's alive." My friend had only the best of intentions, but his story was one that I would have far preferred not hearing. Another man with the same diagnosis with whom I was urged to speak commented, "You know we're going to die." Still another CML patient, whom a well-meaning friend recommended I call for solace, appeared unannounced at my office at the temple, in the midst of a hectic day, and in the course of our conversation, when he saw how upbeat I was, remarked, "Hasn't anyone told you that our illness is terminal?" Ironically, some time later, when I saw him again and reminded him of his words, he apologized, inferring to me that he had not yet reached the place at which I had already arrived. Oh, how I have learned that having the same illness as others does not mean you are in a position to speak to others about it. Furthermore, I have truly come to believe, beyond empirical data, that one's outlook on and approach to the diagnosis and prognosis may in fact have a profound impact upon the course of the illness and the road to healing.

Most important of all is how your spouse, partner, or the people closest to you respond to the diagnosis. My wife, Susan, my soul mate and best friend, never questioned for a moment that all would work out. As she has commented, "We just needed to find the right answers." Determined to search under every stone from the moment we received my diagnosis, Susan contacted the Leukemia and Lymphoma Society (LLS). Shortly after, I received a phone call from an LLS "First Connection" volunteer, a peer who has experienced a similar diagnosis and calls the newly diagnosed patient to share support and express encouragement. Darin Bell, a contemporary, had been first diagnosed with CML some ten years prior to our first conversation. As with my situation, a perfect match for a bone marrow transplant had not been found, so Darin was treated with a drug aimed at keeping the disease at bay. When the medication began to fail him, Darin was able, after much effort, to enter an early clinical trail for the same "miracle drug" of which I had read and to which I was hoping to gain access.

Darin and I spoke for hours that night—I was not only the first rabbi he had ever encountered but also the first individual to ask him so many questions, ranging from the concrete to the personal to the philosophical. For the first time since the "scarlet L" had been placed upon my neck, I began to feel some ray of hope. Without a doubt, Darin, whom I now call my "blood brother," was among the first of the angels whom God sent into my life. As a result of that initial positive, nurturing, and life-affirming conversation, Darin and I have become close friends, and he has inspired me to become a First Connection volunteer. Within time I became a speaker for the LLS and even posed in my rabbinic garb as the "poster boy" for the pharmaceutical company that manufactures my medication. Indeed, God's blessings continue to show themselves, for through this journey with personal illness I have encountered some of the most beautiful human beings you can imagine and discovered untapped dimensions within myself.

Other friends and even congregants who were cancer patients have deeply touched me with their caring, but Darin's encouraging words helped put me on the right track emotionally, in a way that no one else's could. Indeed, although he knew all of the horrors associated with our illness, he so valiantly and triumphantly chose life. Darin's upbeat words and thoughts impelled me as cancer patient to move forward and inspired the rabbi within me to perpetuate such work. Within a short amount of time, I began a similar experimental protocol of this same medication, and weeks later no trace of the chromosome associated with leukemia could be found within my body. Although some people use the word *remission* to indicate the lack of presence of a disease, it is a word I choose not to use, for remission suggests something of a temporal nature. The reality is that life itself is ephemeral. However, if we use language that constantly reinforces such a fact, it might possibly hold us back from following our dreams. Having this diagnosis has reminded me that I am mortal, and that I must not waste time. Rather, I must live each day fully and pursue my passions.

For the agnostic who had always loved the poetry of the liturgy and its inherent ethics, the voice of God truly began to speak. All around me, the full spectrum of colors within the world appeared more brilliantly than ever before, and I was moved to tears as I rejoiced over the beauty of the world with which God graced humanity. I began also to understand that those who are central to my life are truly blessings from God. As I celebrated life, I came to the realization that it was time for me to make the most of each day in every way possible. My professional life took on greater clarity, as I worked to filter out the petty and often dysfunctional aspects of congregational life. On the personal level, I decided that it was high time to plunge into the things I had long yearned to do but had never found the time. I now practice yoga, I have become an avid cyclist, and, after many years, I have returned to playing piano as well as studying guitar and voice. There is no doubt in my mind that, had I not been visited with this "terrible gift" nor accepted that the old me was "dead," I would have never begun to view life as a adventure to be so fully lived every day.

Words, as we know, are incredibly potent tools with the ability to raise or lower vibrations.[7] In addition to the miracles of science and modern medicine, which I have come to believe occur through the inspiration of the Divine, words are among the most powerful of instruments for healing. Perhaps the most beautiful of gifts that I received from many, including congregants, were cards or letters in which they shared their affection and prayers for me. Such upbeat, loving sentiments raised my spirits, reinforced a sense of purpose in my existence, and gave me the strength, courage, and drive to move forward in this frightening new life chapter. Whereas negativity and allegedly well-meaning, though insensitive, comments made by others, which I was forced to endure, created a sense of defeat in my trying to fight this "demon," which I felt was attempting to take control of my body and kill me, positive words and loving thoughts, which did not mention ei-

---

7. See in this book Chapter 2, "Language As a Relational Tool: Using Your Mouth with Your Head?"

ther diagnosis or prognosis, validated the work that I had done thus far and propelled me to partner with God in conquering my illness, both physically and spiritually.

As I mentioned earlier, the efficacy of prayer had always raised serious questions for me, yet music had always been my inspiration. I now understand that music serves as a vehicle for my spirituality.[8] Some years back, after hearing the *Mi Shebeirach* set to music by composer Debbie Friedman, I brought it into my congregation. From then on, at every service, I have asked worshippers to rise and share the names of those in need of healing, followed by the singing of the *Mi Shebeirach*. Though I have refused to have my name recited on any list while I am present, I have come to feel bathed in positive energy, knowing that it is recited in synagogues, as well as in churches and other spiritual homes, around the globe. Immediately following my diagnosis, my then president and vice president, two dear friends, composed a beautiful letter to my congregation:

Dear Congregants,

Just over four years ago, Rabbi Andrew Sklarz joined our temple and introduced the *Mi Shebeirach* to us. Now it is necessary to include Rabbi Sklarz in our thoughts and prayers.

Recently, Rabbi Sklarz underwent a routine physical examination that included standard laboratory tests. The results of the tests indicated an irregularity that required additional testing and analysis. After a thorough review of all information and data, Rabbi Sklarz has been diagnosed with leukemia. He is currently taking medication and will begin substantive treatment after the conclusion of the High Holidays.

I encourage each of you to express your concern by sending a card or a personal note to Rabbi Sklarz. In consideration of the nature of his illness, I ask that, at this time, you refrain from calling him at home.

Please consider showing your support and concern for Rabbi Sklarz and his family by attending services, joining in the "Mi Shebeirach," and assisting in the many activities we are planning to ensure the rabbi's renewal of body, renewal of spirit, and let us say, Amen.

Soon after, the cards, letters, flowers, gifts, and even chopped liver and chicken soup began to flow into my house, and, boy, did my cup—or in this

---

8. See Chapter 9, "The Muse of Music and Song," in this book.

case my mailbox—runneth over. On a daily basis, these letters made me laugh out loud, cry with joy, and recall fondly situations in which I had tried to be a source of comfort to others, while reinforcing the many profound and beautiful relationships with which I had been blessed over the years. Although I requested that my name not be recited on the list prior to the singing of the *Mi Shebeirach* when I was present, friends and colleagues from all over the country continually tell me that they hear my name recited. Perhaps the power and efficacy of prayer is far greater than I ever believed.

At the evening service for the Jewish New Year, one year after my diagnosis, I so proudly and lovingly expressed from the pulpit that, although I had been placed on cutting-edge medications, there was no doubt in my mind that words filled with love, positive thoughts, and happy and meaningful memories, not to mention prayers, were indeed very potent forms of medicine. Such words nurtured my spirit, galvanized my entire being within me to choose life truly and thoroughly, and consequently brought healing to my body. Indeed, all human beings need to feel meaning and purpose in their lives, and reminders of such are the most powerful of propellants for moving individuals forward and helping them to see the light in the face of darkness.

A myriad of forces can compel people to become rabbis, but not until certain experiences arise will rabbis confront long-suppressed emotions and well-concealed dimensions. Most of us are drawn to the rabbinate out of our love for our fellow human beings, coupled with, as I came to realize, the desire, if not the undeniable need, to connect with the Divine. Rabbis who need care need what every other human being needs: the miracles of modern medicine; the love, support, and uplifting words of others; and a deeper relationship with themselves, their loved ones, and God—all good reasons for choosing life.

28

Caring for Those Violated
by Child Sexual Abuse and Incest

Rachel Lev

How do we deal with members of our community who have crossed the boundaries and inflicted grievous wounds on others? How do we determine if they have completed *t'shuvah*?[1] My initial response to these questions is, "Ask the ones who have been wronged," and, "Understand the wrongs that were committed."

My focus here is on child sexual abuse and incest—actions that violate a child's human dignity and physical, emotional, and sexual integrity.[2] Other boundary violations need exploration and action, such as other forms of child abuse and neglect as well as abuse of power in adult relationships, including sexual assault, partner abuse, and elder abuse. These are not specifically addressed here.

Understanding the Wrongs That Were and Are Committed

Sexual abuse is a violation of boundaries, at an emotional and/or physical level. It can be overt or covert. It isn't

---

Author's Note: Grateful thanks to Rabbi David J. Zucker for editing the original version of this chapter, which was written for distribution at the National Association of Jewish Chaplains conference, January 2004, Boca Raton, Florida, and published as "Crossing the Boundaries" in *NAJC Journal*, 7(2) (Winter 2005).

1. Repentance; return to the good way, regret, abandoning sin; a return to God and to the right path. See Chapter 22, "*T'shuvah* in Sexual Violations with Direct Implications for Other Situations," in this book for further explanation.

2. Fran Henry defines sexual integrity as sexual activity that is vital and life-giving and causes no harm. Fran Henry, "A Prescription for Change on Child Sexual Abuse," Presentation to National Advisory Council on Violence and Abuse, American Medical Association, Chicago, Illinois, November 1, 2001; available at http://www.stopitnow.com/fh_ama_speech.pdf.

limited to specific acts of fondling and penetration. It occurs across a continuum from invasion of sexual privacy, to comments about your body, to being kissed in a way that feels uncomfortable, being touched in sexual areas, or being encouraged [or forced] to have sex you didn't want.[3]

Being made to view or participate in pornography is another form of sexual abuse. A distinction is made between molestation by a family member (incest) and by anyone else (child sexual abuse).

A conservative estimate of sexual abuse incidents involving physical contact is at least one in three girls and one in six boys before they turn nineteen.[4] At least 81 percent of child sexual abuse happens *before puberty,* and 42 percent of abuse is experienced *before the age of seven.*[5] Children are most at risk with those they know, including family members or people in the community who are trusted by the family.[6]

Stories told in private conversations, or in the newspapers, confirm that some rabbis, cantors, and clergy, as do other human beings, cross boundaries. Some rabbis/cantors/clergy molest their children. Some molest the children in their congregation or community. Some do both. Some collude with the crossing of boundaries by others by staying quiet, saying it doesn't happen, and/or by doing little or nothing because they don't know what to do or fear ramifications if they take a stand.[7]

Denial that abuse happens can make the events of childhood a life sentence of shame and anguish. We need to shed some light on the impact of

---

3. Contribution from L. Nielsen, in Stephanie Covington, *Awakening Your Sexuality—A Guide for Recovering Women* (Center City, MN: Hazelden Information Education, 2000), pp. 165-166.

4. These figures are based on research in Canada and the United States. The prevalence data are based on research by D. E. H. Russell, *Sexual Exploitation: Rape, Child Sexual Abuse, and Sexual Harassment* (Beverly Hills, CA: Sage, 1984). Also see D. E. H. Russell, *The Secret Trauma: Incest in the Lives of Girls and Women* (New York: Basic Books, 1986). Also see Lloyd DeMause, "The Universality of Incest," *The Journal of Psychohistory,* 19(2) (Fall 1991): 123-164.

5. David Finkelhor, *Child Sexual Abuse: New Theory and Research* (New York: Free Press, 1984); J. Michael Cupoli, "One Thousand Fifty-Nine Children with a Chief Complaint of Sexual Abuse," *Child Abuse and Neglect,* 12 (1988): 158.

6. U.S. Department of Health and Human Services, *Child Maltreatment 2002* (Washington, DC: National Center on Child Abuse and Neglect, 2004); http://www.acf.hhs.gov/programs/cb/publications/cmreports.html.

7. A list of rabbis, cantors, and chaplains accused of sexual misconduct and information can be found at the Awareness Center's Web site at http://theawarenesscenter.org. The Awareness Center is dedicated to addressing childhood sexual abuse in Jewish communities around the world.

molestation with the hope that it will motivate all clergy to move this subject higher on their personal and community's priority list of things to address. The devastation caused by even a single act of molestation can have far-reaching effects on individuals, families, and the moral fiber of our communities. This is especially true when we deny or conceal what has happened. Understanding the impact of child sexual abuse and incest seems essential before determining what is fair and just *t'shuvah.*

We have an illusion that incest and sexual abuse happen to "them," and that those who molest are recognizable, somehow different from us. They are not members of our synagogues or churches. Certainly, they are not our leaders. Yes, sometimes they are. My father was president of the synagogue's men's club, a B'nai Brith[8] man of the year. To this day, people approach me with stories extolling my father's virtues, thinking I will want to hear them. Occasionally I will say, "Yes, he did many good things for people." Sometimes I will say, "My father was a Jekyll and Hyde." No one has ever asked what I meant.

As a little girl, I hated what my father did to me and I adored him. My father died several years ago. I do not miss him. That saddens me. He betrayed and violated me. He never said, "I'm sorry." His passion for his children caused my mother to feel jealous and in competition with us. I have told her that I wish he had adored her more and me less. It's really complex.

Molestation is not love. Violating boundaries is never about love. It is about power, control, and self-absorption. It is selfish. I believe it comes from deep wounds.

When sexual abuse is involved, the worst thing we can do is to look for simple, formulaic answers. We can identify some elements of the complexity, in part, through examining the lives of people who were molested. The following are real stories from Jewish adult survivors of child sexual abuse and incest. They represent every region of the United States and different Jewish affiliations.

Jonathan writes:

> At the age of twenty-one a world-famous rabbi tried to seduce me. It totally retraumatized me and left me not wanting to have anything to do with Judaism. I'd been raised secularly and came to this rabbi for help in learning about my heritage and religion. Instead, he used his position of power to try to use me. It was awful, and just like what had happened to me at home. A decade later, I was finally able to try again, and this time I found an incredible *shul*[9] with a rabbi who is wise and

---

8. Major National Jewish Fraternal Organization.
9. Yiddish for "synagogue."

real and humble. She listened to my story and has been there to reassure me and root [*sic*] me on ever since I met her. Finally, just this year,
for the first time in my life, I joined a congregation.[10]

Sonya went to a visiting rabbi to receive a blessing. She told him, "My father molested me." The rabbi said, "It can't be. Jews don't do that." She was
devastated.[11]

Ten-year-old Nancy was molested by a neighbor on her way to school
one day. When she arrived at her Jewish day school, she spoke with the
principal/rabbi. As they waited for her mother to arrive, the rabbi said this
would not have happened if her mother were at home rather than working.
Nancy said she felt he was blaming her mother for what this man did to
her.[12]

Four young men at a Jewish fraternity party raped Heather, a college student and rabbi's daughter. Her parents insisted she tell no one for fear of the
impact on the rabbi's reputation.[13]

Carla told me:

I am a survivor of incest. Growing up it was like Mengele lived in our
house. I am also a rabbi. . . . When I speak with rabbinic colleagues
about sexual abuse of Jewish children, they recoil in horror. . . . My
openness about my history has hurt me professionally, as if I were not
the innocent child. Some days, I am sure that my incest experience
has shaped me more profoundly than my identity as a Jew.[14]

The Impact

Each child comes into this world whole and holy. When raised in relative
safety and love—allowed to wonder, explore, and discover—a child develops the capacity to think, to discern, to relate, to self-soothe, and to do so
much more. What happens, then, when safety disappears?

---

10. Rachel Lev, *Shine the Light: Sexual Abuse and Healing in the Jewish Community* (Boston, MA: Northeastern University, 2003), p. 135.
11. Based on research for Lev, *Shine the Light*.
12. Based on research for Lev, *Shine the Light*. Another version of this story is in Chapter 2, "If It's There, Why Don't We See It? Denial, Silence and Some of Their Costs."
13. Based on research for Lev, *Shine the Light*. Another version of this story can be found in Chapter 12, "Defining Community."
14. Lev, *Shine the Light*, pp. 30-31.

Those of us who were molested as children face a fourfold risk of a major depressive episode in our lives and a five times greater risk of suicide. We are five times more likely to be diagnosed with an anxiety disorder. The younger we are when first abused, the greater the likelihood of devastating impact.

In an attempt to manage the unmanageable, survivors display significantly more insomnia, sexual dysfunction, dissociation, anger, suicidality, self-mutilation, drug addiction, and alcoholism than other patients do.[15] Research finds that "[56] percent of psychiatric inpatients and 40 to 60 percent of outpatients report childhood histories of physical or sexual abuse or both."[16]

People molested as children show alterations in brain chemistry and social distress, evidenced in higher risks for teen pregnancy, HIV infection, runaway behavior, substance abuse, eating disorders, and vulnerability to yet more sexual victimization, domestic violence, and prostitution. When sexual abuse leads to behaviors such as eating disorders, smoking, and alcohol and drug abuse, the consequences become physically dangerous, for example, increased risk for heart attacks and cancer.[17]

When Is T'shuvah Done?

How can someone achieve *t'shuvah* when the wounds of sexual abuse can impact a lifetime? In some ways, I don't think it is ever done. I think those who violate boundaries need to spend some part of the rest of their lives repairing the world. Molesting a child isn't something you can close the book on and say, "Next issue" or "That's done." People who have been abused are not obligated to forgive.

Those who molest can be forgiven, but depending upon what they did and to whom, the impact never goes away. Consider the Holocaust. Those who survived go on, and some live abundant lives, but Holocaust survivors

---

15. John Briere, presentation at Advances in Treating Survivors of Sexual Abuse: Empowering the Healing Process II, San Diego, California, March 1994; cited in Lev, *Shine the Light,* pp. 78-79.

16. A. Jacobson and B. Richardson, "Assault Experiences of 100 Psychiatric Inpatients: Evidence of the Need for Routine Inquiry," *American Journal of Psychiatry* 144 (1987): 908-913; J. B. Bryer, B. A. Nelson, J. B. Miller, and P. A. Krol, "Childhood Sexual and Physical Abuse As Factors in Adult Psychiatric Illness," *American Journal of Psychiatry,* 144 (1987): 1426-1430; A. Jacobson, "Physical and Sexual Assault Histories Among Psychiatric Outpatients," *American Journal of Psychiatry,* 146 (1989): 755-758; J. Briere and M. Runtz, "Post Sexual Abuse Trauma: Data and Implications for Clinical Practice," *Journal of Interpersonal Violence,* 2 (1987): 367-379.

17. Fran Henry, "A Prescription for Change on Child Sexual Abuse"; see n. 2.

still have those experiences as a core of their identity. Survivors of other traumas, be it by combat, rape, incest, or partner abuse, do as well. The impact is written in their bodies and souls.

What Can We Do?

First, take responsibility. Dr. Abraham Twerski says, "Nowhere is the denial (about abuse) as intense as in the Jewish community." He tells a story which concludes that the mouse which steals the cheese is not the guilty party. The hole in the wall where the mouse takes refuge is the guilty one, as are those who did not seal up the hole. If the mouse didn't have a place to go and hide, he wouldn't steal the cheese. He continues, "Crime can exist only in a community which tolerates it. Wife abuse is a crime."[18] To which we must add, all abuse is criminal.

Doesn't this mean that, whatever the responsibility of individuals who cross the boundaries, the community carries responsibility for giving them places to hide? Rabbi Mark Dratch tells us that community denial about abuses of children is a "sin of omission" for which "our entire community must give *din v'cheshbon.*[19] And it is to protect the bodies and souls of our innocent children that we must speak out and act."[20]

How can we do that? Stop concealing and minimizing the problem. Acknowledge the wrongs that have been done, give voice to the stories of those who have been violated in order to help them and our communities heal, create rituals for healing from trauma, develop policies for how we'll address boundary violations of any kind and work to prevent them. It is time to open our hearts, minds, and doors to those who have been violated. It is time to invest whatever energy, time, and money are necessary to prevent future molestation of anyone, child or adult.

Judith Lewis Herman, MD, identifies three central tasks in healing from trauma: (1) establishing safety, (2) remembering and mourning, and (3) reconnection with ordinary life. She underscores that "recovery can take place only within the context of relationships; it cannot occur in isolation."[21]

Have you been molested or abused? Could you discuss it publicly? How safe would you feel? How do you imagine others would react? If someone

---

18. Taken from an audiotape of a keynote address given by Rabbi Abraham Twerski at the SHALVA dinner, Chicago, Illinois, 1996.

19. A complete and unequivocal reckoning.

20. Rabbi Mark Dratch, "The Physical, Sexual, and Emotional Abuse of Children" [Proposal to the RCA Roundtable], *Nissan* 5752; cited in Lev, *Shine the Light,* p. 46.

21. Judith Lewis Herman, *Trauma and Recovery: The Aftermath of Violence—From Domestic Abuse to Political Terror* (New York: Basic Books, 1992), p. 133.

close to you has been molested, can you talk about it with the person? How do you imagine others would react to hearing these stories? If you or others have felt safe to speak of your experience, what helped you to do so?

Our communities can be places of healing and hope. To make that happen, individuals need to ask, "Is it really safe for those being violated to speak with me or others in this community?" Organizations must create safe environments for those who have been abused to turn to for help.

We ask children and adults who have been molested to step forward without any certainty that it will be safe. How do we make it safe enough to tell? Acknowledge that incest, sexual abuse, and other forms of abuse happen in our communities. Understand the issues. Listen. Work in partnership with experts in dealing with abuse. We need to work to be aware and to ask the right questions, so that the responsibility for raising the issue is not left to children or adults who have been victimized. The organizations, boards, and associations with which we are affiliated need clear policies concerning abuse.[22]

When it comes to the role of rabbi/cantor/clergy, Rabbi Elliott Dorff writes:

> Do not assume that you can handle the situation alone. . . . Clergy, educators, and others who work with youth must learn how best to inquire about the possibility of abuse as well as what to do when they detect or suspect it. While such people can be critically important in helping victims and perpetrators of abuse, they should not try to do this alone. If abuse is to be stopped and its effects ameliorated, professionals of various sorts must be called upon. . . . As religious leaders, unless we are trained to understand and intervene in the areas of child sexual abuse, incest and adult survivors, we should not do therapy with victims or perpetrators. . . . [E]ven volunteers working in domestic violence agencies are required to go through extensive training before they can answer phones or have contact with clients. Certainly, we have a role as spiritual counselors. In that role, our interaction with victims and perpetrators should focus on confirming that we believe the victim and that neither Judaism nor the Jewish community countenances the abuser's behavior. We should also put the victim in touch with trained therapists and volunteers who can help. Creating a net-

---

22. See examples of healing rituals in Lev, *Shine the Light.* Policies and guidelines for abuse prevention have been developed by the Coalition Against Abuse with Shalom Bayit: Bay Area Jewish Women Working to End Domestic Violence. For information, contact Shalom Bayit, P.O. Box 10102, Oakland, CA, 94610; 510-451-8874 (510-451-7233); http://www.shalom-bayit.org.

work of experts who help victims and perpetrators of abuse is an essential part of our role. Working in partnership, we can provide what is best and right.[23]

Many states have laws that address the issue of mandated reporting, including reporting by clergy. If you are a mandated reporter, know what that requires of you.

Healing Our Communities and Ourselves

We are moved by stories told from the heart—stories of challenge, loss, healing, and ways people find the strength to face what life brings. As leaders, teachers, parents, and friends, we often use life experiences as teaching examples. When we've done something for which we're sorry, about which we're ashamed, we take the steps to make things right, and we talk about what happened, what we learned. When we have been wronged, our boundaries violated, we need to talk about what happened. Rabbis, cantors, and all clergy can help communities become healing places by sharing stories in ways that (1) give permission to talk aloud about these issues, (2) identify the ways in which boundaries can be crossed by anyone, in any community, and (3) offer compassion while establishing an expectation of honoring boundaries.

Those who have crossed a line should be expected to talk with a lay or religious trauma expert about how they crossed the boundaries and what they're doing to make amends and to prevent future problems. These sessions could provide material for case studies for discussion in rabbinic, cantorial, or caregiving training. Some of those who have crossed boundaries may also have ideas to help stop these abuses.

We cannot solve this problem by labeling those who abuse as monsters. They aren't. They are human beings who sometimes do monstrous things—things I believe they learned by example, by having them done to them, and/or as a twisted attempt to release their own pain. Those who have molested will have to work hard to heal whatever is inside that leads them to molest. The deeper their wounds, the more complicated the issues—including defenses against seeing the pain they cause and feeling their own pain—and the more time it will take for healing to occur. Resources must be available to help those who have been molested, as well as those who have molested. However, we have no obligation to allow those suspected or known

---

23. Rabbi Elliot Dorff, "The Role of Rabbis, Cantors, and Educators in Preventing Abuse and Repairing Its Consequences"; cited in Lev, *Shine the Light,* pp. 179-180.

to molest to be in situations where they might harm others (e.g., working with youth). In fact, we are obliged to protect people from being violated. No treatment guarantees that an abuser can or will stop abusing. We can hope and work toward that end but cannot risk the well-being of children or, indeed, the well-being of anyone.

As I wrote this, I wondered what my father could have done to complete *t'shuvah* with me. He died before I was able to confront him. Here's what I imagine: He would acknowledge what he did, say he was sorry, and listen as long as I needed to what it was like to be his daughter. Then, perhaps, we would hold each other and weep. What he did to me was a tragedy for both of us. Later, he might tell me of the hurts that happened to him as a boy and we might weep some more.

The answers to our questions about dealing with those who molest, including how to determine if they have completed *t'shuvah,* suggest the need for (1) a long-term commitment to understanding the complexity of the issues, including identifying the healing needs of both those injured when their boundaries are crossed as well as those who cross the boundaries; (2) identifying the role of the community in *t'shuvah,* healing, and prevention; and (3) above all, taking *action* to fulfill our role and meet those needs.

JEWISH RELATIONAL CARE WITH THE IMPAIRED

– 29 –

Relating Gently and Wisely with the Cognitively Impaired

Cary Kozberg

With the death of former President Ronald Reagan after long suffering from Alzheimer's disease, there has been a renewed focus upon the tragic losses that this insidious malady inflicts on its victims and the emotional toll it exacts from their loved ones. The stories were heartbreaking.

Contrary to popular belief, Alzheimer's disease is *not* the only form of dementia, nor is dementia a disease. Rather, dementia is a condition that robs people of their cognitive abilities and is not a synonym for insanity or "being crazy." The causes of progressive, irreversible dementia are numerous, but Alzheimer's disease accounts for most of its occurrences in this country. Among the changes brought on by dementia and cognitive impairment is the eventual loss of both memory and sequential thinking—the ability to remember beloved and long-familiar faces and to independently complete simple tasks, such as dressing one's self or tying one's shoes. During the last ten years of his life, the former president, once leader of the free world, eventually could no longer play golf and gradually could no longer recognize friends and, as the disease progressed, even his children or his beloved and devoted wife, Nancy.

Yet, despite Mr. Reagan's "losing his mind" (as some indelicately put it), he never lost his spirit or his characteristic affability. Despite no longer

339

"knowing" the people who were around him and being unable to put names with faces, still he "knew"—in an *affective* way—that they cared about him; he *felt* their love and concern and responded with his signature graciousness and humility.

Listening to the news reports about Mr. Reagan's battle with Alzheimer's reminded me of other people affected by progressive, irreversible dementia and their families with whom I've worked over the past fifteen years. One individual who continues to intrigue me is a man I'll call "Joe."[1]

A regular *shul*-goer[2] in healthier days, Joe was, until recently, a resident in our dementia care neighborhood. Although he is even more impaired now and requires more care, he still continues to respond to the overtures of other people with affability and appreciation. Every Friday afternoon as we began kabbalat Shabbat,[3] Joe would remind everyone, "It's time to talk to the Boss!" On a good day, Joe still responds to a blessing, a song, or a prayer with a joy and enthusiasm that is nothing less than contagious. In the words of Stephen Post, his religious capacity has been "disinhibited by dementia."[4] Without the self-censoring filter of "rational mind," Joe spontaneously expresses enthusiasm for, and gratitude to, God. Though he can no longer think clearly, he continues to sing most sweetly.

With deep philosophical roots in Descartes's *cogito, ergo sum,*[5] our culture teaches that our capacity to reason and remember is so much a part of our "personhood" (our *Tzelem*[6]) as to be identical with personhood itself. It is a safe bet that most of us find little comfort in the prospect of a heightened spiritual awareness as a consequence or result of our suffering from cognitive impairment. On the contrary, the fear of losing one's cognitive abilities is often a fear worse than that of death itself. Thus, this sentiment is articulated by many: "If I ever get to be that way, just take me out and shoot me!"

That personhood is so identified with healthy cognitive abilities has led certain philosophers[7] to conclude that the absence or loss of cognitive ability (or its potential)—self-awareness, self-control, a sense of the future, and a sense of the past—is tantamount to having no moral/legal claim to

---

1. Compare Cary Kozberg, "Letting Go to Trust God," *Jewish Spectator,* Summer 2001.

2. Synagogue attender.

3. Friday evening service welcoming the Sabbath—a day for rest and renewal.

4. Stephen Post, "God and Alzheimer's," *Park Ridge Bulletin,* January/February 2001, pp. 9-11.

5. I think, therefore I am.

6. The capacity for thought, form, and direction. See Chapter 1, "Premises of Jewish Relational Care," pp. 10-14, in this book.

7. For example, Peter Singer of Princeton.

"personhood." Within this "hypercognitive" definition of personhood, human beings with significant cognitive disabilities no longer have the moral or legal right to be regarded as "persons" and thus should not be under the protective principles of nonmaleficence and beneficence.[8]

Needless to say, such a belief is not, nor has it ever been, part of a *religious* ethic, which tends to be more inclusive in its definition of personhood and what constitutes human worth. But in a time when our society is aging, a fitting response to the increasing incidence of dementia would seem to be to enlarge, not diminish, our definition of personhood and our sense of human worth—as do the *religious* ethics, particularly of the three monotheistic traditions. To be sure, this is why in the midst of our "hypercognitive" culture, the myriad of nursing homes sprinkled coast-to-coast with roots in Protestant, Catholic, and Jewish traditions of care for the weak and vulnerable testify to the sanctity of the *whole* person—not just their capacity to reason or remember.[9]

That sanctity is based on the fundamental belief that a human being is comprised of body, mind, *and* spirit, all of which are God given. The whole person is not only *guf*[10] and *Tzelem* but also *N'shamah*.[11] Dementia indeed causes confusion, limited judgment, and loss of memory, thus robbing people of their minds. It steals the *cogito*.

It does not, however, steal the spirit; it does not encroach upon the *soul*. With the continuing (and amplified) presence of the spirit/soul, the *sum* continues to be affirmed. Put another way, the "soul-full" responses of people with progressive, irreversible dementia highly recommend that the notion of "I think, therefore I am" be replaced with the more inclusive "I feel and relate, and, above all, *I am*."[12]

Responding to the challenges that accompany Alzheimer's and other forms of dementia, clergy are often called upon to be emotional and spiritual caregivers, offering constant and reliable support as the families of these individuals experience (without being able to prevent) two "deaths," usually over the course of several years: the death of the "personality" they knew and loved, and then the death of the physical person. During the course of those years, the cognitively impaired person will need more personal supervision and assistance in the activities of daily living. As long as that person remains at home, providing supervision and assistance falls to

8. Stephen Post, "God and Alzheimer's."

9. Stephen Post, *The Moral Challenge of Alzheimer's Disease* (Baltimore, MD: Johns Hopkins Press, 1995), p. 3.

10. Body.

11. Our breathing, somatic self; from the Hebrew root *N-Sh-M,* meaning "breath."

12. Post, *Moral Challenge of Alzheimer's.*

family members. Indeed, caring for a person with dementia has been called a "36-hour-a-day" job.[13] However, most people who are not familiar with the phenomenon and consequences of dementia do not have a clue about how physically and emotionally draining it can be on the individual's loved ones. Because demented persons loses the ability to care for themselves over time, being a caregiver means always being "on call." To be sure, it often happens that the more caregivers do, the more they feel guilty for not doing more. As one observer has noted, it's not like in the movies, where more caregiving engenders more love. In real life, more caregiving can also spawn more resentment:

> Movie caregivers may feel love. For real life caregivers, abuse and anger are more like it. . . . In the movie "Marvin's Room," the character Diane Keaton played . . . speaks about the love that she receives from her bedridden father and senile aunt, but I hear very different reactions from caregivers: anguish, as love, hope, expectations and life itself erodes in tiny increments.[14]

With all of this in mind, clergy need to be available for caregivers as resources for support and solace, along with their congregations (to be discussed in the following).

The real challenge for clergy sometimes is not ministering to the families but, rather, to cognitively impaired individuals themselves. For many, this is a formidable challenge. How *does* one give meaningful emotional and spiritual care to persons whose cognitive capacities and self-awareness have significantly decreased? How *does* one respond in ways that are helpful and purposeful (ways that *they* experience as "helpful and purposeful")?

Before we address these questions, some preliminaries are necessary. First, it should be noted that the spiritual needs of people with cognitive impairment are not always acknowledged, even by professionals in the field of dementia care. Indeed, in some care settings where interdisciplinary teams create specific strategies to respond to the physical, social, emotional, and psychological needs of their residents, spiritual concerns may receive little more than a perfunctory response—a weekly one-size-fits-all worship service and (maybe) occasional visits from outside clergy, most of whom have little, if any, training in working with this population. These efforts are at

---

13. N. Mace and P. Rabins, *The 36-Hour Day* (Revised Edition) (New York: Warner, 1991). This is the classic text on dementia care.

14. Jane Bendetson, "I Am More Than Hands," *The New York Times Magazine,* April 20, 1997, p. 96.

best inadequate for clinical plans of care that are supposed to be comprehensive and holistic.

Unfortunately, some professionals doubt that such individuals still can relate to matters of the spirit, that they still have the capacity to respond to religious/spiritual stimuli and to resonate with the rituals, words, and symbols of their respective religious traditions. After all, if a person has lost the capacity for self-reflection, can that person really appreciate what religion is about? But although dementia causes a person to lose the capacity to "understand"—to respond *cognitively* to these stimuli and cogently articulate their meaning—there are other noncognitive, yet no less authentic, responses to matters of the spirit, as suggested by this *midrash:*[15]

> "The voice of the Lord is powerful (lit. "in strength"), the voice of the Lord is stately."[16] According to Rabbi Hama bar Hanina, this means that the voice of the Lord was heard as a powerful voice by those who were younger, and as a voice with measured stateliness by the elderly. Agreeing with Rabbi Hama, Rabbi Levi taught: Had the text been written "the voice of the Lord is in *His* strength," the world could not have withstood it. Therefore, Scripture states "the voice of the Lord is in *the* strength—that is, appropriate to the strength of each and every person: the men according to their strength, the women according to their strength, the young according to their strength, and the elderly according to their strength."[17]

No matter how "with it" we may or may not be, each of us hears the Divine Voice in our own particular way, with our own particular capacities. Those who are cognitively impaired may not hear the Voice in the same ways they once did. Nevertheless, they can still hear it, albeit in different ways. And similar to my friend Joe, they can respond to it—sometimes in ways that are not only authentic but also spontaneous and inspirational, as in these examples:

- A man in our care center rarely says a word but always raises his *tallit*[18] to kiss the Torah[19] as it is carried through the synagogue, or

---

15. Discovery of meanings other than literal in the Bible.
16. Psalm 29:4.
17. Midrash Tanhuma, Parshat Yitro.
18. Fringed shawl worn by worshipers in synagogue.
19. The scroll containing the Five Books of Moses; used in a synagogue for liturgical purposes.

one woman, whose conversations never "make sense," always joins in to chant *Sh'ma Yisrael.*[20]

- Russian ladies sit in the front row in the synagogue every Shabbat morning, never letting their inability to understand the English or Hebrew, or to keep up with the service's progression, interfere with their joy over simply being in *shul.*
- A Lutheran woman, when offered Communion wine, took the cup in her hands, raised it as if offering a toast, and declared to the chaplain, "Well, here's to you and me!"
- One significantly impaired woman's family took her to their church's Nativity pageant one Christmas Eve. During a climactic scene, one of the characters standing at the manger asks, in the most urgent voice, "Could this child born in a manger truly be the Messiah? Could this infant really be the Promised One?" To which the woman responded by jumping up out of her seat and shouting at the top of her voice, *"Of course he is, you idiot! Any dumb son-of-a-bitch knows that!"*[21]

As a *midrash* teaches and these examples testify, despite their inability to articulate clearly feelings associated with being spiritually connected, even persons with advanced dementia can still *feel* that connectedness, perhaps more genuinely than those of us who rely only on our rational "filter" to process religious/spiritual experiences. As the examples show, those feelings may be expressed at any given opportunity, at any given moment. Because they can, and do, experience God through the love of those around them, it behooves those of us who are messengers and representatives of Divine love to be aware and open to responding appropriately.

For many rabbis/clergy, responding to people with cognitive impairments in meaningful ways may seem to be somewhat of a stretch. For younger clergy, it is sometimes difficult enough to relate to older adults, and all the more so with those with progressive dementia. As I've been told, sometimes just being in their presence is daunting. It is not uncommon for the most well-intentioned rabbi, priest, or minister to feel discomfort, frustration, and even fear, perhaps daring to ask in their heart of hearts, "Is what I'm doing really doing any good?"

---

20. Watchword of the Jewish people. Literally, "Hearken O Israel, YHWH Our God, YHWH is One." Deuteronomy 6:4. Translation of Torah text by Everett Fox, *The Five Books of Moses: A New Translation with Introductions, Commentary, and Notes* (New York: Schocken Books, 1995), p. 880.

21. A true story and my personal favorite.

To be sure, spending even a little time with the cognitively impaired can be very disconcerting to the uninitiated. We clergy are a group that values the cerebral, sometimes over the spiritual; our work is usually with those who are able to respond with some self-awareness and ability for systematic thinking. Thus, when we are called upon to minister to people who no longer have these capacities, even the most dedicated clergy may find themselves a bit rattled.

Visiting a facility that provides dementia care can make us feel like a stranger in a foreign country. Our discomfort is amplified by a profound unfamiliarity with the language and culture. New visitors to this foreign land often do not understand most of what is said or done by its residents, nor will the residents necessarily understand the visitors. For example, being unfamiliar with the "culture" of this place may cause our patience to be severely tested, particularly when we answer the same question over and over and over again because the questioner does not remember asking the same question only a minute ago.

Such an experience can be not only disorienting and frustrating. It may even feel a bit dreadful. Yet, it is an experience that Jews, particularly rabbis as Jewish relational caregivers, need to have and, perhaps, even seek out. This is true for two reasons.

Our mandate as a faith community committed to providing Jewish relational care calls on us to promote and increase sanctity in the world, even in those places that seem beyond the pale. Although people with dementia may no longer be as sharp and as vibrant as they once were, although they may need constant care and supervision, although they may live in places that are mostly ignored and deemed godforsaken by most of us, still they remain precious; their lives are God given and, thus, unconditionally sacred. Even though they may no longer behave and communicate in ways that "make sense," still their gibberish may be interpreted as sacred in itself, coming forth as it does spontaneously, like the angelic song that affirms "the *whole* world is full of God's glory," found in even those places which seem to be beyond God's provenance. Certainly, spending time with demented individuals gives one the opportunity to apprehend more fully this important spiritual truth: sometimes it is *precisely* in the midst of what is dreadful that one may experience what is "awe-full."[22]

Furthermore, one of the ways we Jews are commanded to promote sanctity in the world is by responding, not just to the physical and material needs of the elderly, but, more important, to their *emotional* needs, specifically,

---

22. From my reflection article: Cary Kozberg, "The Whole World Is Full of His Glory," *Journal of Pastoral Care,* Spring 1994, pp. 88-90.

showing them respect and deference,[23] paying attention to them, and continuing to relate to them as people, rather than ignoring or marginalizing them. It is probably not a coincidence—especially for those who believe the Torah to be inspired by God in some way—that the commandment to love and welcome the stranger (because of our own experiences as strangers in Egypt) immediately follows the one mandating proper treatment of the elderly.

The juxtaposition of these two *mitzvoth*[24] suggests a most important insight. Focusing on the *midrashic* wordplay of *Mitzrayim*[25] and *m'tsarim*,[26] we learn that growing old and frail suggests an existential experience of being "in Egypt"; it is not about suffering physical slavery and servitude, but rather about being "stuck" and coping with the loss of independence and autonomy that accompany physical and cognitive decline.

Taken together, the two verses remind us that we must not treat the frail elderly as strangers in their own communities. They are *not* to be treated as "other." On the contrary, whatever efforts will keep them connected while affirming their presence are not only welcome but are indeed a religious obligation of the community.

That the commandment to love the stranger assumes an affirming love for all is significant. As do many of the *mitzvoth,* it calls for behavior that goes against the human penchant for the xenophobic. It is "unnatural" to love and welcome those who are not "like us." It is more natural to attack, marginalize, or ignore them. The commandment to love the stranger commands behavior that is unearned and unmerited by its recipient. In this spirit, the juxtaposition of these two verses suggests that how we honor and care for the elderly, particularly frail and demented individuals, is not conditional on how attractive, productive, or sharp they are. Rather, entitlement to the community's concern comes from a Higher Authority, as evidenced by the fact that each of the verses concludes by invoking that Authority (". . . I am the Lord").

It follows then that the love and caring experienced by these individuals depends not on the recipient's worthiness but rather on the giver's intentions. Indeed, when family, friends, and professional staff freely and enthusiastically offer love and caring to those who are severely cognitively impaired, the spiritual connections for both givers and receivers will be greatly nurtured. In this way, the *Shechinah*[27] is present and directly experienced.

---

23. Leviticus 19:32.
24. Plural of *mitzvah:* in Hebrew, fulfilling God's command; in Yiddish, a good deed.
25. Egypt.
26. From "narrow places."
27. Divine Presence, often represented as the feminine, caring aspect of Divinity.

Such nurturing is genuinely sacred, especially when one believes that being in relationship with other people is what is most important for people with dementia. As Reverend Elbert Cole learned as he cared for his wife who also succumbed to Alzheimer's, people with dementia are still people. They have the same needs as other people:

- They need to feel good about themselves.
- They need to have the approval of others.
- They need to be stimulated in body and spirit.
- They need to celebrate the joy of life.
- They need to be needed.
- They need to feel secure.
- They need to be included, and not alienated or marginalized.
- They need to be respected.
- They need to know they are loved.

Jewish relational caregivers help provide for all of these needs. However, it must be remembered that because of decreasing capacities over time, these individuals will respond less and less to normative types of relational care. Normative relational care depends on the counselee's having reason, memory, and cognitive integration. It is based on counselors helping counselees to get in touch with their concerns, enabling them to utilize interior resources—resources that are increasingly absent in people with dementia. When working with cognitively impaired individuals, a somewhat different model is required.

Such a model of Jewish relational care focuses on people's capacity for *affect:* their ability to feel and respond to feelings, even when the capability to articulate them or their causes is absent. What is needed in relating to these folks is a "ministry of presence," that is, a model that moves away from a listening/reflective stance, to one in which the rabbi/clergy supplies the energy and substance of the relational exchange *l'hatchilah,*[28] initiating the conversation and, when necessary, giving cues to the person in order to elicit a response.

Faced with a limited repertoire of responses, Jewish relational caregivers must respond to the demented individual out of a stance of total acceptance and a more heightened sense of being "fully present": responding empathically to whatever comes out of a person's mouth, even when nothing said is based on "reality" or makes any sense, which is often the case. Rather than try to bring demented persons "back to reality" by attempting to

---

28. To begin with; for starters.

convince them of the facts, it is more appropriate to accept their reality and respond to it, no matter how outrageous it may seem. Providing effective caring here means that honesty is *not* always the best policy because "reality" is in the eye of the beholder. What makes for effective relational caring is total acceptance of the *person,* not the facts. It is also important to be especially mindful of nonverbal signs: tone of voice, facial expressions, signs of agitation. When words are unavailable, body language often communicates more clearly what is going on with the person. In a word, providing effective emotional and spiritual care to people with irreversible dementia is like listening to a song in a particular way: the "melody" is more important than the "lyrics."

Rather than focus on what to say or what to do, a ministry of presence is more about the Jewish relational caregiver just *being* there for the person, and being okay with just being there. Indeed, it is our rabbinic/clergy *presence,* representing a caring faith community and the One with Whom the community is in covenant, that communicates a message of hope and abiding concern to the cognitively impaired individual: no matter how overwhelmed, abandoned, or rejected you may feel, you continue to be special and you continue to be sacred, and you have *not* been abandoned by God or by us.

Just how strong the desire to remain connected can be in a person with dementia became apparent to one Jewish relational caregiver who, concluding a Shabbat service, invoked God's blessing with the familiar words of the traditional "priestly" formula: "May the Lord make His face to shine upon you and give you peace." To which one of the residents in attendance spontaneously responded, "Oh, I hope so!"

Being fully present with a demented person calls for communicating an affirming caring and reassurance through touch, tone of voice and a visual focus that is consistent. Although such persons may no longer have their cognitive capacity in tact, their intuitive capacity is often more keen, and they can better sense what another person is feeling—often with a response that is spontaneous and unabashed. Therefore, it is essential that Jewish relational caregivers direct their undivided attention to the person being visited and leave any distractions outside.

When diagnosed with a dementia of the progressive, irreversible variety (i.e., Alzheimer's), that person may express feelings of loss, grief, anger, and fear at the beginning, when self-awareness and articulation are still intact. Moreover, similar feelings of despair are to be expected among loved ones and friends. The diagnosis itself may be overwhelming, perhaps triggering a response of depression and a questioning of self-worth: Why is this happening to me? What did I do to deserve this? What good am I now? Am I still worth anyone's time and effort—even God's?

When questions and feelings such as these are brought to us, offering a presence which is affirming, empathic, and accepting, which validates their feelings and takes their spiritual and emotional concerns seriously, may be the most important gift we can give. As they enter the "valley of the shadow," our commitment to help shepherd them in this difficult journey can help make the Divine Shepherd's *ahavat olam*[29] a genuine and authentic experience. And when we are successful, we are witness to the truth that, although human beings may forget, God never does.

To be sure, there are certain "dos and don'ts" that should be observed when visiting individuals with significant cognitive impairment. What follows might be considered a "shepherd's manual" of sorts:

1. Approach the person from the front, so as not to startle and possibly upset the individual unnecessarily. Stand where you can be seen clearly and not turned into a shadow.

2. Asking "Do you remember me? Do you know who I am?" is *not* helpful. Such questions needlessly challenge the person's memory and may result in frustration and embarrassment. Introduce (or re-introduce) yourself and clearly explain the purpose of the visit.

3. Make an attempt to talk *to,* not around, the person. Use a calm tone of voice, and be on the same eye level with the person (don't stand if the person is sitting, and vice versa). Because persons with dementia have lost the ability for more sophisticated reasoning and often can no longer connect ideas together, use short sentences with simple words and ideas throughout the visit, but in a way that does not "infantilize." Unless the person has a hearing loss, it is not usually necessary to raise your voice.

4. It is important to address the person by name and expect a response. There is, however, no fixed rule as to whether a person should be addressed by the first name or in more formal, respectful terms (Mr./Mrs., Dr., etc.). Some believe that using a person's first name communicates a certain familiarity and a desire to be closer to the person. Others recommend using more formal terms, not only out of respect for the person, but also for the benefit of the addressor, who is thereby reminded of the necessity to show respect and deference

---

29. Ever-present love and caring.

to this person, as well as of the person's entitlement to being valued.[30]

5. Smile and be sure to touch the person in some way—offering a hug,
a touch on the shoulder, or the holding of a hand. All of these gestures communicate: "I'm here. I will listen to you. I care about you."

6. A gentle orientation to reality is not always a bad thing. However, if
the person doesn't agree with you, accept the person's perception
and don't argue.

7. To maximize the time spent with a demented person, it is important
that any adaptive devices (eyeglasses, hearing aids) be in clean
and/or in working order and in place.

8. Because dementia robs a person of short-term memory and attention
span, be aware that the person may repeat himself or herself over
and over again; also be prepared to repeat yourself over and over and
over (and over) again.

9. Listen to and validate feelings, even if the words are inaccurate or
inappropriate; there is always a kernel of truth in the person's perception (remember: "melody" over "lyrics"), and, for the demented
individual, it is the *perception* of reality that is real. Therefore, validate the perception.

10. Last, value and celebrate the *moment* with that person!

Similar to other experiences with the sacred, the anticipation may call forth
dread, but the experience of sharing soul to soul can fill one with awe.

Because these folks respond so keenly to sacred experiences and moments due to their heightened capacity for affect, worship, rituals, and religious ceremonies can be quite powerful for them. And because ritual and
ceremony strengthen relationships—with God, community, and surroundings—they help nurture and reaffirm a continuity of self, thereby promoting
a healing of the soul (even in the absence of a cure for the brain). For these

---

30. A personal note: Several years ago I visited one of my seminary professors who
had moved into a long-term care center in Cincinnati, Ohio, where he spent his last days.
He had been a brilliant Talmud scholar and the author of numerous books and articles,
and one of the most gentle human beings God ever made. It would never have occurred
to anyone who knew him or his reputation to refer to him as anything but "Rabbi" or
"Doctor." Yet the young nursing assistant, who albeit provided wonderful care for him,
did not know about his earlier life or his reputation and so consistently called him by his
first name. Yes, the assistant did mean it to be endearing, and my teacher responded
warmly to him. Nevertheless, from my vantage point, such familiarity was somewhat of-
fensive, for it did not show this great man the respect he deserved as an older person,
much less as a great scholar.

reasons, ritual and ceremony are also excellent vehicles for offering effective Jewish relational care.

As with my friend Joe, individuals with dementia are often much more edified by worship experiences than are "healthy" people who attend religious services; therefore, they should be encouraged to attend and participate whenever possible. However, when the majority of people in the congregation are cognitively impaired, the service will "speak" to them only if it is adapted to facilitate their participation. Here, *familiarity* and *simplicity* are the watchwords.

Blessings, prayers, and songs that are traditional and familiar should be included over newer versions that are likely to be not as well known. Because a demented person's long-term memory is usually the last to go, aspects of a worship service that have been known and recited from one's childhood are most available. Old, familiar melodies to such songs as *Shalom Aleichem*,[31] *Adon Olam,* and *Ein Keloheinu*,[32] which may seem "tired" to some, will get more of a response from this cohort than the newer, more modern ones.[33] Because "everything old is new again," the more repetitive, the better.

In addition, *keep it simple!* Decreased cognitive and intellectual abilities (not to mentioned decreased attention spans) render sermons (which rely on systematic thinking and scholarly erudition), not only a waste of time, but also counterproductive. Instead, sharing stories and experiences that are more sensory based will be much more appropriate and effective in a discussion on *parashat hashavua*[34] than sharing brilliant homiletical insights.

Unfortunately, this rule of thumb is lost on too many clergy. They don't understand the importance of simplicity when facilitating worship experiences, not just with those who suffer from dementia, but with the frail elderly in general. Instead of believing that what works in a congregational setting is effective everywhere, they would do well to remember the words of the Psalmist: "the testimonies of the Lord . . . make wise the simple."[35]

As in any religious service, the use of religious items, ritual symbols, and music is necessary, but even more so in this setting. Religious items and symbols also serve as visual cues that remind participants that the experience is a religious one. In addition to using written texts (even for those who can no longer read, the experience of holding a prayerbook can be pro-

---

31. Friday night hymn.
32. Hymns that conclude the Saturday service.
33. Because of the need for using what is most familiar, our service continues to refer to God in traditional, masculine language.
34. Weekly Torah portion.
35. Psalm 19:8.

foundly edifying), other traditional symbols for Shabbat and the holidays are important for people to experience. Again, the more all five senses can be utilized, the richer the experience for the participants.

As was discussed regarding one-on-one visits, the worship experience will probably go more smoothly if certain "dos and don'ts" are followed:

1. Begin with an introduction and a simple "reality orientation": "Good afternoon, everyone! I'm Rabbi ——. Today is Friday, [the date], and we're gathered together for our weekly Shabbat service."
2. Schedule worship at the same time, on the same day, and in the same place, remembering that routine and familiarity are important.
3. Smile and use humor and touch. Again, because people with dementia are more intuitive and sensitive to "body language," smiling and the use of humor is essential, as is offering warm greetings and/or hugs, as well as keeping one's voice upbeat and one's body animated. These help foster an atmosphere of joy, enthusiasm, comfort, and trust.
4. Keep directions simple and use as many cues as necessary; hand motions may also be effective.
5. Provide written materials that are in large print and easy to handle. (*Note*: spiral-bound books stay open better than standard books.) Illustrations and graphics on the pages are also good cues for those who can no longer read. In addition, putting the service on large sheets of newsprint may also be helpful.
6. Make sure that everyone can see and hear to the best of their ability: eyeglasses and hearing aids should be working and in place, and the environment should be spacious, well lit, quiet, and generally conducive to a worship experience.
7. Be patient while folks find the right page. Help *everyone* to feel a part of the experience.

Yet another way in which Jewish relational caregivers can provide effective care for people with dementia and their loved ones is to maintain and strengthen the connections between them and their respective congregations. Regrettably, our youth-oriented culture has managed to seduce even faith communities, regardless of denominations, into believing that younger and more vital is always better. A common consequence of this attitude is that clergy and congregations often pay too little attention and devote too few resources to addressing the needs of their older adults, with even less directed to the needs of those who are coping with dementia. Old people aren't "sexy," and they do not elicit the kinds of programmatic and policy responses from congregational decision makers that children and young people do. Certainly, sufficient resources need to be directed toward keeping the youth connected for the sake of the congregation's (and entire community's) future. However, a mind-set that consistently views outreach to the congregation's older adults as a lower priority shortchanges these members, who probably have contributed much to a congregation's growth and welfare over the years. Moreover, it violates the spirit of the commandment that calls for giving them their due deference, not to mention hindering their ability to "hear the Voice" more clearly.

People with progressive, irreversible dementia, especially in its early stages when some self-awareness is still present, and their loved ones understand what the future holds: eventual placement in a nursing home; being marginalized and treated as a "stranger" by others; being abandoned to their own personal *mitzrayim* from which they will most likely not be delivered. For these people, outreach from rabbis/clergy and their congregations is absolutely critical to their emotional, psychological, and spiritual welfare. Indeed, outreach to those who are suffering from dementia is a way of fulfilling the commandment to heal, as understood by the rabbis: "From where do we know that one must save his neighbor from the loss of himself? From the verse *'and you shall restore it* [a lost possession] *to him.'*"[36] Certainly, broad and substantive programs of outreach by congregations to nurture and maintain spiritual connections with those coping with dementia can go a long way toward helping to prevent this "loss of self."

Reaching out to demented individuals and their families may take various forms. Because caring for a demented person can be extremely difficult and frustrating for families, rabbis/clergy may be called upon to be an objective voice and/or an advocate for the person, making sure that the person is receiving proper care and is in the proper place, whether it be at home or in a care facility. In such a situation, it may be necessary to ask several key questions:

- Is the person's cognitive impairment reversible or not?
- Is the person receiving adequate medical supervision?
- Are the person's physical needs being adequately met?
- Is the family environment nurturing or detrimental to the person's welfare?
- Is the caregiving environment nurturing or abusive?
- How are the individual family members coping?
- Is some sort of long-term care indicated? If not now, when?

---

36. Sanhedrin 73a, quoted in F. Rosner, *Modern Medicine and Jewish Ethics* (New York: Ktav, 1991), p. 91.

Regarding this last question, it is important for rabbis/clergy to be aware of how difficult it may be for family members even to consider long-term care placement for their loved one. When compared to remaining at home, long-term care placement would seem to be more favorable, especially when the dementia is advanced, if only because such facilities are specifically designed and equipped to meet the unique needs of these individuals. However dedicated and devoted individual family members may be, they are susceptible to burnout, which is less likely to happen in a long-term care facility with round-the-clock staff. Despite this objective fact, family members may still resist placement, feeling ambivalent and/or guilty, or simply being stuck in denial. Thus, it may be the Jewish relational caregiver who helps families work through these feelings so that they can do what is ultimately best for the individuals needing this kind of care.

Programmatically, congregations have much to offer in helping cognitively impaired individuals and their families stay connected, particularly in the areas of worship, education, and outreach. In the area of worship, efforts should be made to encourage and assist cognitively impaired individuals to continue worshipping with their communities for as long as possible. Alternatively, more user-friendly services might be created specifically for this population, utilizing some of the suggestions offered earlier. Also important is for services designed to accommodate the needs of persons with cognitive impairments to include strategies for responding to episodic incontinence and/or agitation. Including people with dementia and their families in the congregational *Mi Shebeirach,*[37] and in other familiar prayers, not only keeps them connected and not marginalized, but also keeps them in the memory of the congregation itself.

Learning about dementia and how it affects families and communities and what Judaism offers in the way of response can be a significant addition to a congregation's educational program. Through sermons, classroom curricula on the multifaceted aspects of dementia, family education programs, and organized visits to long-term care centers, congregants will be able to observe the *mitzvoth* of honoring the elderly and loving the stranger in new and significant ways.

As with all *talmud torah,*[38] more learning is supposed to lead to more doing. Hopefully, in congregational settings, learning more about the needs of the cognitively impaired will lead to a heightened willingness and enthusiasm to participate in various outreach programs. Such programs might include these activities:

---

37. Prayer for healing.
38. Jewish religious study.

- Highlight a member who has dementia in the congregational newsletter; include a picture and a short biography to keep that person in the forefront of the congregation's awareness.
- Organize visits to a person's place of residence, whether the family's home or a care facility. Leave a sign-in book with the names of those who visit, along with time and date and a place for a short message. Audiotaped or videotaped messages of greetings from congregants can be played over and over again, reminding the person that he or she has not been forgotten.
- Set up congregational day care programs and respite support for family members. Many synagogues have day care for young children. Why not create programs for older adults with dementia? As noted earlier, the demands of caregiving can be physically and emotionally draining; caregivers need assistance with caregiving tasks and opportunities for rest and relaxation to recharge their "batteries." Day care and respite programs under congregational auspices can not only be a boon to families but also teach volumes to the congregation as a whole about another aspect of *chesed*[39] and *tikkun olam.*[40]
- Set up support groups that utilize distinctly *Jewish* resources. Although local chapters of the Alzheimer's Association sponsor support groups for caregivers, congregations might partner with the association, tapping into their expertise to create their own "caring communities." Including prayer, *torah*[41] study, and opportunities for individual relational counseling, congregational support groups can offer unique opportunities to cope with the many problems, frustrations, feelings, and questions of why that accompany this awesome responsibility.

Although our Sages may not have possessed a sophisticated knowledge of dementia, they nevertheless affirmed the value and worth of those coping with cognitive impairments, cautioning against marginalizing or devaluing them: "Be careful with a scholar who forgot his learning because of his troubles, since it is said that both the holy tablets and the fragmented tablets lie together in the Holy Ark."[42] Centuries later, our teacher Danny Siegel offers further comment on this text as a reminder to us:

---

39. Loving-kindness; loyalty.
40. Repairing and renewing the world.
41. All of Jewish learning.
42. Menachot 99a.

Treat with respect old people
who have forgotten the grandeur of Life
because of sickness and senility.
Were not the shattered fragments
of the First Commandments
also in the Ark?
Were not the smallest chips of Holy Stone
carried by the Jews for forty years
through wilderness and waste
to the Promised Land?
If a man's brain shrivels at eighty
and a grandmother's cells degenerate with age,
is this a reason to throw them away,
to torture them still more
with bare, cold ostracism?
Treat with honor the elders,
though they rave
or act like infants,
silly and shameful.
Feel no shame,
Make no apologies.[43]

As the baby boomers age, the number of people affected by dementia and cognitive impairment in the next several decades is expected to rise significantly. This increase in the number of people stricken by dementia will certainly lead to increased knowledge and awareness of the causes and consequences of dementia. As teachers of *torah,* we need to prepare ourselves as well as those we teach. If we are to be effective caregivers for those with dementia and cognitive impairment, we need to learn how to better preserve their dignity as human beings and their sanctity as having been modeled after and molded by Divinity, and how to restore some sense of relatedness and wholeness to those who have been shattered and fragmented in this way. We have to teach our communities how to make such persons feel honored and not rejected; how to embrace and not ostracize them; how to continue to revere them as sacred and not reject them as useless.

May God help us to fulfill this task faithfully, and may we be worthy of the honor of helping to shepherd them and their loved ones toward the constant and nurturing presence of the Divine Shepherd.

---

43. Danny Siegel, "Senility," in *Between Dust and Dance* (New York: United Synagogue of America, 1978). Copyright 1978 Danny Siegel and Allan Sugarman. Reprinted with permission.

30

Caring for the Mentally Ill

Judith Brazen

A Vignette

Grace,[1] a thirty-five-year-old Caucasian female, was being treated for paranoid schizophrenia. A devout Christian, Grace was aware of my rabbinic background. Nevertheless, she longed to share a religious connection with a chaplain and was receptive to my visits from our very first meeting. Grace identified herself as Christian, yet her fears prevented her from taking the elevator to the hospital chapel for Sunday worship. I discovered that Grace was overwhelmed with religious ruminations, which made a visit to "church" a truly complicated endeavor.

Over the course of weeks, Grace shared her understanding of her relationship with God. Grace felt ashamed before God. She had not been able to live the way one modeled after and molded by Divinity should live. She was not independent like she was "supposed" to be. She had not had her own family or contributed to society in ways similar to her parents and siblings. God must have had a reason for giving her a different soul and a different brain; God must have been trying to teach her a lesson that she could not otherwise learn. Sometimes Grace felt that she received special messages from God, reserved for a confidant or prophet. More often, Grace felt that God was angry and displeased with her and even tried to punish her. Grace both feared God and longed to please God.

When I first visited with Grace, I asked her if she thought these shameful feelings were possibly symptoms of her illness. Grace acknowledged paranoia as a symptom of her illness on a cognitive level but was unable to sustain this acknowledgment on an emotional level. I realized that my continued reference to her fears as symptoms of illness erected a tremendous barrier between us. Grace's paranoia was her innermost reality. Our relationship deepened only after I accepted this reality. Our encounters evolved only af-

---

1. Grace is not a real person. The vignette represents a conglomeration of experiences that I have had in my work with chronically mentally ill individuals.

ter I remained with her fears and her deep sense of shame, inhibiting that
constant urge I felt to bring her more closely into my realm of thinking.

Grace and I concluded each visit with prayer. Although Grace liked to tell
me what she wanted to pray, she always requested that I lead. The prayer
was always the same. Grace asked God for discernment: to know the difference between people who lie to her and people who tell her the truth, to
know when the voices she heard were "real." She prayed to know the difference between truth and falsehood, health and disease. She prayed explicitly
for mental health. I concluded each prayer with my own words: "Oh, God,
please be with Grace and bless her with your divine presence. Help Grace to
see that in your divine, compassionate, and forgiving presence, she is a
beautiful person. Help Grace to see this inner beauty as she struggles to live
a good life. When she is afraid, help her to feel a sense of peace and of calm.
Help her never to be afraid, for You are always with her." Then together we
would say, "Amen."

I now realize the degree to which my relationship with Grace clarified
the essence of my rabbinic presence. I am challenged to meet the patient
where she lives, replete with her cognitive ruminations and innermost fears.
My task is to offer a complete and affirming acceptance of the patient's
whole self. I approached Grace with recognition of who she is, rather than
who she is not. In my acceptance of her reality, I like to believe that I allowed Grace to safely offer her whole self to God.

An Alternative Relationship with God

At the same time that I establish my spiritual caregiving presence and
trust, I symbolically offer an alternative relationship with God. I offer a notion of God that is accepting and understanding of even the most socially
unacceptable thoughts and feelings. I thereby suggest a divine presence
who accepts Grace's fears with love, who helps allay her confusion, and
who ultimately (if only momentarily) strengthens her resolve to find a sense
of meaning in her existence.

In my experience, I have found that many patients approach God with the
opposite understanding: God can be negatively judgmental, unforgiving,
and angry. As with Grace, many patients approach God with a deep sense of
inadequacy and shame, feeling that God has abandoned them in their illness. One patient shared with me, "I offer my prayers up to God and the
prayers are slammed right back down to me." Another patient pointed to the
window and said, "My relationship with God is not good. I feel like I don't
have the faith that I used to. . . . See that window out there? I used to believe
that if I jumped out the window, that God would save me. I don't believe
that anymore. I don't believe that God would save me." Some patients can't

understand why God seems to be punishing them. Others struggle for awareness of meaning in their existence, when they have been unable to sustain relationships, careers, and a variety of other responsibilities. In light of a sense of overwhelming failure as human beings, many struggle to grasp and hold on to reasons for continuing to live.

As a rabbi caregiver, among the most important things I do is enabling patients to engage in sacred relationship with God by providing insights on alternative interpretations of patients' current situations. In offering such a connection, however, I have found some obstacles in the way. One barrier I face is the general lack of acknowledgment of mental illness in our Judeo-Christian prayers and religious texts. Facing a void in traditional resources, I am drawn to alternative ways to help patients connect with God. I think "outside the box" in working with the mentally ill.

Working with the Mentally Ill: Specific Guides

I start by investigating how my patients have spiritually connected in the past. I listen very carefully; I am welcoming; I find out what and who is important to them; I find out if they have any favorite prayers or religious texts. Then I take out my "tools." I have found concrete tools and approaches to be invaluable in my relational caregiving work with the chronically mentally ill. I select prayers and biblical passages that are meaningful to patients. I always carry around index cards on which I write down simple phrases or isolated words to leave with patients at the conclusion of our visits. When patients are too depressed to get out of bed or engage in conversation, I leave an index card with a prayer or phrase at their bedsides. I have had patients recover from incapacitating depression and thank me for these cards. One of my favorite passages—"I will fear no evil, for You are with me"—is a passage from Psalm 23 that addresses the fear and alienation so many patients experience. I encourage my patients to repeat these phrases when they are anxious or depressed, and to engage in relaxation breathing as they do so.

Another way that I think outside the box relates to lessons I have learned from my Christian patients and colleagues. I often depart from fixed prayer and engage in spontaneous prayer with patients. As I did with Grace, I offer prayers to God from the heart. Sometimes I lead these prayers and sometimes patients lead. The content of these prayers evolves from our visits. A patient may be feeling remorse over "sins" that they committed in the past. I might offer a prayer of forgiveness on behalf of the patient, using the patient's own thoughts and sentiments. I integrate traditional phrases or words, yet the core content of the prayers remains personal and spontaneous.

I write prayers with patients. I had one patient who was always eager for my visits. At a certain point, however, our conversations were stagnating. I asked him how he would feel about writing a prayer together. He was immediately receptive. This young man had been expressing concern about achieving a sense of inner peace. He heard voices that were "threatening to destroy him." So we wrote a prayer together about achieving peace. I would start a line and he would finish it, or he would share his feelings with me and I would help shape those feelings into words. Some lines were exclusively his words. We never mentioned the word *voices,* yet he and I both knew that his prayer was referring to the destructive voices that threatened his inner peace. I gave him a copy of the prayer when we concluded. When I saw him next, he approached with a warm smile I had never seen before. He thanked me and told me how much he liked the prayer. Our relationship had reached a new level.

I bring prayers that I have written, or ones others have published, to patients. After working with this population for some time, I can discern common concerns of mental health patients. For those who have a more intellectual approach to God, I bring poems and passages to read and discuss together. One patient who suffered from bipolar disorder was soothed by Victor Frankl's reflections on suffering.[2] I am forever searching for new texts to offer!

I have learned that there is no one formula for all patients. I had a patient who was very reticent and awkward with words. I discovered that he liked to play pool. We played pool during our visits and concluded with a brief conversation and a prayer. I get to know my patients and then intuitively offer the best medium for facilitating a sacred connection to God.

These are only some of the ways I offer my patients opportunities for sacred relationship. I offer a compassionate, reliable, and accepting rabbinical presence. I facilitate a line of communication between the patient and God. I offer hope for a God who is accepting, compassionate, and present with them in their suffering.

An Alternative Relationship with Community

The rabbi's role, as one of support and acceptance of the patient's whole Self, including those obstreperous internal other *"selves,"*[3] which make life difficult for the patient, is crucial for the rabbi to reaffirm. This perspective

---

2. See Victor E. Frankl, *Man's Search for Meaning* (New York: Pocket, 1997).

3. For further explication, see "A Guide for the Reader" and Chapter 1, "Premises of Jewish Relational Care," in this book.

can symbolize a God who, having fashioned them, accepts and loves all creatures and creation. Conveying a message of acceptance allows the spiritual relational presence to bestow a strong representation of a supportive religious community—one that is receptive, accepting, and open to all. Far too often, our religious communities reinforce the unrelenting stigma that society maintains toward people with mental illness.

Family members, co-workers, and friends are not always enlightened about mental illness. One man stated that his brother would have nothing to do with him. Another family member expected him to "snap out of it" and "take care of himself" or "pull himself up by his bootstraps." Family members may blame the mentally ill person, expect the person to be able to control the illness, or deny the illness altogether. One patient stated that it would be better if she had cancer, for at least then people would acknowledge her illness as real and sympathize with her.

Many patients feel alienated and ostracized by their churches and synagogues. One ruminated about the insensitive treatment and cruel teasing that he received from counselors and campers at a Jewish camp. Another turned to Jews for Jesus for a welcoming community. During an initial visit, one patient listed the names of the churches that had asked him to leave. As he reported, the churches feared that he was going to harm their children.

To preach acceptance of mental illness is one matter, but to practice acceptance is much more complex. The problem is complicated by the dual role that shame plays in the lives of many with chronic mental illness. On the one hand, some people with chronic and persistent mental illness are overwhelmed by shame and inadequacy. They feel persecuted and humiliated by their communities. On the other hand, many of these same ill people display an astounding lack of shame. They are unable to fully grasp many key aspects of social convention. One symptom of schizophrenia is a lack of social inhibition and social appropriateness. Another is a lack of personal hygiene and organization, or the ability to understand the nature of one's illness. People frequently react with alarm and discomfort to these manifestations of mental illness. Stigma can be both overtly and subtly active in religious institutions.

Ruth was diagnosed with schizophrenia at the age of eighteen. Her family members were active in the Protestant church in their small town. One Sunday morning, Ruth's enlightened father went up to the podium at church and explained her diagnosis publicly. He wanted to minimize rumors, normalize her illness, and, most of all, ensure that church would be a safe and welcoming place for Ruth. Ruth and her family were able to continue their participation in church events without the shadow of a "shameful family secret."

I focus primarily on my spiritual relationship, as opposed to broader social implications. I am afforded a unique role as a hospital chaplain. In this role, I am cognizant that my encounters symbolize religious community to the individual patient. Genesis provides me guidance: We are all creations of the same God. We are all equal before God. Each one of us has our imperfections and our challenges. If religious institutions don't legitimize and welcome people with mental illness, who will?

The Rabbi

Society perpetuates the notion that perfection is a sign of mental health. We are ashamed of problems; we are taught to present perfect selves to the public. When others manifest their problems in public, we feel threatened because many of us work tremendously hard to isolate our personal struggles to a private arena. In any spiritual caregiving relationship, we are inclined to feel that the patient has the problem and the rabbi has the answer. One of the greatest challenges in our work is to overcome any feeling of superiority with patients; we are all equal before God. I may offer guidance and strength and hope, but I am not a superior creation.

My training in clinical pastoral education has taught me that, to be effective in this work, one has to be self-aware at all times. Self-awareness is a key element in developing a spiritual caregiving relationship with anyone, and especially with a mentally ill population. I must be cognizant of how my personal struggles interface with the struggles of the patient in the individual encounter. I don't burden the patient with the details of my personal challenges, yet I convey an understanding of suffering in the manner in which I relate. As I approach the relationship with respectful acceptance, I convey that both patient and rabbi are equal before God.

Self-awareness is especially important because the encounter involves highly personal matters. It is not unusual for strong feelings of intimacy to develop in both the patient and the rabbi. The encounter often deals with some of the most sensitive and provocative issues of human existence. It is only natural to expect feelings of intimacy to emerge. Nevertheless, there must be limits in expressing these feelings:

- When is it appropriate to hold the hand or touch the arm of a patient?
- When is it appropriate to hug a patient?
- Is it ever appropriate to meet the patient's mother for coffee outside the hospital setting or communicate with a patient after treatment?
- When is it appropriate to challenge a patient's thoughts and feelings?
- How do I answer personal questions that patients pose?

A fundamental challenge in relational caregiving work is awareness of these struggles. At times, sharing personal details in my life may not be helpful to the patient. On the other hand, when I don't share of myself, I may create a barrier in the relationship.

Given these complexities, definitive answers are impossible. I can describe the process in which I engage when confronting such questions. First, it is important to always remain aware of my own personal thoughts and feelings. When I am struggling with these issues, this suggests a need to weigh my next steps carefully. Second, it is invaluable to consult experienced colleagues who have confronted similar issues. An experienced colleague, removed from the intensity of the situation, can offer more objective guidance. It is important to acknowledge that rarely are responses absolutely correct or incorrect. The greatest error one can make is in failing to acknowledge the complexities of the issues involved.

In addition to self-awareness, forgiveness plays an integral role in my caregiving relationships. Forgiveness is at the core of my strength as a rabbi. I visited with a patient who longed to seek forgiveness from God. She insisted that God was "turning His back" on her, and that she was being punished for her "sins." I asked her if she felt unforgivable. I then asked if she could forgive herself. I suggested that before she can seek and receive forgiveness from God, she needed to forgive herself.

I bring these same questions to my own life. My struggle has been to forgive myself for my own "imperfections" and personal challenges. Only when I accept all of my *"selves"* can I model forgiveness for my patients and bring a fuller understanding to the internal struggles of my patients. Self-awareness and forgiveness are key foundations for the sacred relationship.

Conclusion

In any arena, the spiritual encounter represents one of the most complex, intricate rabbinic relationships. The complexity of this relationship stems from the diversity of experiences that our patients face, coupled with the fact that we meet people at a time when they are particularly vulnerable. In this role, we simultaneously stand for the relationship with God, the relationship with the religious community at large, and the relationship with the current medical setting where the patient is receiving care. These complications are confounded when we are dealing with mentally ill patients, due to the additional burdens brought on by mental illness. These are conditions for which both religious and secular societies continue to harbor considerable stigma.

As a rabbi, one must constantly struggle with the complications inherent in general aspects of relational interchanges as well as with interchanges related to the unique demands associated with mental illness. I have found that specific techniques facilitate my effort to meet these challenges. Using specific prayer techniques and engaging in spontaneous prayer have both proved invaluable methods for facilitating encounters with the mentally ill. However, more important than using these techniques, rabbis must come to this work with a firm understanding of their own feelings, emotions, and prejudices. Encounters with mentally ill individuals will evoke strong feelings in rabbis. However, when rabbis can learn to use these reactions to the benefit of the patients, these feelings and emotions provide a unique opportunity for a genuine spiritual healing by the individuals with whom we work.

31

Caring for the Institutionalized Developmentally Disabled

Bernie Robinson

Participation in communal worship for institutionalized persons with developmental disabilities is virtually the only avenue that they have to actively identify with the Jewish People and tradition, other than what their families are able to provide. Visitation by rabbis with individuals on their residential units, while an essential act of friendship and support and also a reinforcer of Jewish identity, is not as effective a vehicle to transmit Jewish values or community as is group programming.

We all come to know ourselves as part of environments bigger than ourselves: our family, the schools from which we have graduated, the organizations we've joined, the causes we've supported, the avocation or vocation we've chosen, the place where we reside, and so on. Each of these helps us to fit into the fabric of society, to find a secure place there, and to feel good about ourselves. Although a few of these associations may be available to the person with retardation, many are not due to limited capacity to comprehend, narrow life experiences, or constraints upon opportunities to participate. Some are simply too abstract to claim meaningfulness. How very important then to facilitate self-identity and self-esteem through avenues that do lend themselves to concrete expression and meaning.

Jewish communal worship and celebration is a most effective means to enhance self-worth, engender feelings of inclusion in a greater whole, and promote meaningful personal and religious values in the life of an individual with developmental disabilities, just as it is for those of us with fewer disabilities. Jewish tradition relishes concrete expression: the sound of the *shofar*,[1] the scent of the *etrog*[2] and the sway of the *lulav*,[3] the color and bril-

---

1. Ram's horn blown on the High Holydays.
2. Citron, used on Tabernacles.
3. Palm branch waved on Tabernacles.

liance of the *chanukiyah,*[4] the grating of the *gragger,*[5] the flavor of the *matzah*[6] and *maror,*[7] and the grandeur of lifting a Sefer Torah[8] from the ark, and, more than anything else, songs and more songs. These are the makings of a joyous Jewish experience and a real sense of specialness and belonging.

The worship services at the developmental centers I serve emphasize song, interchange, and celebration. The worship themes usually derive from holidays, both Jewish and American. The talk and dialogue we share are mostly about the blessings each of us receives and the kindnesses we can bestow upon one another and those dear to us. The prayers are mostly those of thanksgiving. The songs we sing have familiar Israeli and liturgical melodies for which English lyrics have been especially written, in appropriate language with didactic intent, to emphasize Jewish values and holiday content. Song is clearly the most important single vehicle that can be used to communicate Jewish identity and community. Even though the words may not be sung aloud by some of the participants, the music binds our spirits together. Positive assent and pleasure show even on the faces of those whose lips never move. We take about thirty to thirty-five minutes for song and prayer and then change from seats in a circle to seats at a table for refreshments. The food is an awaited positive reinforcement, not unlike the *oneg*[9] after a late Friday night service out in the community.

The key to success is in approaching people with retardation on a level to which they can relate. As explained in the Passover *Haggadah,*[10] the Torah bids us four different times to teach our children about the exodus because there are four different kinds of children: the wise, the rebellious, the simple, and the ones who do not know how to inquire. The message is that each child and each Jew is to be addressed and taught at his or her own level. Proverbs 22:6 also teaches this when translated: "Teach your child according to his way"—that is, his way of learning, not ours. Ours is so often abstract, subtle, verbose, and intellectual. My congregation understands what is direct and concrete, and what especially appeals to the heart.

In the course of time, reverence and love of God, respect for the Torah, loving-kindness and fairness toward other people, the value of family and community, the dignity of work, the value of learning, wonder at the world,

---

4. Eight-branched candelabrum used on Chanukah.
5. Noisemaker used on Purim.
6. Unleavened bread used on Passover.
7. Bitter herbs used on Passover.
8. The scroll containing the Five Books of Moses: Genesis, Exodus, Leviticus, Numbers, Deuteronomy.
9. Collation.
10. Special book used for Passover *seder.*

and appreciation for simple blessings are rehearsed and learned. These become the stuff of what being Jewish is all about. These constitute our Jewish spirituality.

Of course, individuals relate and absorb according to their abilities and limitations. Some can appreciate the rhythmic melodies, the special attention they receive when they attend services, and the refreshments at the end. A few acquire a real sense of pride in their special identity as Jews, an awareness of the Jewish calendar cycle, and the values rehearsed throughout the year. Yet others find an opportunity for self-expression and a deeply felt relationship to God who made the world and who loves each person in it.

The families of the retarded gain as well. Parents who see that their children are being exposed to the values and ways of our people know that their children are not being shortchanged again. They reap comfort from knowing that the tradition handed down to them is in some way being passed on as a blessing to their children.

Our *minyanim*,[11] modest, unknown, and almost never publicized, embrace a population that deserves greater inclusion by the Jewish community. Serving them in a large institutional setting where they reside and are aggregated is, of course, much easier than out in the general community. Large residential developmental centers for people with retardation are currently being fazed out and closed, however, and their former residents scattered to small group homes disbursed throughout the general community. The *minyanim* of which I have spoken may soon be a thing of the past. This presents our Jewish community with the increasing challenge of integrating this uncelebrated and fragile segment of our people into the synagogues and other institutions of the Jewish community.

---

11. Plural of *minyan,* a quorum of ten Jews required for public prayer.

JEWISH RELATIONAL CARE
AT LIFE'S END

– 32 –

Relating to the Sick and Dying

Steven Moss

The [*Tzelem*⇔*N'shamah*]¹ relational model, described in Chapter 1 of this book—"The charge each of us caregivers is faced with is to search out, tune in to, stay focused on, respect, nourish, sustain, and sponsor the [Breath-Taking⇔Model of Divinity], first in all our *"selves"* and then in others"—finds itself manifest in caring for the sick and dying, for, by definition, this caring must be relational. In Hebrew, the phrase for this *mitzvah*² is *bikur cholim,*³ meaning "visitation of the sick." Taking note of the word *visitation,* the relational dynamic between the person visiting and the person visited becomes evident. You must be in some kind of physical relationship, at least a sharing of a space, during the visit. Although an individual or a congregation, without the ill person present, can offer a *Mi Shebeirach,*⁴

---

1. [Breath-Taking⇔Model of Divinity]. See *ABC's of Jewish Relational Care* in this book; for further explication, see Jack H Bloom, *The Rabbi As Symbolic Exemplar: By the Power Vested in Me* (Binghamton, NY: The Haworth Press, 2002), especially Chapters 6 and 8.
2. In Hebrew, fulfilling God's command; in Yiddish, a good deed.
3. Visitation of the sick.
4. A specialized prayer in the synagogue liturgy often, but not exclusively, used for healing: "May the God of our Ancestors bless (and heal) So-and-So, the child of So-and-So."

this prayer does not fulfill the *mitzvah*. The *mitzvah* can be fulfilled only when the visit occurs, as it says in the *Code of Jewish Law:* "When a person gets sick, it is the duty of every man to visit him, for we find that the Holy One, Blessed be He, visits the sick."[5]

Although some people wish to be alone when they are ill, most people enjoy the company of visitors, at least in measured numbers and for limited periods of time. Most sick people certainly appreciate a caring phone call. Often an ill, hospitalized person finds even the brief visit of a nurse, or other hospital personnel who show care and concern, desirable because it is preferable to being alone in that room for hours on end, and it says to the patient that someone does care. Many patients have said that, as important as the medical expertise of their physicians is, the physicians' "bedside manner" is of equal, if not greater, importance. They want doctors who, through a relationship expressed by a listening ear, an attentive voice, and a caring heart, will be there for them. This is especially true when patients are dying; they know that while the doctors can no longer bring a cure, the doctors can still bring a caring presence expressed by the dynamic of a relational movement between *"selves,"* the *"self"* that cares and the *"self"* that yearns for that care.

As to dying itself, although it is an "alone experience," in that a person, even when surrounded by others, dies alone, for no one can die for another person, most people do not want to die lonely. They desire relationships until the very end, particularly when these are caring relationships that affirm the person as a Self, one with dignity and worth, created by the Eternal One, [*Tzelem*⇔*N'shamah*]. Although the physical breathing body might have changed, the *Tzelem* is still vital (in the absence of Alzheimer's) and remains so until the last exhalation. The dying desire relationships in which there is recognition by deed and word that the dying person is still a person.

This is true for the sick as well. I will always remember the patient who was so pleased to see me walk into her room. After I introduced myself as the hospital's rabbi, she said, "I am so glad you are here. I know that unlike the other staff, you will care for me from the top of my head to the bottom of my toes." In other words, she believed that I, as rabbi, would bring to her a spiritual relationship of caring that would affirm her Self as a whole Self. For her, the fragmented *"self"* that had been poked, prodded, and examined was not the Self that she wanted to be. This is Jewish relational caring, *"self"* for *"self."*

Those visiting the sick and dying have many ways to enhance and intensify the relational caring that they are affirming. I would like to suggest two

---

5. Rabbi Solomon Ganzfried, *Code of Jewish Law,* Volume 4 (New York: Hebrew Publishing Company, 1963), p. 87.

of them that I believe are vital to the relational model being offered here. I will present them by sharing two stories from my hospital visits as a chaplain.

As a young twenty-three-year-old rabbinical student, I was asked by a floor nurse to visit a nineteen-year-old young man who was dying of leukemia. As I walked into his room, the family members who were standing by his bedside looked up at me. Their faces expressed both sadness and anger. They also questioned where I had been during the past three weeks while Gary had been in the hospital. "Now that he is dying," they said, "you show up!" As I was only substituting for the authorized rabbinic chaplain, I neither made excuses for his not visiting nor defended my visit now. I simply stated that I could not offer any explanation as to why no one had previously visited, but that I was here now to visit Gary.

I then walked over to Gary's bed and immediately took his hand. I have always found touching to be a very important bridge in the relational experience of caring for another human being. Particularly for those who are severely ill or dying, it is a way of bridging the physical chasm between two bodies and saying in a powerful nonverbal way, "I am here with you." I then sat down next to him. He turned to me and through his oxygen mask asked, "Rabbi, where is the justice in what is happening to me?" Still holding his hand and without any hesitation in my voice, I said, "Gary, I'd be a fool to give you an answer." He then closed his eyes and I left the room, offering to the family my telephone number if they needed to reach me.

The next morning, although it was not scheduled, I chose to visit Gary before going to my classes. I never made it to classes that day because Gary would not let go of my hand while I stayed with him for the next eight hours until his death. His family also remained in the room, standing around the bed, crying and taking turns holding his other hand. During this time, he asked me to talk to him to fill the void that was silence, which meant to him the arrival of death.

I officiated at Gary's funeral, and I visited the family during *shivah*.[6] I asked them why they thought Gary had wanted me to be with him during those last hours of his life. I remember the answer they gave me, as if it were today: "Gary wanted you with him because of the answer you gave to his question. You did not offer an intellectualized theological response to his question. Rather, you offered yourself in your own questioning and faith, and that was what he wanted and needed: honesty."

The first imperative in caring for the sick and dying is to be yourself. When you are, you show them the respect they need. You are treating them relationally, as the words of the Torah can be rephrased: "You will respect

---

6. The seven-day (hence *shivah*, Hebrew for "seven") period of mourning, following interment, spent at home receiving visiting consolers, called "sitting *shivah*."

your neighbor, as you respect yourself."[7] Since all is on the line for them, particularly the dying or the person facing the potential of a catastrophic diagnosis, they do not have the time for cerebral responses or responses that do not come from the heart, soul, and gut. To offer such a canned response is to cut off the relationship. It says to the person, "You are dying and I am not." This is an [I–It] relationship. There is a failure of any of the *"selves"* of one to bond with any of the *"selves"* of the other. But when the words and/or actions of the visit are offered with sincere honesty of Self, made up of multiple *"selves,"* then it is from an [I–You][8] relationship that you are saying, "You are dying, but I could be too."

Whenever I visited Douglas, a seven-year-old who was suffering from a brain tumor, his mother would be sitting in the corner. She barely looked up at me when I entered, and she never acknowledged my entry with a greeting or words of good-bye when I left. During each visit, however, I walked over to Douglas, who would be sitting in a wheelchair with his upper body slumped over, got down on one knee so that we would be at eye level, took his hand or put my arm around his shoulder, and talked to him for a few minutes, usually about baseball. Before rising, I would give him a kiss on the forehead and tell him I would see him later in the week.

This went on for a few weeks in exactly the same way. There was never any acknowledgment of my presence or visit by Douglas's mother. One day, as I came onto the floor, I was greeted by a nurse who told me that Douglas had been discharged, but his mother had asked that I call her at home. I was surprised by this request, but I, of course, called anyway. After saying hello to each other, I asked her what I could do for her. She said, "I would like to ask you to officiate at my son's funeral when the time comes." After a moment of silence, I responded, "Of course I will, but I must tell you I am surprised by this request. With all my visits, I never thought we had a relationship." She then said, "That's where you are wrong, for we did." She then explained that as I accepted her in her anger at me, as God's representative, I gave her the space that she needed. I did not allow her anger to keep me away from expressing my care, love, and respect for her son. This was why she wanted me to be at his funeral, for him, and also for her.

The second imperative in caring for the sick and dying is always accepting others where they are, without negative judgment and with affirming love. This, too, is the manifestation of the [I–You] relationship. It says to the other Self: I am not here to make you in the image of myself, for, after all,

---

7. A rephrasing of Leviticus 19:18.
8. After Walter Kaufmann, in "I and You: A Prologue," in Martin Buber, *I and Thou: A New Translation* (New York: Simon and Schuster, 1970); see also in this book "A Guide for the Reader," p. 2, n. 3.

only God can do that; rather, I am here to accept you for your Self, wherever and however that is. This is difficult for many caregivers, even those who are truly caring, for we think of ourselves as doing "for others," helping them to get to the place others think they should be, rather than just "letting them be" in the place where they are. However, to let them be where they are is the greatest gift one person can give to another. It is the basis of all mutuality of relationships, for it declares, "I am with you. I am not here to remake you."

Martin Buber wrote:

> A being to whom I really say "You" is not for me in this moment my object, about whom I observe this and that or whom I put to this or that use, but my partner who stands over against me in his own right and existence and yet is related to me in his life.[9]

What the sick and dying truly need is a partner with them on their journey. To be this partner is a great *mitzvah,* probably the greatest we can offer to someone else.

---

9. Martin Buber, "Responsa," ed. and trans. Maurice Friedman, in *Philosophical Interrogations,* ed. Sydney and Beatrice Rome (New York: Holt, Rinehart and Winston, 1964), p. 21.

33

The *Vidui:* Jewish Relational Care for the Final Moments of Life

Alison Jordan
Stuart Kelman

Jewish tradition responds to the death of a Jew with well-defined structures of liturgy and ritual. From the moment we learn of a death, through the following hours, days, months, and years, specific words, such as the mourner's *kaddish,*[1] and specific actions, that is, the laws of mourning, are provided for the bereaved and for the extended Jewish community. The system of laws and customs is complex, and specific to relationship and time.

In contrast to the detailed *Halachah,*[2] which sets procedures for mourning, relatively few words and practices are associated with the end of life itself, and those which exist are not widely known or observed in modern American Jewish practice. Although the subject of death is of fundamental theological interest, and despite the inevitable confrontation of every human being with this highly charged emotional, physical, and spiritual passage, there is little Jewish structure to support us during this liminal period. Some questions to consider:

What does Judaism have to offer the person who is dying?
How do biblical images and rabbinic ideas affect our use of prayer and ritual during the time preceding death?
Why are there few specific prayers or behaviors currently in use for those who are in the presence of one who is dying?
What liturgy or ritual can be of help for loved ones, caregivers, and clergy?
How may we acknowledge the presence of God at the bedside?

---

1. Doxology recited often throughout the service, and also said by mourners: "May God's name be hallowed and exalted throughout the world."
2. For traditional Jews, the proper path of religious observance.

Based on our own values and experiences at the bedside, we are concerned with the relative absence of words and practices to accompany the *goseis*[3] and those in the presence of the dying. We will attempt to address these concerns through presentation of traditional and innovative prayer forms that may be of help as death approaches.

We begin with a brief look at some biblical and rabbinic responses to the final moments of life, seeking insight into traditional practices. We will discuss the *Vidui*[4] and the recitation of Psalms, as well as noting positive uses of silence and apparent silences of omission. We will conclude with some traditional as well as innovative approaches to Jewish practice in the final moments of life.

Torah and Midrash: Silence and Words

"Vayidom Aharon"[5]—"and Aharon[6] was silent." Not only is there a deafening silence as Aharon's sons, Nadav and Avihu, are consumed in the fire brought forth by God, but even Aharon, the bereaved father, is silent in the face of the loss of his children. One might say his silence is an appropriate response, perhaps the only response, to the tragedy of the death of two children. In fact, the silence of Aharon is traditionally given as the reason for not speaking upon entering a house of mourning. This understanding gives legitimacy to silence as the most appropriate response to grief. It reflects a sensitivity to the bereaved, to be spared the distraction of mundane talk in a time of unspeakable loss.

Interestingly, Moshe does speak to Aharon immediately following the deaths[7] and at least one *midrash*[8] challenges silence as the only response to bearing witness to death. This *midrash*[9] puts words into the mouth of Aharon. He cries out to God:

> All Israel saw You at the Red Sea as well as Sinai without suffering injury; but my sons, whom you ordered to dwell in the Tabernacle—a place that any layman may not enter without being punished by

---

3. The dying person.
4. Deathbed confessional.
5. Leviticus 10:3. Translation of Torah text by Everett Fox, *The Five Books of Moses: A New Translation, with Introductions, Commentary, and Notes* (New York: Schocken, 1995), p. 548.
6. Names of the biblical figures follow Everett Fox's translation and are closer to the original Hebrew. Fox, *The Five Books of Moses,* p. 548 and throughout the book.
7. Leviticus 10:3.
8. P'sikta Rabbati 47, 189b.
9. Discovery of meanings other than literal in the Bible.

death—my sons entered the Tabernacle to behold Your strength and Your might, and they died!

This cry is not the silent acceptance of a divine decree that some interpret from the biblical passage, but rather an expression of outrage and a bold questioning of God. God immediately responds to Moshe (not to Aharon), saying, "Tell Aharon . . . I have shown you great favor and have granted you great honor through this, that your sons have been burnt." God proceeds with a detailed explanation through Moshe. Upon hearing Moshe's recitation of God's words, the bereaved Aharon offers praise and thanks to God "because Your loving-kindness is better than life."

Perhaps God's explanation helps Aharon; perhaps the very fact of God's hearing Aharon's pain soothes him; perhaps it is the nearness and compassion of his brother that brings comfort. The result is that Aharon, in the throes of grief and the midst of consolation, gives thanks to God.

In this same *midrash,* Moshe then offers consoling words of his own, saying, "Now I perceive that your sons were nearer to God than we," and these words: "sufficed to induce Aharon to control his grief . . . he silently bore the heavy blow of fate without murmur or lament." Whereupon God "rewarded Aharon for his silence by addressing him directly."

Indeed, God pronounces the essential rules and requirements that would keep Aharon and his surviving sons safe while uplifting him through conferring his priestly responsibility for the life and holiness of the tribe.[10] In this way, this *midrash* demonstrates a process of moving from stunned silence to the silence of acceptance and awe.

The *midrashic* Aharon, God, and Moshe are expressive and communicative. Aharon calls out in anger and confusion. God responds (albeit not making eye contact) with the person who holds Him accountable. Moshe, loving brother and faithful messenger of God, serves as a bridge between Aharon and God. Moshe facilitates Aharon's movement from alienation from God as arbitrary destroyer to restoration of the capacity to experience God as loving and just. The all-knowing and merciful God offers Aharon the Jewish context within which to cope with bereavement.

Aharon was silent. His first reaction was not *"baruch dayan haemet,"*[11]— our tradition's prescribed response upon learning of a death. Rather, the *midrash* reveals a much more complex experience. Aharon called out in distress and received the magnificent gift of compassion and understanding before accepting God's judgment.

---

10. Leviticus 10:8.
11. Praised be the true judge.

As with Aharon's encounter with the death of his children, the death of Moshe[12] is a dramatic and pivotal moment, both for the man as well as in the story of the Jewish people. While the Torah offers significant narrative related to stages and events around the end of a life, it is spare in contrast to the many *midrashim* on the subject. Again, we find in the *midrash* an acknowledgment of the fullness and complexity of human response to death.

There are other such stories.[13] One example is the detailed description of the human response to the death of a beloved leader: shock, disbelief, a kind of seeking of the lost person.[14] Another is the extensive and poignant treatment of the difficulty Moshe encounters facing the end of life and the many interactions necessary to help him come to terms with letting go.[15] Yet another is the not so well-known *midrashic* response of God, which appropriates and therefore highlights human reaction by claiming that the death of Moshe is God's own loss, not Joshua's.[16]

In addition to the biblical blessing that Moshe confers upon the people, Moshe, in an extended *midrash*,[17] asks forgiveness, saying, "You have had much to bear from me in regard to the fulfillment of the Torah and its commandments, but forgive me now." The people reply, "Our teacher, our lord, it is forgiven." In turn, the people ask forgiveness, saying, "We have often kindled your anger and have laid many burdens upon you, but forgive us now." Moshe says, "It is forgiven." Toward the end, Moshe offers encouragement to the people, who fear life without him. Moshe says, "Put your trust in Him through whose word arose the world, for He lives and endures in all eternity. Whether you are laden with sin, or not, 'pour your heart before Him,' and turn to Him." The people of Israel respond, "The Lord, He is God; the Lord, He is God. God is our strength and our refuge." In the final moments, Moshe and the people weep, together.

Liturgy and Ritual in the Final Moments of Life

We are not sure why our tradition developed explicit requirements for mourners but did not create a vibrant liturgical response to death, even

---

12. Deuteronomy 34:5.

13. Many of these *midrashim* may be found in Louis Ginzberg's seven-volume *Legends of the Jews* (Baltimore, MD: Johns Hopkins University, 1928), as well as the shorter version, *Legends of the Bible* (Philadelphia, PA: Jewish Publication Society, 1975). For further commentaries, see Michael Swirsky, *At the Threshold* (Northvale, NJ: Jason Aronson, 1996).

14. Sifre Deuteronomy 357; Midrash Tannaim 227.

15. See Ginzberg, *Legends of the Bible,* pp. 471-506.

16. Midrash Tannaim 225; ARN 12:51 and 57:1; Sifre Devarim 305.

17. Midrash Tannaim 14-15.

though the *midrash* and Torah (e.g., the aging and death of Yaaqov) clearly sensed the need. In our experience, we have found that people seek appropriate words, formulas, and prayers to accompany them during this emotionally challenging time.

Prayer is an attempt to establish relationship. We believe that prayer helps many people feel closer to God and those who came before them. We are in a position to facilitate relationship by our presence, through sharing information about Jewish tradition and offering to pray together.

Prayer may be silent and personal, as was possibly the experience of Aharon, as well as public and formalized, as in liturgy that addresses particular moments in life.

The Jewish tradition suggests the recitation of specific Psalms as a source of comfort in times of crisis. Verses from Psalms such as 49,[18] 42,[19] 63,[20] as well as the familiar Psalm 23[21] stand as well-known examples. We would add Psalms 30[22] and 90[23] as well. In our practice, we encourage people to find other Psalms that are particularly meaningful to them.

Finally, the rabbis created a form of liturgy called the *Vidui,* the core of which is the notion that death is an atonement for sin.[24] As we have seen in the *midrash* about the death of Moshe, interactions around forgiveness and parting are complex and multilayered. We propose additional forms of the traditional *Vidui,* which take into account the *goseis,* those standing near the bedside, and the caregivers.

Standing by the bedside, we engage the *goseis* in conversation, finding an appropriate way, based on the dialogue, to acknowledge the reality of the situation, that is, that the end of life is near. Often, a handshake or a touch is enough to begin this process, recognizing that our intention is to bring comfort and is not seen as contributing to the hastening of death. This is a time to help the *goseis* say whatever is on his or her mind. It may be about fear, about unfinished business, be about leaving loved ones behind, or about readiness to die.

---

18. "But God will redeem my life from the clutches of Sheol, for God will take me. Selah." Psalms 49:16.

19. "Like a hind crying for water, my soul cries for You, Oh God. My soul thirsts for God, the living God; Oh when will I come to appear before God!" Psalms 42:2.

20. "For Your loving-kindness is better than life; my lips shall praise You." Psalms 63:4.

21. "Though I walk through the valley of the shadow of death, I fear no harm, for You are with me." Psalms 23:4.

22. "Adonai, my God, I cried out to You, and You healed me." Psalms 30:3.

23. "Teach us to treasure our days, that we may obtain a heart of wisdom." Psalms 90:12.

24. Sanhedrin 43b.

In the course of this intimate conversation, we talk about the existence of the *Vidui* in our tradition and ascertain if some form of the *Vidui* would be appropriate to recite together with the *goseis*. At this moment others may be in the room or a waiting area and we help the *goseis* articulate a preference for privacy or for gathering others to the bedside. Before we begin, we state quite firmly that the purpose of this prayer is to bring closure to this part of one's existence, and that in no way does it imply that death will immediately follow. We encourage the person to make use of the vehicle of the *Vidui* for bringing closure to life, as Jews have done for centuries. However, when individuals do not wish to recite the *Vidui,* their wishes are respected and we try to assist in bringing closure in a way that brings comfort. When the *goseis* does wish to recite the *Vidui,* the next step is to determine which version from those which follow is most appropriate and whether the language to be used will be Hebrew or English. If the *goseis* cannot engage in this kind of decision making, we choose a version and language based on our best understanding of this person. If the *goseis* is unable to speak, it is traditionally appropriate to recite it for him or her as a proxy. At the conclusion of saying the *Vidui*, we sit at the bedside to respond to any needs of the *goseis* that arise before we leave.

Versions of the Vidui

This traditional version is adapted from the Hertz Siddur:[25]

> I acknowledge before You, *Adonai* my God and God of my ancestors, that both my cure and my death are in Your hands. May it be Your will to send me a perfect healing. Yet, if my death be fully determined by You, I will in love accept it at Your hand. May my death be an atonement for all my sins, iniquities, and transgressions of which I have been guilty against You. Bestow on me the abounding happiness that is treasured up for the righteous. Make known to me the path of life: in Your presence is the fullness of joy; in Your right hand bliss forevermore. You, who are the father of the fatherless and judge of the widow, protect my beloved kindred with whose soul my own is knit. Into Your hand I commend my spirit: You have redeemed me, *Adonai,* God of truth—Amen and Amen.

> *Adonai* is ruler; *Adonai* was ruler; *Adonai* will be ruler forever and ever (to be said three times).

---

25. Dr. Joseph Hertz, *The Authorised Daily Prayer Book* (New York: Bloch Publishing Co., 1959), p. 1065.

Blessed be God's name whose glorious kingdom is forever and ever
(to be said three times).
Adonai is God (to be said seven times).
Hear, O Israel: *Adonai* is our God, *Adonai* is One.

Th following is an alternative and more contemporary version of the
Vidui, which includes the morning liturgy to emphasize the continuity of
living and dying:[26]

VIDUI #1

I acknowledge before You, my God and God of my people,
that my life and my death are in Your hand.
The soul you placed within me is pure:
You breathed it into me.
You have guarded it all these days;
You take it from me;
You will restore it in time to come.

In Your hand are the souls of all who live and die
and the breath of every being.
Into Your hand I release my spirit.
I am thankful before You, my God, I have treasured my days.
Sustained by times I lived well,
touching others with goodness and beauty.
I am glad for choices that lifted me up,
and for the opportunity to be a spark of light to the world.
I am grateful for the help and kindness that has always accompanied me.

I regret the times I did not choose well:
times I was too hurt or frightened to see my way,
times I was too confused or angry to follow my best intentions.
My heart aches for words I could not say
and for those better left unspoken; for actions I could not take
and for those I might rather not have taken.

Comfort me with forgiveness, *Adonai,*
and let me be remembered for the good.
Gather me to my people,
and grant me my portion in *Gan Eden.*[27]

---

26. This, and all original prayers in this chapter, copyright 2002-2004 Alison Jordan.
27. The Garden of Eden; in Middle English, Paradise.

My God, please sustain my family.
In Your endless compassion
please bless each one and protect them.
Bring comfort to my loved ones and to all who mourn,
and let their spirits be renewed in the fullness of your love.
Sh'ma Yisrael, Adonai Eloheinu, Adonai Echad.

The following is a more meditative version that does not include traditional Jewish God language:

VIDUI #2

breathing in breathing out
contemplating living dying living dying

wonder *arises passes* sadness *lingers fades* anger *flares softens*
grief gratitude terror *here now floating*
every moment   each breath   new

suddenly restless frantic grasping
thoughts feelings crowd collide
TRAPPED
only dread only sadness only anger
how can I surrender into something I don't understand!
how can I die?
meet the unknown? say good-bye? leave everything!
words spoken and left unsaid,
mistakes made and actions not taken?
confused and afraid, alone, I do not feel ready to give up this life

seeking forgiveness and reconciliation, an open heart,
I return to breath clear light of awareness
gratitude for times of wholeness
knowing in my truest heart that everything living will also die
my self has dis/appeared in the roar of the ocean,
crashing waves gentle waves foam returning to sea
dis/appeared in the forest, streams steam ancient moss fallen leaves rocks
breathing in
continuous embrace
separate and connected
my self has dis/appeared in love and in the colors of the sky

recalling these things (I) am one with all that changes

have been am now forever will be part of the great mystery
that was is will be
no more trembling I, no fear, just each breath entering
into Breath returning, reentering the all,
it has always been so! deathless! One!

In the following version, the *goseis* has an opportunity to speak out loud
in the presence of loved ones, who may join in responsively:

VIDUI #3

I give thanks, Infinite Spirit, Undying Hope.
You return my soul to me faithfully, I am grateful.

I know that life and death are in your hand;
in your hand are the souls of all who live and die,
the spirit of every being.

In your embrace I seek refuge for my restless spirit.

Sometimes I am not ready to let go.
In distress I think: I have not completed what was set out for me to do.
I long for connection with my God, myself, and with others.

Please hear my prayer, comfort me in your embrace.

Although I have meditated on the mystery of life and death, still,
sometimes I feel afraid.
As I contemplate dying, stay with me, be my help!
I am calling to You, be near me!
Reveal to me the Oneness, release me from fear.

Please hear my prayer, comfort me with love.

O God, grant me a healing of peace.
Help me to turn from my mistakes,
both intentional and unintentional,
to return with a whole and unburdened heart.
Help me to forgive and be forgiven; let me be remembered for the good.

Please hear my prayer, comfort me with compassion.

Kiss me and release me;
gather me to my people,
guide me lovingly into the shelter of your peace.
Grant me my portion in the fullness of your love.

Please hear my prayer, lift me and deliver me!

My God, bring comfort to my loved ones
and renew their spirits in compassion.
I am grateful,
Eternal Spirit, Keeper of all souls.

Sh'ma Yisrael, Adonai Eloheinu, Adonai Echad.

We move now to give voice to the feelings of those standing near the bedside of the *goseis:*

MI SHEBEIRACH
FOR THOSE GATHERED AT THE BEDSIDE

May the One who blessed Abraham with seedlings
as countless as the stars and infinite as the sands
bless us, the generations of the blessing.

May the One who comforted Abraham, Sarah, Hagar, Ishmael, and Isaac
comfort us now, and hear us in our distress.

May we, too, be remembered with compassion, laughter, and miracles,
and be blessed to welcome the visiting angels in our midst.

May we be like Abraham when he knew grief.
Abraham wept out loud and mourned for Sarah,
he praised her and he buried her.
And it is written of Abraham: "He was blessed with everything."

May the One who blessed Abraham, who promised Abraham:
"You shall come to your ancestors in peace,"
grant that (_____, and) each of us in our time
shall come to our ancestors in peace.

As we are gathered together today
may we be gathered someday in *Gan Eden*.
May it be so, and let us say, Amen.

Often, the mourner who has had a difficult relationship with the deceased
faces particular challenges during the bereavement period. The following
addresses this situation:

VIDUI #4

FOR MOURNERS OF PAINFUL RELATIONSHIPS

My God and God of the generations of my people,
I am distressed and confused.

> *Hear my prayer, answer me with compassion.*

During my lifetime I have experienced misunderstanding, hurt,
and harm in my relationship with _____, who is dying (has died).
Though I have sought help and understanding, I have not found
peace nor recovered from painful experiences and memories.
I have been unable to forgive _____; neither have I found the ways
to forgive myself for my own confusion, anger, and suffering.
Some days I feel no hope for connection and reconciliation.

> *This is a painful passage;*
> *I have no answers, but my questions cry out:*

How can I approach this period of mourning?
How shall I mark this death?
How can I fulfill my obligation as a _____ to one
    who has been a source of my grief?
How can I find solace in my community if I feel different
    from other mourners?
Without a community, where will I find my help?
With whom can I share this particular pain?
How can I be most true to myself, for my own sake?
What do I need at this time?

> *From a place of narrowness I cry out; please free me!*
> *Breathe into me the breath of healing spaciousness.*[28]

---

28. Psalms 118:5.

Meditation on prayer and Psalms can lead to new openings and consolation. Listen for poetry/liturgy that touches you. Saying *kaddish* with others can support the ongoing process of putting the relationship to rest. These passages from the weekday *Amidah*[29] and Psalm 19 may be helpful:

> Sustainer of the living with kindness,
> supporter of the fallen, healer of the sick,
> Bring me near, wholehearted;
> help me find compassion and reconciliation.
> Look upon my pain and release me.
> Heal me and I shall be healed, deliver me and I shall be delivered.
> I am thankful for my life
> and for the daily miracles that accompany all of us
> morning, noon, and night.
> May I, among the mourners of Zion and Jerusalem,
> be blessed with comfort and peace.
> Guard my tongue from harmful speech,
> and help me to ignore the speech of those who speak ill of me.
> May my soul be humble and compassionate
> and my heart be open to the wisdom of Torah.

> *Errors, who can comprehend? From hidden faults cleanse me.*
> *Also from willful sins spare your servant, let them not rule me.*
> *Then I will be strong and will be cleansed of my transgression.*
> > *May the words of my mouth*
> > *and the meditations of my heart*
> > *be acceptable to you, my rock and my redeemer.*[30]
> **Sh'ma Yisrael, Adonai Eloheinu, Adonai Echad.**

Once death has occurred, the need is certainly present for expression of grief and the initial emotions following the loss of a loved one. The following is appropriate here:

VIDUI #5 FOR MOURNERS

My God and God of the generations of my people,
please hear me in my distress:

---

29. The eighteen, the silent devotion, on weekdays consisting of eighteen prayers, hence the name.

30. Psalms 19:13-15.

I am grieving for _____.
whom you gave life and length of days,
but I was not ready for _____ to die.
Though I know I must eventually live with this bitter loss,
today I feel crushed,
and cry out for just one more moment with _____!
I yearn to be in the presence of my loved one.
Help me to reflect on what was left unfinished.
To say what I haven't said, to hear what I didn't hear.
My heart is heavy with grief, and regret, and full with love.

_____, let me talk to you now as I grieve for you.
Allow me to feel you with me and honor you.

Please forgive me for what I didn't say, and for what I may have said
intentionally or unintentionally that caused you pain.

Please forgive me for what I didn't do, and for what I may have done
knowingly or unknowingly that caused you pain.

Forgive me for the ways I held myself apart and didn't know you.

Release me from the pain of my failures in compassion;
for not forgiving you, and myself, when there were hurts between us.

For the times of disconnection I want to say out loud that I am sorry.

Remembering the good times brings you closer, it soothes me.
May the love in my heart serve as atonement and reconciliation,
bringing comfort to our souls.
I am grateful for our lives intertwined.

I pray for the strength to live each day without you,
to comfort others, and to honor your memory
with *tzedakah*[31] and deeds of loving-kindness.

God grant you your portion in *Gan Eden,*
and give you shelter, and give you peace.

---

31. Charity.

May the endless source of being bring comfort to every soul and renew our spirits in compassion.

I am grateful, infinite spirit, keeper of all souls.

Sh'ma Yisrael, Adonai Eloheinu, Adonai Echad.

34

Jewish Relational Care with the Grieving

Mel Glazer

Jackie called me last week to schedule an appointment. When I asked what we were going to talk about, she told me that her mother had died a year ago, and she was still having "problems." I told her that I would be honored to see her, and that we would spend an hour together to see if we both thought we could work on helping her. She thanked me and we set a date to meet.

Oh, Lord, I thought, not another "mother" issue. As I began to think about Jackie's mother, my thoughts were drawn once again to my own mother. This is a reaction that is, I am sure, shared by many. Whenever I officiate at the cemetery, those present inevitably begin to think back and recall the last time they were there, or they begin reminiscing about their own loved ones. Our minds are associative; we connect the present to the past, which is why we are often asked to chant *El Malei*[1] for other relatives.

My mother and I had a typical Jewish mother-son relationship, which means that it was rocky, with many complicated "issues." She died almost thirty years ago, after a long illness. I knew for sure that while I would be speaking to Jackie about her mother, I would be thinking about mine too. The two mother issues, hers and mine, are clearly related. I needed to be clear about my own inner relationship, before I could begin to help Jackie with her mother.

I am a Congregational rabbi and a grief recovery specialist. I began this work, I now realize, as a response to my own parents' deaths. Call it transference, if you like, but it is my reality. In my rabbinic practice, I find myself

---

1. Prayer offered in memory of the deceased: "Exalted, compassionate God, grant infinite rest in your sheltering presence . . ."

constantly returning to my personal life experiences as I try to help those who will need me to deal with their own life baggage. The challenge in all the grief counseling I do is to keep the focus on "their" grief because Mom is sitting right there with me, too, wanting to speak. I always experience a tug-of-war between my professional head, which knows what is needed in this setting, and my personal heart, which teases me all the time and reminds me that my grief work is never ever finished. Personal and professional issues blur. I must be vigilant not to bring my mother to the table as we discuss Jackie's mother; that would be unprofessional in light of my charge to focus on her well-being. Though we have inherited a perspective that a "counselor" needs to be a blank sheet, yet my openness about my own grief may indeed be useful in the healing relationship. But given the nature of that relationship, I am charged, when she's present with me, with attending to *her* needs, not my own. I need to use my own inner processes with great discretion. At the same time, I constantly keep in mind that, as I counsel Jackie, I cannot deny my own experiences. As Rabbi Jack Riemer likes to say, "I preach to myself because I need to hear what I have to say. If anyone else wants to listen, *mah tov.*"[2] It is the same for me. First, I have to be clear in my own head and heart before I can help Jackie. My "job" is to assist her in grieving her mother, to keep the focus on her loss. Nevertheless, her grieving brings back my own grieving; it reminds me that I, too, have more work to do. Helping her helps me. My challenge is, on the one hand, to keep our respective griefs separate and, on the other hand, to know that they are related.

How to Do Relational Grief Caregiving

When Jackie arrives, we sit together in my study around a small and comfortable conference table. No desk and couch for me—they are much too intimidating. We are not here to discuss a business venture, nor to do psychotherapy. I am not a therapist; I am a rabbi, with extensive expertise in grief recovery, and there is a difference. We are here to create a special relationship that will lead to the beginnings of healing. Sitting around the table, we are equals, two children of God who come together to grieve Jackie's mother. I always have a box of tissues available, so that Jackie will not be interrupted while she is crying.

My opening words are always "What happened?" She needs to talk; I need to listen. Most grief caregiving is reflective and responsive listening. Each of us needs a place where our voices can be heard, and, for reasons that I will elaborate upon later, our society is reticent about providing such

---

2. That's fine.

places. My study is a safe haven for Jackie, where she can tell me anything and everything, without fear of being censored or shut down. For an hour each session I will, as it were, create a container for her pain. I will allow her to share it and grieve it and come out the other side, hopefully hurting less and ready to reenter the world without paralyzing emotional, and sometimes physical, pain.

Jackie begins to talk to me about her mother's life and death, and as is common in mother-child relationships, all was not well. Numerous bumps and roadblocks arose along the way. She and her mother were sometimes at peace, but usually turbulent. I ask her why she is still bothered by something that happened a year ago, and she cannot answer. As we talk more over the next two weeks, I realize that Jackie came to me to grieve her mother's death, but, more important, to grieve the mother-daughter relationship that she never had. It was the lost opportunity for relationship, not the death, that Jackie was most grieving, and the sadness was that she had never been able to confront her mother about the lost hopes, dreams, and expectations. Jackie and her mother had lived a masked life, a life of pretending, and now that mother had died, Jackie is haunted by the superficiality of what has been, and the time that could not be recovered. Going back and living her life over with her mother is not an option. The past is now gone forever. Even worse, Jackie has not been able to voice any of her pain. This is what Jackie came to me to grieve.

I tell Jackie my favorite Zen story, the story that vividly illustrates my grief work: Two monks were traveling together in the rainy season. They came to a small creek, overflowing with heavy rains. There they saw a lovely young girl in a silk kimono, unable to cross. One of the monks offered to carry her across on his shoulder and did so. The monks walked on silently for a long time, until the other monk could not restrain himself and said, "We have been taught that it is forbidden to touch a woman. How could you so blatantly carry that girl on your shoulders?" The first monk replied, "Oh! I put that girl down a long time ago. Why are you still carrying her?"

Precisely. Jackie (and all the rest of us) is still lugging her mother around on her shoulders, and the weight is spiritually crushing. My task is to help Jackie "lay her gently down," not to forget about her mother, but to heal the pain of the past so that Jackie can move forward toward joy and happiness and fulfillment. I am Jackie's "hope giver."

The world is not an easy place for those who have lost someone or something dear to them. Loss shows up in many diverse forms: the death of a loved one, the loss of a job, moving from one city to another, the death of your first pet—these are all examples of life losses that are painful and leave us unaccountably numb.

Every transition in life involves a loss, and every loss is itself a transition to a new reality. We are aware of the inherently sad loss moments, such as funerals, but even joyous occasions, such as *bar mitzvahs,*[3] weddings, and college graduations, are grief experiences and must be seen through that lens. All of them have to do with letting go of children who will then begin to discover their own, new paths in the world. Letting go is tough, and no one does it easily. The past must be allowed to transform itself into the present, so that the future can be a joyful one. The river of life, with all its vicissitudes, will continue to flow. When I speak to brides and grooms, I spend most of the time asking them about their parents' ability to let go of them and allow them to find their own way in the world that they will now create together. It is normal for parents to want to hold on to their children forever; it is that desire to stop the flow which causes substantial, sometimes irreparable, damage to the new couple.

The world in which we live teaches us very well how to acquire things and relationships, but it does not teach us what to do when we lose them. Losses abound in our lives, and so we need to learn as much as possible about how to lose. I believe that loss is a painful gift and that many of life's most important lessons are learned only through loss. Our successes, although pleasurable for a while, serve mostly to feed our egos. From our losses we learn who we are; where our power and strength reside; what values matter most to us; and what we truly believe about life, hope, and God. Losses must be named and they must be blessed. There is nothing wrong about feeling pain; on the contrary, the ability to feel pain is the beginning of healing. We must help those for whom we provide care to identify and grapple with their losses; it is the only way to heal from them. We help them to become lighter because they can now compartmentalize their pain without its being all-controlling. Pain is normal; they are normal. They are scared of giving up that pain, however, because it has been their companion for so long. They are used to living with it, they are secure with the devil they know, and they are loath to exchange the known for the unknown. That, however, is exactly our holy task: to help them shift and redirect their ways of responding to death and loss, enabling them to embrace God's gifts of life and hope.

Positive Grief Language

What do we say when grievers come to talk? Rather than "preach" to them, we must help them find their authentic voice that reflects the painful

---

3. At age thirteen, a young person is obligated for the fulfillment of God's commands. The occasion is marked by being called to the reading of the Torah, and participating as an "adult" in the service.

feelings in their hearts. We rabbis like to solve problems, but grievers need much more than that from us; they need us to hear them, to validate and respect their feelings. Here are some suggestions on how best to do that.

My All-Time Favorite Beginning:
"What Happened?"

When we begin this way, we can be totally open to their agenda. The grief is theirs not ours, and so they will tell "the story," the way they want us to hear it. Until we hear what is in their hearts, we cannot be effective hope givers. Let them talk as long as they need. The main issues will soon surface, and you will be better able to respond to their needs. Pay attention to the major themes; try to make connections between the current loss and previous losses in their lives. Ask them about their childhood, and about their earliest life loss. Definite similarities will exist between previous losses and current ones. The way they handled early losses is precisely how they will handle current ones. People have loss ("leaving") styles, which do not change over their lifetimes, so that knowing details of grievers' early losses will help you help them.[4] Remember, their hearts are broken, not their heads. They "know" that when cancer comes, death often soon follows, and they "know" that ninety-year-olds are supposed to die. Speak to the heart— that is what is broken.

> What happened?
> You must feel so . . .
> > crushed; devastated; overwhelmed
> > heartsick; heartbroken; exhausted; painful
> > confused; drowning; trapped; scared
> > sad; lost; abandoned; numb; surprised
> > relieved that your loved one's pain is over
> I cannot imagine what that was like for you:
> > You really loved this person.
> > This was likely difficult for you.
> > It sounds so sad.
> > It sounds as if the illness lasted a long time.
> > You were so concerned with your loved one's well-being.
> > This person meant a lot to you.

---

4. To learn more about your own "leaving style," read Roy M. Oswald, *Running Through the Thistles: Terminating a Ministerial Relationship with a Parish* (Bethesda, MD: Alban Institute, 1978).

The very best thing you can *say* to grievers is, "Tell me a story about your loved one." The very best thing you can *do* for grievers is to give them a hug!

Negative Grief Language

In the first three days after a loss of any kind, 141 clichéd comments are heard by grievers. Out of those 141, 122 are unhelpful because they either give advice or appeal to the intellect. The intellect, the mind, is not broken; the heart is broken. To touch another's heart we must speak only the language of feelings. We should have learned all about grief when we were children, but we did not. What we did learn was how to avoid grief, how to pretend that loss does not hurt, when in fact it hurts plenty. No one truly understands the mystery of life and death, and so we cover up by attempting to intellectualize, which never suffices. These are some of the grief responses that the world has taught us to say when someone we know experiences a loss. None of them is helpful. Avoid them at all cost.

Negative Grief Language #1: "Don't Feel Bad "

> "She was sick for such a long time; it is better this way."
> "She is not suffering anymore."
> "You did the best you could."
> "He was such a good person."
> "You shouldn't feel guilty."

Such comments are wrong because feeling bad is a necessary first step in grieving and healing; thus, we must never deny the feelings of hurt and loss. When we ask grievers, "How are you feeling?" and they say, "Fine," do not believe them. They want to be fine, but right now it is difficult for them. Their hearts are shattered, and they want and need us to empathize with them. Our empathy is the first step to helping them feel whole again.

Negative Grief Language #2: "I Know How You Feel"

> "My mother died from the same disease."
> "I know, it is a terrible hospital."
> "Dad had the same symptoms before he died."

Comments such as these are wrong because every single death is personal and unique and is mourned 100 percent. My mother's death hurt me just as much as your mother's death hurt you. No comparisons are possible where grief is concerned. You cannot know how anyone else feels after the death of a loved one, so do not pretend. "I know how you feel" takes the power of grief away from grievers; it diminishes their right of ownership over their personal struggles. In their worlds, which have lurched out of control, they need to assert at least the semblance of having some control, even if only over their personal grief. This is why mourners stand for *kaddish;*[5] it is a statement: "This is my pain. I rise so that you can recognize me and support me and comfort me." Where they have no ultimate control, still they have self-dignity. Allow them to "own" their grief; this is a gift you can give them.

Negative Grief Language #3: "Replace It"

> "Don't worry. You can always get another one."
> "We'll get you another one tomorrow."
> "There are plenty of fish in the sea."
> "You are still young. You'll find somebody else."

Such sentiments are wrong because they totally ignore the initial grief response, which is numbness. Aharon's silence, *"Vayidom Aharon,"*[6] at the death of his sons, Nadav and Avihu, is the typical first response to death. Whether death comes without warning, as in Aharon's case, or is expected makes little difference. None of us is quite prepared; none of us knows what to say. Even when death marks the end of a life of pain and suffering, even when the Angel of Death is not always an enemy, we are still numb. The present must be attended to; the future must wait its turn. To immediately concentrate on the future, without processing the loss feelings swirling around the griever's heart, makes attending to the grief even more difficult. Remember how badly you felt right after the loss of _____ (fill in the blank)? It hurt, it was serious, and you were in no mood for anyone to tell you that "the next one" would be better.

Negative Grief Language #4: "Grieve Alone"

> "You just need to be alone for a while, and you will be fine."
> "Go to your room and cry. Nobody wants to hear about it."

---

5. Doxology recited often throughout the service, and also said by mourners: "May God's name be hallowed and exalted throughout the world."
6. Leviticus 10:3; Aharon was silent.

Such statements are wrong because, in fact, the very best treatment we can offer grievers is to bring them into relationship with others who are in pain. This, as we all know, is the power of the daily *minyan*.[7] Most everyone in attendance is part of a magical grief recovery club, a community where feelings can freely surface without fear of rejection or embarrassment. The camaraderie matters to the mourners; it is an essential healing ingredient, which is probably why so many mourners have a difficult time stopping saying *kaddish*. It also explains why so many mourners continue to be "regulars" even after the eleven months are over. When we are together with those who share our healing journey, somehow the trip goes easier. Our synagogues benefit from the presence of the mourners; they help make up our *minyan;* they need us and we need them. To mourn alone is impossible; it cannot happen. As children we were taught to keep quiet about our feelings, especially the painful ones. Now we know that is an incorrect response. Mourners need to talk; our job as rabbis is to help them relate to others who can listen. Death leads to community, and community leads to healing.

Negative Grief Language #5: "Time Heals"

> "Just give it time, and you will be fine."
> "You'll feel better soon."
> "It's been a year. You should be over it by now."

Such comments are wrong because grief recovery happens when time is filled with recovery actions. Mourners will be unable to progress along the recovery journey without being conscious of the goals that must be achieved. Those who are grieving must first make the decision to heal, and they must partner that decision with specific, definite healing acts. Otherwise, they will remain in the same emotional place, in a holding pattern that will lead them nowhere. On every birthday we get older, whether we consciously choose to or not, but if grievers choose not to heal, they will remain in exactly the same place, similar to a jetliner stranded on the runway, waiting to take off. While there is no clock for the soul, and ultimate healing takes as long as it needs to, grievers must make a commitment to heal or nothing can happen.

---

7. Technically, the quorum of ten Jewish adults required for public prayer; in this instance, the daily service attended by mourners for eleven months after their loss.

Negative Grief Language #6: "You Must Be Strong"

"Your family needs you."
"If the children see you acting strong, then they'll be strong."
"You can't fall apart now."

Why is this wrong? When my father died, Uncle Jack said to me, "Melvin, you are the man of the house now. You have to take care of the family." I was all of twelve years old! I understood nothing, only that my father had died, and I had no idea what to do. What did he mean? Should I cry? Take charge of the house? What? I didn't understand any of this, nor did my mother or my sister or brother. I did know my feelings, even if I could not express them: despair, fear, loneliness, childlike depression. What I wanted to do was get in bed, cover up under the blankets, and never come out again. I wasn't interested in seeing anyone or talking to anyone. It fascinates me that at that precise moment, when all mourners want to do is disappear, Judaism says that they must eat and be with people, for otherwise they are liable to cut themselves off permanently from all those who care about them. *S'udat havra'ah*[8] returns mourners to the world of the living and allows them, forces them (!), to be cared for by those who love them. This is a time to trust and to be nourished by others. But "be strong"? Not a chance!

Negative Grief Language #7: "Keep Busy"

"Go on a cruise. You won't think about it."
"Go back to work. It will keep your mind off of it."
"Volunteer for lots of organizations. You'll feel much better."

Such advice is wrong because, in our world, we stay well longer thanks to better treatments, heightened medical intervention, and advanced hospital care. As a result, death arrives later for most than it once did. When the final illness comes, families often sit a "virtual *shivah*"[9] for extended periods of time. The relatives are weary, exhausted, and, after the funeral, immediately ready to reenter the world of the living. They sometimes think that their debt to their loved one has been paid in full over the sometimes

---

8. Meal provided for mourners by sympathetic neighbors on return from the funeral; the meal of health and consolation.

9. The seven-day (hence, *shivah*, Hebrew for seven) period of mourning, following interment, spent at home receiving visiting consolers. Called "sitting *shivah*," it is one of the great inventions of Judaism.

months and years before death arrived. How many folks do we know who do not sit *shivah,* but who go right back to work as if nothing important has happened? Nevertheless, value exists in stopping to reflect on the person who has left this world. We may miss the one who has died, but what we are truly missing is that special relationship we had with that person. With death comes the end of a degree of intimacy that will not ever be repeated in quite the same way. Each relationship is unique and must be mourned as unique. Often we think we need not pause to reflect upon these relationships, but we are wrong. They must be given our attention; that is why we sit *shivah,* even if the death has taken a long time. To go back to work immediately not only ignores this truth but also postpones the inevitable grief that will come. That is in part why it took a whole year for Jackie to come to see me after her mother had died.

Negative Grief Language #8: "It Was God's Will"

> "God needed her in heaven more than we did on earth."
> "She's one of God's angels now."
> "We should never question the ways of God."

Such explanations are wrong because they often elicit this response: "Then I hate God." If we hate God, we cannot call upon God for help. If God is the problem, God cannot also be the solution. Never put anyone in that position! When they start to ask why God allowed this, I turn the focus onto their feelings instead and say, "It sure hurts a lot, doesn't it," and give them a hug.[10]

Helping Children Grieve

This is the overriding principle with children: "If it's unmentionable, it's unmanageable."[11] Children need to know that they are an important part of the family, with rights and privileges that they are allowed to express. When death visits a home, it visits children as well, and they must be included in the final arrangements. Children have a pivotal need to focus on their experience; they need to be paid attention to when death enters their lives. They also need to know that they are safe, that they can share feelings and fears without being shunned or silenced. Home must be a place where children

---

10. Advice from my colleague Rabbi Richard Plavin, Jewish Theological Seminary of America, Rabbinical School Senior Homiletics Class, 1974.

11. Maria Trozzi, *Talking with Children About Loss* (New York: Berkley Publishing Group, 1999), Chapter 17, p. 271.

can talk about anything, where nothing is so sad or terrible that they cannot discuss it with their parents. Such openness makes a permanent, large-scale, and wide-ranging difference in their lives, allowing them to survive the family crisis and remain intact. In addition, this openness helps them learn to manage *all* of their normal fears, and they become stronger and more resilient throughout their lives as a result. Children will eventually become adults, but they will hold on to their first death experiences for as long as they live. The way they see early losses "handled" by their family members will become the way they respond to every subsequent loss. That is why the first experience of death is of such importance; its impact will remain with them long after childhood is over.

This learning experience can be enhanced by encouraging children to attend funerals and cemetery services. Children who do attend funerals accompanied by their parents will feel safe and unafraid; they will begin to intuit that death is a part of life that holds no fear, only sadness. Children (older than four or five) who do not attend funerals might have nightmares imagining what went on at the cemetery. As we know, the fantasy is usually worse than the reality, but children need to be present to find this out for themselves. Another danger is that children will feel left out and begin to wonder why they are not included in this critical family event.

Before each funeral, I invite children to a private room at the funeral chapel and I explain to them exactly what will happen at the funeral. I have invited grandchildren to write something about their grandparents to be read at the funeral by them or by an older relative, or to draw a picture to be placed in the coffin, or to be in charge of giving out *kippot*[12] at the service. At the cemetery I ask them if they have any questions for me. This keeps them involved and also models to their parents the appropriate way of dealing with death, in as straightforward and honest a way as possible. When we take care of the children, we also take care of their parents, who are always afraid and unlettered in the ways of appropriate grief response.

Our Jewish rituals empower us. Although we have little power over death, we have much control over how we respond to it. We use Judaism's rituals of death and mourning to support children who are in serious pain and unable to know how to express that pain. As we teach children about death and the proper response to death, so we are preparing them for the next death and the one after that. Each time death visits, they will know how to respond. We can literally save their lives and change the way of the world at the same time.

What a blessing!

---

12. Skullcaps, known in vernacular Yiddish as *yarmulkes*, worn when involved in acts of holiness or worship.

Frames for Blessing All *"Selves"*
As [Breath-Taking⇔Models of Divinity]

Jack H Bloom

Blessings are a crucial part of Jewish relational care. This chapter includes poems useful as blessings. The editor hopes to transform this chapter into a booklet for wider use and distribution by Jewish and non-Jewish caregivers alike.

The majority of the following blessings were written by the editor and so are presented without attribution. Originating over the years as the text on the editor's New Year's greetings, these blessings use various parts of the body as starting points.

The other poems, readings, and songs attributed to other authors have touched the editor deeply and so find their way into this chapter, which my editor, in her inimitable fashion, originally referred to as the "appendix."

In the beginning, only one person was created
a demonstration of God's greatness.
A human being mints many coins from a single mold
all are duplicates
interchangeable with one another.
Yet, God creates everyone in the mold of the first person
there are no duplicates
each human being is unique.
Therefore
each and every one of us is obligated to affirm
For my sake, the world was created.

Sanhedrin 4:5
Translation by Jack H Bloom

To begin
from the beginning

And so—be blessed anew

In the dark, the party over
the trumpets having taken leave of the violins
the midnight watch saluting the morning dew
we long to awaken on the morrow
with a new song in our heart.

To sing our song with fervor
to sing our song through pain
to hear the echo of our unfettered spirit
a flute's melody on the morning wind . . .

Hebrew Lyrics by Naomi Shemer
Translation by Jack H Bloom

Ain't no sense in worrying about things you got control over, 'cause if you got control over them, ain't no sense worrying about them.

And there ain't no sense worrying about things you got no control over, 'cause if you got no control over them, ain't no sense in worrying about them.

Mickey Rivers

To know that difference is
to know a difference that in truth
makes a difference in how
we live with each other and the world around us.

May knowing the difference be your blessing.

A PARABLE

A man is lost in the forest. He has been wandering many days
and nights and cannot find his way. Finally he meets another
man—and says to him: "My friend, I am lost. I have been trying to find the way for many days and nights, but I cannot.
Can you show me the way?"

The other man answers: "I too am lost. Yet I can tell you this:
Do not go the way I have gone—that way does not lead any-
where. Let us search for the way together."

> *Rabbi Hazyim of Zanz (nineteenth century)*
> *Translation by Jack H Bloom*

Since it is unlikely that we will be out of the woods
this moment
let this amongst all needs be our desire:

That traveling the road to we know not where
we go side by side, hand in hand, heart to heart
—alone yet together—
and so lighten our steps and brighten our days.

BREATH

Out of breath from the chase
endless demands breathing down our neck
we suspend our breath in fear
breathless in the commotion

In a single breath both proud and humble
"not worth it" we mumble under our breath
yet dare not breathe a word of it

Take a breather and
breathe new life into your Being
giving yourself and others room to breathe
letting each breath be a blessing

Embrace your breath and affirm:

God the breath You have given me is pure
From first to last
mark of my life
source of my being
breadth of my existence
because of Your breath I am
Breathe new life into me
Let every breath confirm my Being
a [Breath-Taking⇔Model of Divinity]

MIND

Hope you don't mind my
reminding you of what's on my mind
though it may boggle your mind
you are modeled after and molded by Divinity
and so embrace multiple minds

Some say
pay him no mind
that is only a mind game
it is mindless to think that
Mind you—
make up your mind! Now!

Never mind what they say
while mindful of others
keep an open mind
to all that is on your mind
the presence of mind
to speak your mind
even from the back of your mind.

Put your mind at ease
bearing in mind that
your mind is yours
you can change your mind

Keep in mind that it is
mind expanding and life enhancing
to be of more than one mind

BODY

Afraid of being nobody
striving mightily to be somebody
now and then anybody will do

Everybody has a body
hardly ever the "right" body
we body-build and body-pierce
body-paint and body-mold
in quest of a celestial body
that feign will provide an out-of-body experience

There are limits to all bodies
no matter how body centered we are
our body clock ticks
the body politic falls short
the corporate body deceives
alien bodies promise hope and disappear
the best bodyguards cannot protect

Embody who you are
modeled after and molded by Divinity
embodiment of God's unique presence in the world

Your body language will hold true as you enjoy
the full-bodied melody of a life that is yours

BONE

Bone chilling it is when bone tired of
the glut of bones of contention
all the bones we pick
with our *"selves,"* with others, with God
we lose touch with the bare bones of our creation
knowing in our bones that we are each
a [Breath-Taking⇔Model of Divinity]

Rest your weary bones and bone up on this
it is bone of our bone, mind of our mind, flesh of our flesh
it is who we are
yet not only
that with the Psalmist you may say

Every bone in my body proclaims God's majesty

And may God bless every bone in your body

BLOOD

It makes the blood run cold
to witness the bloodletting
that bad blood brings
the bloodfeuds
and bloodbaths
yet too many idolize blood and guts

Getting blood from a stone is simpler than
traversing the blood-brain barrier on this
Need a bloodhound to sniff out the
the words that are our lifeblood
Though blood is thicker than water
we are each and all blood brothers and sisters
the same blood flowing through us
each the other's flesh and blood
not one bloodless
all in need of new blood
so we know in our blood
that each
is modeled after and molded by Divinity
And that's the bloody truth

SKIN

Makes the skin crawl
behaving like mice in a Skinner box
pressing the lever for skinny rewards

Our love only skin deep
no skin off our nose
skinning the other
acting skinflint with those
whose skin is a different hue
getting under their skin
leaving them skinless and boneless

Save our own skins by the
skin of our teeth
We are thin-skinned
when we need be thick-skinned
and thick-skinned when
soaked to the skin
our skin shivering and blue
Know that it is more
than just a skinned knee

Wear the other's skin and know
the skinny on the news is that we are
modeled after and molded by Divinity

HAIR

Let's not split hairs
much of life hangs by a hair
We sign on to harebrained schemes
just to win by a hair

Hair raising to admit that
our own receding hairline
the weird hairdo our hairdressers gave us
the hairbrush that brings no order
a bad hair day
stands our hair on end
we tear our hair out
and fancy sticking a hairpin in others

Know that life is a hairy enterprise
a hairbreadth difference
between winning and losing

No need to don a hair shirt
just let your hair down
and acknowledge that which
the tortoise and the hare have taught us
that slow and steady wins the race

It's good to be in the race at all

HEAD

Headline reveries turn our head
proclaiming us head of the line
head and shoulders above the crowd
miles ahead of the flock

Head over heels bewitched with control
we head out with no clear heading
plunging headlong into the headwind
pursuing a headlock on life

Over our head
head start lost
headway pitiable
headquarters baffled
headed off at every turn
heads ache in confusion

Heads or tails—it matters not
Yet having a head for
seeking life's headwaters
we return with head held high
that the Ultimate Headmaster
grant us both headrest and headlights
as we head on our way

FACE

It is told that before the
expulsion from Eden
our first ancestor's entire body
radiated divine light
providing astonishing clarity
adding to the brilliance of God's world

In us the descendants
no longer residents of Eden
a trace of that divine light
is still found in one place only
—-our face—
which glows warmly in moments
of joy, peace, and inner tranquility
a physical manifestation that we are each of us
modeled after and molded by Divinity

Face it!
Doing an about-face and facing each other
face-to-face is the way to face what will be
When we face up to that, the light in our face
and the faces of those we face will surface
giving creation a face-lift
forcing God to again turn to face us in love
so that together
we might brighten the face of the world.

May your face shine forth . . .

EAR

The hearing ear and the seeing eye
Divinity has shaped them both

Up to our ears in earsplitting din,
earfuls of heartache and hearsay
so much in one ear and out the other
earthling ears ache
grow hard of hearing

Set the world on its ear
earmarking this time for hearty hearing

Play these by ear
to your own heart's yearning give ear
to those near and dear be all ears
to the mute fears of others weary of tears
lend an ear

Keep an ear to the ground of all being
that earnest prayers a gentle hearing earn

EYE/I

Blessed be the I

An I opener it is that having I's for others
we say aye to God's creatures
If inner I be nurtured, allowing open I's
we celebrate your public I
and cherish your private I
detecting the primeval I
whom we are modeled after

Let an I for an I be reward not retribution
Have a good I for all
an evil I for none
an I out for those who see
I to I

As time unfolds
be the apple of God's I
an I full of delight
And if tempest must be
calm be your I

MOUTH/LIP/TONGUE

Mouthpieces for lip service
tongues tied by fear
we lip-synch "truths" not ours

When others' lips distort and deceive
beguile and betray
our mouths stay sealed
though on the tip of our tongue
our muted self does lie

Now
let us lip-read others' silenced voices
and with lips that frame what's actually so
kiss the others' essence

Mouth words that heal self and others
so mouth to mouth
resuscitate the "image"
revive its living breath
that our untwisted tongue
might taste the truth
the sweet savor of love engulf us

NOSE

Nose to the grindstone
huffing and puffing to win by a nose

Everyone knows the trouble we've got
—nose out of joint—
we pay through the nose doing a knows job
counting our knows and others' knows not
looking down our nose at
who knows who and who knows what
who knows more and who knows less
thumbing our nose at those who have taken a nosedive

Yet with a nose for what's so
each of us knows
that when God counts noses
each is unique and all modeled after Divinity.

And God knows what we do with this fact
that's plain as the nose on our face

May The One who knows bless you and yours

SHOULDER

Straight from the shoulder

The road we travel affords no safety on the shoulder
to shoulder that to which you are called
rub shoulders with those head and shoulders above the rest
who shoulder God's covenant yoke

Modeled after and molded by Divinity

Without a chip on your shoulder
firmly on the shoulders of those who went before
trust the good head on your shoulders
turn not a cold shoulder to any who to life's errant wheel
would offer their shoulder

That shoulder to shoulder
sparse tears on other's shoulders
burden offset on all shoulders
we traverse our destined path

And so shoulder on

HEART

This is the heart of the matter:

That we set our heart on taking to heart
that which at heart is wholeheartedly ours

That while knowing our heart's true yearning
we be yet aware of the heartache in others

That heart-to-hearts with sweethearts and others
unfetter our heart
and for them be heartwarming

That ours be the wholeness of heart
of the brokenhearted
without the heartrending that framed it so

That we be softhearted where right
hardhearted where needed
lighthearted mostly
and fainthearted seldom

That heart and soul
we learn this by heart
that heart and hearth be filled with love

HAND

As the clock hands turn
reckoning at hand
we take in hand the hand we are dealt

On the one hand molded by Divinity
on the other hand, but clay
and a handful of hand-me-downs
offhandedly left us

Yet having in hand all we require for the handiwork of our lives
we walk hand in hand with our handpicked

Merely hands on God's crew
yet each of us handy
let your handbook be love
that handicaps be handholds
hand-me-downs handicrafts

Be evenhanded with all
highhanded with few
and underhanded with none
that by lending a hand and living hands on
we hand on to others
handwritten in our hand
a handsome chapter in our life's book

May God's hand touch you and yours
that the works of your hand
be blessed

HEEL

Head over heels in love with your Creator
be heel to none—healer to self
trod not under heel those down at heel
if well-heeled
let that not be your Achilles heel

Proud scion of Jacob, first heel holder
take not to heel at first fright
dig in your heels for your birthright
to heel in a direction worth going

Knowing that you are healable
speak and attend to words that heal

That as time marches on
you may joyfully kick up your heels
having come home to your
[Breath-Taking⇔Model of Divinity]

FOOT

Your word is a lamp to my feet
a light for my path

Foot soldiers not footnotes
footsore from life's footrace
weary of fancy footwork
with footlights too bright
spent putting best foot forward
sitting at great ones' feet
all feet of clay

Underfoot no solid footing
yet footfalls of our essences call
for a foothold on the foothills of our dream

Unsteadily venturing footsteps
life measured by the moving foot
we mold footprints worth following

On this footbridge to somewhere
your words lighten and balance

With footpaths thus lit
footwork more sure-footed
today perhaps, tomorrow for sure,
a foot in the door

BACK

Back at square one
too many stabs in the back
no comeback in sight
our needs on the back burner
we go back to our usual ways
a throwback to how we once were
hesitating to talk back,
backing off from long-held vows
so many drawbacks
the back of their hand
their turned back
backbiting without end

In the dark
a flashback to the future
a pat on the back
backing your ability to bounce back
no more laidback about
getting back into life

Let setbacks not be rollbacks
turning you backward from your chosen path

Let your fallback position be
you are backed by knowing that you are
a [Breath-Taking⇔Model of Divinity]

Let this serve as backbone

THUMB

There are those who thumb their nose at others
giving thumbs-down to those overwhelmed in life's struggle
applying the thumbscrews however they can.

Thumb through the sacred text of your life
and let this be your rule of thumb
Okay to stick out like a sore thumb
by thumbing a ride with those
who give thumbs-up to folks
who emerge with their integrity intact

Be not under another's thumb
rather than twiddling your thumbs
imagining you are all thumbs
no bigger than Tom Thumb

Be a green thumb for human growth and flowering

TOE

On your toes—life is calling

To get a toehold
toe the mark
take your dreams in tow
What you have in tow may bless
Towing too much can be a drag

When you crash
the tow truck can tow you even as
you are taken in tow by those who
stand toe-to-toe with you—
grasp their rope tow
as you tiptoe cautiously
in tow with others like-minded
till your toe is in the water once more
on your designated route
Yet know from head to toe
be careful of toeing the party line

For you are a [Breath-Taking⇔Model of Divinity]

To the very tip of your toes

VEIN

Is it all in vain?
Pursuing vain hopes
offering vain promises
vain exertions?
Vainglorious posturing
the vanity of the vanity's mirror
vain charades to be other than we are
checking the weathervane for the wind's bearing
searching in vain for others guidance—
these blows to the jugular vein
take in vain that which is true

Vanity of vanities?

Mine the vein of truth
the refreshing vein of humor
ride the veins that nourish the heart
glory in the vein of a leaf that gives shade
be amazed at the veins of insect wings
lifting a body too big to fly

And in a courageous and loving vein,
know that all is not in vain
as you follow the hallowed vein of your being
modeled after and molded by Divinity

TOOTH

When the tooth fairy no longer shows up

Too many lie through their teeth
setting our teeth on edge

It's like pulling teeth to get others
to cut their teeth on
and ourselves to sink our teeth into
the reality that truth has teeth

Armed to the teeth
we grit our teeth
fight tooth and nail
in the teeth of oncoming squalls
We'd give our eyeteeth to prevail

Rather than gnashing your teeth
choose friends with a fine-tooth comb
have a sweet tooth for love that sustains

And though there is no tooth fairy
not even for wisdom teeth
get your teeth into this

You are a [Breath-Taking ⇔ Model of Divinity]

THANKS

Thanks for all You have created
Thanks for what You have given me

For eyes and the light
For a friend or two
For a soaring song
For a forgiving heart
For a child's laughter
For blue skies
For the good earth
A warm home
A corner to sit in
And someone who loves me

Thanks for what is mine in the world

These sustain my being

Thanks

For a day of delight
For Innocence and sacrifice
For simplicity and decency
For sad days now vanished
For millennia of survival and salvation
I applaud You

Thanks for what is mine in the world

These sustain my being

Thanks for all You have created
Thanks for what you have given me

Hebrew Lyrics by Chaim Moshe
Translation by Jack H Bloom

If I am I because You are You
and You are You because I am I
then I am not and You are not.

But if I am I because I am I
and You are You because You are You
then I am and You are.

Mendel of Kotsk
Translation by Jack H Bloom

. . . and We can talk.

Carl Whitaker

Once upon a time there was a man who lost his snuffbox. He searched everywhere, for it meant a lot to him. He cried when he could not find it. Searching and crying, he wandered into the middle of a forest. There he came upon a strange, wonderful, and most generous creature—a sacred goat, who roamed the roads of time. And each midnight he touched the heavens with his immense horns, awakening the stars and inspiring them to shine and sing. "Why are you so sad?" asked the goat. The man told the truth: that he had lost his snuffbox. "Is that all?" the goat asked. "It's foolish to cry; I'll help you. Just take your knife, cut yourself a piece of horn and make yourself a new snuffbox." The man did as he was told.

Upon returning to his village, his neighbors marveled: his tobacco had the smell of paradise. Harried with questions, he admitted that it was not the tobacco but the snuffbox, and he told them the whole story. They all immediately ran into the forest, found the amiable and generous creature and cut his horns, which shortened by the minute until they were no more. And so the goat could no longer touch the sky to wake up the stars. He could only look at them from far away, with longing and a little remorse.

Mendel of Kotzk
Translation by Jack H Bloom

Though we know that our vision exceeds our reach
and our knowledge surpasses our wisdom
yet may we—each of us,
live so as to touch the heavens
and so brighten the night
and fill the air with song.

The entire world is a narrow bridge,
and the important thing is not to be afraid at all.

Rabbi Nachman of Bratslav
Translation by Jack H Bloom

For you uneasy and vulnerable
apprehensive and anxious
for you a full and complete healing
and for you and your loved ones
relief, release, and renewal.

Behold,
the Winter is past
The rain is over,
gone
Spring blooms
having appeared in the land
The time for singing is here

Song of Songs
Translation by Jack H Bloom

May your song be one of healing and love.

Index

Page numbers followed by the letter "n" indicate notes.

Aaron, 112
Abortion
    barriers to, 177
    genetic abnormalities, 181
    personal ritual, 117
    pregnancy counseling, 176, 177, 181
    reproductive counseling model, 187
    rituals for, 189
    single women, 185-186
    stigma of, 165-166
Abraham, strangers' visits, 94. *See also*
    Avraham
Abrams, Judith Z.
    background of, 307-308
    illness of, 308-310
Acceptance, visitation with the dying,
    372-373
Ad Hoc Committee on Human
    Sexuality, 241
Adon Olam, cognitively impaired, 351
Adoption
    pregnancy counseling, 176, 177
    reproductive counseling model, 187
    stigma of, 166
Adult education, interfaith
    relationships, 162-163
Adultery, [*Tzelem⇔N'shamah*]
    relationship, 263
Adulthood, Jewish tradition, 193
Affect, cognitively impaired, 339-340,
    347
Aging
    blessing for, 304-305
    Jewish relational care, 278-279
    "new" old, 277
    personal rituals, 117
    pursuing your passion, 300-303
    Simchat Chochmah, 118, 118n.13,
        121-122

Aging *(continued)*
    Vaillant's study, 294-295
    values of, 297-298
    visiting the, 87-88
Aging Well, 289
Agreement, 48
Agus, Jacob B., 256
Aharon
    numb response, 395
    silent response, 376-377
Ahavah (love), spontaneous prayer,
    135, 135n.19
Ahavat olam (loving care), 349,
    349n.29
AIDS, mourning ritual, 120
Aleph of Anochi, 146
"Alien" attacks, 37
Alien reality, 38-39
All Options Clergy Counseling
    description, 175-176
    domestic violence, 179
    fetal health, 179-181
    infertility, 182
    maternal health, 181-182
    reproductive choices, 177-178,
        186
    session model, 186-188
    single women, 186
"Alone experience," 370
Alzheimer's disease
    caregiver exhaustion, 341-342
    needs of people with, 347
    prevalence of, 339
Amalek text
    in Christian tradition, 271
    Hebrew passage, 273
    traditional view, 269-270
Amicus curiae, 149
Amidah (weekday prayers), 386

Anger
  brokenness and healing, 229, 238
  divorce reaction, 165, 166, 169
  visitation with the dying, 372
Ani Adonai, 287
Anti-Semitism, 163
Anxiety, 68
Anxiety disorders, 333
Appreciation, 28
Ariel, David, 279-280
Arzt, Ray, 292
Arzt, Roz, 292
Ashkenazim, musical tradition, 110
Auditory language, 31
Avinu Malkeinu, t'shuvah
    (return/answer), 247
Avraham, blessings, 209, 212, 216,
    217, 301. *See also* Abraham
Ayin (nothingness), spiritual world, 85,
    85n.18, 86

Back, blessing of, 424
Bahr, Raymond, 109
Baltes, Paul, 300
Baltimore Hebrew University, 307
Bar Abba, Rabbi Chiya, 88-89
Bar mitzvah (entry into adulthood
    ceremony)
  gay congregant, 191, 191n.1
  personal ritual, 117, 117n.2
Baruch dayan haemet (praise be the
    true judge), 377
Bat gil (peer to patient), 127, 128
Bat mitzvah (entry into adulthood
    ceremony)
  personal ritual, 117, 117n.2
  Rabbi Sklarz, 320
Bateson, Gregory, 19n.2
Be gone, 56, 58
Be honest, 56-58
Be present, 56, 57
Be there, 56, 57
Beck, Evelyn Torton, 196
Behavior
  first-order reality, 40-41
  reframing examples, 42-46
  skillful reframing, 46-49
Being present, visiting guidelines, 90,
    91-92

"Being there," 88
Being there, visiting guidelines, 90, 91
"Beingness," 8
Beit din (rabbinic court)
  bill of divorce, 174
  congregants, divorce tips, 170, 170n.2
Bell, Darin, 324
Ben gil (peer to patient), 127, 128, 138
Ben Meir, Rabbi Baruch, of Barcelona,
    135
Bereavement, 165
Beth Chaim Chadashim, *Simchat
    Chochmah* (aging ceremony),
    121
Beth El, divisions, 215
Beth El Synagogue Center, 291
Beverages, rituals, 125
Beyn adam l'atzmo, 262-263
Beyn adam l'chaveiro, 262-263
Biale, David, 256
Bikur cholim (visitations), 88, 369-370
Bimah (officiating area), 154-155,
    155n.3, 230
Binah (hard-earned knowledge), mental
    world, 84, 85
Binah (understanding), in *Chabad*
    system, 84, 84n.11
Birchat Hagomel (prayer), miscarriage/
    abortion, 188, 188n.28
Blame
  divorce reaction, 168
  throw out, 27-28, 32
"Blamer's debris," 28
Blessing
  as Jewish rituals, 118
  of sons, 192-193
Blessing others
  forefathers, 212-218
  rabbinic obligation, 210, 212
Blessings
  of the Back, 424
  of the Blood, 410
  of the Body, 408
  of the Bone, 409
  of the Breath, 406
  of the cognitively impaired, 351
  of the Ear, 415
  of the Eye/I, 416
  of the Face, 414
  of the Foot, 423

Blessings *(continued)*
   of the Hair, 412
   of the Hand, 421
   of the Head, 413
   of the Heart, 420
   of the Heel, 422
   of interfaith relationships, 162
   of the Mind, 407
   of the Mouth/Lip/Tongue, 417
   of the Nose, 418
   Sanhedrin 4:5, 402
   of the Shoulder, 419
   of the Skin, 411
   of Thanks, 429
   of the Thumb, 425
   of the Toe, 426
   of the Tooth, 428
   of the Vein, 427
   visiting guidelines, 90, 94
Blood, blessings, 410
Bloom, Rabbi Jack H
   on being a rabbi, 62
   CCAR Director of Professional
      Career Review, 292
   on divorce, 169
   first position, 291-292
   psychology internship, 292
   at the Rabbinic Training Institute,
      303
   symbolic exemplar, 136
   [*Tzelem* ⇔ *N'shamah*] model, 64
Body
   blessing of, 408
   dimension of reality, 72-73
   SSP exercise, 76
Bokser, Ben Zion, 256-257
Bone, blessing of, 409
[Both/And] position, and relationship,
   251
[Both/And] thinking,
   and [Either/Or] thinking, 249-250
   and sex, 261
   ⁄ and *t'shuvah,* 249-250, 259
"Bowling ball approach," 321
B'rachah (blessing)
   music, 106
   spiritual world, 85, 85n.16
B'rachah l'vatalah (empty blessing), 58
Bradley, Reverend Patrick, 112
Breath, blessing of, 406

Breath work, 111-113
Breathing
   and chanting, 111
   expressive differences, 32
   SSP exercise, 76, 77
Breath-Taking Somatic self
   (N'shamah), 5, 11. *See also*
   N'shamah
Brener, Anne, 188
Brevity, visiting guidelines, 90, 94
B'rit (infant welcome ceremony),
   personal ritual, 117, 117n.1
B'rit ahuvim (commitment ceremony),
   same-sex couples, 203,
   203n.26
Bronfman, Edgar, 290, 299
B'tulta (virgin), 261
B'tzelem Elohim (in the image of God),
   sexual values, 13-14
Buber, Martin
   [I–You] relationship, 255-256, 265,
      316
   listening, 102
   on the other, 373

Campbell, Don, 108
Cancer, *mikveh* (ritual bath), 121
Candles, 118
Cantor
   healing trauma, 336
   as sexual abusers, 330, 330n.7
   time management, 51, 56, 58, 61
Caregiver
   and dementia, 341-342
   relationship model, 8-9
Caring, difficult congregants, 205-206
Carla, incest survivor, 332
Celebrations
   foundation myths, 140
   op-ed piece, 162
Centering, 264-266, 302-303
Central Conference of American
   Rabbis (CCAR)
   Director of Professional Career
      Review, 292
   staff, 292
   violator norms, 241-242
Chabad system, mental world, 84,
   84n.11

Challah (bread)
  ritual item, 90, 90n.9
  Sabbath service, 106-107
Chameitz (leaven), 118, 118n.7
Chant, 110
Chanting, 111
Chanukah
  Jewish rituals, 118
  visiting guidelines, 90, 90n.10
Chanukiyah (candelabrum), 365-366,
  366n.4
Chaplaincy, time management, 51, 56,
  58, 61
Character building, reframing example,
  43
Charitable gift, *Simchat Chochmah*
  (aging ceremony), 122
Chatan (groom), 155, 155n.4
Chatimah (seal), 131, 131n.12, 137
Chavrutah study, 233
Chemotherapy, *mikveh* (ritual bath), 121
Cherem (excommunication), 264
Chesed (flowing, endless, giving love)
  and cognitively impaired, 355
  emotional world, 83n.8, 83-84
Child Custody Protection Act, 183-184
Child sexual abuse
  impact of, 332-333
  and *t'shuvah*, 329, 337
Children, grief experience, 398-399
Chochmah (flash insight), mental
  world, 84-85
Chochmah (wisdom), in *Chabad*
  system, 84, 84n.11
Christian Coalition
  partial-birth abortion, 184
  size of, 183
Christians, diversity among, 160-161
1 Chronicles 6:31, musical
  demarcations, 109
Chuppah (canopy)
  blessing of sons, 192-193
  Jewish marriage, 155, 186
  Jewish rituals, 118, 118n.12
  same-sex couples, 203-204
Churches, and mentally ill, 361
Churchill, Winston, 290
Clergy
  caregiver support, 342
  cognitively impaired support, 342,
    344, 345

Clergy *(continued)*
  healing trauma, 336
  interfaith relationships, 162-163
  as sexual abusers, 330, 330n.7
  sexual orientation counseling, 193
  time management, 51, 56, 58, 61
"Climbing the Tree," 81-82
Clinical pastoral education (CPE),
    visiting guidelines, 94
Cognition, and personhood, 340-341
Cognitive impairment
  losses of, 339, 341
  programs information, 355
Cognitive self-mindfulness *(Tzelem)*,
    role of, 3, 5, 11-12, 209. *See
    also Tzelem*
Cognitively impaired, 343-344
Cohen, Jack, 291
Cohen, Mark S., 253
Cole, Reverend Elbert, 347
Coming out
  expanded concept, 195-196
  gay congregant, 191
  process steps, 196-198
  recent LGBT youth, 200
Communal norms
  foundation myths, 140
  interfaith relationships, 162
  and non-Jews, 146-148
Compassion
  description of, 69-71
  dimensions of, 72-73
  practice of, 75-79
Compassion fatigue, 67-68, 73-75, 79
Complementary relationships, 9-10
Concern, skillful reframing, 47
"Concerning the Conflict of Opinions
    and Beliefs," 258
Confirmation, personal ritual, 117
Congregation Ner Tamid, *Simchat
    Chochmah* (aging ceremony),
    121
Congregational church, 160
"Congregational triage," 207
Connection, music, 106-107
Conservative Judaism
  get requirement, 174
  job listing, 291
Constructive criticism, 47
Container, 391

"Containers," 169
Contemplative practices, 76-76, 77-78
Control, Mickey Rivers, 404
Copyrights, rituals, 125
Corman, Debra Hirsch, 4
Counseling, relational listening, 103
Courage, 47
Cousins, Norman, 108
Covering exchange, 63
Covey, Steven
    on self-care, 68
    on time management, 55
Creation
    Sanhedrin 4:5, 402
    Third Era myth, 145-147, 150
    [*Tzelem*⇔*N'shamah*] model, 248.
        See also [*Tzelem*⇔*N'shamah*]
        model
Credit, 28, 29-30, 32
Cronkite, Walter, 299
"Cross the street," 92
Culture, as frame, 34
Curtin, Ari Mark, 250-251

Daat (enlightened understanding),
        mental world, 85
Daat (knowledge), in *Chabad* system,
        84, 84n.11
Dan (Rabbi)
    alternative scene, 238-240
    cleansing, 234-236
    healing, 231-232, 234
    Jonathan's death, 224, 225, 226-228
    new congregation, 221, 222-224
    postdeath period, 229, 230, 231
Daniel, brokenness and healing, 227
David, brokenness and healing, 227,
        234
David, King of Israel
    divisions, 215
    psalms, 110
Death
    as gift, 311
    in Jewish tradition, 375
    responses to, 376-377, 379
"Death zone," 310, 312
Dementia
    cognitive loss, 339, 341
    diagnosis of, 348-349

Denial
    child sexual abuse, 330-331, 334
    divorce reaction, 168
Depersonalization, Amalek text, 273-275
Depression
    child sexual abuse, 333
    divorce reaction, 166, 168
Descartes, Rene, 340
Developmental Tasks and Education, 293
Developmentally disabled, communal
        worship, 365
Difference, poem/blessing, 404
"Dim eyes," 213, 214
Din v'cheshbon (reckoning), 334
Dina, blessings, 214, 217
Disabilities, in Jewish tradition, 307
Disabilities in Judaism from the
        Tanakh Through the Bavli,
        307
Disenfranchised grief, 169
Distractions, listening guideposts,
        101-102
Divided loyalties, divorce, 166
Divine Breath *(N'shamah),* 11-12,
        209-210, 248. *See also*
        N'shamah
Divine Source of Healing, chants, 113
Divine Spark
    as image, 130
    Third Era myth, 146
Divorce
    behaviors to avoid, 171
    helping role, 165-166
    life-shattering event, 165
    mikveh (ritual bath), 119-120
    reactions to, 166-170
    sign of healing, 172
"Divorce crisis," 166
Domestic violence, 178-177
Dorff, Rabbi Elliot, 255, 335-336
Douglas, visitation with the dying, 372
Doveir emit bil'vavo, relationships, 263
Down's syndrome, fetal testing, 180
Dratch, Rabbi Mark, 334
D'var (text commentary), 123, 123n.28
D'veikut, relationship with God, 282,
        282n.11
Dying
    Jewish response to, 375-376
    visitation of the, 370

Ear, blessing of, 415
Education
    differential, 366
    mental illness support, 361
Efrayim, 215, 216, 218
Eid ne'eman (trustworthy witness),
    263, 263n.87
Ein Keloheinu, cognitively impaired,
    351
Ein Sof (that without limits), 85, 85n.15
[Either/Or] position, 249, 251
[Either/Or] thinking
    and [Both/And] thinking, 249-250
    in foundational texts, 271-272
    and fundamentalist thinking, 254
El Malei (prayer), 389
El Na R'fa Na Lanu ("Please Divine
    One Please Heal Us"),
    113-114
Emotional world, Kabbalah, 82,
    83-84
Emotions
    language production, 20
    SSP exercise, 76-77
Empathy, 102, 394
Endorphin, 108
Erickson, Milton H., 219
Erikson, Erik, 296, 300
Esav, 212, 215, 217
Essence, relationship model, 15
Ethics Committee on the CCAR,
    violator norms, 241-242
Etrog (citron), 365n.2, 365-366
Evangelical church, 160
Events
    first-order reality, 41
    foundation myths, 140
Evil, modern view of, 245
Exodus
    foundation myths, 140, 142, 143,
        150
    Third Era myth, 146, 148
Exodus 3:14, relationship with God,
    280
Exodus 18:18, time management, 53,
    54, 56, 59-60
Exodus 31:17, rest from work, 65
Experience, code words, 20, 21
Eye/I, blessing of, 416
Ezra, foundation myths, 143

Face, blessing of, 414
Falk, Marcia, 122
Family. *See also* Jewish family
    as frame, 34
    visiting ill/aging, 87-88
Fear
    divorce reaction, 169
    self-compassion, 68
Fear of God, Amalek text, 270, 271,
    273-274, 275
Feedback, lay leadership, 207
Feeling words, 31
Fetal health, 179-181
First Church Congregational, 160
"First Connection," LLS, 324
First Temple, foundation myths, 143
First-order reality
    description, 24, 25
    reframing, 41
Fitch, Victoria, 298
Five Books of Moses, The, 3-4
Fleishig (meat), 63, 63n.33
Flexibility, 39
Foot, blessing of, 423
Forgiveness
    death of Moshe, 378
    divorce healing, 172
    mental illness support, 363
Foundation myths
    change of, 140-141
    communities, 139-141
    layers of, 141-144
    Third Era, 145
Fox, Everett, 3-4
Frames
    aging values/resources, 297-298
    limiting, 34-35
    reality construction, 32-34
    useful, 36
Frankl, Viktor, 286, 360
Free will, RaMbaM, 247-248
Freedom, 297, 299
Freud, Sigmund, 97
Friedan, Betty, 298
Friedman, Debbie, 120, 122, 123, 326
Friends, visiting ill/aging, 87-88
From Age-ing to Sage-ing, 298
Fundamentalism
    Christian diversity, 160
    reality construction, 25

Gan (nursery school), 292, 292n.12
Gary, visitation with the dying, 371
Gay rights, and religious right, 183
Gender differences, 30
Gender identity, 192
Gender roles, 192
Generalizing, Amalek text, 275
"Generativity vs. Stagnation," 296
Genesis 1:26-27, creation of humans, 3-4, 10, 13, 281
Genesis 2:5, creation of humans, 281
Genesis 2:7, Divine Breath, 10-11, 13
Genesis 2:18, creation of Eve, 9-10
Genesis 5:1-2, creation of humans, 3-4
Genesis 9:6, modeled after God, 64
Genetic testing, 179, 180
Gentiles, 159, 160. *See also* Non-Jews
Ger toshav (resident alien), 146
Get (bill of divorce), 173
Gilligan, Stephen
    clinical psychologist, 1
    relational *"self"/"selves,"* 70
    on sponsorship, 2
Gillman, Neil, 303-304
Gladys, Miriam, 122-123
Glaser, Rabbi Joseph, 292
G'milut chasadim (loving-kindness to others), 89
God
    alternate reality of, 358
    evolving relationship with, 280-283
    human response to death, 376-377
    journey to, 317, 318-319, 325-326, 327
    mystery of, 71, 71n.8
    parental image, 279-280
    plural self-references, 250-251
    quintessential visitor, 88
    relationship with, 7, 11-12, 76, 163
    in relationships, 16
    response to grief, 398
    and *t'shuvah* (return/answer), 245-246
"Going meta," 45-46
Golovensky, Rabbi David, 291
Gomel (thanksgiving prayer), 118, 118n.9
Goodness, [*Tzelem⇔N'shamah*] model, 211

Gordis, Daniel, 280-281
Gordon, Gil E., 62-63, 65
Goseis (dying person), 376, 379-380, 383
Grace
    Jewish rituals, 118
    mental illness, 357-358
Gragger (noisemaker), 365-366, 366n.5
Gray, Peter, 39n.15
Greek Orthodox Church, 160
Greenberg, Rabbi Yitzhak, 142, 143-144
Grief
    brokenness and healing, 228
    communal needs, 395-396
    divorce reaction, 169
    mikveh (ritual bath), 121
    ownership of, 395
    positive language, 392-393
    recovery actions, 396
    responses to avoid, 394-398
    silent response to, 376
Grief counseling, 390
Grief recovery specialist, 389-390
Grossman, Rabbi Susan, 61
Group prayer, 123-125
Group programming, developmentally disabled, 365
Guf (body), personhood, 341
Guided imagery, 133-135
Guilt, 168
G'vurah (strength and boundaries), 83n.9, 83-84

Hadassah Medical Center, 292
Hadrachah b'dugma (leadership by example), 61, 61n.25
Hair, blessing of, 412
Halachah (Jewish law)
    foundation myths, 143, 143n.16, 151
    mourning rituals, 375
Halakhic Man, 253-254
"Hammer on the Rock," 162-163
Hand, blessing of, 421
Hand washing, 118
Hanley-Hackenbruck, Peggy, 195
Havdalah (sacralization), 118, 118n.5
Havdalah blessing, *Simchat Chochmah* (aging ceremony), 121, 122

Havighurst, Robert, 293, 296
Head, blessing of, 413
Health care institutions, 98, 108
Health Insurance Portability and
     Accountability Act (HIPAA),
     93
Heart, blessing of, 420
Heather, rape of, 332
Hebrew Bible, 163
Hebrew Union College—Jewish
     Institute of Religion, 307
Heel, blessing of, 422
Hei, in *N'shamah,* 281, 286-287
"Help as curing," 87
Hemenway, Reverend Joan, 128-129
Hemphill, Barbara, 54-55
Herman, Judith Lewis, 334
Hertz Siddur, 380
Heschel, Abraham Joshua, 283,
     283n.14
Hillel, self-care, 60-61
Hinei Mah Tov, 157
Hineni, "I'm Here," 219, 304
Hitlavut ruchanit (spiritual
     accompanying), 127-128
Hod (humility)
     emotional world, 83-84
     physical world, 82-83, 83n.6
"Holarchies," 72
"Holding pen," 310
Holmes, Oliver Wendell, 303
Holocaust
     foundation myths, 142, 143, 144
     impact of, 333-334
     observances, 163
Holub, Rabbi Margaret, 127
"Holy sparks," 28, 256
"Hope giver," 391
Hospitals, interfaith chaplaincy, 154
Human beings
     personhood, 341
     Self/*"selves,"* 251-252, 255. *See
         also* Self/*"selves"*
     shared connection, 71
Humanity, exploration of, 7-8

Identity, and *t'shuvah,* 254
"Identity vs. Identity Diffusion," 296

[I–It] relationship
     compared to [I–You] relationship,
          255-256
     with the dying, 372
Illness
     gains from, 312-313
     as life-shattering event, 165
     and loss, 312
     and pain, 311
     positive affirmations, 323
     relating to those in agony, 313
     support groups, 323-324
Ima, Yesh Li Mashehu L'Saper Lakh,
     196
"Image," 3, 12-13
Image of God, sexual values, 13-14
Incest, and *t'shuvah,* 329
Infertility, 182
"Informed consent" laws
     and abortion, 177
     and religious right, 183
Institutionalized developmentally
          disabled, communal worship,
          365
Integrity, 47
"Integrity vs. Despair," 296
Intention, 41
Intentions
     and outcomes, 36-37
     positive, 29-30, 47-48
     skillful reframing, 46-49
Interfaith Mission Trip, 163
Interfaith relationships
     follow-up steps, 162-163
     introductory efforts, 162
     necessary qualities for, 161
Interfaith spouses, 154-156
Intimacy, 362
"Intimacy vs. Isolation," 296
Into Thin Air, 310
Island image, 128-129
Israel (State of)
     Bloom visit, 292
     foundation myths, 142, 143-144
     interfaith relationships, 163
[I–You] relationship
     between *"selves,"* 254-255
     compared to [I–It] relationship,
          255-256
     with the dying, 372-373
     and intimacy, 265
     and sex, 261

Jackie, grief counseling, 389, 390-391
Jacob, Walter, 278
Jasper, Jan, 55-56
Jethro, time management, 53, 56, 59-60
Jewish Board of Family Services, 153
Jewish community
  child sexual abuse, 334
  foundation myths, 139-141
  and rabbinic success, 207
  sexual abuse examples, 331-332
Jewish Encyclopedia, "Repentance,"
    246
Jewish family
  abortion attitudes, 185-186
  and domestic violence, 179
  "gender-normative" dating, 197
  and LGBT coming out, 195,
    198-199
  procreative model, 192-193
Jewish feminist movement, personal
    rituals, 117
Jewish Home and Hospital Lifecare
    System, 153, 156-157
Jewish Hospital, 153
Jewish relational care
  cognitively impaired, 347-349,
    350-353
  dos and don'ts, 349-350, 352
  with the mentally ill, 359-360
  visitation of sick/dying, 370-371
Jewish relational caregiver
  building rapport, 26, 27
  reframing, 43-45, 49
  rituals, 117
  second-order reality, 26
Jewish Theological Seminary, 291
Jewish tradition
  concrete experiences, 365-366
  death liturgy/ritual, 375
  learning's role, 354
  sexual conduct, 260-261
  singular/plural God, 251
  spontaneous prayer, 135-138
Jews, minority status, 196
Job, visiting friends, 87
Joe, dementia, 340
Johnson, Philip, 290
Jonah, *t'shuvah* learning, 264
Jonathan, rabbinic sexual abuse,
    331-332

Jonathan (brokenness and healing)
  death of, 224-226
  early life, 221-222
Josiah, King of Israel, 142
Judaism
  abortion views, 181, 182, 184, 185
  earlier foundation myths, 139-144
  LGBT response, 192
  and modern culture, 144
  musical tradition, 109-110
  mystical use of silence, 99
  number symbols, 113, 114n.13
  relationship model, 11-12
  reproductive counseling model, 187
  second-order reality, 26
  Self-Relations model, 1-2
  strangers' visits, 94
Jungreis, Rebbitzen Esther, 319

Kabbalah
  dimensions of reality, 72
  Tree of Life, 82-85
Kabbalat Shabbat (Sabbath service),
    106-107
Kaddish (mourner's prayer), 223,
    223n.1, 375, 375n.1, 386, 396
Kadosh Baruch Hu (Holy and
    Bountiful One), 82, 82n.3
Kahal (Jewish community), 145
Kane, Saralee, 264-265
Kaplan, Mordecai M., 291
Karet, punishment, 263
Karov Yisrael, Third Era myth,
    148-151
Kavanah (intention), 74
K'dushah (holiness), prayer, 130-131
Keaton, Diane, 342
Kedushah, holiness/sanctity, 14
"Keeper of the Meaning," 296-297, 301
Keter (crown), 85, 85n.14
Ketubah (marriage contract)
  in divorce proceedings, 173
  interfaith couples, 155, 155n.5
  same-sex partners, 202, 203
  and *t'shuvah,* 261
Kiddush (sanctifying prayer), 107,
    107n.8, 119

Kiddushin (Jewish marriage ceremony), same-sex couples, 203, 203n.25
Kierkegaard, Soren, 68
Kishkes (visceral self), 74, 74n.11
Kittel (white garment), *Simchat Chochmah* (aging ceremony), 121n.25, 121-122
K'lei Kodesh (Holy Vessel), service provider, 195, 195n.11, 198
Knowledge, modes of, 72
Kohler, Kaufman, 246
Kol Nidrei (prayer), 234
Kook, Rav Abraham Isaac
  holy sparks, 28, 267-268, 302
  on *t'shuvah*, 256-259
Korban (sacrificial offering), 148-151
Kotre, John, 297
Krakauer, Jon, 310
Krane, Charles, 295
Kraus, Rabbi Pesach, 317-318
K'rovei Yisrael, Third Era myth, 149, 150, 151

Lamed, in *Tzelem*, 281, 283, 285, 286
Landsmanschaft, 292
Language
  expressive differences, 29-30
  as frame, 34
  and reality construction, 25
  relational tool, 17
  in relationships, 21-23
  role of, 9, 18-19
  use capacity, 17-18
Law, foundation myths, 140
L'chah Dodi, Sabbath hymn, 107
Lea, blessings, 213-214
Leib, Rabbi Moshe of Sasov, 102
Leow, Rabbi Judah (MaHaRal), 282, 282n.13
Lesbian, gay, bisexual, and transgender (LGBT) rights movement, 192
Lesbian Rabbis, 196
Leukemia and Lymphoma Society (LLS), 324
Lev (heart), 283, 285

Lev, Rachael
  sexual abuse of, 330
  on *t'shuvah*, 337
Levi (Joining), impaired blessings, 213, 218
Levinson, Daniel, 293-294
Leviticus 19, *Ani Adonai*, 287
Leviticus 19:2, blessed visitor, 95
L'hatchilah (relational exchange), 347
Life cycle events, 171
"Like a Gangster on the Night of the Long Knives, but Somewhat in a Dream," 15
Lip, blessing of, 417
Listening
  congregants, divorce tips, 170
  grief counseling, 390-391
  guideposts of, 101-103
  role of, 101
"Living-Room Dialogues," 162
Loneliness, 168
"Longevity generations," 282-283, 284
"Longevity revolution," 277, 278
Loss, pain of, 391-392
Loss styles, 393
Love
  differential treatment, 206
  Jewish tradition, 283, 284-285
  symbolic exemplars, 207-208
Lulav (palm branch), 365n.3, 365-366

Ma'aseh Avot Siman l'banim, 215
Ma'asim tovim (good deeds), 192-193, 193n.4
Maimonides, Rabbi Moshe ben Maimon (RaMbaM)
  on *t'shuvah*, 247-248
  on *Tzelem*, 3, 12, 209
Malchut (kingdom/reign), 82, 82n.2, 85
Manipulation, definition of, 22
Map image, 129
Marian, brokenness and healing, 223, 226
Maror (bitter herbs), 365-366, 366n.7
Marriage
  Jewish view of, 192-193
  personal ritual, 17
"Marvin's Room," 342

Matzah (unleavened bread), 365-366, 366n.6
Meaning
  aging population, 277
  second-order reality, 41
Medical tests/procedures, 309
Meditation, prayer, 133-135
Mem, in *N'shamah*, 281, 285-286
Memorial Sloan-Kettering Cancer Center, 316, 317, 318
Memory, and dementia, 339
Menashe, blessings, 215, 216, 218
Mendel of Kotsk, 7, 430, 431
Mental world, Kabbalah, 82, 84-85
Mentally ill
  alternative view of God, 358-359
  guides for working with, 359-360
  and religious institutions, 361
Methodist Church, 154, 160
Mi Shebeirach (prayer)
  for bedside gatherers, 384-385
  for healing, 313, 316, 326, 327, 354, 369-370
  Jewish rituals, 118, 118n.8, 120, 123
  for miscarriage/abortion, 188
"Midlife crisis," 20
Midrash
  cognitively impaired, 343, 344, 346
  death of Moses, 378
  images of, 128-129
  on silent response to death, 376-377
Mikveh (ritual bath), 119-121
Milchig (dairy), 63, 63n.33
Minchah services, 157
Mind
  blessing of, 407
  dimension of reality, 72, 73
Mindfulness. *See also Tzelem*
  compassionate practices, 75-76, 78
  as *Tzelem*, 64
Minyan (*minyanim*, plural form) (quorum)
  congregants' divorce, 171
  developmentally disabled, 367
  and grief, 396
  at *shivah* house, 228
Miriam
  as *hitlavut ruchanit*, 127-128
  healing of, 113
  illness of, 112

Miriam *(continued)*
  musical tradition, 110
  Simchat Chochmah (aging ceremony), 122
Miscarriage
  personal ritual, 117
  prayers, 188
Miscommunication, 22
Mishkan, foundation myths, 142
Mishnah Avot, 64, 64n.38
Mishpachah (family), prayer, 135, 135n.19
Mitzrayim
  cognitively impaired, 346, 353
  servitude, 156
Mitzvah (*mitzvoth*, plural form)
  and cognitively impaired, 346
  meanings of, 60n.22, 88n.2, 160, 160n.2, 266, 285, 302, 346, 346n.24
  and *N'shamah*, 285-286
  visitations, 369-370, 373
  visiting guidelines, 94
  Yosef's visit, 215
Mo'achin d'gadlut (expanded mind), 84-85, 85n.12
Mo'achin d'katnut (small mind), 85, 85n.13
Molestation
  familial/stranger, 330
  impact of, 333
  as power/control/self-absorption, 331
Monotheism, [Either/Or] view, 249, 271-272
Montague, Ashley, 297
Mood, SSP exercise, 76-77
Moralnet, 130, 130n.9
Moses
  chant of, 112
  death of, 378
  relationship with God, 280
  response to death, 376-377
  songs of, 110
  time management, 53, 54, 56, 59-60
Moshe. *See* Moses
Moshe, Chaim, 429
Mother-daughter relationship, loss of, 391
Mothers, relationship issues, 389

Mourning, laws of, 375
Mouth, blessing of, 417
Mozart Effect, The, 108
M'tsarim (narrow places), 346
"Multiple spiritual paths," prayer, 135
Music
    lessons of, 105-110
    and prayer, 131-133
Music therapy, 108-109
Mystery, divine, 71, 71n.8

N'shamah
    Breath-Taking Somatic self, 5, 10-12,
        65, 209-210
    letters of, 281, 282-287
    personhood, 341
    relationship with God, 281
    soul, 113, 114n.11
Numbers 12:1-13, revolt against Moses,
    112
Numbness, grief response, 395
Nun, in *N'shamah,* 281, 282, 286

Naches (good feelings), 304, 304n.49
Nafash (rest), 65, 65n.41
Name change
    mikveh (ritual bath), 120
    Simchat Chochmah (aging
        ceremony), 122
Naming, rabbinic obligation, 210, 211
Nancy, brokenness and healing, 224,
    225, 226-227
Nancy, child sexual abuse, 332
National Public Radio, 59
Nation-state
    foundation myths, 143, 144
    Third Era myth, 147
Nefesh (physical/mental spirits), 65,
    65n.42
"Negative nullifier," 29
Negatives, 28-29
Nelson, Rabbi Harry, 291-292
Ne-man (faithfulness), 282, 282n.12
"Nested hierarchy," 72
Netzach (victory)
    emotional world, 84
    physical world, 82-83, 83n.5
New Jewish Publication Society,
    Amalek text, 270, 272-273
New York Times, The, gut brain, 249
Nice Jewish Girls, 196
Niggun (melody without words), ritual
    element, 119, 119n.14, 133
Nitzotzot k'dushah (holy sparks), 256,
    266, 267, 301
Non-Jews. *See* Gentiles
    foundation myths, 140
    Third Era myth, 146-147, 148-149
    working with, 154-158
Nose, blessing of, 418

Observance, 140
"Off time." *See* "Time off"
"O Guide My Steps *Haskiveinu,*" 132
Olam Ha'asiyah (physical world),
    82-83
Olam Ha'atzilut (spiritual world), 82,
    85
Olam Hay'tzirah (emotional world),
    82, 83-84
"Old," 278
Omission, dying person, 376
Oneness, [Either/Or] view, 249
Operative ideals, foundation myths,
    139-140
"Oral torah," 312
Organization, time management, 54-55
Orthodox Judaism
    abortion, 185
    get requirement, 174
Outcomes, 36-37
Overcompensation, 169
Oz, Amos, 15

Pagers, 58, 59
Pain
    fleeing, 75
    and healing, 392
    patient agony, 313-314
    and suffering, 311
    unavoidability of, 74
Palimpsest, 141
Palm pilots, 58, 59
Parable, lost way, 405
Paranoid schizophrenia, rabbinic
    presence, 357-358
Parental consent laws, 177

Parental notification, 177
Parenting
    pregnancy counseling, 176-177
    reproductive counseling model, 187
Partial-birth abortion, 184
Passing, LGBT youth, 198
Passion, 69, 301
Passover
    foundation myths, 142
    Jewish rituals, 118
    visiting guidelines, 90, 90n.12
Passover *Haggadah*, retardation, 366
Past, aging values/resources, 297, 298
Pathos, 67-68
"Patient uniform," 309
Pentecostal church, 160
"Percentages," 86
Perry, Grant, 246
Person, Rabbi Hara, 4
Personal ritual
    abortion/miscarriage, 188-189
    divorce supports, 171
    purpose of, 117
    same-sex ceremonies, 200, 201,
        203-204
Personhood, 340-341
"Pervasive panic," 169
Physical world, Kabbalah, 82-83
Physicians
    "bedside manner," 370
    time with, 310
Piyutim, musical tradition, 110
Place of Light, A, 52
Planning, visiting guidelines, 90-91
Plaskow, Judith, on Amalek text, 272
"Please Divine One Please Heal Us,"
        113, 114-115
"Poop in a pouch" theory, 84
Pornography, as sexual abuse, 330
Post, Stephen, 340
Praise, 28
Prayer
    creation of spontaneous, 131-138
    dying person, 376
    efficacy of, 326
    foundation myths, 142
    and mental illness, 359-360
    response to death, 379
    spontaneous, 130
    visiting guidelines, 94

Prayers
    abortion/miscarriage, 188-189
    cognitively impaired, 351
Precedent, role of, 141
Pregnancy, unwelcome, 175-176
Pregnancy counseling, 177-186
Presbyterian church, 160
Presence
    cognitively impaired, 347-348
    interfaith relationships, 161
    mental illness, 358, 359, 360-361
Privacy
    time management, 58
    visiting guidelines, 93
"Professional persona," 223, 224, 230
Projection, 97
Prophets, 163
Proselytizing, visiting guidelines, 93
Proverbs 22:6, on teaching, 366
Psalm 9:2, musical tradition, 109
Psalm 19, mourning, 386
Psalm 90, musical tradition, 110
Psalm 121, rage ritual, 123
Psalms
    dying person, 376
    response to death, 379
Psychology, 72-73
Punishment
    mentally ill, 358-359
    and suffering, 311
Purim, visiting guidelines, 90, 90n.11
Purpose, aging population, 277

Rabbi(s)
    abuse of, 206
    blessing charge, 209
    brokenness and healing, 221,
        223-224, 230, 231, 234, 238
    cognitively impaired support, 344,
        345-346, 353-254
    compassionate practice, 75-76, 78
    congregants' divorces, 170-172
    divorce "container," 169
    divorce reactions, 166
    grief recovery specialist, 389-390
    healing trauma, 336
    interfaith relationships, 161-162
    life cycle participant, 67

Rabbi(s) *(continued)*
mental illness support, 358, 360-361, 362-363
non-Jewish congregants, 157-158
reflection of God's self, 221, 234
reproductive counseling model, 187-188
responses to personal illness, 319-323
role in illness, 313-314
same-sex ceremony, 204
same-sex counseling, 200-201
as sexual abusers, 330, 330n.7, 331
sexual orientation attitudes, 193-195
sexual orientation counseling, 193
symbolic exemplar, 52-53, 57, 65, 98, 159, 169, 206-209, 210
time management, 51, 53, 56, 58, 61
t'shuvah role, 262-263, 266-267, 268
unwelcome pregnancy counseling, 175-186
visitation of sick/dying, 370, 371
witnessing obligation, 210-211
work with Gentiles, 159-160
Rabbi As Symbolic Exemplar, The, 2
Rabbi Chanina, 89
Rabbi Hazyim of Zanz, parable, 405
Rabbi Moshe of Kobryn, listening, 101
Rabbi Nachman of Bratslav, 432
Rabbi Yochanan, 88-89
Rabbinate, requirements of, 52, 64
"Rabbinic egos," 207
Rabbinic Training Institute, 303
Rabbinical Assembly list, job listings, 291
Rabin, Yitzhak, 163
Rachamim (Merciful One), 124, 124n.30
Rachmanim b'nei rachmanim (merciful children of merciful parents), 242
Rage, ritual for, 122-123
Rahel, blessings, 214
Rapport
breakers of, 26-27
building of, 26, 27-32
five skills of, 32

Rapport dance, 32
Rationalization, 41
Reading, *Simchat Chochmah* (aging ceremony), 122
Reagan, Nancy, 60-61, 62
Reagan, Ronald, 339-340
"Reality," 9, 23
Reality
construction levels, 24
definition of, 24
dimensions of, 72
and language, 23
Reassessment, 172
Rebirth, Rav Kook's view of, 259
Reciprocity, 256
Reconnection, 334
Reconstructionist movement, 291
Redemption
foundation myths, 142, 143
Third Era myth, 146, 147
Referrals, visiting guidelines, 90, 94
Reflection, 172
"Reform Jewish Sexual Values," 13-14
Reform Judaism
and *get,* 174
Taxonomy on Sexual Behavior, 241
on *t'shuvah* (return/answer), 246
Reframing
description of, 40-42
examples of, 42-45
"meta level," 45-46
skillful frames, 46-49
Reincarnation, 311
Rejection sensitivity, 167, 168
Relabeling, 48
Relational grief caregiving, process of, 390-391
Relationship, unit of, 9-10
Relationship model. *See* [*Tzelem*⇔ *N'shamah*] model; [*Tzelem*⇔ *N'shamah*] relationship
Relationships
clergy/congregants, 60
rabbinic guardianship, 262-263
trauma recovery, 334
Religion
and religious right, 183
second-order reality, 25
use of silence, 97

Religious Coalition for Reproductive Choice (RCRC), 175, 185, 186
Remember/mourn, trauma healing, 334
Rena (brokenness and healing)
    alternative scene, 238-240
    chaos/despair, 228-231
    cleansing, 235, 236-238
    healing, 232, 233-234
    Jonathan's death, 224-226, 227, 228
    Jonathan's life, 221-222, 223
Renunciation, and *t'shuvah*, 252
"Renunciation and Wisdom," 296
"Repentance," 246
Repentance
    meaning of, 243-244
    and self-creation, 254
Reproductive rights, 183
Respect
    visitation with the dying, 371-372
    visiting guidelines, 90, 92-93
Responsibility, 172
Retardation, communal worship, 365, 366-367
Retirement years, maturity tasks, 293-295
Revelation, Third Era myth, 145-146
Re'uven (See a Son!), impaired blessings, 213
Revenge, 169
R'fuah (healing), 135, 135n.19
Riemer, Rabbi Jack, 390
Rigidity
    divorce reaction, 169
    and old age, 299-300
Rituals
    caveats, 125
    elements of, 118-119
    Jewish traditions, 118
    purpose of, 117
Rivers, Mickey, 404
Robertson, Paul, 108
Rodeif (pursuer with intent to harm), 181
Roman Catholic Church, 160, 184
Rosenzweig, Franz, 145
Rosh Hashanah (New Year), brokenness and healing, 230
Rossel, Rob, 293

Ruesch, Jurgen, 19n.2
Ruth, schizophrenia, 361

Sabbath services, 162
Sacrificial system, 141-142
Safety, trauma healing, 334
Same-sex ceremony
    normalizing, 200, 201, 202
    ritual elements, 203-204
Same-sex context, Jewish tradition, 192
Sanctuary, interfaith relationships, 162
Sarah, *Simchat Chochmah* (aging ceremony), 121, 122
Saul, King of Israel, 110
Scents, rituals, 125
Schachter, Zalman, 298
Schneider, Lawrence, 113
Scholoessinger, Max, 246
Seasons of a Man's Life, The, 293-294
Second Temple, foundation myths, 140, 141, 143
Second-order reality, 24-25, 41
Seeber, J. J., 283-284
Sefer Torah, 365-366, 366n.8
Self/*"selves"*
    aging, 303
    brokenness and healing, 221
    human beings, 251-252, 255
    human relationships, 284, 286
    of the mentally ill, 360
    multiplicity of, 7-9
    relational, 70
    relationship with God, 280, 281, 282, 284
    t'shuvah (return/answer), 248, 249-250, 254-255
    [*Tzelem⇔N'shamah*] model, 15-16, 159-160
    visitation of sick/dying, 369, 370, 371-372
Self-acceptance, 198, 363
Self-awareness, 362, 363
Self-care
    compassion fatigue, 67-68
    time management, 60-62
Self-creation, and *t'shuvah*, 253-254
Self-esteem, developmentally disabled, 365

Self-identity, developmentally disabled, 365, 367
Self-presence, compassion, 70, 75-77
Self-Relations model, 1
Separation, ritual element, 118-119
Sephardim, musical tradition, 110
Sequential thinking, dementia, 339
Sermons, listening guideposts, 102-103
Setel, Drorah, 122
Sex, somatic urge, 259-260
Sexual abuse
    denial of, 330-331
    description of, 329-330
    impact of, 332-333
    mikveh (ritual bath), 119-120
    prevalence of, 330
    recovery rituals, 117
Sexual infidelity, [*Tzelem*⇔*N'shamah*] relationship, 261-262
Sexual orientation, congregants, 192, 193, 194-195
S'firot (divine spheres), balance of life, 82, 82n.1
Shabbat (Sabbath), 63, 63n.32, 90, 90n.8, 175, 175n.1
Shalom, spontaneous prayer, 135
Shalom (brokenness and healing)
    alternative scene, 238, 240
    healing, 232, 234
    Jonathan's death, 224, 225-226, 227, 228
    postdeath period, 229
Shalom Aleichem, Sabbath hymn, 107, 131-132, 351
Shalom bayit (domestic peace), 179, 179n.9
Shame, 166, 168
"Sharpening the saw," 68
Shavat vayinafash (rest and refreshment), 65
Shavuot, foundation myths, 143
Shechinah (Divine Presence)
    and cognitively impaired, 346
    group prayer, 124, 124n.29
Shehecheyanu (thanksgiving), 118, 118n.4
Shemer, Naomi, 403
Sheva B'rachot (Seven blessings), same-sex couples, 203, 203n.27

Shim'on (Hearing), impaired blessings, 213
Shin, in *N'shamah,* 281, 285
Shirat Hayam, song of redemption, 110
Shivah (mourning ritual)
    brokenness and healing, 225n.2, 225-226, 227
    grief response, 397-398
    visitation with the dying, 371, 371n.6
Sh'leimut (soundness), 285
Sh'loshim (mourning period), 228
Sh'ma (prayer), 14, 283, 283n.17
Shock, 168
Shofar (ram's horn), 365n.1, 365-366
Shomayr hab'rit (guardian of the covenant), 263, 263n.88
Shoulder, blessing of, 419
Shul (synagogue)
    brokenness and healing, 230, 233
    Jewish music, 106-107, 107n.4
Siege of Leningrad, The, 274
Siegel, Danny, 355-356
Silence
    dying person, 376
    impact of, 97
    spiritual care, 98-99
    theological aspect, 99
Simchat Chochmah (aging ceremony), 118, 118n.13, 121-122
Simon, Dvorah, 14
"Sin of humility," 227
"Sin of omission," 334
Sinai
    foundation myth, 141, 143, 150
    Third Era myth, 146, 147, 148
Singer, Muriel, 265
Singing, universality of, 107
Skin, blessing of, 411
Sklarz, Rabbi Andrew
    leukemia diagnosis, 315-317
    spiritual comfort, 317
Social distance, 206
Social justice, 183
Society for the Advancement of Judaism (SAJ), 291
Solace, 170, 171
Solomon, King of Israel, 215
Soloveitchik, Joseph, 253-254

Song at the Sea, 110
Song of Songs, blessings, 433
Songs
    and cognitively impaired, 351
    Jewish folk rock, 133n.16
    worship services, 366
Sonograms, 179
Sons, blessing of, 192-193
Sonya, sexual abuse denial, 332
Sound, 19-20, 105
Space, marking of, 109
Spiegel, Marcia Cohn, *Simchat
    Chochmah* (aging ceremony),
    121, 122
Spirit, 72, 73
Spiritual care, 97-99
Spiritual needs, cognitively impaired,
    342-343
Spiritual world, Kabbalah, 82, 85
"Sponsor," 1
Spontaneous prayer, pastoral visit,
    130-131
Stein, Rabbi Jonathan, 241, 242
Steinsaltz, Adin, 252-253
Stevenson, Robert Louis, 129
Stigma
    of divorce, 165
    of mental illness, 361, 363
    of unwelcome pregnancy, 165-166
Structured self-presence (SSP),
    exercise, 76-77
Study of Adult Development, The,
    294
Success, redefinition of, 206-207
S'udat havra'ah (mourners' meal),
    397
Suffering
    as punishment, 311
    sharing of, 71
Suicide, contemplation of, 311
Suicide risk, child sexual abuse, 333
Symbolic exemplar
    aging passion, 301-302
    rabbi as, 65, 98, 137, 159, 169,
        206-208, 210
    role of, 52-53, 57, 57-58n.18
Sympathy, and compassion, 68
Synagogues
    and the mentally ill, 361
    and older Jews, 279

Take Back Your Time, 55-56
Talking, divorce reaction, 168
Tallit (prayer shawl)
    Jewish rituals, 118, 118n.11
    Simchat Chochmah (aging
        ceremony), 122
Talmud, "being there" vignettes, 88-89
Taylor, Rabbi Bonita E, 62
"Teachings," 159-160
Technology, time management, 58-59
Teenagers, domestic violence risk, 178
Temple, foundation myths, 142, 150
Temple of Jerusalem, divisions, 215
"Terrible gift," 317-318, 325
Terror, divorce reaction, 169
Teubal, Savina, *Simchat Chochmah*
    (aging ceremony), 121-122
T'fillin (phylacteries), 261
Thanks, blessings, 429
"Theology of relationships," 277, 281
Third Act, The, 290
*Third Great Cycle of Jewish History,
    The,* 142
*This Is My Beloved, This Is My Friend:
    Sex and the Family,* 255
Thoracic outlet syndrome, 308
Thumb, blessing of, 425
Tiferet (balanced, abundant love),
    83n.7, 83-84,
Tikkun olam (repair/renew world),
    cognitively impaired, 355
Time, marking of, 109
Time management
    need for, 51-53
    and organization, 54-56
    as sacred work, 65
    and technology, 58-59
    wearying people, 59-60
"Time off," 51, 59, 60, 62-65
"Time on," 51, 56-58, 60
"To begin," 403
Toe, blessing of, 426
Tongue, blessing of, 417
Tooth, blessing of, 428
Torah
    blessing of sons, 192-193
    emotional world, 84, 84n.10
    foundation myths, 140, 143, 150
    interfaith relationships, 163
    and Jewish rituals, 118
    visiting guidelines, 92, 92n.14

Touch
  congregants, divorce tips, 170
  with grievers, 394
  mental illness support, 362
  in rituals, 125
  and silence, 99
  visitation with the dying, 371
  visiting guidelines, 93
"Toward a Taxonomy for Reform Jews
      to Evaluate Sexual Behavior,"
      241
Tower of Babel, 19
Transitions, difficulty of, 391-392
Transliteration, guidelines, 4
Treasure Island, 129
Tree of Life, Kabbalah, 82-85
Tree planting
  rage ritual, 123
  Simchat Chochmah (aging
      ceremony), 122
"Triune formulae," 161
T'shuvah (repentance), 69, 69n.4
T'shuvah (return/answer)
  [Both/And] thinking, 249-250, 259
  Buber's view, 255-256
  and child sexual abuse, 329,
      333-334, 337
  covenant community, 264
  Dorff's view of, 255
  important questions, 242-243
  meaning of, 243, 244-247
  Rav Kook's view of, 256-257
  and sexual violators, 241-242
  Soloveitchik's view of, 253-255
  Steinsaltz's view of, 252-253
  traditional understanding of,
      246-252
Turn It Off, 62-63
Twerski, Abraham, 334
Twice Blessed, 196
Tzedek (justice/equality/worth), in
      Tzelem, 281n.10, 281-282,
      286
Tzelem (cognitive self-mindfulness)
  letters of, 281n.10, 281-282, 283, 286
  and personhood, 341
  relationship with God, 281
  role of, 3, 5, 11-12, 64
  on *t'shuvah* problem, 252

Tzelem Elohim (image of God)
  cognitive being, 3, 12, 209
[*Tzelem⇔N'shamah*] model
  aging population, 284-285, 286,
      287-288
  blessing, 209-210, 212-218
  centering, 265-266
  description of, 11-16
  naming, 211
  relationship with God, 281
  self-attacks, 37
  self-care, 64
  and *t'shuvah* (return/answer), 248,
      249-250, 254-255
  visitation of sick/dying, 369, 370
  witnessing, 210, 211, 214
[*Tzelem⇔N'shamah*] relationship
  midrashic images, 128-130
  music/song, 132-134
  and sex, 261
  spontaneous prayer, 137
  work with Gentiles, 158, 159-160

Unblessed, 210
Union for Reform Judaism, 4
Union of American Hebrew
      Congregations, transliteration
      guidelines, 4
Uniqueness, 37-39
University of Massachusetts Medical
      Center, 108
Unnamed, 210
Unwell, visiting the, 87-88
Unwitnessed, 210
Urgent, time management, 55
Uveyn adam lamakom, relationships,
      262-263

Vacillation, 168
V'ahavta, love, 283, 283n.18, 284
Vaillant, George
  adult development study, 294-295,
      296, 297, 301
  on aging, 289, 290
  wisdom, 303
Value concepts, 139-140
Vein, blessing of, 427

V'heyeh b'rachah (be a blessing), 209, 209n.2, 211, 268, 303
Vidui (deathbed ritual/prayer)
   alternative version, 381-382
   for consolation, 386
   imminent death, 132-133, 133n.15
   meditative version, 382-383
   for mourners, 386-388
   for mourners of painful
      relationships, 385
   rabbinic practice, 376, 376n.4,
      379-380
   responsive version, 383-384
   traditional version, 380-381
Violence, *mikveh* (ritual bath), 119-120
"Virtual *shivah*," 397
"Visitation of the sick," 369
Visiting
   guidelines for, 90-95
   sacred task, 88-89, 369
   suffering reduction, 127
Visual language, 31

Waiting periods, 177
Watzlawick, Paul, 24
Weaning, personal ritual, 117
Weinstein, Rabbi Aryeh, 319
Wells, David, 8-9
"What happened?," grief language,
   393-394
Whitaker, Carl, 430, 431
Wholeness, goal of, 14
Wilber, Ken, 72
Wisdom, aging, 297, 299-300
Wisdom literature, 163
Witkowski, Reverend Joan, 111-112
Witnessing, 2, 210
Women, personal rituals, 117
World-to-Come, rewards of, 88

Worship, developmentally disabled,
   365-367
Wrestling with God and Men, 196

Yaaqov
   blessing of favorites, 215-216
   impaired blessings, 212-215, 217-218
Yaaqov's Blessings, 214
Yehuda (Giving thanks)
   divisions, 215
   impaired blessings, 213, 218
Yekkeh rebbitzen, 274
Yesh (being), 85, 85n.17, 86
Yesh g'vul (There is a limit!), 58, 61
Yiddish expressions, 153
Yisrael, blessings, 212
Yissachar (There is hire), impaired
   blessings, 213-214
Yitzhak, blessings, 212, 213, 216, 217
Yod, letter, 305
Yom Kippur (Day of Atonement), 230,
   231-232, 233, 234-235
Yosef
   blessing of, 216
   impaired blessings, 214, 215, 217
   visit to dying father, 215
Y'sod (core identity), 82n.4, 82-83

Zachor ()remember, 269
Zaiman, Ann, 291
Zaiman, Rabbi Joel, 291
Zen story, grief counseling, 391
Zevulun (Prince), impaired blessings,
   214
Z'mirot (festive songs), 109
Zucker, Rabbi David J., 112

Order a copy of this book with this form or online at:
http://www.haworthpress.com/store/product.asp?sku=5440

JEWISH RELATIONAL CARE A-Z
We Are Our Other's Keeper

_____ in hardbound at $69.95 (ISBN-13: 978-0-7890-2705-4; ISBN-10: 0-7890-2705-4)

_____ in softbound at $39.95 (ISBN-13: 978-0-7890-2706-1; ISBN-10: 0-7890-2706-2)

Or order online and use special offer code HEC25 in the shopping cart.

COST OF BOOKS_____	☐ **BILL ME LATER:** (Bill-me option is good on US/Canada/Mexico orders only; not good to jobbers, wholesalers, or subscription agencies.)
POSTAGE & HANDLING_____ *(US: $4.00 for first book & $1.50 for each additional book)* *(Outside US: $5.00 for first book & $2.00 for each additional book)*	☐ Check here if billing address is different from shipping address and attach purchase order and billing address information. Signature_____
SUBTOTAL_____	☐ **PAYMENT ENCLOSED:** $_____
IN CANADA: ADD 7% GST_____	☐ **PLEASE CHARGE TO MY CREDIT CARD.**
STATE TAX_____ *(NJ, NY, OH, MN, CA, IL, IN, PA, & SD residents, add appropriate local sales tax)*	☐ Visa ☐ MasterCard ☐ AmEx ☐ Discover ☐ Diner's Club ☐ Eurocard ☐ JCB Account # _____
FINAL TOTAL_____ *(If paying in Canadian funds, convert using the current exchange rate, UNESCO coupons welcome)*	Exp. Date_____ Signature_____

Prices in US dollars and subject to change without notice.

NAME_____

INSTITUTION_____

ADDRESS_____

CITY_____

STATE/ZIP_____

COUNTRY_____ COUNTY (NY residents only)_____

TEL_____ FAX_____

E-MAIL_____

May we use your e-mail address for confirmations and other types of information? ☐ Yes ☐ No
We appreciate receiving your e-mail address and fax number. Haworth would like to e-mail or fax special discount offers to you, as a preferred customer. **We will never share, rent, or exchange your e-mail address or fax number.** We regard such actions as an invasion of your privacy.

Order From Your Local Bookstore or Directly From
The Haworth Press, Inc.
10 Alice Street, Binghamton, New York 13904-1580 • USA
TELEPHONE: 1-800-HAWORTH (1-800-429-6784) / Outside US/Canada: (607) 722-5857
FAX: 1-800-895-0582 / Outside US/Canada: (607) 771-0012
E-mail to: orders@haworthpress.com

For orders outside US and Canada, you may wish to order through your local
sales representative, distributor, or bookseller.
For information, see http://haworthpress.com/distributors

(Discounts are available for individual orders in US and Canada only, not booksellers/distributors.)

PLEASE PHOTOCOPY THIS FORM FOR YOUR PERSONAL USE.
http://www.HaworthPress.com   BOF06